T0354525

Books in the series 'The Colonial Economy of NSW 1788-1835'

A Brief Economic History of NSW

The Colonial Economy of NSW 1788-1835–A retrospective

The Government Store is Open for business–the commissariat operations
in NSW 1788-1835

The Enterprising Colonial Economy of NSW 1800-1830–Government
Business Enterprises in operation

Guiding the Colonial Economy–Public Funding in NSW 1800-1835

Financing the Colonial Economy of NSW 1800-1835

Essays on the colonial Economy of NSW 1788-1835

Industries that Formed a Colonial Economy

A BRIEF ECONOMIC HISTORY OF COLONIAL NSW

The Golden years of the Colonial Era re-examined

GORDON BECKETT

For book orders, email orders@traffordpublishing.com.sg

Most Trafford Singapore titles are also available at major online book retailers.

© Copyright 2012 Gordon Beckett.
All rights reserved. No part of this publication may be reproduced, stored in a retrieval system, or transmitted, in any form or by any means, electronic, mechanical, photocopying, recording, or otherwise, without the written prior permission of the author.

Printed in Singapore.

ISBN: 978-1-4669-2804-6 (sc)
ISBN: 978-1-4669-2805-3 (hc)
ISBN: 978-1-4669-2806-0 (e)

Trafford rev. 08/17/2012

 www.traffordpublishing.com.sg

Singapore
toll-free: 800 101 2656 (Singapore)
Fax: 800 101 2656 (Singapore)

CONTENTS

The economic history of Colonial Australia is in need of re-examination. It is almost 20 years since the death of the wisest exponent of that period—Professor N.G. Butlin, and the publication of his posthumous book 'Forming a Colonial Economy'. The operations of the colonial economy are reconsidered in terms of new findings.

Published For
The Colonial Institute
Gatton 4343

CHAPTER 1

INTRODUCTION TO THE COLONIAL ECONOMY

The economy of the colony (between 1788 and 1856) is by far the most interesting chapter of early Australian history after settlement, and within that chapter the Macquarie economy and its growth and major accomplishments is the most interesting segment. Why those particular dates? Settlement commenced with the arrival of the First Fleet, and their goal of being a self-sufficient penal colony, and full self-government arrived with the Constitution Act of 1855.

Of the Macquarie economy, we can see the economy in transition (from penal, towards a free, settlement); we see the exploration over the mountains, a barrier that was both physically and psychologically a severe limiting factor to the growth of the economy; we see the dramatic changes in agricultural production with the opening up of the Western Plains (both the Bathurst and the Liverpool Plains) and the advent of foreign (British) investment. The growth of manufacturing accompanied a change of policy with the Commissariat, and the financial institutions grew in accompaniment to the British absentee landowners, and the rise in livestock numbers. The desire and need to earn an adequate return on the investment in these pastoral enterprises, created a surge in exporting, as well as the diversification of enterprises and the decentralisation movement (the expansion of settlement boundaries).

The most significant change during the Macquarie Administration was the great movement of convicts into the colony and the Macquarie policy of putting these people to creative work; the by-product of these policies was the investment in public infrastructure of roads, bridges, public buildings and private housing.

The economy flourished and operated at full steam. The Hunter and Bligh years had witnessed very little capital investment in buildings and roads, so Macquarie had a lot of catching up as well as fulfilling his own expansionary plans.

The central theme of the era was not the official congratulations to Macquarie but the unceasing urging by successive Secretaries of State to curb expenditures even those annual local revenues tripled during the decade of 1810 to 1820 and over 50% of those revenues found their way into the public building program.

Consternation that the local revenue and taxing powers had been invalid since 1802 (Gov. King's first revenue raising to re-build the local jail) led to a validating Act in 1819 by the Westminster Parliament, who unctuously appointed a select committee into transportation to review government activities in the colony but then directed Bathurst to send a Commissioner (Bigge) to the colony for a more first-hand and in-depth investigation.

This story is firstly about the growth of the Colonial economy between 1788 and 1856, then about the key aspects of the Macquarie economy between 1810 and 1821 and finally to review the civil and criminal codes under which the colony operated and the variety of statutes imposed on the colonial governance.

There are some notable contributions to studies on many aspects of the colonial economy–that is the period between 1788 and about 1830. This period covers the setting up and establishment of the penal colony to the transition period when most of the economic development and structuring of the economy took place.

The major contributors to our knowledge of the colonial economy and its growth and structure are Professor Noel G. Butlin (late of Australian

National University) and his brother Professor S.J. Butlin (late of Sydney University). Collectively they have contributed numerous books and monographs to the literature His contributions come in his books (two are published posthumously)

My studies have been into more particular issues of and within the colonial economy. I commenced with an assembly and analysis of the financial statements of the two 'funds' from 1802 to 1822, followed by a biography of the first colonial acting treasurer and auditor-general–William Lithgow. Two important structural aspects of the economy as detected by N.G. Butlin are dealt with–the Commissariat and the Government Business Enterprises that commenced in 1802 and were not abandoned as Government policy until about 1830. This led to an analysis of the growth of manufacturing and the role of the early entrepreneurs. One of the most interesting aspects of the early economy (as directed by the British Treasury) is the establishment of 'land grant companies for development of land and pastoral enterprises. The first two are the AA Pastoral Company established in NSW in 1823 and the Van Diemen's Land Company, established in Tasmania in 1824. Both companies operated in the pastoral industry and in pursuit of wool interests held by their major stockholders. Whereas one was successful whilst the one studied in this volume–the VDL Company was close to ruin for much of its existence even though it survives to this day.

I have assembled as a companion volume, 20 of the best essays and writings on the colonial economy. This volume includes writings by N.G. Butlin and other exponents of the development and growth of the economy between 1788 and 1830 and includes my own study of the Aboriginal economy as of 1788.

DEFINING ECONOMIC HISTORY

A good definition of Economic History (relating to Australia) is taken from Colin White '**Mastering Risk, Politics in Australian Economic History**'

3

'(Man's economic activities which define those parts of the environment relevant to him, and which he can select as being those parts of the environment which can be described as resources'. P. 3)

White spends a large amount of print on questioning the key elements of colonial economic development and concludes (p.78)

"Most accounts of 19th century Australian economic development assume homogeneity with characteristics of uniform government attitudes to development finding expression in common economic policies, and an economic system in which exports of staples are important and that the all-pervasive capitalist system with its associated class struggle"

White is correct that these attitudes are prevalent amongst social; and political historians and for good reason. The colonial society was surging ahead on solid bedrock of private enterprise guided by the government wanting to encourage private and foreign investment and minimize government social expenditures.

However, White could offer an alternative guide to the colonial economy. The size of the economy dictated government involvement at the embryonic stage of private enterprise. It was not only Macquarie's encouragement of private enterprise that fuelled growth but his intervention in cleverly putting government assigned convicts to productive work in the GBEs and then transferring those activities into private hands that created a strongly growing secondary sector and further fuelled foreign investment and loans into the economy.

The encouragement of education, job training and productive labour were the driving force behind development. The conduits of the commissariat and the GBEs gave expression to a successful secondary sector and profitable outcomes.

50 ASPECTS OF (AUSTRALIAN)
COLONIAL ECONOMIC HISTORY 1788-1835

Aspect	Period	development	planning	natural resources	Social	Political
Commissariat Operations	1	1				
convict assignment	1				1	
Crime & law enforcement	1				1	
Developing a welfare program	1				1	
Development of export industries	1		1			
Development of Infrastructure	1		1			
Development of Staples	1		1			
discovery and settlement of Australia	1					
Fishing & Whaling	1		1			
Government farms	1		1			
Growth of Population	1				1	
Growth of religion	1				1	
Growth of the colonies	1					1
military traders	1	1				

CHAPTER 2

INTRODUCTION AND CHAPTER OUTLINE

THE COLONIAL ECONOMY–an outline of operation

Defining the colonial economy and creating a mission statement; *the purpose for this volume is to try to explain many financial aspects of the colonial economy between 1800 and 1830, based on numerous journal articles by leading Australian Economic Historians interested in this era. By selectively quoting from these sources and providing a summary of all conclusions, this volume may become, as intended, a comprehensive, detailed analysis of the colonial economy and for it to become synonymous with a full study of the topic, in supplement to that by Professor. N.G. Butlin.*

Land Grant Company: Heavily involved in the Australian pastoral investment was the Van Diemen's Land Company (VDL Company) who selected in exchange for an investment by shareholders of only half a million pound, 350,000 acres on the north-west cape of Tasmania. Both companies made rocky progress and both failed to fulfil the expectations of the British stockholders.

Population Growth; the purpose of this segment of the study is not of a demographic nature, although a section includes reference to the elements of population increase, but relates more to the economic history of the country and of the causes and circumstances of the changing population in the colony. Topics such as the catalysts of economic change and therefore of the growing population are meaningful, and these include, the immigration sponsored by the colonial governors, the exploration that opened up the western plains, and which led to new towns and much speculation from foreign investors, the entrepreneurs that encouraged trade, both export and import, and the pastoralists that risked all by extending the limits of settlement further and the Colonial Economy. The description 'bridgehead economy' was used by one of Australia's foremost economic historians, N. G. Butlin to refer to the earliest decades of British occupation when the colony was essentially a penal institution. The main settlements were at Port Jackson (modern Sydney, 1788) in New South Wales and Hobart (1804) in what was then Van Diemen's Land (modern Tasmania).

The colony barely survived its first years and was largely neglected for much of the following quarter-century while the British government was preoccupied with the war with France. An important beginning was nevertheless made in the creation of a private economy to support the penal regime.

Above all, agriculture was established based on land grants to senior officials and emancipated convicts, and limited freedoms were allowed to convicts to supply a range of goods and services. Although economic life depended heavily on the government Commissariat as a supplier of goods, money and foreign exchange, individual rights in property and labour were recognised, and private markets for both started to function.

In 1808, the recall of the New South Wales Corps, whose officers had benefited most from access to land and imported goods (thus hopelessly entangling public and private interests), coupled with the appointment of a new governor, Lachlan Macquarie, in the following year, brought about a greater separation of the private economy from the activities and interests of the colonial government. With a significant increase in the numbers transported after 1810, New South Wales' future became more secure. As labourers, artisans and craftsmen, clerks and tradesmen, many convicts possessed the skills required in the new settlements. As their terms expired, they also added permanently to the free population. Over time, this would inevitably change the colony's character.

Starting in 1788 <u>the economy had a plan for growth</u>–based on both economic and sustainable growth built around the establishment of a settlement with homes, barracks, store houses, food provision and obviously retail establishments and the need to perform much like any other new founded towns within colonies

<u>The Aboriginal economy</u> in 1788 was actively supporting the million or so natives living within the national borders. The native economy had it manufacturing and trading aspects, much like a regular economy. There many similarities would end, however, estimates have been made of the GDP of the Aboriginal economy and it is likely that this closed economy outperformed the white economy until somewhere about the mid-1820s. Barnard writes "through many thousands of years the aborigines adapted themselves to the continent of their choice as surely and as perfectly as the eucalypts. Except in the far north where they may have had some contact with Papuans and Malays, no outside influence worked upon them". What the aborigines did bring to their new country was an adaptability, which spelt survival and the spiritual inheritance of a dream.[1] A.G.L. Shaw describes them as 'Stone Age people' and 'the only race which could serve as a common ancestor for all mankind'.[2]

The first connection between the white and dark people after Phillip arrived was for economic gain and benefit. Phillip, however, soon found that no advantage was to be reaped from the aboriginal except occasional succour when white men lost themselves in the bush, nor could he estimate their numbers with any accuracy.[3]

Lord Glenelg raises an interesting point in his conveyance of the results of the 1836 (February 9th, 1836) House of Commons Select Committee Report into Aborigines.

The aim of the Enquiry was "to secure for the aborigines the due observance of justice and the protection of their rights, to promote and

---

[1]   Barnard *ibid* p.648
[2]   Shaw, A.G.L. *The Story of Australia*
[3]   HRA 1:1:29

spread Christianity among them and to lead them to the peaceful and voluntary reception of the Christian religion . . ."

Glenelg advised, "They (the natives) are to derive the highest possible claim from the Sovereignty which has been assumed over the whole of their ancient possessions. If the rights of the Aborigines as British subjects be fully acknowledged it will follow that, when any of them comes to his death by the hands of the Queen's officers, or persons acting upon their command, an Inquest should be held to ascertain the cause which led to the death. Such proceeding is important not only as a direct protection to Society against lawless outrage, but to impress on the public the value of any human life". The flaw in this proclamation was that the natives were not Christians, they did not understand the nature of white man law and so 'the treatment of Aborigines remained a matter of grace rather than of justice'.

Staples: it was imperative that the local economy produced an export range of commodities, which would provide the all important export income against which to offset import expenditures. Eventually in the 1820s, wool was to take its place as head staple but before that time, sealskins, seal oil; timber and whale products would be tested in Britain. Staples would produce the commodities much needed to create and sustain a vigorous export market. The economic managers were bound by the convention that imports and exports had to match so that there were essentially neither 'surpluses nor 'deficit' in the economy.

Economic Growth in the colony, upon emergence from penal status, would become the lifeblood of the fledgling economy. The terms sustainable development and sustainable growth have become very familiar while their meanings have remained vague. A first step toward clarity would be to adopt the dictionary distinction between growth and development. Tel grows means to increase naturally in size by the addition of material through assimilation or accretion. To develop means to expand or realize the potentialities of; bring gradually to a fuller, greater, or better state. In short, growth is quantitative increase in physical scale, while development is qualitative improvement or unfolding of potentialities. An economy can grow without developing, develop without growing, or do both or neither. Since the human economy is a subsystem of a finite global ecosystem, which does not grow, even though it does develop, it is clear that growth of the economy cannot be sustainable over long periods. The term sustainable growth should be rejected as a bad oxymoron. The term sustainable development is much, more apt. Qualitative development of non-growing systems has been observed for long periods. The goal of this survey is to synthesize disparate strands of literature to link entrepreneurship to economic growth. This will be done by investigating the relationship between entrepreneurship and economic growth using elements of various fields: historical views on entrepreneurship, macro-economic growth theory, industrial economics (Porter's competitive advantage of nations), evolutionary economics, history of economic growth (rise and fall of nations) and the management literature on large corporate organizations. Understanding the role of entrepreneurship in the process of economic growth requires the decomposition of the concept of entrepreneurship. A first part of our synthesis is to contribute to the understanding of the dimensions involved, while paying attention to the level of analysis (individual, firm and aggregate level). A second part is to gain insight in the causal links between these entrepreneurial dimensions and economic growth. A third part is to make suggestions for future empirical research into the relationship between (dimensions of) entrepreneurship and economic growth.

Contours and segments in the growing economy Every economy is cyclical and this chapter examines the cyclical nature of the early colonial economy. The economic impact of droughts, floods, food shortages and the growing number of convicts in the settlement all impacted on the cyclical nature of the colonial economy (N.G.Butlin)

Establishment and progress of Banking The fact that there was no treasury in the colony was of course detrimental to the growth and diversity of the economy. Governor Macquarie, whilst on his way to the colony, stopped off in Cape Town and saw first-hand how the banking institutions operated and how important they were to economic development. He could not get support from the British Treasury to issue a banking licence, but decided anyhow to issue a local but illegal license hoping that when the institution was successful and irreplaceable, it would be granted an operating licence by the British Treasury.

<u>Pastoral Land Grant companies;</u> Circumstances in Britain, following the Napoleonic Wars created investment opportunities in the new colony. There was a need for sourcing of wool within Britain rather than Germany (Saxony) and Spain. This led to owners of woollen mills consorting with the British Government to take over a large land grant in the colony of NSW suitable for large-scale wool production, followed by shipment to British woollen mills to replace the imports from the two former European countries supplying Britain but not meeting the new levels of demand. The first of the Land Grant companies was the Australian Agricultural company (AAC) that offered to invest one million pound in the colony in exchange for a grant of one million acres and a supply of convict labour. The company took up the offering of land in mid-central NSW but within a few years determined the Liverpool ranges area was more fertile and beneficial and was given permission to transfer its selection. The second company further west.

Production ASPECTS OF THE COLONIAL ECONOMY

Convict Work Patterns

Convict transportation commenced with the arrival of the First Fleet in 1788. They were an important aspect of the early settlement and its growth. At the start, they were responsible for clearing land by cutting trees, erecting buildings, stores, forming cart-racks and unloading ships. Then they were employed with the cultivated of the cleared land, followed by its planting and then harvesting any crop. Shortly after the turn of the century, the governor, Phillip Gidley King, established a Maintenance Yard so that convicts became responsible for the storing, borrowing, returning and maintaining of tools. This became the predecessor of establishing and working in the Lumber Yard, the Timber Yard, Naval Yard, Stone Quarries, Government Farms and numerous other *government owned business enterprises*.

<u>GBE's;</u> the GBE's were essentially created for two purposes—firstly import replacement and to create productive type work for the growing number of convicts arriving in the settlement.

The Commissariat; this government store was the most important economic driver in use between 1788 and 1830.

The storage and supply of food, liquor, hardware and other goods was initially in the hands of the Commissariat Department. The Commissariat was an arm of the Civil Administration responsible for the supply of goods to colonial establishments of the British Empire. It held a strategic role in the economy of the early colony. Supply of food and other necessities was under the direct control of the Commissariat, particularly in the early years. It was a role which, though it diminished through time, was a significant function within the Town of Sydney and the Colony for many decades. The Commissariat had access to credit in Britain via the use of Treasury Bills to pay for overseas purchases; this was an important avenue of finance which aided the development of commerce, banking and even agriculture.

Due to the lack of ready cash in the Colony, and the high 'credit rating' of the Commissariat Store, receipts issued by the store had a ready circulation throughout the colony, and along with the barter system, became the currency of the colony as it moved from a convict to a market system.

By 1815 the role of the Commissariat was changing. Macquarie abolished the custom of supplying the needs of the inhabitants from the Commissariat on credit. Not only did this protect the government from a large number of bad debts, but he felt that 'All their wants may now be fully supplied by the Free Merchant Shipping, frequenting this port from England and other countries.' The 1812 Commissariat Store was built as part of the rearrangement of the store's function and role. In 1813 the Commissariat was reorganized as a branch of the army commissariat in London, a sub-division of the English Treasury. Thereafter the Commissariat was controlled by the Lords Commissioners of the Treasury whose instructions were superior to those which the Governor might give in his capacity as Captain-General. Until these changes the Governor directed the Commissary, was dealing with each situation as it arose. There were no full and complete set of rules for procedure, a situation that the Governors up to Macquarie seemed to struggle with.

There were two buildings which were used as Government stores, the first appears to have been designed in 1809 and built in c1810 this was the 'U' shaped building constructed next to the shoreline. The other building was constructed in 1812 to the west of the first, next to George St and it is this building that the stone came from. This building was a long rectangular structure and is almost covered by the footprint of the MCA building, although it appears that there may be archaeological evidence of this 1812 building still extant.

The 1812 building appears on various plans as Naval stores, Ordnance stores and is referred to as the Taxation building in the 1930s. It is possible that both these buildings had the convict stonemason's initial carved into every sandstone block. These blocks may have been purchased by St Philips church to build a church hall (Sydney Morning Herald July 6 1939) the hall has been subsequently demolished and it is not know the whereabouts of these blocks.

The foundation stone marked the foundation date of the building and it was located over the doorway. There were protests about the demolition of the buildings and when it became obvious that they could not be saved the Historical society requested the preservation of the foundation stone and the keystone. The foundation stone was placed in the park as part of the landscaping works for the Maritime Services Board Building.

Government Administration

The weight of evidence suggests that the colonial governments played a positive and active part in encouraging economic enterprise, whether trading, pastoral, agricultural or experimental. It seems justifiable to dispute the validity of statements in the British government's instructions to Commissioner Bigge in January 1819, for even if it could be argued in 1788 that the colony 'had not been established with any view to . . . commercial advantage, its economic growth up to 1821 had frequently not been regarded by governments as 'secondary consideration' to its function of 'receptacle for offenders'.

Macquarie's building program seems to have been necessary for both skilled and unskilled labourers. The government was in 1820 employing 3300 out of 8900 male convicts in NSW, whilst the remaining 5600 were assigned, but the greatest demand was still for farming men. It was these that the government could not supply—it only had about ¼ of the number requested. In addition to the 9000 convicts there were a further 5000 male emancipists and about 1300 who had arrived free or who were born free in the colony. Thus in 1820 the participation rate had grown from 40% to over 60%, adjusted to about 45% if adjustment for productivity is included and this is compared to only 30% in 1814 and 40% in contemporary England.

'Assignment' appealed to the civil servants of Whitehall, who considered the inducements of special rations for good behaviour and 'tickets'. Macarthur told Bigge, 'being involved in rural work, there is much time for convicts to reflect and self-examine themselves'. On the other hand, in government work, threat of punishment was greater, though the skilled man was often put on piecework. Bigge recorded 'a convict servant costs his employer between £20 and £25 a year for rations, supplies and wages; the unskilled free labourer costs £40 per annum and he was often paid more. Bigge concluded that 'if the convicts were only 2/3rds as efficient as a free man he was worth having and when wages of free men were higher than those quoted by Bigge, the convict could be even less efficient and still be an economical servant.

Manufacturing before 1821, except for Simeon Lord in the production of cloth and a few domestic articles, attracted little capital. There were notable exceptions—brewing and flour milling. Perhaps the greatest restraint on manufacturing arose from the way in which capital was raised for colonial enterprises. Few settlers brought actual capital to the colony. Most depended on mercantile credit, which merely encouraged the decision to persist with trade. Once capital had begun to accumulate, its transfer to pastoralism was more attractive as the otherwise heavy investment in land could be avoided through lease, grant, or a modified form of squatting. Perhaps it was the difficulty in getting large grants of land that channelled a large proportion of emancipist capital into manufacturing. Though most raw materials were available, manufacturing was restricted to replacing imports by an absence of skills and sometimes of equipment.

A transition of manufacturing from the public to the private sector was a further encouragement to investment in and contributing capital to manufacturing. Overall, it remained more profitable to import goods than to make them.

It has been shown that a 'great concession' as Wentworth termed it–in other words the commercial slump of 1812-1815, was as much a result of external factors as the scarcity of local money. The domino effect of pressure for payment moved from Britain to India, to Sydney and onto Sydney customers. The flow of capital in the form of credit extended to local merchants was cut off, and the volume of imports fell during this commercial slump from the high levels it had reached immediately before its onset. It was from wool exports that the local market sought salvation. Sheep numbers were expanded, rising from 34,550 in 18140 to 74,825 in 1814, a total not exceeded until 1819. Exports of wool to England, began with 3-4,000 pounds shipped by Marsden in 1812, 35,000 in 1813, 17,000 in 1714 and 35,000 in 1815

The paradox of promoting long-term economic growth gives rise to the observation by Wentworth in 1820 'the colony has been in a state of retardation for the last 15 years; an assertion not easily reconciled with the increase in population, and in the cultivated lands and in the number of sheep and cattle'. Wheat had trended upwards in total production terms but needs to be weighted by annual increases in yield per acre. Yield initially was estimated at 12.5 bushels per acre in the Parramatta region but had climbed steadily in the Hawkesbury region to 25 bushels according to Bigge. Sheep numbers steadied reflecting an increase in the consumption of sheep meat, and a tendency to breed lighter carcasses.

Because of the lack of precise data concerning changes in agricultural and pastoral yields only a broad indication of the rate of growth of real output in the farming sector can be made For the period 18/10 to 1820, indications are that wheat production incr4reasefcd at a rate of 5Z%whilsat met and wool, rose by about 10%. Before 1808, imported supplies met most of the colony's meat needs. This rate of growth in physical output would have been consistent with the observed growth in the capability of the colony to supply its own food requirements. From a dependency on imported grains and meat until the mid-1990s, the King period worked towards and met self-sufficiency in grain by 1802and meat by 1810.

Summary

By 1821, NSW was a diversified economy, encouraged by the government. It was also not the case, claims Joyce, that economic expansion to this time was the result of defiance of Gov. Regulations by private enterprise, or the challenge to the monopoly by the East India Company. Nor is it the case that the penal function slowed or restricted economic development. Before 1821, the role of the gov was usually positive. On occasions it restricted or opposed certain types of enterprise on the grounds it was in conflict with gov and private enterprise. The fundamental challenge facing early governors was to feed and clothe not only the convicts but also the military and many of the free settlers. Even during the Macquarie years, government despatches describe food shortages in much the same terms as earlier governors did. Ensuring a sufficiency of food against the perils of floods, drought and the excess transfer of prisoners was the immediate and immense problem the governors faced. Thus, they remained concerned mostly with the short-term rather than the 'distant scene'. Whilst the governors faced the task of feeding the colony, private enterprise turned its focus on other not so necessary consumables. There became a close proximity between government and private enterprise

One problem faced by the British Board of Trade in protecting the interests of the East India Company was that many boats owned partially by Campbell, Macarthur and Simeon Lord were also partially owned by British residents and registered in England. The question asked by Lord Auckland, the president of the Board of Trade of Prime Minister Grenville was Is NSW a colony and don't its inhabitants have a right to trade. Grenville decided that British interests could not be used as an excuse to prevent the development of the colony and he sought a solution, which preserved the interests of the company. However, the privileges of the company were not ended by legislation until 1814, except for trade with China and trade in tea. The general colonial response was 'official policy still preferred to maintain existing British interests rather than to encourage colonial trade and commerce', but in fact colonials had gained much by these negotiations. Only on one staple could the colonial governor and the British government both completely support rival economic interests–the exception was wool. Since 1788 sheep had been underpinned for meat production, and Secretary Dundas stressed that the increase in livestock, chiefly sheep and cattle must be a primary objective. A Governor King enquiry in 1805 into the types of sheep owned in the colony concluded that income from meat production was the main goal of most owners. Each governor had to stress the need for agricultural expansion for subsistence, and no governor opposed pastoral expansion, nor can any governor be blamed for other defects in the industry such as inefficient shepherds. Hunter was aware of these and other problems whilst Bligh gave priority to agriculture and supported grain production for food and recognised the shortage of labour. He also gave priority to sheep production for meat rather than for wool. Although agreeing that the wool trade would eventually improve.

Enterprise does not lend itself statistical analysis only reinforces the tendency to 'discount the economic significance of anything that cannot be numerically expressed'. Enterprise is the catalyst that converts inert land, labour and capital into functioning factors of production. The entrepreneur is the agent of change, who with initiative and persistence exploits resources in new ways, thereby increasing efficiency. Economic development depends on the existence of the entrepreneur as much as on the availability of sufficient capital, land or labour. Because of his pioneer activities the colonial entrepreneur holds the key to the growth of a colonial economy, and it can be expected that the nature of that economy, will reflect the character and experience of the men who first accepted economic risk. There had to be the ambition to investigate and exploit the resources of the new world. Another characteristic of colonial enterprise was the spirit of economic speculation which found its strongest manifestation in trade. The glamour and consequence of the successful merchant provided a target for all men of ambition. The most alluring test was the speculator were the new settlements outside Europe.

Before the colonial hinterland had been settled fifty miles from the coast, commercial frontiers of trade had been reached with the Pacific Island, India, China and South America. Free men came to the colony to engage in trade, and convicts stood by awaiting an opening. The four classes of colonial society by 1819 were:

1. Civil and military officers and private gentlemen in mercantile pursuit
2. Transferees from England of credible habits who came free to trade
3. many persons who are householders and traders
4. free labourers and prisoners

Since specialisation was not yet economically feasible, the term merchant described a function rather than an occupation. Merchanting was a risk, but it was wiser to spread them than for one man to risk everything. Variety provided the means of dabbling in a number of small commissions. Many merchants and treaders kept a farm on which to raise grain and livestock. These piecemeal activities raised many a fine entrepreneur–those people who from the successful commercial activities amassed the capital that was later invested in the development of sealing, whaling, grazing or manufacturing. The first to indulge were the military officers of the NSW Corps but it began modestly earning the odium of *The Rum Corps*.

Introduction

A good definition of Economic History (related to Australia) taken from

Colin White **'Mastering Risk, Politics in Australian Economic History'**

'(P. 3) Man's economic activities which define those parts of the environment relevant to him, and which he can select as being those parts of the environment which can be described as resources'.

White spends a large amount of print on questioning the key elements of colonial economic development and concludes (p.78)

"Most accounts of 19th century Australian economic development assume homogeneity with characteristics of uniform government attitudes to development finding expression in common economic policies, and an economic system in which exports of staples are important and that the all-pervasive capitalist system with its associated class struggle"

White is correct that these attitudes are prevalent amongst social and political historians and for good reason. The colonial society was surging ahead on solid bedrock of private enterprise guided by the government wanting to encourage private and foreign investment and minimize government social expenditures.

However, White could offer an alternative guide to the colonial economy. The size of the economy dictated government involvement at the embryonic stage of private enterprise. It was not only Macquarie's encouragement of private enterprise that fuelled growth but his intervention in cleverly putting government assigned convicts to productive work in the GBEs and then transferring those activities into private hands that created a strongly growing secondary sector and further fuelled foreign investment and loans into the economy.

The encouragement of education, job training and productive labour were the driving force behind development. The conduits of the commissariat and the GBEs gave expression to a successful secondary sector and profitable outcomes.

THE ENTERPRISE ECONOMY

The enterprise economy was the foundation for solid entrepreneurial action. The circumstances of the new settlement gave rise to many needs, and therefore man resolutions to the new circumstances—only few of which could be used or taken seriously. It is a clears understanding of the economy that allows us to understand, interpret and draw conclusions on the success or otherwise of the entrepreneurial outcomes

A significant omission in packing for the First Fleet was any real equipment, other than four forges, for making small items in the new settlement. The type of items required locally, if Captain Phillip had put his mind to it, were axe heads and handles, adzes, picks, shovels, hand-hoes, and mattocks. All these items had been brought out with the other food and rations, but the quantity and quality were inadequate and inappropriate.

It took 14 years or so from the foundation for the colony to become a settlement and before government minds turned to a 'manufacturing' centre. What took place in this intervening time was land clearing, the building of barracks, basic housing, a church, cart tracks, bridges a brick-making facility, and a second settlement at Parramatta;. This concept of government ownership of any means of production was anathema to the British government, but rather essential in a penal settlement in NSW. Obviously, there were precedents in the settlement—government-owned and regulated farms had been in existence since 1788. This necessity was due to there being no free settlers available to carry on the work of farming and being committed to the raising of grain, livestock, vegetables and even fruit from trees. The plans for settlement had not hit their stride at this early time and so there were insufficient numbers of prisoners to create specialisation and all prisoners were on rotation to any task assigned on a daily basis. Building was in great demand and thus timber was in equally great demand. Phillip had already created the basic tenets of government-sponsored *enterprises* by establishing public farming, timber harvesting and processing off public lands, and the construction gangs. These gangs for land clearing, road making and building construction were a central theme of the colonial economy and government enterprises until well into the 1830s. Therefore, government enterprises were an early theme of economic growth and development.

The GBEs were a government instrument to control the farming, manufacturing and communication sectors of the public economy. If organised and operated successfully, the public operation could throw doubt on the expected expansion of the settlement into a private sector. Butlin in *Forming* terms it a bridgehead economy, but as a public sector economy it was essentially closed; why then encourage settlers for agricultural pursuits?; why encourage free mechanics and labourers for a private sector—why not just train the government workers for these tasks?; why encourage entrepreneurs, traders and even speculators?; why worry about a transition from penal to directed economy, which denial would remove the need for a bridgehead? Could a public sector economy with access to almost unlimited numbers of government labourers and access to the almost limitless supplies of natural resources be able to sustain itself and survive without free enterprise planning and capital? Was a private sector essential to economic growth and a successful economy?

This then is the story of the evolvement of fully-fledged government enterprises and their operation. Government Business Enterprises (GBEs) were the backbone of the colonial economy between 1800 and 1830. They were the planning arm of the commissariat operation of the settlement, which really began in 1776 with the assembly by Captain Phillip in England of the supplies and provisions of the First Fleet in readiness for the initial settlement. Being a relatively low-level officer in the Royal Navy, Phillip's association with the settling of the new colony sets the scene for a relatively low-key planning and operation exercise. It was outside the competency, training, experience and general expertise of Phillip to undertake such an assignment [although in retrospect, he was a superb selection as an administrator], and so the oversight by the Naval Board in the procurement process further undermined the quality of the provisioning side of the expedition. The Naval Board was being challenged to keep the costs of the expedition to a minimum and to Phillip's later regret the quality of the tools and supplies were of a lesser quality [and in many instances, also of quantity] than the exercise deserved.

This level of second-rate provisioning long pervaded the commissariat operations in the settlement. Plates and mugs as well as tools, were inadequate and sub-standard and not of sufficient quantity for the 1000+ personnel in the settlement. The tools supplied to convict workers for land clearing were unsuitable and inadequate in the field and most failed in service. In the same vein, food supplies had been underestimated and there was great pressure on Phillip to replenish the victuals in stock with fresh supplies produced locally. By 1800, much of the initial planning for land utilisation had been completed. At this time Hunter felt comfortable in thinking that, some form of local revenue would be useful in supplementing British Treasury appropriations for the colony. His approach, in order to remain within the law of England and follow his own instructions, was not to generate revenue as such, but rather he planned to 'seek reimbursement for providing government services'. His plan was to rebuild, as a community activity, the original wooden gaol.

Hunter's successor, P. G. King, was not as reluctant in his revenue generating plans. He selected another project, which the Treasury would not support with funding,-the socialising of the orphans and abandoned children of the settlement. For this, he planned a governor's discretionary fund—one for the orphans, which he called the Orphan Fund, and a second for rebuilding the gaol, which he called the Gaol Fund. The obvious point here is that the colony had no treasury, and was considered under-funded in terms of establishing a new settlement and of creating a wide-range of infrastructure and there was the beginning of a move to transfer certain British treasury responsibilities to the colonial governor.

This funding shortage and transfer of fiscal requirements to the colony was to be a trademark of the colony for the first fifty years of its life. These two aspects of colonial administration were also to be a standard of policy and practice during much of these fifty years. The two underlying mainstays of local public policy were firstly, the raising of local revenues and of using convicts for much of the public labour requirements. Thus, convicts assigned to government service carried out building and construction of public buildings [barracks, civil service housing, government office buildings, hospitals and churches] and all public works [roads, bridges, wharves, stores, water delivery].

The same policy planning that created local revenue for official purposes, and created the usage of a declining percentage of convicts for government service, also planned to find a staple export commodity to create foreign exchange. The generation of foreign exchange was to try to offset the growing importation of consumption and capital goods in an increasingly trade-oriented economy. Foreign exchange can be effectively generated in two ways-firstly, by the sale of goods and services outside the economic frontiers. The second way is to save on the importation of goods and services by making them within the local economy. Successive governors actively pursued both policies from Phillip to Macquarie. The encouragement of exports was necessarily limited because of the unavailability of goods, other than basic, unprocessed natural resources and then primary agricultural goods. Coal and timber were the first such export commodities, followed closely by staples such as sealing and whaling products. Transfers between VDL, Norfolk Island and NSW were considered inter-governmental, but over time became quite substantial and important to each settlement.

Obviously, the first need in a fledgling economy was to support its victualling requirements as much as practicable. The concept of public farming must have been anathema to the colonial secretary's office in London. Britain had built its international economic prowess on private enterprise and thus public farming was a novel if an unwelcome necessity. Equally, resentment would grow in London towards a government manufacturing operation. Then the London authorities did not have to manage a settlement with instant demands, and remoteness from the real world of about 18 months.

However the necessity of both forms of public business enterprise (i.e. in the primary and secondary sector) sponsored by government became inevitable once the colony got on its feet. The circumstances became that labour, in the form of a large [and growing] number of convicts, was available for work; there was a definite and often dramatic need for fresh rations for this growing population; and the enormous turn-around time from British suppliers was equally cumbersome to manage and accept. There became an immediate need for local skills and local repair/ replacement capability if these circumstances and strictures were to be satisfied. Phillip had brought in his initial store inventory on the First Fleet, a forge, brick moulds, and a variety of axes, hoes, picks, adzes, and other tools, as well as various grinding wheels. Phillip had the makings of basics industries. It was the poor quality of these tools that became a limiting factor in moving ahead with development of the infrastructure required in the settlement. Thus, the first workshop for repairing, sharpening, renewing and replacement of tools and equipment took shape quite early in the timeframe of the settlement. This move also coincided with the establishment of timber camps, the timber yard with its sawpits and kiln, brick making and the public farms. What a multi-faceted economy Phillip was trying to operate. This initial repair and maintenance facility, was only an adjunct to the main 'store' which provided the rations, issued the initial tools and spare parts, in addition to the receiving, storing, inventorying issuing and collecting all the normal items required by government and kept by the commissariat. Without the skills and machinery available in Britain, the commissariat before Macquarie's arrival in 1810, at which point the whole structure and philosophy of government business enterprises, in particular government manufacturing, was changed, could carry out only basic repairs and replacements.

Even the concept of public farming changed. After 1814, the government participated in not only vegetable growing and small livestock management within the Country of Cumberland, but commenced broad acre grain growing and the management of large livestock herds outside the county. The colony depended very heavily on government grain supplies, both for price management and regularity of supplies Macquarie set the purchase price of grain from the private sector at the beginning of a planting season and in an effort to keep his convict maintenance costs low, often underbid for grain with the result that less than necessary supplies were available. Private growers often complained that a price of only 8/–(eight shillings) per bushel did not cover their costs. Yields on small acreages were insufficient to make any price less than 10/–attractive. The commissariat officials in conjunction with other senior planning officials in the Macquarie Administration gave a great deal of thought to the location of the 22 identified government farm facilities. Usually the locations were adjacent to or near flowing rivers, and the variety of locations balanced the almost annual management challenges of droughts, floods, insect pests and other vagaries of nature. It was thus avoidable that all public farm crops failed in the one season. A well-designed practice that took hold from the early days was that of running livestock on farming areas alongside vegetables and grain. In this way, the livestock waste was used as fertiliser of the cropping areas. Such farming practices were learnt from local experience for few convicts or free settlers with British farming experience came the way of either the Principal Superintendents of Works or Convicts. The next step in progressive public farming was when crop rotation practices and basic equipment were put to use.

To supplement a rather slow beginning under public farming, Phillip commenced a system of land grants to interested emancipists, military personnel and in the case of James Ruse, of convicts who showed interest in working for themselves on farming activities. Naturally the intent was to take these people 'off the store' and make them subsistence farmers on a 30-, 50–or in the case of the military, 100-acre farmlets. Phillip acknowledged that any output from these ventures would hardly cover the needs of the farmer himself let alone offer a surplus for the government store. However, he pressed ahead for every possible person to be taken 'off the store', and save that amount of rations for another day. The system also opened the way for a limited number of convicts to be allocated to these minimalist farmers and with such allocation came the hope that these extra workers could also be supported 'off the store'. Lack of skills and experience, small acreages, underperforming land and lack of commissariat credit for seed, made such a hope almost pointless. Such a policy of convict assignment to private masters with private full support was not to become official policy until Macquarie's arrival in 1810. Although not as successful as first thought, public farming made a significant contribution to the settlement's economy. Government farms kept growing in every respect.-more locations were opened within both the County of Cumberland as well as the nine counties within the approved limit of locations; whilst more convicts were utilised in working on the public farms. A number of the farms [but not all] provided barrack accommodation for onsite convicts. Without a treasury in the colony, any farm output such as grain etc, had to be bartered for a sale to be consummated. In the absence of a currency, settlers were willing to accept 'store receipts' which could in turn be bartered either with the government store or with most merchants for face value. Obviously, output from the government farms had priority of acceptance with the stores, although few surviving records identify transfer from a specific farm to a store location.

The needs of a rapidly expanding economy and its demanding population set the scope of operations for the government business operations. The various farms provided the settlers with fresh grains, vegetables fruit and dairy products. The demand for housing and public buildings created a continuous need for stone blocks, bricks, tiles and timber framing for floors, walls and roofing. With interior fit-out essential the need for doors, hinges, windows and even furniture was also met by a government business enterprise–the Lumber Yard. Therefore, a pattern of operations emerged. The enterprises commenced in the new settlement with brick and tile facilities–on Brickfield Hill and then on the south bank of the Parramatta River at Rosehill, followed by the timber camps, timber yard, lumberyard and the stone quarries. The rather attractive sandstone was used for construction of the grander government office buildings and the most elegant of private houses. In time, the majestic colonial buildings still standing today used the historic Sydney sandstone–for example The Lands Department building, the colonial secretary's office, the Sydney Hospital, the King Street church and Law Courts and Hyde Park barracks.

Therefore, the evolvement of the public enterprises came from humble, but essential beginnings, born of necessity, and grew into an integrated series of government service centres. They were mostly output oriented although spreading the enterprise over the work gangs-road-making, land-clearing, grass-cutting and ferrying services took the enterprises squarely into the realm of delivery of both goods and services. Then followed the adjunct services, such as boat building, ship loading and provisioning, watering and repair work. A multitude of products, services and outcomes, with surprisingly little criticism or official questioning—for even the most hardheaded free enterprises proponent would have recognised that there would not have been private entrepreneurs with sufficient capital to start most of these businesses on a timely basis. It took the genius of Macquarie to underpin the future secondary industries of the new colony by planning for a post-Bigge transition and hand-over between the public sector and the private sector, of methodology, equipment and skilled labour.

The value of government enterprise output continued to increase as a growing number of convicts became available for government assignment and the demand expanded for the broad range of products produced by the various enterprises-the lumber timber, brick, dock and stone yards, the naval yard, the government farms, and the various gangs used for construction, land-clearing and road-making. Towering over these subsidiary operations was a complex organisation and planning operation. Consider the planning involved here. There are over 5,000 labourers available. Therefore, the potential output is considerable. To achieve such output, raw materials have to be available on site. The labourers need to be trained, fed, and ready to work. They need proper and adequate supervisors. They need roofed facilities and access to plenty of equipment. There needs to be storage facilities for finished products and an inventory system based on clerical recording of production. The most important aspect of the planning work is to know what public works are in the pipeline, and from this the materials quantities will be assembled. Therefore, for instance, Greenway had the designs ready for the Hyde Park barracks. We know that only Governor Macquarie was intending to inspect and approve the working plans. So once approved the planners assembled a materials list setting down the number, dimension and finish of sandstone for the Quarry supervisor. The number of bricks, roofing tiles, timber framing and flooring, the wall sections, the roof-trusses were also listed and circulated to the other supervisors. Once received by the supervisors and depending on the lead-time involved work would commence. The principal enterprise supervisor would inform the sub-supervisors of the production schedule and an area set aside for finished output. The more demanding work of loading carts and pulling laden carts full of materials to the worksite would also be completed to a schedule so that construction workers were not delayed by any shortage or unavailability of materials. Such planning was a massive exercise under the control of the commissariat and such work was a credit to the stewardship of the senior commissariat officials.

In my introduction, I speculated on the success or otherwise of a closed public sector economy. However without growth provided by free settlers, and therefore from a private sector, such an economy would fail. It could not generate growth, for consumption could only match the rate of growth, otherwise an internal tangible surplus would result, which would be a wasting asset. However if certain circumstances were somewhat different, the colonial economy could well have surged forward both financially and structurally.

So what were the limiting circumstances?

1. There was no treasury in the colony before 1824
2. The British treasury was starting to limit its appropriation to the colony and put more responsibility on the colonial revenues for the funding of local needs, rightly the duty of the conquering power.
3. A growing number of convicts were being transported to NSW from Britain.
4. The best turn around time for orders from NSW to British suppliers was still 12-18 months
5. However, the most negative and therefore limiting factor facing the colonial administration was the British treasury placing 'nil value' on convict labour or on their output

GDP projections

In addition to the value of output from the GBEs set down in the summary, one enormous tangible contribution came from the public works program. Macquarie's rather peevish last letter to Early Bathurst in July 1822 [HRA 1:10:671 offers a list of 266 items of construction in a ten-year public works programs during his administration. This list can be costed in terms of 'valuing' the items. Greenway's archrival, Henry Kitchen informed Commissioner Bigge that the labour 'value' alone was valued at over £950,000, so by adding the estimated value of the materials used, the total project cost of all items would be more than £2 million. In this way, it can be seen that the convict and transportation program paid its way many times over, if the Colonial office and British Treasury had been sufficiently creative to analyse that putting the convicts to work would produce an outcome of public value.

The government business enterprises played an important, essential and pivotal role in colonial economic development. In much the same way, the commissariat filled the role of a quasi-treasury for the first 35 years of the settlement the enterprises filled a need for timely production of tools, goods and services, during the same period. The government farming enterprise kept the settlers alive and in food for several early years, and without this public conscience it is doubtful if the construction work or the communications or the delivery of rations would have succeeded. The convicts were beneficiaries as well. The opportunity existed for convicts to be assigned to private masters or to government service and those convicts, accepting government service usually learnt important skills for when they were emancipated.

The only way we can assess the contribution of the GBEs is in terms of output achieved, services performed, and the use made of that output. As referred to above, output can be measured in two ways. The first is to assign a daily rate to the convict working population, in government service, and there from value the amount of labour performed. From previous computations, labour represents approx. one-third of the total value of production. The alternate method is to value the individual items produced within the GBE system. Both methods have been tested at this point and the results are proximate to each other, thus verifying the results.

The results are as follows:

1. In 1817, there were 4747 convicts in government service with an estimated annual production value of £916,408
2. During the Macquarie administration, the value of labour used in construction gangs, was over £950,000, with a value assigned to the public works program of over £2 million.
3. The GBEs as part of the commissariat system were an important economic driver of the colonial economy.
4. A 'valuation' of the secondary industry items confirms that the manufacturing economy, before 1830, [at least between 1810 and 1830] outperformed the agricultural economy, even after the government farm output is considered.
5. The GDP figures for the period 1810 to 1830 are really much higher than previously estimated by N. G. Butlin, because he did not include the value of convict output. Butlin followed the British Treasury methodology and made no allowance for 'valuation' of convict labour or convict output.
6. So in summary, the tangible benefits of the GBEs included not only an extraordinary value that can be placed on production, but on the whole value of the public works program, before most of the materials used in the PW program were produced by the GBEs and therefore paid for from the convict maintenance allowance rather than any direct appropriation from the British Treasury.

Then followed a most important transition–the gradual transfer of manufactures from the public sector [the GBEs] to the private sector, which in turn underpinned the future growth and prosperity of this secondary industry component of the colonial economy. Pressure for items to fit into the daily work pattern often resulted in fresh thinking and a novel approach to entrepreneurship. Innovation in the small settlement was important and contributed to a new type of entrepreneur–innovation without huge capital investment. Progressively a range of new local manufacturing industries came about, including the manufacture of farm equipment suitable to local conditions. The manufacture of boats was brought about out of the need to service a new industry of sealing and whaling. The intangible benefits from the GBEs were just as numerous although not quantifiable in direct value terms. The development of a broad skills base, the development of government services such as hospitals, schools, churches, outlying villages, ferry services etc. These socio economic benefits would not have arrived until much later if innovation, local revenues and the development of convict jobs had not evolved as they did. Other Macquarie innovations such as a more formal town planning system and a systemised system of trade and commerce assisted in the development process and can be attributed to the growing business approach to components of the colonial economy.

Industries that formed a colony

What a huge plan; what a gigantic undertaking; production planning, market planning and a comprehensive business plan of the finest sort. A mammoth undertaking in an advanced economy, but for a small settlement of relatively few permanent free settlers, an unwilling military, and the challenge could easily seem overwhelming. The needs were not extravagant—a building design, plenty of labour, suitable raw materials, some limited equipment and off the project could go. Of course, a small number of basic government sponsored operations were already underway. A brick and tile site was initially built in the *Brickfields* are of Sydney and then Phillip commenced a second site in Rosehill on the east side or southern bank of the Parramatta river; the first stone yard was commenced just off the eastern side of Observatory Hill and the main timber harvesting site had been developed east of the Lane Cove River in Castle Hills. In addition to the small secondary industries, the early government-sponsored business enterprises included the building activities of the prisoners, the government farming activities and the livestock management. So there was some precedent for planning a convict labour driven commercial operation. The first step was the planning aspect. Lieutenant G.T.W.B Boyes who was experienced in the British commissariat of Mauritius was transferred to the colony of NSW to take control of the Finance, accounts, and planning branch. However, we have jumped ahead to the time of Boyes' arrival in the colony in about 1820. Our story commences in about the middle years of the Macquarie Administration when the first surge of prisoners arrived in the colony. Macquarie appointed two Principal Superintendents of Convicts–the first being Major Druitt, and the second a Major Ovens. Both men were dedicated to the task and made giant improvements in convict work practices.

During the early days of the Macquarie Administration, one of the benefits of Major Druitt's planning was more output from fewer labourers. With assignment under way, about 50% of the arriving prisoners were sent into the employ of 'masters', who had grazing and agricultural properties to work. Druitt commenced work with the government land clearing gangs and the government road-making gangs. This harsh work was usually left to the more unruly of the prisoners. So when the big rush of prisoners commenced arriving shortly after the Napoleonic Wars ceased in 1815, some work was available for them, but the real planning for growth commenced. Whilst the commissariat was planning to upgrade and expand the government business enterprises, Macquarie himself was planning for the extensive public works program. One needed the other. Macquarie's public works program badly needed the GBEs for cost reasons as well as the practical supply side, whilst the commissariat needed to plan its production around specific guidelines and objectives. Thus the GBEs commenced in 1802 long before Macquarie's arrival with the forerunner of the Lumber Yard (called the convict workshop), followed by a variety of subsidiary or associated operations–the Timber Yard, the Stone Yard, an expanded Brick and Tile Yard, a Dock Yard. The Lumber Yard's site was selected in a prominent location on the corner of High (George) Street and Bridge Street. Most raw materials used were despatched to the main commissariat store on George Street North, in a three-storey brick building fronting George Street. Logs were floated down the Lane Cove and the Parramatta Rivers and then on to the main commissariat wharf before being moved to the Timber Yard and onto the Lumber Yard. Metal strips were brought on ships travelling from, England and transferred to the Lumber Yard. Convicts were initially housed in private quarters until the Hyde Parks Barracks were completed at which time they were marched to the Lumber Yard and other work sites each morning at 5 AM.

i. Enterprises

Not surprisingly, the Commissariat became the prime storekeeper of materials and supplies used within the Colony. Out of necessity, the demand for timber products, bricks, tiles, stones, rude furnishings and carts needed to be and could be supplied locally. There was a need for local building materials, because of the length of time it took to order and receive supplies from Britain, and the urgency of building accommodation for military and civil personnel, a secure storehouse and essential infrastructure such as wharves, bridges, and housing for both settlers and convicts. Suitable local materials had been identified, including good clay deposits for brick and tile manufacturing and grain suitable for liquor production was being produced All that was needed was labour and basic equipment. Thus, the government business enterprises were assigned as a planning responsibility of the Commissariat and, in conjunction with the Superintendent of Convicts, Commissariat personnel planned for equipment, materials, transport and the provisioning of remote convict camps.

These government business enterprises covered a great deal of activity ranging from the making of bricks and tiles, basic forged tools, slops (clothing), shoes, furniture and timber frames for buildings to timber felling camps, vegetable and meat production, abattoirs, boat building, provisioning visiting ships and stevedoring. In addition, convicts were organised into gangs to clear land and build cart tracks. Ferry services were established to cross the harbour from north to south and link the Sydney and Parramatta settlements by river.

The Commissariat was not only about being a storekeeper; it also became responsible for business services, and a means of exchange was created by the store in the form of store receipts, whilst negotiating payroll bills and consolidated bills for remittance overseas. A foreign exchange facility was also created, and it became a catalyst for a local free market for agricultural products for settlers and emancipists.

    a.   Pastoral
    b.   Government Farms
    c.   Wool

    d.   Sealing & whaling

    e.   Boatbuilding (ref Th. Moore & Kings Dock Yard)

v. Business Development (Simon Ville)

vi. Social or Human Capital

In his useful 2003 summary of the theory of social capital, John Field claims that the central thesis of social capital theory can be summarised in two words: relationships matter.

By making connections with one another, and keeping them going over time, people are able to work together to achieve things that they either could not achieve by themselves, or could only achieve with great difficulty. People connect through a series of networks and they tend to share common values with other members of these networks; to the extent that these networks constitute a resource, they can be seen as forming a kind of capital. As well as being useful in its immediate context, this stock of capital can often be drawn on in other settings. In general, then, it follows that the more people you know, and the more you share a common outlook with them, the richer you are in social capital. (Field 2003, page 1)

Field suggests that social capital consists of informal networks, in contrast to formal procedures and responsibilities. When people want to make something happen, they will "ignore formal procedures and responsibilities and set off to ask someone they know . . . Calling on trusted friends, family or acquaintances is much less stressful than dealing with bureaucracies, and it usually seems to work faster and often produces a better outcome." (Field 2003 page 2).

Though this does not necessarily achieve a fairer outcome. As Field observes "Social relationships can sometimes serve to exclude and deny as well as include and enable." (Field 2003 page 3) He gives the example of 'old boy networks' that are said to dominate parts of the British Civil Service.

Field concludes "People's networks should be seen, then, as part of the wider set of relationships and norms that allow people to pursue their goals, and also serve to bind society together." (Field 2003 page 3)

Field's account of social capital appears to be the standard view. The OECD defines social capital as networks together with shared norms, values and understandings that facilitate cooperation within or among groups (Australian Bureau of Statistics page 1).

CHAPTER 3

TOWARDS SELF-SUFFICIENCY

Early Intentions, Policies & Plans

It was British policy to retain the concept of a prison settlement but only if the colony could pay its own way. Such dual desires were in conflict. Autocracy (as in being necessary to operate a prison) would destroy any freedom of enterprise, which in any other circumstances was essential to the growth of colonial income. Would social and political progress come with economic advances?

Wealth would increase continuously between 1802 and 1850, not due to any industrialisation, but due to an entry into a cycle of investment in pastures and sheep–'the golden age'. Wealth was measured in purely tangible forms–Coghlan in *The Wealth & Progress of NSW–1886'*, computed the wealth of the colony at that time, in terms of the value of rural holdings, the value of residential town developments, the value of government buildings, of roads and other infrastructure, plus the value of all usable plant and equipment. Needless to say, this measurement got unwieldy and did not last as a statistical guide to the success of the colony. Probably Coghlan was being forced to compare the colony of NSW with other colonies in Australia as well as with similar countries overseas, for political purposes. Coghlan produces a table comparing the NSW wealth per head with that of numerous overseas countries, with little point except to comment that measuring standards were different elsewhere.

The cycle rolled forward–opening up new land, adding the grazing of sheep, adding to 'national income' followed by more investment–and the cycle rolls around again. Diversification of the economy soon followed and led to an ever-increasing standard of living, which, in itself sustained further growth.

Capital formation followed, mostly in agriculture but increasingly in manufactures[4]. Such steps usually relied on borrowing externally, but such borrowing must have been accompanied by development of financial institutions.

A society, which cannot by its own savings finance the progress it desires, must strive, in the alternative, to make itself credit worthy and will only succeed if it follows market opportunities and adopts comparative advantage.

Because future prospects depend so much on present imports, the colony must look for profitable export industries[5]. It must also offer prospects of gain to people of enterprise.

Let me restate the salient points of the above synopsis.

The main characteristics of the colonial economy in transition [6](before 1832) are

The Colonial Government adopted the policy of free enterprise and free trade, during and following the administration of Lachlan Macquarie.

Out of necessity there was a dominance of agriculture in the economy–this was a social phenomenon because of the needs and availability of convict labour.

Social problems with bad treatment of aborigines and convicts curbed the otherwise 'clean' image of a successful economy.

---

4   Butlin–Forming the Colonial economy
5   Based on Hainsworth–The Sydney Traders
6   Beckett, G 'The economics of Colonial NSW' (colonial press 2003)

Lack of catalysts for British private investment prevailed until Macquarie converted the colonial image in the 1810-1820 period with new buildings, cleaning up the slums of the 'Rocks' area, and encouraging new enterprise.

Wealth creation was taking place through capital investment and speculation.

The growing need for financial institutions came with the commencement of borrowing and capital migration.

The need for private borrowing overseas occurred because of the lack of savings, wealth and financial institutions in the economy before 1830.

On the other hand the key factors of the (gradually) maturing colonial economy changed slightly (after 1832)

Transportation and the convict labour program was the catalyst for growth until growth plateaued and transportation became more of an economic burden that could not continue to be tolerated

The importance of the on-going British treasury support payments was that there was a steady flow of funds arriving in the colony, not only as support payments for the convicts, but they also had a flow-on effect through the commissary into the pockets of small farmers, pastoralists and vegetable growers as well as to the numerous cottage industries springing up throughout the settled areas of Sydney, Parramatta, Liverpool, Newcastle and the Hawkesbury.

The role of free immigration and the accompanying capital contributions was essential to the constant demand for labour, enterprising operators and the capital formation within the colony. They brought capital goods, capital ideas and just plain capital to the colony.

The role of land sales[7] was that it provided the colony with the funding boost it required to diversify the colony. Land revenues provided the direct funding for immigrants, aboriginal support, and a small amount of supplemental discretionary funding for the governor.

The rise of the pastoral industry was crucial for trade, attracting immigrants, British investment and then to the attracting of manufacturers associated with the agricultural industries, including the extraction industries.

The growth of manufactures[8] closely followed the growth of the agricultural sector and attracted another source and variety of capital and direct investment

British capital investment and speculation was encouraged by the creditworthiness of the colonies, by direct investment of landowners from Britain and by migrant flow. British newspapers gave many column inches to events in the colony and there was a constant stream of books being written about life and exploits and successes in the colony.

Population growth[9] was constant and fast and was supported by emancipated convicts, and convicts whose sentences had expired, by free immigrants and even by British ex-Military personnel attracted to the colony from India and post-Napoleonic Europe.

The importance of education cannot be overstated. The illiteracy rate between 1788 and 1802 was high, but Marsden led the movement for schooling young people as well as creating literacy programs for the mature aged worker[10].

Statistics collected for the period come from a variety of sources such as 'The blue books' original records held by the (NSW) State Records Office, from the HRNSW and the HRA. Some of the pre-1822 statistics are questionable but with nothing better, they offer a limited picture of life in the colony. Coghlan was the official collector of statistics for over

---

[7]   Butlin 'Forming the colonial economy'
[8]   Hainsworth 'The Sydney Traders'
[9]   Hartwell 'Economic Development of VDL'
[10] Abbott–Chapter 3 in Economic Development of Australia

30 years and his 'Wealth & Progress' provides a vital contribution to our understanding of fiscal events, trends and achievements within the colony as well as a graphic comparison of the six colonies.

Each of these elements contributes to the growth of the colonial economy.

Thus, this is 'how' the economy grew[11], the 'why' is another matter. The why was, in reality, to further the goals of British colonial policy–to create a strategic base for defence and foreign policy rationales, as an investment outlet, as a source of trade, both with raw materials being exported to Britain and British goods being imported–a Navigation Act scenario, and mostly, in practice as a transference of some of the worst social ills in Britain to a colony' out of sight'. Wrapping all these aspects together was the goal of self-sufficiency and self-support.

As in any modern economy, the colonial economy had practical and physical limitations[12].

The trade and economic cycles in the colony were influenced by events overseas, as well as local.

Droughts and floods, insect plagues and livestock disease.

Grazing land had limited availability until explorers found a way across the Blue Mountains in 1816.

The Depressions of 1827 and 1841-1843 were manmade and largely the result of British speculators, but the negative effects were largely offset by the boom times which attracted the investors and speculators, improved the trading between the two countries and improved the overall standard of living at a rate far greater than if there had been no cycles.

---

11 Beckett 'The Economics of Colonial NSW' Chapter 3–Policies & Planning
12 Based on Beckett, G 'The Public Finance of Colonial NSW' (colonial press 2002)

To offset these limitations[13], there were a number of positive aspects within the economy

There was a continuous and growing flow of convicts between 1820 and 1842. In all over 160,000 convicted souls found their way to the colonies in Australia.

Ever increasing physical and fiscal resources were provided by Britain to the colonial economy.

There followed the creation of basic capital accumulation by individuals.

Sustained higher living standards were underpinned by British fiscal support.

The growing population was underpinned by the progressive freeing of prisoners, as well as by sponsored immigration, which in turn brought a constant social change.

Other commentators and writers comment on the source of growth in the colonial economy. Abbott and Nairn[14] introduce a number of specialist economic historians in their edited version of 'The economic Growth of Australia 1788-1820'; Hartwell[15] writes of the Economic Development of VDL 1820-1859, and Fitzpatrick[16] offers another opinion in 'The British Empire in Australia'.

Butlin, N.G.[17] suggests his own formula of economic growth factors in 'Forming the Colonial Economy'.

However, Abbott in his Introduction[18] points out the dearth of any written treatment of the early phases of Australian economic development

---

[13] Based on Butlin, S.J. 'Foundations of the Australian Monetary System 1788-1851'
[14] Abbott & Nairn (eds) Economic Development of Australia
[15] Hartwell 'Economic Development of VDL'
[16] Fitzpatrick 'The British Empire in Australia'
[17] Butlin, N.G. 'Forming the Colonial Economy'
[18] Abbott & Nairn 'The Economic Growth of Australia'

in publication between 1939(Fitzpatrick) and Shaw's Convicts and Colonies[19] in 1966. Abbott & Nairn try to fill that gap through a collection of short papers, usually an abbreviated version of the author's full account elsewhere in print. They believe (as stated in their Introduction) that the 'economic advantages to the colony included the resources made available by Britain, although the convicts provided merely the means, not the end of settlement'[20]. They also insist that the economic and strategic motives ascribed to Britain in the settlement of the colony must include the 'examination of the decision to transport convicts to Botany Bay in terms of British colonial policy before 1786, and of the prevailing social and economic conditions in Britain and their possible relation to crime[21]'.

Having considered the how of the equation seeking to determine the contribution to growth of the colonial economy, now we need to consider the reasons why.

The economic growth of the colony was but one of the considerations necessary to meet the defence, foreign policy, economic and social goals of the British settlement plan. An undeveloped colony did not gain the British any credibility in meeting their goals, and it was the transfer of the convicts to this alternative penal settlement that provided the workhorses of development to meet their full objectives. In addition, at least in Governor Phillip's settlement implementation plan, the convicts would be used to develop the infrastructure whilst at the same time encouraging the extraction and utilisation of available raw materials ready for shipping back to Britain.

We will now consider the key factors set down above, within the space constraints of this exercise. Each one would be the subject of a broad study in chapter length[22], under a number of category headings viz. Colonial Economic Statistics; Capital Formation in the Colonial Economy; Sequencing the Growth (an Abbott concept); The Patterns of Growth and The Cottage Industries.

---

19   Shaw, A.G.L. 'Convicts & Colonies'
20   Introduction to Economic Development of Australia 1788-1821
21   Abbott & Nairn (eds) 'The economic Growth of Australia 1788-1821'
22   Refer Beckett who includes chapter length discussions in 'The Economics of Colonial NSW'

A. Statistics

The statistical[23] summaries[24] show numerous highlights of the colonial economy and can be listed as follows:

The population growth[25] was regular and challenging, although the surplus of males over females was disparate and potentially detrimental. We should be mindful of the number of children and their specific needs. The nexus between total population and those 'on the store' was broken and reduced year by year. This progress affected the role, influence and operation of the commissary. Two other observations on the population growth can be made. Firstly, the growth rates in the Town of Sydney followed similar trends to those later found in Parramatta, Liverpool and Windsor. This means that selected decentralisation locations were attractive to new settlers and met the needs of these settlers. Secondly, as the earliest settlement outgrew its natural boundaries (of the Blue Mountains, the Hawkesbury to the north and the Nepean to the south), the new expansion settlements of Bathurst (ten (10) small land grants were initially made 1815-1818) and Newcastle (twenty-three (23) small agricultural grants were made in 1821) supported Lord Bathurst's policy of large-scale land grants to be a catalyst to growth.

The number of convicts[26] arriving in New South Wales made a big difference to the colony in transition

The volume of treasury bills[27] drawn by the colony, especially in those first important 30 years, reflected two facts—the amazingly low cost to the British Treasury of operating the colony (that Treasury goal was being achieved) and of just where the 'capital formation' in those early years was coming from.

---

[23] Sourced from Beckett, G 'Handbook of Colonial Statistics' (colonial press—2003)

[24] Reproduced in the appendix to this study

[25] Source HRA, *passim*

[26] Shaw, A.G.L. *Convicts & the Colonies* pp363-8

[27] Bigge, J.T.—Appendix to Report III (1823)

The return of livestock[28] shows the successful pasturing of sheep and cattle and the quality of management, climate and husbandry proffered this burgeoning industry.

Trade statistics[29] (imports) shows the source of such imports and the need for securing the Asian trade routes, for the majority of imports arrived from India and China and only in 1821 were the majority of imports from Britain.

From as early as 1810, private farming[30], based on evidence to the Bigge enquiry as contained in his subsequent report, was dominant, successful and essential to the needs of the colony. The accuracy of some of the statistics is questionable but they are the only statistics available. The total acres appear to be well balanced between grazing (sheep, cattle and hogs all grew rapidly with little sign of breeding loss or slaughter for food) and grain, with wheat and maize sharing the farming land.

By reviewing the prices obtained at the London auctions of NSW Wool between 1818 and 1821[31], we can understand Bathurst's goal of growing 'fine' wool, which he thought would have averaged 12s per pound rather than the 2s 10p it actually achieved.

Wool shipments[32] soared between 1807 and 1821 and grew from 13,616lb to 175,433lb annually during that time.

An early 1821 map of Sydney[33] shows the location of the emerging manufactures of the colony. The second slaughterhouse had opened, a sixth mill was opened and we find the locations of boat-building, tanneries, salt works, furniture, candles, earthenware, tea and tobacco and a brewery, all serving the colony. Manufacturing was not the largest employer but in terms of import replacement goods, was the most important employer.

---

[28]   Source: Select Committee of the House of Commons on Transportation 1838

[29]   Wentworth, W. C. 'History of NSW '

[30]   Bigge evidence

[31]   Macarthur Papers Vol 69

[32]   ibid

[33]   NLA Map Collection–Sydney Map published 1822

Agriculture won the export stakes and supported the colonial local revenue base by allowing imports to match exports, and supporting a duty and tariff on all imports. This local discretionary revenue started off small and convenient, but grew rapidly into a major government source of revenues to cover every expenditure apart from the direct costs of the convict system.

A listing of major Public Works[34] helps us understand the benefits to the colony of the free settlers, the convicts, the contractors and the entrepreneurs. In summary, the period between 1817 and 1821 witnessed the development of 6 main roads, of major government buildings, of churches, of military barracks and growing infrastructure. Mostly the period witnessed the success of the Macquarie administration and his major contribution to the colonial economic growth.

This writer's assembling of raw colonial economic statistics[35] (refer appendix) suggests a positive balance of payments growth during the 1826-1834 period with growth, but sometimes negative balance of payments at other times. Imports took a dip in the depression years of 1827 and 1828 but grew dramatically until the next depression of 1842-1844. Local revenues, which the British treasury relied upon to replace contributions from Britain, also grew as a reflection of the burgeoning colonial economy. If we use 1826 as a base year then growth to 1834 became a cumulative factor of 280% over those 8 years or a remarkable 4% per annum.

All in all, the statistics acquaint the reader with a fairly comprehensive picture of 'how' (much) the colony was growing, especially during those important formative years. The colonial establishment had laid the basis for a successful colony and for supporting the future rounds of convict transfers.

---

[34]   Cathcart, L–Public Works of NSW
[35]   Beckett 'Handbook of Colonial Statistics (colonial press 2003)

CHAPTER 4

LOCAL TAXATION

A reader may ask, why 1800 and why 1810. As we saw in the first chapter of this study on the rise of public finance and public accounting in the colony, 1802 was the first attempt to record either income or expenditure in the colony. The British Treasury had for the years between 1788 and 1801 recorded all of the expenditure in equipping and moving the first and second fleet, and for the provisioning and victualling the colony for this same period. However, with the necessary, but loose, mechanism of drawing Bills on the Treasury for most purchases, there is a great deal of doubt in the mind of Butlin, Shann and even Clark, that the published figures of the period are accurate.

For this study we are relying on the source documents–the hand-written documents prepared by Reverend Samuel Marsden and Asst Surgeon Darcy Wentworth, 'audited' by the Lieutenant Governors each quarter and then published for all settlers to read in the *Sydney Gazette*.

In a splendid work, edited by James Thomson in 1881, the resources of the Sydney Morning Herald were used (since the Hansard transcription service had not yet commenced in the New South Wales Legislative Chambers) to assemble the Treasurers statements between 1855 (the First Parliament) and November 1881 (the Tenth Parliament).

Thomson wrote in the Preface "Some years ago it was considered desirable that all the Financial Statements made since the inauguration of Responsible Government should be collated and printed for future reference, and for distribution amongst the Public Libraries, Schools of Arts and other literary institutions of the colony. The task of editing these Statements was entrusted to me, I presume, of the experience, which I had acquired, during a long course of years, of the financial affairs of the colony, and the practical knowledge which I possessed of its public accounts generally. Until recently (when Hansard commenced a reporting service in 1880) no authorised copy of any of the Financial Statements (by the Colonial Treasurers) was in existence, so that in the discharge of the duty imposed upon me I had to carefully revise the reports that were given of them in the *Sydney Morning herald*, which I found extremely accurate. In revising these statements I had to compare the Herald's figures with the published printed documents,–a labour which necessarily involved much trouble and occupied a considerable amount of time.

I have placed, as an Appendix to the Financial Statements, a memorandum explanatory of the financial system of New South Wales and an account of the rise, progress and present condition of the public revenue, as it is considered they may be found useful to those who take an interest in the financial affairs of the colony. I prepared these two papers in 1876 and 1879 for the information of the Imperial Government, who had it in contemplation at the time to publish some kind of official work on the defences, financial resources, and general condition of the several Australian colonies."

Why 1810? This was the year during which Lachlan Macquarie arrived in the colony, as the successor to William Bligh, whose failure to govern for all residents led to a slackness and sickness in the colony, which would take many pains from Macquarie to make better and allow the deep wounds to heal. Macquarie reformed the Commissary operation firstly, then 'reformed' the public finance and the public reporting of the colony, but tightening up the currency movement, creating a bank to assist both the traders and the colonial merchants, and 'regularising' the accounting mechanism of the 'Orphan Fund' and the 'Police Fund'.

The period between 1802 and 1810 was highlighted by a change of governor (King to Bligh) in 1806. This date marked a social decline in the colony, with Macarthur turning into a bitter enemy of the governor, followed by a re-alignment of the NSW Corps allegiances away from the governor and towards the rampant self-serving individually profitable trading activities of the military officers.

The colonial economy had been running in freefall. Little government support, a touch of entrepreneurial activity and a few governor declarations that urged the emancipists onto a self-supporting 30 acres and off the general stores. By the end of the King era, he could account for only 180,246 pounds in 'value' of assets as a 'credit against expenses'.

The value of grain and supplies in the commissary stores of about 62,000 pound

The value of buildings completed by King, could only account for 6,500 pound

The value of public livestock owned by the governor would amount to 112,000 pound

The contribution of King to the colonial economy was little (especially when compared to Macquarie). He was not even the able administrator that Phillip had encountered in the time prior to 1792, and other than a few social welfare titbits, King managed to let the colony run without much interference by government. Many more persons were dependent on the government store in 1806 than when King accepted his appointment in 1800. Hunter had led the social decay during his years of 1795 and 1800, but much of his era was spent undoing the damage completed by the interim administrators (between Phillip and Hunter)–Captain Grose (upgraded from Lieutenant Governor for two years, and then Captain Paterson, acting as Lieutenant governor for the next year. These three years allowed the military officers to become dominant in the colony and run things on their own terms–the assignment of the convicts; the run-away trade in spirits; the use of spirits as the means of exchange; the absolute domination of the military in buying shiploads of goods for re-sale. It took the shipment of Macquarie's own regiment to the colony and the withdrawal of the NSW Corps to finally put a stop to the military occupation of spirits and trade. Bligh saw the problem but appeared powerless to intervene.

H.V.Evatt describes these years well in his study 'Rum Rebellion'. In a forward to the 1938 edition, Hartley Grattan (a Carnegie Scholar 1937-38), and an American who became enamoured with Australian History wrote" the law can become a weapon in the social struggle and the courts a battleground of opposing class interests on which justice is weighed in favour of one side. This is in response to Justice Evatt's assertion that 'the Courts were the true forum of the little colony . . . . there was no legislature, no avowed political association or party, no theatre and no independent press' but the major social issues are generally apt to be subverted to the interest of the dominant class in the community." This class struggle pitted Bligh against Macarthur even though the English Government's economic plan for the colony envisaged the strong establishment of a small-holding peasantry in the country, the bulk of the peasants in any future of the colony then visible would be limited to time expired and emancipated convicts. Grattan suggests this economic plan was merely the projection on virgin Australia of an economic pattern being disrupted by the industrial revolution, which plan was destroyed after Phillip's departure from Sydney by the military officers.

The military, in the period between Phillip and Hunter, manipulated their own plan into full operation. They wanted a trading monopoly which was a combined with land holding on an extensive scale along with the ruthless exploitation of convict labour. Rum became the established medium of exchange and it was monopolised to raise its price, whilst consumption was pushed to the limit, thus allowing the monopolists to make huge profits. The defence of the system became the Rum Rebellion' of 1808-09. The struggle over the rum traffic was merely symptomatic of a deeper issue. The small landholders only existed to be exploited until economically exhausted and then removed through inevitable bankruptcy.

Grattan records in his Forward that "since the officers held, in their hands, the military power, as well as such minimum civil as had been developed, whilst the Courts held the supreme economic power, the combined power made them masters of the community. They directed it in a fashion that benefited themselves, but allowed for no progress" The 'brains' of the system was John Macarthur though he was far from being the sole initiator, beneficiary or protagonist. These monopolists broke three governors–Hunter, King, through complete lack of scruple and set a pattern for any successor, even though Bligh had been instruction to break up the monopoly and return the small landholders to the place in the community originally planned for them. Setting about his orders, Bligh quickly fell afoul of Macarthur and his associates

Macarthur came through this relatively unscathed, especially in latter-day public opinion, and his legacy, as muted through John Thomas Bigge in 1822 was to create a third economic program of foreseeing a broad acre pastoral industry, utilising the free labour of the convicts, but repaying the costs of the colony afforded by the British Treasury through the export of raw wool and the resulting strengthening of the woollen industry in England.

A review of significant events will show that the 'Rum Rebellion' was not the only big event that affected the colony.

When Phillip arrived in the colony in 1788 and established the penal settlement, he came with the authority to raise taxes. This was part of his instructions dated 2nd April 1787.

"Our will and pleasure is that all public monies which shall be raised be issued out of warrant from you and disposed of by you for the support of the government and for such other purpose as shall be entirely directed and not otherwise".

Phillip had been instructed to create a local commissary (he was provided with a commissary officer) in order to acquire, stock and furnish supplies within the colony to victual convicts, the military and the 40 military wives and families that had arrived with the Fleet. The commissary thus became the heart of the local economy for at least the first 20 years of settlement. The commissary was responsible for planning the rations required for the number of persons to be provisioned, based on the governor's decision on individual rations. The role of the commissary was to purchase supplies from visiting ships or, when available, local suppliers and pay a bill of exchange drawn on the British Treasury. This system provided the supplies needed but promoted great inaccuracies in the recording area, and thus, according to N.G. Butlin, the figures from the British Treasury for the tooling and victualling of the colony during the first few years are questionable and likely inaccurate. Phillip had been authorised to draw a bill at the Cape on route with the First Fleet, in order to purchase fresh supplies for the remainder of the voyage. It would have taken many months for this bill to be presented in London, and so, even if accurate, it is unlikely that the expenditures via bills presented would have reflected the correct time period.

There were many items that became short in the first few years and since there were no local persons to provide a source of supply, the governor stepped in and provided the labour within a government-inspired operation. The governor created his own vegetable patch and orchard in the 'governor's domain' and on 'Garden Island'. The governor organised a 'government farm' for watching over the livestock that had arrived and to grow grain that appeared to do well in the colony. It was to take a convict experienced in English style farming to cross grain strains and achieve a suitable local strain of wheat, barley, corn and maize. Clothing had become a major difficulty, with convicts going around in an advanced state of undress and shoeless. The answer was to establish a clothing factory in which the female convicts could be utilised. This answer would also segregate the male and female convicts as already the fear of growing numbers of illegitimate children running around the colony occupied the governor's mind. Children meant education, as well as extra mouths to feed and this was a penal colony with growing numbers of convicts expected. Phillip's planning for the colony had not included social or political matters. He had not anticipated free settlers, other than military or civil officers needing to retire and wanting to remain in the colony. Phillip himself had planned only to return to England at the end of his official term.

There were many opportunities for small business in the colony. For a start, very quickly it became apparent that the tools and equipment supplied with the First fleet were neither entirely suitable or in sufficient quantity. The felling axes were of little use against the standard trees in need of clearing around Sydney Cove and the Rose Hill settlements, and naturally, each new 30-acre farmer required a set of tools if he was to clear his land and become a farmer supplying produce to the commissary. But the second most important need was that of transportation. Since there were no working horses there was no need for carts, but there was an urgent need for boats for fishing and movement of people and goods between Sydney and Rose Hill. It took until 1790 for the first locally made boat to be ready to cover the Sydney-Rose Hill (Parramatta) link.

The first mill assembled on Observatory Hill could only grind 6 bushels of wheat each day. Mills were to play an important role in the colony and from just one operating mill in 1795, the number grew rapidly so that by 1848, there were 220 operating mills of which 79 were steam powered, and the remainder were horse, wind or human driven. Mills accounted for over 50% of total industry by the middle of the 19th century.

New industry was to be the mainstay of the fledgling colonial economy. The growth of industry was slow but creative and ranged from road making and road repairs to boat building, whale and seal hunting to a broad range of farming–vineyards, brooms, clothing and linen (from locally grown flax).

Other developments that created work for convicts and a trading and export opportunity were the discovery of coal. Newcastle became a convict centre as well as the main provider of coal for export to South America, England and Calcutta. The discovery of seals in Bass Strait gave encouragement to a large sealing industry, which led to a dramatic growth of the local boat-building industry. Exporting commenced in 1800 with the first shipment of sandalwood, wheat and pork. Obviously trading was expected to grow and become quite important to the colony, because Governor King built the first Customs House on the edge of Sydney Cove.

Funding for the first twelve years of the colony had come from the British Treasury but keeping in mind that the colony was instructed to become self-sufficient as quickly as possible, and also that the governor had been given taxing powers, King decided to impose tariffs on spirits, wine and beer in 1800 to complete the new Sydney Gaol that could not be completed by subscription as originally planned by Hunter.

Thus, by 1800, the colony was finding a sense of direction. King was not the right man for the times and there was more neglect during the Bligh times until Macquarie arrived with enthusiasm and a resolve to build the colony into the giant economy that was expected by the British Treasury.

One of the last acts of Phillip before he left the colony for his home in Britain was to proclaim the hours of work to be adopted by the convict labourers.

Phillip set "from sunup to sundown, with a break of 2 ½ ours during the day". When food was particularly in short supply, Phillip had expected that the finishing hour would be 3 o'clock in the afternoon, which would allow time, before dark, to tend to a vegetable patch or such food sources (livestock) that was being set aside for nutrition apart from foodstuffs supplied by the Commissary.

Hunter era was unremarkable for any positive gains in the colony. He claimed at one time that the Combination act in Britain of 1799 would restrict economic activity in the colony, but this piece of legislation intended by Westminster to stop formation of unions and prohibit strikes, was of little, if any, interest to colonial settlers, who went on their own way building homes, farming, trading, protecting what little they had and being subjugated to the military officers. The only relief or release would come from orderly organisation of the convict work gangs but since the military decided it was not their role to supervise convicts the work supervision was left to independent supervisors, but mostly to other convicts. The system did not work well, at least until Macquarie came to the colony.

Both Hunter and King arrived in the colony with instructions from the British Government to break the trade monopoly by the military, but reform was slow to gain any foothold at all. Even King sought relief from the military activists. King decided to rebuild the government herd of livestock, which was a noble enough plan and designed to provide food in the event of another severe drought and food shortage, but in order to implement his plan, he purchased cattle from the very military officers who were rorting the system and King paid far in excess of their real worth. Lackadaisical supervision of both cattle and convicts saw the cattle escape and until near the end of the Macquarie years, build into a substantial herd worth a goodly sum to the settlers when finally recaptured.

King did introduce a ticket of leave system for the convicts who were in good stead with the military, their direct supervisors, the commissary, and the law. It was King's way of removing convicts who could be trusted to be good colonial citizens from the commissary ration list.

King's other contribution was to foreshadow the usefulness to the colony of a local vineyard, and upon receiving two Napoleonic War prisoners in 1801 put them to work in establishing a wine industry for the colony.

The Hunter River area received a boost when it was found that locally grown flax could be used to produce linen. It was not the best quality but the governor thought it could be of great interest to the English government. In this way King recognised the conflict he was in the middle of. He was the British representative in the colony, was paid (rather handsomely as it turns out) by the British Government from the Civil List, but was usually respected and befriended by the settlers to whom he felt a moral and ethical, if not a legal responsibility. In the event of a conflict between the colony and the crown whose side would he choose?

The flax exercise should have been beneficial to both sides, but King knew in his heart that the local product was not of a high quality and would not be accepted by the British public or the British manufacturers. Likewise in declaring in 1801 that all coal and mineral reserves in the colony were the property of the Crown, he knew that only lackadaisical convict labour would be used to extract, load and work the coal removed from the Newcastle coal–fields. King was a free enterprise man under his gubernatorial cloak and invited Robert Campbell (from India) to set up a warehouse and trading post in the colony.

Campbell brought immediate gain and benefit to the colony by shipping a load of colonial coal from Newcastle to Calcutta.

The British encouraged free enterprise in other ways. The English government was going through one of its phases of privatisation. After the second fleet was thought to be much more expensive that Matra had projected, the Colonial Office decided to ship via contractors future prisoners to the penal colony, for a fixed fee. Competition brought a high price for the privately transported prisoners. Savings were encouraged by the contracts on the ship's captains by cutting food (both quantity and quality), limiting appropriate clothing, eliminating exercise and generally creating deplorable conditions for the prisoners, not least being the overcrowding. As a result the death rate of prisoners between England and Botany Bay was nearly 50% in the third fleet. The Government was only mildly offended by the charges of unlawfulness by Wilberforce and his ilk. But the resolve was to make failure to deliver healthy humans instead of human misery hurt the contractor's pocket. Surgeons were included on each shipping manifest with a bonus of 10/6 for each convict landed in healthy condition and a bonus of 50 pound to the ship's captain for assisting the surgeon to land healthy convicts. The problem may not have been solved but was made much better by these incentives.

With the sealing industry showing great promise, the whaling industry was given new strength mostly by the arrival of American whalers into Sydney Harbour. The local industry got underway in 1802 with 7 ships operating from Port Jackson. The Bass Strait area was using half of the 22 ships operating by 1803. The others were successfully operating in New Zealand and South Australian waters.

The colony by this time was moving through turbulent times. The settlements were mostly rural in nature and relied mainly on produce grown with the assistance of assigned convicts. By governor regulation these assigned persons were to be fed, housed, clothed and generally maintained by the 'master'. This was not an inexpensive program for the masters, especially where smallholdings were involved. King ordered that the commissary purchase all produce from these landholders and set a minimum price at which wheat and other grains would be purchased. In this way the landowners could be seen to receive adequate compensation to meet their obligations to their convict workers. As the colony grew demand for 'luxury' items as well as a broader range of staples also grew and this attracted a growing number of 'speculative' ships into the port of Sydney. A price war developed between the traders, the military and those wanting to participate in the purchasing of imported goods. Governor King, having set the original tariff collections on only spirits, wine and beer, decided to impose a 5% ad valorem duty on all imports in 1802. This immediately created a steady revenue stream that needed accounting for. King assumed that this was discretionary income available to him to dispense, as he considered fair and not as an offset to what the British Treasury was providing to the colony.

King had identified a growing social problem as the one where street children were in large numbers, and decided to do something about it. King formed the female Orphan Committee, with the object of housing, feeding, clothing and educating these children until they could be put into service in the colony. The committee included the Reverend Samuel Marsden who had really been instrumental in recognising the problem and finding a partial solution. King appointed Marsden the Treasurer of the committee and decided to use certain Treasury funds to buy the house of the departing Lieutenant Kent, who made it known that he (Kent), had the finest residence in Sydney. Kent was leaving the colony to return to England and take up another posting and he negotiated with the governor for the government to buy his house at 'valuation'. The valuation was based on a replacement cost, whether or not another house like Kent's would ever be built again and the valuation came to 1,700 pound. Kent received his money via a bill drawn on the British Treasury, which King prayed would be accepted by the Treasury. The bill was negotiated and the Female Orphanage got a residence for about 80 waifs off the streets, although a revenue-raising plan came about when Marsden accepted destitute children from single fathers for a lump sum of 5 pound. It was not as though Marsden or the Orphan Committee were short of revenue. With the growth tax imposed by King, the amount of revenue raised by the Harbour Master from imported goods, especially the alcohol trade, Marsden was constantly looking for ways to spend his money.

King sent Lt-Governor David Collins off to open a settlement at Port Phillip but Collins decided that the Mornington Peninsula was not an ideal place to commence a colony and crossed the strait and selected Hobart instead. Van Diemen's Land had been settled first in 1803, just as the *Sydney Gazette* newspaper was being founded by King as a means of keeping the settlers informed. He would make many proclamations to the free settlers as well as advertising that certain convicts had gone bush. The scourge of the importation of spirits could not be handled but King decided that 32,000 litres of rum brought to the colony from Bengal by Campbell should be returned and he accepted no counsel to the contrary although Marsden led a group to announce how great noble and strong the governor was becoming. It was at this time, with minimum imports transferring from the colony into Britain that the British Government decided to impose a tariff on all colonial imports. Sealskins had yielded either to the colony or to the British merchants over 100,000 skins between 1800 and 1806. This could be considered an ecological disaster or a trading triumph, depending on one's viewpoint, but then the British Government cashed in on the colonial 'success' by imposing this levy on all imports.

In the colony, prices were heavily influenced by local conditions including droughts and floods, and English economic conditions all affected events in the colony. The drought of 1804 for instance affected the wheat crop and thus the price of wheat within the colony. King decided to increase to price the Commissary would purchase private farm grain but even so the shortages were reflected in the price of bread. A settler could buy a loaf of bread for 4p or barter it with 2 ½ pound of wheat.

By 1805 Macarthur could see the writing on the wall for his days as a military officer and accepted his grant of land available to all military who intended to settle in the colony and opened his estate at the Cowpastures, probably the best grazing land within the 1805 limits of the colony.

King's next contribution to the social needs of the convicts was to proclaim a 56-hour workweek for all assignees in return for bed and breakfast, tobacco and tea. The convict rations from the commissary would meet their needs for lunch and dinner.

The first free settlers were wealthy Britons who were enticed into relocating by the offer of free land grants, convict labour to work the land and an allocation of government livestock. The Blaxland brothers responded to this enticement in 1805. In that same year the first colonial built whaler was launched so that greater local participation could be realised.

Pressure on the colony was coming not only from outside the territory but inside as well. We have accounted for King's sudden interest in the growing orphan numbers in Sydney town, but the cause of the problem raises concerns as to the type of society the colony could develop into. Two measures offer some indication of the underlying movement.

In 1805, there were 1400 women in the colony but there were only 360 married couples

Of the 1800 children, under 18, over half were illegitimate

The crime rate in the colony was by 1807, 8 times the rate in England.

The 1806 drought made the wheat crop fail, and the grain became scarce. The price of wheat rose from 1/1/–to 3/14/–per bushel and the price of bread rose 12 fold from 4p to 4/–per loaf. The new governor, sent to replace Phillip Gidley King arrived in Sydney. Tales of the Bounty mutiny and its remarkable voyage of skill and endurance had foreshadowed William Bligh's arrival across the Pacific.

Having outlined the many events, which both curtailed and encouraged the colonial economy, it is time to review the impact on the financial situation brought about by these economic conditions.

N.G. Butlin reports in *Forming a Colonial Economy*

"British decision makers were far from consistent in their attitudes to fiscal obligations to and from the colonists. All governors to 1821 left with at least his fiscal reputation tarnished. Intermittent and at times irascible and condemnatory intervention in colonial expenditures reflected, in part, British ignorance and suspicion. In fact, complex colonial fiscs operated almost from the beginning of the settlement. By 1830, local revenues were offsetting expenditures for everything except convict and defence functions.

"The transfer of prisoners was, from a colonial Australia view, a capital transfer, even if, from a British perspective, the human capital involve had a negative vale. Britain was determined to constrain the British contribution to the colonial operations and to narrow the range of support. It sought ways of ever reducing, to the British taxpayer, the per capita costs of prisoners landed in the colony and to limit the total budgetary costs of sustaining colonies. One way, they decided to achieve this was through auditing public accounts and criticising local behaviour. Other ways was the adoption of a policy of private development of the country, and make the country no longer dependent essentially on convict transfers. A second they decided would be to encourage the emergence of a freed society from a freed population. Thus part of the funds could be diverted from the convict population to the funding of public activity.

"The question remains is the extent to which the colonists could be encouraged to enter the colony and how much of the burden could they bear".

A study of the types of public and private British Investment in the colony is the subject of another exercise, but it can be said here that a wonderful model could be constructed of the formation of a colonial economy.

Consider the inputs: British investment of capital and goods, the transfer of industry–the branch office in the colony, the use of the colony as a source of raw materials–the colonial garden, ripe for the picking. British ships transferring people and goods.

Consider the restraints of population to adopt and utilise the investment

Consider the ultimate limitations of human personality–the convicts forced to labour, when their colleagues back 'home' were lounging in a prison cell. Why should they work in exchange for a limited freedom?

If all this sounds farfetched let us consider the role of free trade and its benefits to Britain.

This is a piece by Sir T. H. Farrer (Bart) from his 1887 book 'Free *Trade versus Fair Trade*'. The notation on the front-piece of the book shows the Cobden Club emblem with the words 'free trade, peace, goodwill among nations'. We will discuss Cobden a little later when we review the work of the Federation Senator Edward Pulsford–another outspoken supporter and devotee of the Cobden philosophy, and free trade and open immigration.

"The amount of English capital constantly employed abroad in private trade and in permanent investments, including Stock Exchange securities, private advances, property owned abroad by Englishmen, British shipping,

British-owned cargoes, and other British earnings abroad, has been estimated by competent statisticians as being between 1,500 and 2,000 million pounds, and is constantly increasing. Taking the lower figure, the interest or profit upon it, at 5 per cent, would be 75 million pounds, and at the higher figure it would be 100 million pound."

Farrer then equates this income figure to the spread of imports over exports and finds that the two compare. But then he argues there is the question of freights. "A very large proportion of the trade of the United Kingdom is carried in English ships, and these ships carry a large proportion of the trade of other countries not coming to England. This shipping is, in fact, an export of highly-skilled English labour and capital which does not appear in the export returns of the 19th century, and considering that it includes not only the interest on capital but also wages, provisions, coal, port expenses, repairs, depreciation and insurance; and that the value of English shipping employed in the foreign trade is estimated at more than 100 million pound per annum, the amount to be added to our exports on account of English shipping, must be very large". But he goes further, "add to this the value of ships built for foreigners amounting to over 70,000 ton per annum, worth together several millions, and all these outgoings, with the profits, must either return to this country in the shape of imports, or be invested abroad—I believe 50 million pound is too low an estimate of the amount of unseen exports. In addition there are the commissions and other charges to agents in this country, connected with the carriage of goods from country to country, but each of these items do not appear in the statistics of exports. I can only assume that we are investing large amounts of our savings in the colonies, such as Australia".

The Farrer argument in favour of 'free trade' then turns to the 'fair trade' objections to foreign investments.

Farrer writes "When we point to the indebtedness of foreign colonies to England as one reason for the excess of imports, they tell us that we have been paying for our imports by the return to us of foreign securities; and at the same time they complain bitterly that, instead of spending our money at home, our rich men are constantly investing their money abroad, and thus robbing English labour of its rights here"

But we know that is not the whole story.

If England investors remit capital to the colonies, it is not only in the form of cash (which would come from savings) but it is more often in the form of capital goods. England sends iron; the shipbuilders who make the ships that carry the goods, and the sailors who navigate them. When they reach the colonies, what happens then? They return with grain, or coal, or wool, or timber, and that makes those commodities cheaper in England. The investor receives the interest or profits on that capital invested which would generally be greater than what could have been earned if the capital had been invested in England. Now that return can be spent on luxury goods, invested locally or re-invested overseas to commence the whole cycle again. That return will be employed in setting to work English labour, earn a return and so on.

It remains true that on the whole, based on the Farrer argument, the transfer of English capital from an English industry that does not pay to a colonial industry which does pay, is no loss to England generally, and causes no diminution in the employment of English labour. There are at least two drawbacks to colonial investment by a maritime power; one, in the event of a war, the returns would be open to greater risk, and two; the investors can more easily evade taxation by the English Government.

Obviously since 1886, when Farrer constructed this argument, the world has changed, investment opportunities have changed, England has fallen from its pinnacle as a world power and international commercial leader and the improved collection of statistics now recognises movements of goods and investments on both current account and capital account. But the concept helped put the Australian colony on the map and attracted enormous amounts of private capital into the colony to make it grow and prosper.

Farrer concludes his argument with this observation.

"The desire to make profitable investments, however valuable economically is not the only motive which governs rich men; it's the love of natural beauty; interest in farming and the outdoor life; personal and local attachments; all of which are quite sure to maintain a much larger expenditure on English land than would be dictated by a desire for gain. Let these other motives have their way, as these investors still contribute to the welfare of the toilers and spinners who produce the goods, and make a good return that in the end makes England wealthier"

If Farrer really believes his wholesome argument, then the theory of developing a colony economy as espoused by the British Government took on great validity, and if it had been followed through fully, the colony may have developed faster and been self-sufficient long before 1830, but on the other hand, it may or would have emulated the British economy much more than it did.

A closer examination should be made of the original intention of 'local' revenue raising. Phillip's instructions had included the right to raise local 'taxation', however Butlin, in *Forming a Colonial Economy* writes that

"At least as early as 1892, Phillip had sought approval for introducing indirect taxation. The British officials approved the raising of charges but not as 'revenue' for disposition by the governor. It took until 1896 for such charges to be put into operation, when Hunter imposed a charge on access to imports, not a duty on the goods themselves".

Hunter's action, writes Butlin appears devious when put into the context that the British reserved the sole right to raise revenue from duties, tolls, and licences.

Again, in the context of the British policy to make the colony self-sufficient and self-regulated, it does not make sense to have firstly included in the official instructions to Phillip the right, if not the obligation to raise local revenues, to then impose restrictions on the governor by limiting the area, range and amount of taxes, but by 1800 King was raising duties and tariffs, with any restriction on amount, disposition or accounting. Butlin may, himself, have misinterpreted the role and intent of the local efforts and the British policy.

Far from being able to privatise development in the colony and rely on private development, the British Government had to take account of the recommendations of the Select Parliamentary Committee on

Transportation, which reported in 1810 on the need, and benefits of continuing with transportation of prisoners to the colony. This policy would continue to provide workers and population for the colonial economy, since by the time the Committee reported, less than 33% of the population were convicts at this date.

On the other hand, four statistics provided to the Committee should have persuaded the Committee to terminate transportation

The cost of convict maintenance rose to a high of 120 pound per convict per annum. This had risen from the previous average of less than 32 pound

Marsden took the first wool for weaving to England and received a very positive reception

The Commissary was able to buy fresh beef and mutton from farmers for rations, and replace salted imports

The port duties in 1810 had risen to 8,000 pound annually and were making a good contribution towards local discretionary revenue for the governors.

The colony was finally finding its feet. A solid base had been set, one from which Macquarie could build and use a building program with investment opportunities relying on free enterprise. The economy was on the move.

The financial statements for the colony during this period come to us via the *Sydney Gazette* each quarter. The newspaper published the quarterly statements of the Orphan Fund and the Police Fund (the successor by name change) to the Hunter-sponsored Gaol Fund.

The Macquarie years are the most special period—they were dynamic in every respect—economically, socially and politically. After the years of torment during the Bligh era, Macquarie was like a breath of fresh air, arriving in the colony. His role was an important one, and he brought with him, not only a new regiment which would further assist in ridding the colony of the vestiges of the 'Rum Corp' and all it stood for, but the hopes and aspirations of the British Government for Macquarie to complete the transition and transformation of the heavily subsidised colonial operations but the possibility of the colony feeding the British manufacturers with resources of raw materials and grow into a recipient of British manufacture. Wakefield foresaw the British Treasury reaping rich harvests from the sale of pastoral land, whilst the free traders saw the colony as an opportunity for being the outlet for British machinery and in so many ways, the branch office for British manufacturers.

A.T. Yarwood states that Marsden's name once again came to the fore during the early Macquarie years. He writes in 'Marsden of Parramatta'

"During the first few years the relations between Marsden and Macquarie deteriorated steadily, for Macquarie identified him as the leader of wealthy colonists who opposed his policies of self-interested and unworthy motives. Involved in the dispute was Macquarie's vision of the colony as a place where convicts had the chance, on proven good behaviour of regaining freedom and aspiring to social recognition and even official positions.

We will set down some of the major economic highlights of the Macquarie era—those very special 11 years between 1810 and 1821. Obviously the one highlight not to be overlooked is the massive contribution to the economy and the future of the colony made by his building program.

Macquarie told Bigge, in a very understated way that he decided the colony could justify a major building program because it would lift the tenor of the colony, lift the spirits of the residents, set the tone for future generations, use local materials (timber, bricks and tiles, lime and, mortar—all of these items were made by convict labour) and use an ex-convict as designer / supervisor (Francis Greenway). The equivalent value of the labour, using 3/–per day as a base rate is 500,000 pound, whilst the value of materials is approx 420,000 pound. Although Bigge agreed that it was a good use of convict labour, and the results cost very little in cash terms to the British Treasury, the benefits were enormous to the morale and the social well-being of the settlers—they were given a boost that might not have come in ordinary circumstances for another few generations, in fact not until the discovery of gold sand the resulting gold rush.

Macquarie began his administration with a goodly amount of economic passion. He talked about establishing a bank. He discussed with his senior officials the expansion of private enterprise and expansion of local industry. Immigration of free settlers was not high on his list of things to do, since he considered the economy needed lots of attention. In this area Macquarie made good progress. The naval boatyard was carrying out building and repair work. The sealing and whaling industry had established a viable export business and was bringing a regular supply of goods and supplies into the colony with every foreign boat that arrived. Blaxland advertised his locally produced salt for sale at 2p per pound. Thus, in addition to the milling operations, boat building, clothing and boot manufactures; the colony could boast a salt manufacturer.

It is only when things are starting to go right that the Government wanted to make change. The second committee on Transportation recommended in 1812 that fewer ticket-of-leave convicts be created. This would affect the commissary operations as well as expanding the cost of maintaining convicts on government rather than assigning them to private 'masters' and taking their clothing, feeding and housing costs off the government. 1812 also saw a second credit/liquidity crisis due to credit withdrawal by British investors.

The next major event with long-term ramifications was the crossing of the Mountain range (the Blue Mountains) that was boxing in the pastoral and farming prospects of the colony. In 1813, Blaxland, Lawson and W.C. Wentworth proudly advised Governor Macquarie that they had found a way across the mountains and witnessed the open panorama on the other side.

Locally, another drought in 1813 created a scarcity of corn and wheat and drove prices higher. Wool was catching on both at home and abroad. The significance of the crossing of the mountain range west of Sydney can be seen in the record quantity of wool being grown and thus the number of sheep running in the colony. In 1814 the Female factory at Parramatta used over 35,000 pound of wool, rising to 40,000 pound by 1818. In the same year the colony exported 30,000 pound of wool to Britain. Macquarie sent Surveyor-General Oxley and Mitchell to mark the route taken across the mountain and explore the open land on the west side of the range. After the 'explorers' returned Macquarie determined to establish Bathurst as the first plains settlement. Wool exported to England was not only a boon to the colony; it raised revenue for Britain as well. Britain decided to impose a duty on wool. Before 1819, the rate of duty was 6p per pound; during 1819 the rate was halved to 3p. During 1819 a new industry was introduced to the colony. In spite of the tariff, the woollen mills could not buy enough colonial wool and asked the British Government to do whatever it could to lift production.

Local industry demonstrated the capacity for innovation which resulted in productivity gains as reflected in total output increases without accompanying increases in labour input. This gain in productivity led to a mini 'business' boom. New settlements were still in demand and a penal settlement was established at Port Macquarie on the north-coast of New South Wales. For every door that opens another closes. Having supported the concept and operation of private enterprise and having encouraged new industry as well as a favourable setting for progress in the colony, Macquarie was confronted with his adversary Commissioner Bigge recommending the privatising of the coalfields. Consolidation in the pastoral expansion meant that in 1821, 80 owners controlled 60% of all land in the colony. Another sign of the times arose from the coal-mines being placed into private hands. The first free labour was used in the coal-mines in 1821. Settlement was now taking place along the south-coast of the New South Wales colony.

The paper used for the *Sydney Gazette* was now locally produced

The credit squeeze of 1812 was the first time economic hardship or stress had reached the colony since 1788 and was the first occasion that the withdrawal of British investment scrambled the comparative gains being made steadily in the colony. Of course, Macquarie tried to counter the effects of the credit squeeze by encouraging trade, creating the atmosphere for entrepreneurs and encouraged local business to establish and grow. This was an unusual credit squeeze and an even more unusual impact on the new and fledgling economy. Since there was little employment, as we know it today, there was little unemployment created as a result of the downturn. The main impact in the colonial economy was in the level of confidence. After the Bligh years and the constant warring between the governor and the military, Macquarie went out of his way to keep the military in its place. Having come to the colony as head of his own regiment he expected and received strong and loyal support and little distraction from the military officers. As a way of reversing the troubled mindset of the population away from the turbulent Bligh years, Macquarie commenced his four-fold program of

A building program of fine buildings that would make the people proud

A local revenue raising program that would provide a significant amount of discretionary revenue to support his local and almost all unapproved activities

A social revolution whereby convicts who had served their time and returned to the regular community were welcomed into society and seated at his table. Simeon Lord was even appointed a Magistrate by Macquarie much to the consternation of leading citizens including Rev'd Samuel Marsden

Encouraging free enterprise and new businesses: privately capitalised and operated.

The withholding and withdrawal of investment capital had only marginal impact. Mostly the traders lessened their level of speculation, which slowed the introduction of new supplies and stocks of new goods into the colony. The export trade still continued but prices sat their destination were lower and in spite of lower wholesale prices demand was reduced in Britain. For once the Keynesian laws of supply and demand did not work.

Governor Brisbane arrived in 1821 to replace Macquarie who had returned to Britain and his home in Scotland.

These are the years leading up to the great recession of 1842. The foundations of the causes of the recession lay in the British influence on and over the colonial economy.

Naturally 50 years from the founding of the first penal settlement produced more than just one recession, although the term of the day referred to the economic collapse as being a depression. Gipps, as governor of the senior colony, found it difficult to ascribe more than partial blame on the British situation, but modern economic historians including Brian Fitzpatrick, Noel Butlin and A.G.L. Shaw place much if not most of the blame on the withdrawal of British Investment from the colony. The depression of 1842 was a follow-on event from the hiccup of 1827. The credit squeeze of 1812 was the first time economic hardship or stress had reached the colony since 1788 and was the first occasion that the withdrawal of British investment scrambled the comparative gains being made steadily in the colony. Of course, Macquarie tried to counter the effects of the credit squeeze by encouraging trade, creating the atmosphere for entrepreneurs and encouraged local business to establish and grow.

Brisbane's arrival in the colony in 1821, marked the end of the successful Macquarie years, and reduced the growth of activity in the colony to a more normal level.

One of the first steps taken by Brisbane was to approve of and encourage the spread of settlement along the south coast from Sydney. The coast to the north of Sydney had been successfully settled for some time, sponsored by the coal fields around Newcastle, the fertile soils of the Hunter River region and the convict settlement in Port Macquarie.

New investors were showing interest in the colony following the publication in England of the three Bigge Reports. One such investment company was being formed in Scotland to exploit trading opportunities between Scotland and the colony. The Australia Company was formed in 1822 in Scotland to take advantage of the coming investment opportunities in the colony. By 1830 over 33% of all landowners in NSW were Scots born.

To further assist the growth of the settlements, Brisbane built a road from Windsor to Maitland and opened up more of the Hunter River district.

The organisation of the convict labour was consistently a problem in the colony, and although Macquarie had taken a personal interest in the convicts by receiving the convict ships into Sydney Harbour and by directing the assignment of convict labour to public projects, Brisbane

69

chose to transfer responsibility for convicts from the Superintendent of Convicts to the Colonial Secretary.

Brisbane suppressed the first recorded discovery of gold from the Bathurst District in 1823. He was concerned his convicts would be tempted to escape the assignment provided and head for the hills of gold. Thus it took a further 30 years for the official find to be publicly announced.

Upon leaving the colony, Commissioner Bigge recommended to the British Treasury that extra import duties be placed on all colonial products except wool, timber and tanning bark. On these goods he recommended lower duties.

1823 also saw the formation of the NSW Legislative Council authorised by the New South Wales Judicature Act (UK legislation) which also extended the role of the Supreme Court in the colony.

In 1824, William Charles Wentworth commenced *The Weekly Australian Newspaper*. The challenge thrown before Brisbane in the newspaper columns brought about the first threat of censorship to the new publication. This followed Brisbane heavy censorship of the *Sydney Gazette* and forbidden to report on local politics.

A giant boost to the development of the colony and the spread of settlement and the attraction of new investment from abroad came with the formation of the Australian Agricultural Company in 1824. The establishment of the AAC is described in more detail later on.

Another new and promising industry was established, when, in 1824, sugar was produced from local sugar cane.

Brisbane opened the Morton Bay settlement in 1824 and moved to further explore the Brisbane River.

Brisbane was recalled without having achieved much of what he was sent out to do. The post–Macquarie years had witnessed the decline of growth and the decline of British interest in the colony.

General Sir Ralph Darling arrived as Governor in 1825 (Brian Fletcher has written a comprehensive biography of Darling's life–*Ralph Darling–A Governor Maligned*)

The first of Darling's proclamations restored the supervision of convict labour to the Assignment Board.

When the question of legitimacy of import duties imposed under former governors was raised Darling moved to ratify their legality through the new Legislative Council

The AAC utilised their exclusive access to the coal-fields of Newcastle and even though the company was the recipient of both a grant of land (one million acres) and an assignment of many convicts, the company decided to modernise coal hand and laid a tramway in Newcastle to carry and move coal from the fields to the wharf.

We noted a first liquidity crisis in 1812 when British investors withdrew credit from the colony. A second liquidity crisis took place in 1827 and was due to a decline in export prices in Britain and cuts in foreign investment.

Darling introduced the concept of pastoral and commercial land leasing in 1828 just as a significant boost in convict numbers arriving in the colony was creating further investment opportunities and demand for labour. The arriving convicts were mostly assigned to pastoralists and farmers. This boost in transported convicts increased the convict element of the overall population from 29.8 to 46.4

'Bay whaling' was commenced at Twofold Bay on the south coast of the colony in 1828, whilst VDL boasted 5 bay whaling stations.

The only way Darling could try to control squatters and pastoralists were to impose 'limits of location', and by 1829 the limits of location was limited to 219 counties in New South Wales.

Extending the settlements embraced the new colony of South Australia and Edward Gibbon Wakefield published his plan for land reform and the colonising of Australasia.

Labour organisation was underway in Sydney now that the restrictive UK labour laws on association and organisation of workers had been repealed. The Sydney Shipwright's Association was formed as a trade society in 1829. Later, in 1833, the Cabinet Maker's society was formed to maintain piece rates for workers.

New industry attracted many interested entrepreneurs. With over 3 million lb of tea being imported annually from China, tea plantations were first experimented with in northern NSW.

Darling's last acts as governor saw the implementation of the Rippon Regulations which approved crown land sales at 5/–per acre; the Molesworth Committee's recommendation that transportation be suspended, and the funding of immigration into the colony from the Land Fund

Upon the return of Darling to England, Sir Richard Bourke was appointed governor of the colony in 1831.

The colonial governors were still under heavy influence from Britain with Bourke being faced with action being required on the recommendations of the Committee on secondary punishments. Due to the growing crime rate in the colony (it was 8 times the rate in Britain) the UK House of Commons committee recommended more convict discipline and harsher treatment. The crime rate, especially amongst convicts had reached startling levels. In 1835 there were 28,000 convicts and over 22,000 summary convictions against convicts.

Bourke didn't agree with this action but was aware that if free migrants and investment were to be attracted to the colony then the people of Sydney and Parramatta were not to be scandalised by convict misbehaviour, a high crime rate and chain gangs of convicts being paraded through the streets of the principal town.

Due to growing land sales revenue and a strong interest in migration from Britain to the colony, an Immigration Commission was established in London and funded by the Land Fund. Land sales were not the only growth revenue increasing. In 1833 the import duties into the colony exceeded 100,000 (108,466) pound for the first time With the ad valorem duty being set at 5%, this revenue indicated that over 2 million pound of goods were being imported into the colony. With the total population set at 60,794, this level of imports meant that every man, woman and child, civil servant and convict, was importing nearly 33 pound of goods per year. With exports matching imports in value, trade had reached a remarkable level of 65 pound per head per annum in less than 45 years from the original settlement.

The recommendation to cease transportation to the colony was generally welcomed by the town people, but pastoralists bemoaned the fact that they would lose future access to assigned free labour. It was decided that all prisoners convicted to less than 7 years punishment would in future be handled within Britain.

The pastoralists had plenty to be concerned about. The convicts constituted most of their labour, and few free workers were available in the colony to replace them. All this at the same time that wool exports from the colony reached record levels in Britain and replaced whale products as the colony's main export.

They were not welcomed but the first Chinese labourers arrived in the colony in 1837. Plenty of local opposition stopped any large scale transfers of Asian workers to the colonies.

Workers were an important ingredient missing in the colony and that is why the Land Fund was being used to sponsor free settlers into the colony, but they could not arrive fast enough.

The census of 1839 (Sir George Gipps arrived as the new governor in 1838) showed that NSW had 2 distilleries, 7 breweries, 12 tanneries, 3 brass foundries, 77 flour mills, whilst single factories were producing hats, salt, sugar, tobacco and other goods. Bread had become a good barometer of changing prices and cost of living in the colony and in drought or in times of shortage, wheat would rise in cost, and the price of bread would react accordingly. In 1839, the reverse was happening. Good conditions led to a favourable harvest and a good crop so wheat prices fell from 1/2/–per bushel to 2/9 and bread dropped from 4/–per loaf to 1/3p.

By the end of this third period, the colony was making giant strides in growing and acting like a town that was there to stay. Food was plentiful. Jobs were available for everyone wanting to work. The Military was loyal to the Governor and the Legislative Assembly appeared to be acting responsibly. In 1832 the first Appropriation Bills had been provided to the Legislators and it was shown that the colony was in good shape financially. Social problems were being addressed, convict transportation had ceased and less than 1,000 convicts were still under maintenance.

Investment from overseas was being attracted to the colony and there were lots of opportunities for investors and new settlers. There was a cloud on the horizon in 1842 but until that time the colony was under good management.

CHAPTER 5

PUBLIC EXPENDITURE IN THE COLONY

If the statistical summary shows how progress was made in the colonial economy then a brief study of the mechanics of 'capital formation' will evidence the fiscal factors underpinning that progress.

Capital formation in the colony during these early years can be focused on the massive building and construction program. In the new colony, there was a demand for convict and military barracks, housing and government buildings, storehouses for the commissary, docks, wharfs, draining programs, fresh water, and so on. The support services required a supply of bricks, tiles, timber, furniture, roads, boats, agriculture and farming for food production. *The core of government practical economic management between 1788 and 1830 was The Lumber Yard[36], which included The Dockyard, the Stone Quarries, the Female Factory, and various timber harvesting, land clearing and road making enterprises.*

The capital for these government enterprises had been provided by the British Treasury, and certainly in greater quantities than originally estimated. Matra, in his 1776 submission to the British Government estimated an outlay of £3,500 for the first year and from then on self-sufficiency

---

[36] Refer Beckett' The Public Finance of NSW' where a full discussion is made of the Commissary and convict management including the various enterprises of the commissary operations.

and no further cost to the British Treasury.[37] This estimate was not only optimistic but did not allow for adequate infrastructure once the colony was settled. Matra's plan was for a small convict contingent by the shore of the deep water mooring, with a fresh water stream close by, level ground for building log barracks and store buildings. No weather disturbances, no wild animals, no deleterious convicts, and a plentiful supply of wild animals and fruit and vegetables, good soils, and no interference from any natives. Matra's dream world was far from realistic and practical but his projections suited the senior government and parliamentary officials who approved a small impractical budget for the expedition.

The basic economic problem within the growing economy, and thus one of the early limitations to solid or speedy growth, was the provision of savings to sustain the army of unskilled and semi-skilled workers engaged in this construction and development work–this in turn, hindered private construction for other than settlers who had ready money to invest in such work, and thus most early residences were supplied and furnished by the government. However, in the absence of an adequate local supply, the greatest part of these 'investment' funds was to be drawn from outside Australia, in the form of imported British capital. This flow of British capital helps our understanding of the aggregate capital formation in the colony. British capital was important in inducing the smooth expansion during the first four decades of the colony, and it was a key factor in the subsequent economic declines in 1827 and in 1842-1844. For most of this period, prices and wages rose slowly if not persistently and inflation was imported on the back of speculative activities.

Obviously public authorities played an important role in capital formation[38] and the public sector seems to have contributed a declining portion of the aggregate from 100% to approx 50% during these first four decades. Four components dominated overall aggregate capital formation. These are ranked in terms of volume: Infrastructure such as roads, buildings, barracks etc; agriculture such as government farms, grain growing and livestock grazing; residential construction, and finally

---

[37] HRNSW–Copy of Matra's letter to the British Colonial Secretary detailing the costs of establishing the new colony

[38] Based on Hartwell 'Economic Growth of VDL'

manufacturing. In broad terms, we can see that manufacturing investment in workshops and offices matched each other, and it is interesting to note that manufacturing investment did contribute to what was perceived as a dominant agricultural, pastoral and farming economy. It is also noteworthy that the British Government continued to pay for and thus contribute the convict and transportation system, the colonial defence and the 'civil list' for the colonial use.

C. The Role of the State[39]

If capital formation reflected the engine of growth and the statistics reflected the multifarious facets of growth, then the State became the conduit for growth[40]. Competent government policies, capable administration and sound conditions for enterprise were the essential ingredients for colonial economic growth, and even the dichotomy within the colony of 'free enterprise' or 'government enterprise' could not slow the clamour for better living conditions, jobs and a controlled haven for entrepreneurs.

Fitzpatrick in *The British Empire in Australia* reminds us of the transition in 1834 from the point 'where the earliest community was primarily a state-supported establishment to the next point (after 1834) when imported capital applied to wool growing and associated or derivative industries rapidly endowed the community with the character of British private enterprise instead of public enterprise, and appointed the pastoral sector as a field for investment into a profitable colonial territory'[41]. The Forbes Act (by the Legislative Council) in 1834 offered inducements to British capitalists to invest in New South Wales, and as a result the colony of NSW, with three million people, had received twice as much British capital as the Dominion of Canada, with a population of nearly 4.5 million. There are obviously two distinct stages of state intervention in reaching out to overseas investors. Before 1834 the role of the state was to provide British capitalists with free land and labour in the colony, then came the development of sheep-raising of fine wool, and the sequel

39 Based on Fitzpatrick 'The British Empire in Australia
40 Based on Beckett–Chapter 5–'William Lithgow' where capital formation and the role of government is discussed
41 Fitzpatrick 'The British Empire in Australia

was, having facilitated the importation of capital for investment, its role was to provide services which would facilitate the earning of dividends on the capital invested. However, even though initial dividends were sent 'home' in ever-increasing quantities, the time came when local people and institutions were the recipients of these dividends and great enterprises were part owned within the colony.

The state had, according to Fitzpatrick[42], four main functions:

Firstly, to take the responsibility for adjusting claims when the economic system reached crisis, as in 1827 and 1842, although Governor Gibbs acted reluctantly and belatedly in the latter crisis.

Secondly, the state is to administer essential services, in the operation of which private investors could not derive normal profits.

Thirdly, the state must nurture enterprise, including well-capitalised undertakings, by means of tariffs, bounties and other concessions.

Fourthly the State is to take responsibility for restoring to private capital, power, which has been taken away from it.

Fitzpatrick can be challenged on, at least, this last point. It surely cannot be the role of the state to supplant, supplement or fiscally support private capital lost within the colonial economy. If private investment criteria is invalid or faulty, then within a free enterprise economy, even one adopting an extended use of government enterprise, private capital must be supported by or subjected to market forces and not 'restored' by the state.

The introduction of the railways, just outside our time-line is such an example. The British were strongly urging private operators to install and operate in-town rail services. The *Sydney Railway Company* was empowered by the Legislative Council to build a private line with the support of 'government guarantees', with the right of the government to resume operations with minimal compensation to shareholders if

---

[42]   ibid Page 347

the enterprise collapsed. The enterprise did collapse, was taken over by government planners, financially restored to health and the railway system moved on to be become a successful government enterprise[43]. The role of the State, in this typical case, was not to guarantee speculators, but to protect the suppliers and contractors who placed their trust and faith in the free enterprise system. Fitzpatrick is confusing a touch of Marxist policy with a shackled government enterprise.

We can deduce that the state had an important role in the development[44] of the colonial economy and filled this role with supportive mechanisms and policies–especially guidance for financial institutions following overseas borrowing, overseas investment and land speculation.

D. Sequencing Economic Growth[45]

I come now to a brief study of 'in what sequence' did the economy grow, and as N.G. Butlin, in the Preface to *Investment in Australian Economic Development* writes "I have found no guidance on this question from the few essays which examine the early economy in identifying the sequence of economic growth in terms of both aggregate behaviour and the performance of major investment components".

One must fear to tread where Butlin finds weakness or gaps. This essay may still not fully satisfy the larger Butlin type questions but the immediate concern is about the 'hows' and the 'whys' of the colonial economic growth between 1788 and 1850 and as such there is an obligation, albeit ritualistic, to outline the main sectors of investment contributing to that growth. Since this study may cover many areas, methodology and circumstances of sequential development may not matter as much as first thought.

Some facts should perhaps be stated first as the basis for future conclusions:

---

[43] Beckett 'The Public Finance of the Colony of NSW' (colonial press 2002)

[44] See also Butlin, N.G. 'Forming the Colonial Economy' for a discussion of these factors leading to changes in financial institutions

[45] Based on Butlin, N.G. 'Investment in Australian Economic Development

Government enterprise towered above private enterprise[46] at least between 1788 and 1821 because the government had the sole access to capital, land and labour, and government enterprise met the needs of the colony and its community of free settlers.

Government enterprise was based on two facts–survival and self-sufficiency of the colony. From Phillip's livestock and building materials imported with the first fleet (including his 'portable' government house), government had undertaken to be the planner, the contractor, the financier and the provider of all labour and material resources in this new penal colony. That essentially was the nature of a penal settlement[47]. Then King decided he wanted a little 'spending money' outside the purview of the British Treasury, and this was a development unknown in normal prison or penal colonies but became the first step in the transition to a semi-autocratic free settlement. If this is an anachronism, then substitute 'planned economy' into any government encouragement of free enterprise. Then add Governor Macquarie, who as a free spirit, developer extraordinaire and ego driven creator of entrepreneurship[48]. Macquarie's contribution is in itself extraordinary. He applied, wisely, firm private enterprise principals to planning and development and set his sights on bettering the colonists' standard of living, changing the reliance on government hand-outs (the colony had to stand on its own feet, which is subtly different to being entirely self-sufficient, but is a good first step to self-sufficiency) and encouraging entrepreneurship in the colony. In Macquarie's mind, the role of his administration was to reduce British Treasury support payments, increase discretionary local revenues, build desirable government buildings and infrastructure, and create the atmosphere for manufacturing in the colony.

Obviously agriculture was the main objective of economic planning. It could use most of the convicts arriving in the colony[49]; it was minimalist in skills requirements, and relied more on natural events than most other colonial activities, but was mainly the most important of labour intensive undertakings. Agricultural operations would be extended to government

---

[46] A concept of Marjorie Barnard in 'Macquarie's World'
[47] Based on Ellis Chapter 11 'Lachlan Macquarie'
[48] Concept from Barnard 'Macquarie's World'
[49] Refer Shaw 'Convicts & Colonies'

farming, land clearing, timber harvesting and much of the work of the Lumber Yard. Its success was essential to maintaining the colony and making it self-sufficient As was pointed out above, agriculture contributed to more capital formation in the colony than did manufacturing but the rise of manufacturing mostly during and following the Macquarie administration created balance within the economy and created a support structure internally and an import replacement opportunity

The growth of government enterprises such as the government farms, the Lumber Yard,[50] which in turn included the stone quarries, and the timber forests, the Female Factory and the Dockyard, encouraged rather than damaged any move to free enterprise operations. The earliest private enterprises, other than pastoral establishments, were government contractors. Little capital was required, only limited skills (other than a nose for making money) were necessary, and there was plenty of work available and not a lot of competition.

British private capital was uncertain and untried in the colonial context; investment within Britain or in the tropical colonies was considered more profitable and safer; of the hundreds of companies floated in the United Kingdom between 1820 and 1850, only five important companies were formed for investment in Australia. The Land Grant Companies–these were the three (3), plus two banks, within the Australian context–The Australian Agricultural Company (AA Coy), The Van Diemen's Land Company[51] (VDL Coy), The South Australia Coy (SA Coy), Bank of Australasia and The Union Bank of Australia–filled a role as catalyst for attracting new investment and even offered some official sanctioning and support parameters for colonial investing[52].

A question should be posed, at this point, as assistance for understanding the sequence of development. Was the colonial NSW economy in

---

[50] Refer Beckett 'The Economics of Colonial NSW'

[51] Refer Beckett, G. 'The economic circumstances of the Van Diemen's Land Company (colonial press 2003)

[52] Hartwell refers to similar factors in 'The VDL Government' Historical Studies ANZ, Nov 1950

1830 a capitalist economy[53]? It was, as we learnt earlier, an economy in transition before and after that date. In so far as capitalism implies a rational, and acquisitive society, then NSW had been capitalist (urged along by Macquarie) ever since it had broken the bonds of being the self-contained prison promulgated in 1788. Capitalist techniques, as opposed to traditional techniques of economic planning, assisted with the transition from a penal to a free economic society. The transition included the organisation of production by the capitalistic entrepreneur for profit, by the combining of labour and materials into a marketable product. The capitalist enterprise portrayed itself in the banks, the insurance companies, merchant houses and the large-scale pastoral farms–all institutions, which were rationally organised for the pursuit of profits. The most important means of production–land–had fallen by the 1830s into relatively few hands–trade and finance were highly concentrated, most of the population were without ownership of property, and worked for a wage determined by the market. West, in *A History of Tasmania*[54], offers us a quotable insight into the settlement progression "The dignity and independence of landed wealth is Whatever his rank, he dreams of the day when he shall dwell in a mansion planned by himself, survey a wide and verdant landscape called after his name and sit beneath the vineyard planted by his own hands"

Another brief quote may also be in order. Hartwell, writing in *The Economic Development of VDL 1820-1850* thinks "it is impossible to study the trade cycles without reference to general economic development, and the existing economic histories of Australia did not answer the kind of questions I was asking"[55]. His point is that he offered, in his work, a specialist account of economic development, as will this account try to be in relation to the growth of the colonial economy in New South Wales.

---

[53] Butlin, N.G. in 'Forming the Colonial Economy states that the colonial economy was 'capitalistic' This portion of the essay is examining this claim
[54] West,' History of Tasmania–edited by Shaw in one volume
[55] Hartwell 'Economic History of VDL' P.251

E. Patterns of Economic Growth[56]

Although Butlin raised an interesting question on sequences of growth, any reference to sequences can also be raised in terms of 'patterns'.

The highlights of any 'pattern' can be traced to the foundation of the colony. This will also serve to identify some of the 'whys' in the essay topic.

The colony was founded for the multiple purposes of creating an intermediate stopping point for British ships travelling to India and China, of provisioning them, offering some form of back loading for the return trip to Britain, after unloading goods at this Port of Botany Bay. It was also considered to be of strategic value in limiting the expansion of Portuguese and Dutch interests in the sub-Asian region. Bonus reasons were considered to be that the East Coast region could be a source of raw materials for British industry[57], which was at that time coming to the implementation stage of the industrial revolution, and that any future colony would utilise British shipping and be an outlet for future investment and finally but almost as an after-thought any colony in so isolated a region could be a suitable location for a penal settlement.

Thus the growth in the colony followed first the formation of capital, then the importation preferences of capital, then the needs of the colony and finally the desires and preferences of the entrepreneurs and traders. This cycle continued right up to the discovery of gold, but it was not the traditional boom and bust cycle. It was a trade and investment cycle of designating an investment opportunity, bringing together the capital required, filling the opportunity and recommencing the cycle by starting all over.

The pattern changed somewhat in the mid-1830s (the colony was by now almost a mature 50 years of age) when the pattern of growth suddenly had a new spoke–local wealth, local ownership, locally retained dividends and the need for reinvestment. This change in pattern broke into the

---

56 A Beckett concept developed in The Economics of Colonial NSW
57 Proposed by Sir Joseph Banks (HRNSW–Vol 1)

overseas raising of capital, and the overseas distribution of dividends and the overseas domination of manufacturing in the colony.

Local traders were gaining prominence in sealing, whaling, exporting and importing, merchant financing and the commencement of local auctioneering. Traditionally the Sydney markets had favoured enterprising practitioners who had surplus livestock or cottage industry manufactures, and these pursuits often led to more than the public markets as their distribution point. Simeon Lord, the master trader, bought a hat manufacturer in Botany whose rise had been exactly along those lines, cottage industry production, and public markets distribution, rented premises, paid labourers, advertising, then buy-out and take-over.

Government policy fitted largely into this pattern and we have covered already the encouragement of business enterprise, however, the main role of government was to create the climate and the environment for entrepreneurs, borrowers, lenders and a satisfactory circumstance for making a profit and the return of capital. This came by way of successful business ventures, in both the agricultural and industrial enterprises. Because the skill levels within the colony were only gradually expanding and refining, there was official encouragement of British industry expanding with branch operations. Agricultural enterprise was encouraged by offers of land grants and then the cheap sale of land, and later the provision of either cleared land or convict labour.

Abbott[58] discusses the 'constituents' of the New South Wales colonial economy, and lists six. Agriculture; The Pastoral industry; Manufacturing; Trade within the colony; Exports other than wool; Government Works and Services.

Let me turn to some 'constraints' on the growth of the colonial economy; these include[59] Government policy; land, labour and capital.

There was an implied constraint to local colonial growth imposed by the Westminster parliament. The last of the series of Navigation Acts was

---

[58]   Abbott & Nairn 'The Economic Growth of Australia
[59]   Abbott & Nairn 'The Economic Growth of Australia

in 1696 but stood unchanged until after the recognition of American Independence in 1783[60]. In general, until the legislation was passed,

British colonists had been free to trade with any country and to use ships of any nationality, and accept the cheapest freights. Following the passage of the legislation and the numerous amendments, they were obliged to use only British (including colonial) ships, to send all their exports direct to Britain and to import all their overseas goods direct from Britain. In this way, writes Abbott in *Economic Growth of Australia 1788-1821*, the colonists were virtually insulated from direct contact with the world economy.

Growth of Public Service 1800-1825

It is not unexpected that the public service for colonial NSW from 1800 revolved around the growth of the settlement, firstly as a penal colony and then changed as its role required transition into a market-driven economy.

The Governor's establishment changed little before Brisbane and Darling came Ion the scene. Its staffing was hierarchal and was based on the head of state being the governor, his deputy (Lt-Governor), and his heads of nominal departments. Darling referred to this group as his 'kitchen cabinet' or Board of General Purposes, but whatever the name, the role and participants remained the same—the chief judge, the chief surveyor or surveyor-general, the commissary-general, the chief surgeon, the chief chaplain and soon the Auditor-general (appointed 1825 under Darling)

Each governor had appointed a private secretary, and in 1822, this position was re-classified with its role expanded, and its own establishment created. Sub elements included the Colonial Treasurer and the Colonial Auditor-General and their expanding staff. The combined duties included issuing land grants, issuing land titles, collecting and accounting for all revenues, recording expenditures, completing feasibility studies for the

---

[60] Discussed in Hainsworth 'The Sydney Traders'

expanding government services and handling all official correspondence into and from the colony.

Typical of the growing bureaucracy was the roads department. As treasurer of the Police Fund, Darcy Wentworth had been responsible for repairing roads, the Superintendent of Convicts was responsible for their formation and the Police Fund and its treasurer were responsible for payment of all associated costs. The British Treasury did not see the need for significant expenditure on road making, so the making and repairing fell to be supported by local revenues and convict labour. Macquarie increased this expenditure enormously when he designed and constructed the Great North Road (to the Hawkesbury), the Great West Road (to Parramatta and Bathurst) and the Great South road (to Goulburn). Within the colony, such road making was essential if new lands and settlements were to be opened up, and livestock moved around the colony. To raise revenue for the colony and to maintain the new roads, tolls were imposed on users of the road system, and these tolls eventually funded ferries and bridges, where rivers and streams had to be crossed.

This review of the growth of Public service is designed to embrace not on the coming 'Public Service 'system with its teams of public servants, but also the role of serving the public with official services. Obviously what springs to mind is the necessity for hospitals, coal for heating, fresh food, transport and communications, livestock, ferry services (initially between Sydney Cove and Parramatta), building materials, and most importantly, labour for hire.

Macquarie expanded this role by initialising a local manufacturing industry, essentially serving as an import replacement opportunity. He encouraged local entrepreneurs, who turned their hand to consumer imports, dressmaking, hats and apparel, shoes and furniture making.

Macquarie also co-ordinated the burgeoning government convict numbers into specialty trade teams for expanding government services.

The timber-cutters, carpenters, sawyers, bricklayers and blacksmiths were moulded into the full-service mini-manufacturing operation named the Lumber Yard. The boat-builders, boat unloaders and wharf-workers and ferrymen were moulded into the Dockyards, the brick and tile makers were pulled into the Brick Yard, whilst new activities included carriage making, cooper workers, whilst the commissariat grew with its own range of livestock herdsmen, slaughter men, storemen and clerical assistants. The commissariat also managed until 1817, the large government farm operations, used for the growing of government grain, vegetables, and fruit, for the colony as a whole.

The interest in the commissariat operating a more general store was too overwhelming and would have failed if the Treasury had not rejected the concept. The initial approach was along the lines of a catalogue service, whereby consumers ordered and paid in advance, and the commissariat placed the import request and added a sufficient margin to cover shipping, handling and clerical services.

Policing services were commenced under Macquarie band these numbers grew rapidly as the settlement grew in Sydney and outlying areas. Macquarie also appointed the first government printer, who used imported presses to publish official government regulations and orders.

The analysis of Accounts extracted from the 'Blue Books' of 1822 through 1828 allows a number of conclusions to be drawn.

The initial claim by the author that the cost to the British Treasury of establishing and operating the Colony, was NOT the millions of pounds claimed by other historians, is borne out by examination. The accounting records as maintained by Governor Macquarie from 1822 leads to a statement of 'net revenue and expenses' which purports to offset all revenues against all expenses, and includes as revenue certain convict maintenance charges. Even in 1822 the Colony was showing a small operating surplus. This surplus grew through 1828 until, other than for transportation of convicts to the Colony; the charges on account of the British Treasury were less than One Hundred Thousand pounds for protecting, feeding and housing nearly 5,000 fully maintained convicts. Against this cost, the charge for housing, feeding and guarding this same number of prisoners in Britain would have been substantially higher, since in addition to the 5,000 gully maintained convicts there were a further 20,000 being paid for by free settlers and used as supervised labour. Britain surely had found a cheap source of penal servitude for at least 25,000 of its former prisoners, and found a very worthwhile alternative to the American Colonies as a destination for its prisoners.

Revenue from Crown Land sales and rents was used to offset Civil (Crown) salaries and expenses.

It is probably incorrect, at this stage, to say that it cost Britain nothing or at best, very little, to establish and maintain the Colony, but it can be said that from 1842 the costs were limited to maintaining fewer and fewer convicts. But from these convicts great value in terms of agricultural produce, coal and other minerals extraction was derived. Just in terms of coal for lighting, heating, the cost to the government of purchasing these items commercially would have been substantial. The 'Blue Book', however, reflects the use of the coal as a cost rather than a gain as would be the accounting standard today.

A final conclusion could be given that there are much more known records available for this period (the first One Hundred Years) than the author originally thought. The reproduction of the 'Blue Book' by the State Archives Office is a major step forward in understanding the economic challenges faced by settlers and convicts in the early Colony. The sourcing of material from the Blue Book unveils the financial statements and conditions of these early years. It is still considered that finance records of the period 1788 to 1822 are not re-constructible, but the author feels that a deep search through the microfilms forming the Joint Copying Project will provide information on the two Colonial operating funds of the period—the 'Police Fund and the Orphan Fund'. This is a challenge for another time.

An interesting observation is found in 'The Constitutional History of Australia' by W. G. McMinn (1979).

P 33 records "Subject to the need for a vice-regal message, accepting that any locally (Australian Colony) initiated legislation of a money bill nature requires The Sovereign's ratification, the New South Wales Legislative Council was to have a general right to appropriate revenue from taxation, except for an amount of 81,600 pounds, the expenditure of which was to be in accordance with 'three schedules' to the Act; 33,000 pound for the salaries of those on the civil list e.g. Governor et al, the superintendent of Port Phillip and its judges and for the expenses of administering justice; 18,600 pound for the chief civil officers and their departments, for pensions and expenses of the council; and 30,000 pound for the maintenance of public worship. Land and casual revenues were also reserved.

The Sale of Waste Land Act raised the minimum reserve price of crown land to one pound per acre, except that large remote areas might be sold at a lower price, and established a formula for the use of the land revenue; fifty percent was to be spent on immigration, the rest was to be expended by the Governor in accordance with British Government directives from time to time. The Governor was to continue to have power to issue depasturing licences and to make regulations for the use and occupancy of unsold lands, but the existence of the Sale of Waste Lands Act placed an important restriction on the colony by implying a prohibition against the Legislative Council legislating on these matters. The first directive on how the Governor was to spend a portion of the fund, enjoined the Governor to spend a proportion on Aboriginal protection and another on the roads; he was left free to hand any surplus over to the Council for appropriation; but it was made clear that the whole of the fifty percent was to be considered as an emergency reserve if the Council proved difficult". McMinn sheds some further light on the Crown Lands mystery by there still remains the question of how, year after year, were these funds fully used or were they just included as a contribution to general revenue. It would appear that somewhere there is a firm directive from the British Treasury that the revenues from Crown Lands sale were to be used to 'offset' British costs of maintaining the Colony. The 'Blue Book' is evidence that as general revenues, these funds were already being used to pay for the costs of feeding, clothing, housing convicts, and we know they were specifically used to pay for 'sponsored immigrants', aboriginal 'protection', and now roads. The costs of the military establishment were charged against general revenues so in the quite large 'pot', nearly all Colonial expenditures were subsidised or offset by revenues from the Sale of Crown Land. Britain put its hand in the till only; it seems, to pay for the shipping and supplies costs of getting their prisoners to the Colony. After 1828, we know that convict production–both agricultural and mineral–went a long way to paying their expenses, so perhaps the British Treasury did in fact get off very lightly indeed, especially fort the benefits it derived.

The vexing question of Crown Lands revenues still remains. It is apparent from the 'Blue Book' notations that this revenue was 'reserved' for specific allocation by the Crown and remained in the Colony as an offset against British Government fiscal obligations (e.g. Civil List salaries) until self-government in 1855. A relevant quotation from the 1887 Financial Statements of the Colonial Treasurer of New South Wales follows:

"Prior to the passing of the Constitution Act, the Territorial Revenues of the Colony belonged to the Crown, but upon that coming into operation in 1855, they were placed at the disposal of the local Parliament, and together with the taxes, imposts, rates and duties were formed into one fund, under the title of the Consolidated Revenue Fund. In lieu of the Crown Revenues thus given up to the Colony, an annual Civil List of 64,300 pound was made payable to Her Majesty out of the Consolidated Revenues of the Colony." What this means is that the British Treasury allowed the offset of all direct British payments made on account of the Colony against revenues raised by the sale, rent or lease of Crown lands.

Bigge in his first report to Lord Bathurst recommended that 'the number of convicts employed by the Government on public works should be reduced, both in the interests of economy and because it was argued that these men, especially if working in Sydney, were usually idle, and prone to misbehaviour in town. As far as possible, Bigge's recommended, convicts should be assigned to public service in the interior. He did, however, approve of sending convict offenders to penal settlements for further punishment, and he suggested that the settlements be expanded.

After the departure of Macquarie, administration of convicts became more efficient. The number of convict clerks in government service was gradually reduced, although the Marine and Survey Departments, the hospitals and domestic service for government officials became a reward for good conduct, although convicts were often placed in government service for breaches of discipline or failure to work effectively for private masters. In some areas, government service tended to be arduous.

The majority of convicts were 'assigned' to private employment and provided the bulk of the work force of the colony. Those 'assigned' were taken off commissary support and were entitled to be clothed and fed by their master in proscribed quantities of food and garb.

CHAPTER 6

FOREIGN INVESTMENT TO THE RESCUE

EXPLAINING THE COLONIAL ECONOMIC DRIVERS 1788-1856

In order to understand the growth of the colonial economy, we must understand the economic drivers that underpinned, sustained and supported the colonial economy. There are at least six, if not seven, such economic drivers. They include the factors of (a) population growth, the (b) economic development within the colony, the (c) funding sources such as British Treasury appropriations and the (d) revenues raised from within the local economy (for example, taxes and duties on imports) and (e) foreign investment (both public and private). The traditional concept of growth within the colonial economy comes from (f) the rise of the pastoral industry. A seventh driver would be the all-important Land Board, which played such an important role within the colonial economy The Land Board played an important role in co-ordinating crown land policy, controlling land sales, squatting licenses and speculators, re-setting boundaries of location, establishing set aside lands for future townships and for church and school estates, carrying out the survey of millions of acres of land transferred by grant and sale, and offering terms sales for crown lands and being responsible for the collection of repayments, rents, license fees, quit-rents and depasturing fees. In addition the land board was vested with road reserves for hundreds of miles of unmade roads but important rights-of-way that would well into the future protect access to remote pastoral and farming properties. The main thrust of published material about the Land Board is in conjunction with crown land sales policy, but the Board had a much larger role and the overall Board policies sand performances are what are to be reviewed here.

Although an important factor it is no more important that our other five motivators of the colonial economy between 1802 and 1856. Why have I selected these two specific dates? 1802 was when Governor King first imposed an illegal, but justified and well-intentioned impost on the local free community to build a local gaol to replace one burnt to the ground through a lightning strike but which the British would not replace. The local residents thought a more solid and durable prison was a worthwhile community investment. At the other end, the year of 1856 signalled the first real representative and responsible government in the colony, and although it was not the end of the colonial era, it was certainly the end of Britain's financial support of the colony and as such the colony was expected to stand on its own two feet.

These six factors will be discussed as mechanisms for 'growing the colonial economy between 1802 and 1856'

One consideration that must not be forgotten is the externally enforced pace of colonial expansion, particularly through the organised rather than the market-induced inflow of both convicts and assisted migrants. What this means is that instead of market forces requiring additional labour and human resources, extra labour and resources were imposed on the colony and there was an obligatory process of putting these people to work, in many cases by creating a public works program and pushing development ahead at an artificial pace rather than at a time and rate suited to the local economy. In much the same way, the 'assignment' system in the 1810-1830 period forced landowners to create clearing and development programs in order to utilise the labour available rather than only develop land as demand required.

1. Population growth including immigration of convicts & free settlers

The reason the colonial society did not change very much in the 1820s is that relatively few immigrants arrived. During 1823, Lord Bathurst, Colonial Secretary, sent instructions to Governor Brisbane (Macquarie's successor) altering the administration of the colony of NSW in most of the ways Commissioner Bigge had recommended in his reports.[61] One result of the Bigge Reports was that Macquarie was officially recalled to Britain even though he had canvassed his retirement before Bigge's arrival in 1819. Macquarie was distressed by the Bigge Reports and took very personally the recommendations made for change. Although there were many implied criticisms Macquarie considered that the public perception was that he had not acted properly in his role as Governor. Macquarie set to and compared the circumstances of the colony at the time of his arrival in 1810, with the great achievements he had made through 1821. In hindsight, Macquarie had accomplished much, mostly by means of arrogantly pursuing a series of policies without the pre-approval of the Secretary or the Government in London.

The arrival of only a few immigrants was because Bigge and the Colonial Office believed that only men of capital would emigrate. Labourers and the poor of England should not be encouraged and, as these people rarely had money to pay for the long passage to Sydney, few of them arrived.[62] Although the numbers were small, few of them came unassisted. In 1821 320 free immigrants arrived and this increased each year; 903 in 1826; 1005 in 1829, but slipping to 772 in 1830. Mostly they were family groups with some financial security.

---

[61] Commissioner J.T. Bigge had been sent by Bathurst to Enquire into the State and Operations of the colony of NSW in 1819; the House of Commons had demanded an inquiry into the colony and had threatened to hold one of its own; Bathurst pre-empted a difficult government situation by appointing Bigge with a very broad and wide-ranging terms of Enquiry. Bigge held two years of investigations in the colony and reported to the Commons in 1823 with the printing of three Reports.

[62] Australian History–The occupation of a Continent *Bessant* (Ed)

In 1828, the first census (as opposed to musters) of white persons in NSW was taken. 20,930 persons were classified as free and 15,668 were classified as convicts. However, of the free persons, many had arrived as convicts or were born of convicts. In fact, 70% of the population in 1828 had convict associations. However, by 1828, one quarter of the NSW population was native born; 3,500 were over 12 years of age

There was another side to this migration of unregulated souls. Shaw writes" The cost of assistance, the unsuitability of many emigrants, their ill-health, and the numbers of children and paupers that were sent–all these gave the colonists a source of grievance".[63] A large part of the problem was that the English wanted emigration–but those they wished to see emigrate were not welcomed in the colony. A growing opinion in the colony was that free migrants could not work with convicts; the convicts by themselves were too few and with growing expense; therefore transportation must stop and immigration be encouraged. However, immigrants of a good quality were not those the English wanted to send; its preference was for the paupers and the disruptive in the society. To stop transportation would be "attended with the most serious consequences unless there is previous means taken to ensure the introduction of a full supply of free labour". [64] In the next five years, the number of free immigrants increased so much that transportation could be stopped with little political backlash. Between 1835 and 1840, the colony was quite prosperous (it was a case of boom and bust–the great depression came in 1841); sales of crown land were large, and consequently the funds available for assisting immigrants were plentiful.[65]

---

[63] Shaw, A.G.L. *The economic development of Australia* p.44
[64] HRA Bourke to Colonial Secretary *Governor's despatches* 1835
[65] The British Treasury had agreed to put 50% of land sale proceeds into assisting immigrants with shipping costs; a further 15% into assisting Aborigines' and the balance was for discretionary use by the crown. These percentages changed in 1840 when all sale proceeds were spent on immigration but the land fund still ran out of funds in 1842 and no further assistance was made to immigrants other than by the colonial government borrowing funds in the London market through its own credit.

In 1838, land revenue was over £150,000 and assisted migrants numbered 7,400; in 1839, land revenue was £200,000 and assisted migrants 10,000; in 1840 revenue was over £500,000 and assisted migrants 22,500.

Between 1832 and 1842, over 50,000 assisted and 15,000 unassisted migrants arrived in NSW; or they might have arrived as convicts, and over 3,000 arrived that way each year. Thus between 1830 and 1840 the population of the whole of Australia increased from 70,000 to 190,000, with 130,000 of those in 1840 being in NSW. Of these 87000 were men and 43000 were women; 30,000 had been born in the colony; 50,000 were free settlers, 20,000 were emancipists and 30,000 were convicts.[66]

2. Foreign Private Investment

We need to make the distinction between foreign public investment, and foreign private investment. The British Treasury appropriated specific funds for infrastructure programs in the colony, such as public buildings, churches, gaols, roads etc.

One reason that local colonial taxes and duties were imposed on the colony was to give the governor the funding source for discretionary expenditures in order to improve his administration. There were many instances of expenditures which could not be covered by the British funds, such as a bounty to recapture runaway convicts, building fences around the cemeteries and whitewashing the walls of public buildings (for instance barracks) in the settlement. The British Treasury would have considered such items of expense as being unnecessary. Road repair and maintenance was intended to be covered from toll receipts but they were never sufficient to make necessary repairs. Governors Hunter and Bligh did little to improve public and community buildings, roads and bridges and by the time Macquarie arrived in the colony in 1810, there was a major backlog of building work and maintenance to be undertaken. Macquarie expanded the local revenue tax base in order to give himself more flexibility in pursuing improved conditions for the settlers and the population at large.

---

[66] Shaw *ibid*

Although Macquarie did not specifically seek new free immigrants for the colony, word of mouth circulated that the colony was in a growth stage and worthy of being considered for either immigration or investment. Usually one accompanied the other. The first private investment came with the immigrants. Free settlers would either cash up in England or transfer their possessions to the colony, and this small level of private investment was the start of a major item of capital transfers to the colony.

However, private capital formation took many forms; the early settlers, bought or built houses, they built or bought furnishings; they had carriages and often employed water conservation.

As the system of land grants was expanded and farming was encouraged the spread of settlement required a combination of public and private investment.

The government had to provide roads and townships, and the settlers had to provide pastoral investment. This pastoral capital formation consisted of five main types of assets:

Buildings–residence, outbuildings, wool shed or grain storage

Fences–stockyards, posts and rails

Water conservation–dams, tanks, wells

Plant–cultivators, tools

Stocks–food, clothing, household items, materials for animal care and general repairs–livestock

Stephen Roberts offers an interesting insight into the colony of 1835.[67]

"It did not need much prescience to foresee the whole of the country united by settlement–so much had it outgrown the coastal stage of Sydney

---

[67]   Roberts, S.H *The Squatting Age in Australia 1835-1847 (published 1935)*

town. It was a new Australia–a land of free settlement and progressive occupation–that was there, and the old convict days were ending.

Both human and monetary capital were pouring into the various colonies and transforming the nature of their population and problems. Convicts no longer set the tone; even autocratic governors belonged to a day that was passing, and instead, the country was in the grip of a strangely buoyant, and equally optimistic, race of free men".

As part of our private capital formation, we must remember the growth of human capital and the needs for specific labour. Capital requires labour with a specific role. The establishment and expansion of farming meant more than shepherding and ploughing. There was a considerable demand for building skills, for construction and maintenance of equipment such as drays and carts, harness making and repair, tool-making etc. It became important, in order to support and sustain capital growth and economic development to be able to employ labour with multi-skills. This was a new phenomenon for the colony, especially since Britain did not develop these types of broad skills and self-motivation in its criminal class. The Rev. J.D. Lang sought a temporary answer by specifically recruiting 'mechanics' in Scotland as immigrant for the colony.

3. British Public Funding transfers

Public Capital formation is obviously different to private capital formation. I have given an example of rural-based private capital formation elsewhere in this study and will do so again here, in order to demonstrate both types of capital investment.

Private capital formation took many forms; the early settlers, bought or built houses, they built or bought furnishings; they had carriages and often employed water conservation techniques, which included tanks or earthen dams.

As the system of land grants was expanded and farming was encouraged the spread of settlement required a combination of public and private investment.

The government had to provide roads and townships, and the settlers had to provide pastoral investment. This pastoral (rural-based) capital formation usually consisted of five main types of assets:

Buildings–residence, outbuildings, wool shed or grain storage

Fences–stockyards, posts and rails

Water conservation–dams, tanks, wells

Plant–cultivators, tools

Stocks–food, clothing, household items, materials for animal care and general repairs–livestock

Public capital on the other hand was a socio-economic based government asset, and included:

Roads, bridges, crossings, drainage, excavation and embanking, retaining walls

Hospital, storehouses, military barracks, convict barracks, Court-house, police posts, government office buildings

Market house, burial ground, Church, tollhouse, military magazines.

Obviously the list can go on and on.

MAJOR PUBLIC WORKS IN NSW 1817-1821

Roads
Sydney to Botany Bay
Sydney to South Head
Parramatta to Richmond
Liverpool to Bringelly, the Nepean and Appin
Buildings
Sydney
A military hospital; military barracks; convict barracks; carters barracks; Hyde Park

Toll-house; residences for the Supreme Court Judge, the Chaplain and the Superintendent of Police; an asylum; a fort and powder magazines; stables for Government House; a market house; a market wharf; a burial ground; St. James Church
Parramatta
All Saint's church spire; a hospital; a parsonage; military and convict barracks; a Factory; stables and coach-house at Government House; a reservoir
Windsor
St. Matthew's Church; military barracks; convict barracks
Liverpool
St. Luke's church; a gaol; a wharf; convict barracks

4. Economic Development

K. Dallas in an article on *Transportation and Colonial Income* writes, "The history of economic development in Australia is concerned with the transplanting of British economic life into a unique and novel environment. All colonial societies resemble each other in the problems of transplanting, but only in Australia was there no indigenous communal life vigorous enough to influence the course of future development"[68]

Dallas in the same article declares, "The economic effects of the transportation system are usually misunderstood. The real development of Australia begins with the pastoral industry and the export of wool in the 1820s. Until then, penal settlements were a base for whalers, and made the pastoral possibilities known to English capitalist sheep farmers earlier than they would otherwise have known."[69]

Since this is such a major point on which much disagreement exists, an analysis of its merits is required. No less an authority than N.G. Butlin, J.Ginswick and Pamela Statham disagree, and they record in their introduction to 'The economy before 1850 "the history books are preoccupied with the pastoral expansion in NSW. It is reasonably certain from the musters that a great many complex activities developed and

---

[68] Dallas, Keith *Transportation & Colonial Income* Historical Studies ANZ Vol 3 October 1944-February 1949
[69] Dallas *ibid*

Sydney soon became not merely a port town but a community providing many craft products and services to the expanding settlement".[70]

The next section of this study outlines the remarkable contribution of Governor Macquarie between 1810 and 1821, most of the physical development taking place before the arrival of Commissioner J.T. Bigge in 1819. The table of infrastructure and public building development below confirms that the greatest period of economic development in the colonial economy took place under the Macquarie Administration and did not wait until the spread of settlement and the rise in the pastoral industry (which brought with it so many economic problems) in the late 1820s and 1830s.

IMPACT OF THE COLONIAL ISOLATION DURING THE 1800S

The question of isolation was of positive benefit to the British authorities because the concept of creating a *'dumping ground for human garbage'* was synonymous with finding a *'penal wasteland that was out of sight and out of mind'*.

However the disadvantages to the Colonial authorities were numerous

There was the tyranny of distance—the huge risks, of frightening transportation by sailing ship to a land hitherto unknown, uncharted and unexplored, promising huge risks and great loss of life.

Food preservation during the voyage and in the Colony was a challenge with no refrigeration or ice and with the only preservatives being salt and pickling.

Communications between Sydney and London made exchange of correspondence, obtaining decisions and permission tiresomely long. It often occurred that the Colonial Governor wrote to a Colonial Secretary,

---

[70]   The Australians: Statistics Chapter 7 'The economy before 1850'

who during the twelve months of round trip, had been replaced with another person.

Laws and justice, in the Colony, were to be based on British law, but in reality, local laws became a mix of common sense and personal philosophies e.g. Lt Governor Collins, as Advocate-General in the Colony desperately needed law books to practice, but they were never sent. Bligh, as Governor, ruled virtually as a despot and tyrannical dictator, knowing that a sea trip of seven months was between him and any admonishment or complaints being heard.

Factors Affecting British Investment in the Colony

A number of factors affected the level of capital investment into the colony–many were ill informed and relied on delayed newspaper reports on activity in the various settlements.

    a.   The offer of assisted migration
    b.   The failing economic conditions in Britain
    c.   conomic expansion for the pastoral industry due to successful exploration in the colony
    d.   Two other steps had important consequences, one in the colony and the other in Britain.

In 1827 Governor Darling began to issue grazing licenses to pastoralists, and the terms were set at 2/6d per hundred acres, with liability to quit on one month's notice. From this movement grew, writes Madgwick in *Immigration into Eastern Australia*, the squatting movement and the great pastoral expansion, and the idea of the earlier Governors that the colony of New South Wales should be a colony of farmers was thus abandoned. The concurrent event was the floating of the Australian Agricultural Company in London. Development by the AAC and by the free settlers brought increasing prosperity. Exports tripled between 1826 and 1831. k.There is a connection between availability of factors of production and the level of investment. In the early days of the colony, labour was present–bad labour, convict labour, but still labour. The governors had demanded settlers with capital to employ that labour and develop the land. They proposed to limit land grants in proportion to the means of the settler. Governor Darling declared (HRA ser 1, vol 8) that 'when I am satisfied of the character, respectability and means of the applicant settler in a rural area, he will receive the necessary authority to select a grant of land, proportionate in extent to the means he possesses.

Under Macquarie the colony had boomed with new buildings, new settlements, new investment and lots of convicts. Under Brisbane the needs for economic consolidation and new infrastructure would be addressed, together with an appeal for free settlers.

Some significant events took place during the Brisbane guardianship

The British were intent on accessing every available trading opportunity with the colony, and formed in Scotland *The Australia Company*

A road was built to connect the Windsor settlement to the new settlement at Maitland. This decision opened up the Hunter River district to new farming opportunities

The responsibility for convicts was transferred from the Superintendent of Convicts to the Colonial Secretary, although this move was to be reversed within the next decade

The first documented discovery of gold was made. It was hushed in the colony lest convicts run off to find their fortunes.

In Bigge's third and final report, he recommended extra colonial import duties and less British duty on imported timber and tanning bark

The most significant event of all was the confidence placed in Bigge's favourable opinion of the potential of the colonial economy by the London Investment community and the resulting subscription of one million pound for the Australian Agricultural Company. The subscription was accompanied by a grant of one million acres of land around Port Stephens and the allocation of 5,000 convicts, but also brought inflation to livestock prices and availability throughout the colony.

J.T. Campbell wrote about the first decade of the Australian Agricultural Company 1824-1834 in the proceedings of the 1923 RAHS.

"Soon after Commissioner Bigge's report of 1823 became available for public information, several enterprising men concerted with a view to acquire sheep-runs in the interior of this colony, for the production of fine wool.

The success which attended the efforts of John Macarthur and a few other New South Wales pastoralists, in the breeding and rearing of fine wool sheep and stock generally, as verified by Bigge, gave the incentive and led to the inauguration of proceedings which resulted in the formation of the Australian Agricultural Company.

The first formal meeting of the promoters took place at Lincoln's Inn, London, (at the offices of John Macarthur, junior).

Earl Bathurst, advised Governor Brisbane in 1824 that . . . .

His Majesty has been pleased to approve the formation of the Company, from the impression that it affords every reasonable prospect of securing to that part of His Majesty's dominions the essential advantage of the immediate introduction of large capital, and of agricultural skill, as well as the ultimate benefit of the increase of fine wool as a valuable commodity for export.

The chief proposals of the company are:

The company was to be incorporated by Act of Parliament or Letters Patent.

The capital of the company was to be 1 million pound sterling divided into 10,000 shares of 100 pound each

A grant of land of one million acres to be made to the company

That no rival joint stock company to be established in the colony for the next twenty years

That agents of the company would select the situation or the land grants.

The shepherds and labourers would consist of 1,400 convicts, thereby lessening the maintenance of such convicts by an estimated 30,800 pound or 22 pound/per head/ per annum.

The Royal Charter of 1824 forming the company provided for payment of quit-rents over a period of twenty years, or the redemption of the same by paying the capital sum of 20 times the amount of the rent so to be redeemed. These quit-rents were to be waived if the full number of convicts were maintained for a period of five years. No land was to be sold during the five-year period from the date of the grant".

Being important that the investment be seen to have the support of strong leaders in Britain, and democratic governance, the company operated with one Governor; 25 directors; and 365 stockholders (proprietors). The old English structure was retained, that of, Governor and his Court, with the directors being the members of the Court whilst the Governor was the Chairman of the Board or Court

Leading stockholders included

- Robert Campbell
- Chief Justice Forbes
- Son of Governor King
- Rev'd Samuel Marsden
- John Macarthur
- Each Macarthur son, John Jr, Hannibal, James, Charles, Scott & William John Oxley. The Colonial-Surveyor (Oxley) had recommended the area of Port Stephens as an eligible spot for the land grant. The local directors inspected and approved the site but John Macarthur was extremely critical of the selection, the management plan and the extravagance of the first buildings.

This venture was the first major investment into the colony and set the scene for later developments. In 1825 the Van Diemen's Land Company was chartered by the British Parliament and granted land on the northwest corner of the territory.

Both the A.A. Coy and the VDL Coy still operate today after nearly 180 years of continuous operation, a record beaten only by the operation of the Hudson Bay Company in Canada.

Sir Timothy Coghlan was the colonial statistician whilst he was involved in preparing the series 'The Wealth and Progress of New South Wales 1900-01'. He was later appointed as Agent-General in London before compiling the 4-volume set of 'Labour and Industry in Australia'.

Circumstances in Britain contributed greatly to the climate of 'greener pastures' over the seas.

Conditions were never more favourable for emigration than they were during the 1830s. The decade had opened with rioting in the agricultural districts in the south of England. This was followed by the upheavals of the Reform Bill of 1832, the Factory Act of 1833 and the Corn Laws, which kept wages low and unemployment high. The Poor Law of 1834 withdrew assistance from the poor and re-introduced the workhouse. The Irish rebellion was creating both upheaval and poverty

These conditions were met by the enthusiastic reports coming from Australia of the progress being made in agriculture, commerce and the pastoral industry. The assistance granted to emigrants as a result of Edward Gibbon Wakefield's reforms made possible the emigration of people who had previously been prevented by the expense. It is almost certain that free passage would not have been a sufficient enticement if conditions in Britain had not been unfavourable. It is significant that years of small migration coincided with good conditions in England accompanied by unfavourable reports from the colony.

4. Creating Opportunities in the Colony

Availability of land and labour to yield profit on invested capital is the constant decisive condition and test of material prosperity in any community, and becomes the keystone of an economy as well as defining its national identity.

British Government policy for the Australian colonies was formulated and modified from time to time. Policies for the export of British capital and the supply of labour (both convict and free) were adjusted according to British industrial and demographic and other social situations, as well as the capability and capacity of the various colonial settlements top contribute to solving British problems.

By the 1820s there was official encouragement of British Investment in Australia by adopting policies for large land grants to persons of capital and for the sale of land and assignment of convict labour to those investors. Then followed the reversal of the policy of setting up ex-convicts on small 30 acre plots as small proprietors. The hardship demanded by this policy usually meant these convicts and families remained on the commissary list for support (food and clothing) at a continuing cost to the government. It was much cheaper to assign these convicts to men of property and capital who would support them fully–clothe, house and feed them.

We can ask, what led directly to the crash of 1827? a. Firstly, the float of the Australian Agricultural Company raised a large amount of capital, mostly from the City of London investment community, and this contributed to speculation and 'sheep and cattle mania instantly seized on all ranks and classes of the inhabitants' (written by Rev'd John Dunmore Lang) 'and brought many families to poverty and ruin'. b.When capital imports cease, the wherewithal to speculate vanished; speculation perforce stopped; inflated prices fell to a more normal level, and wrote E.O. Shann in Economic History of Australia 'because those formerly too optimistic were now too despairing, and people had to sell goods at any price in order to get money; men who had bought at high prices were ruined, and perforce their creditors fell with them'. c.In 1842, it was the same. The influx of capital from oversees, pastoral extension, and large-scale immigration, caused much speculation. The banks, competing for business, advanced too much credit. Loans were made on the security of land and livestock, which later became almost worthless; too much discounting was done for merchants (Gipps, HRA Vol 23).In the huge central district on the western slopes, along the Murrumbidgee and the Riverina, the squatters triumphed, as was inevitable. He had the financial resources to buy his run–especially after the long period of drought. Four million acres of crown land was sold for nearly 2.5 million pound. The confidence of British investors was waning. A crisis in the Argentine and the near failure of the large clearinghouse of Baring's made them cautious. Stories of rural and industrial strife in the colony were not inducements to invest: and wood and metal prices were still falling Loan applications being raised in London were under-subscribed, at the same time; the banks were increasingly reluctant to lend money for land development, which was so often unsound.

5. Assisted Migration

The dual policy of selling land to people with sufficient capital to cultivate it, and keeping a careful check on the number of free grants was adopted after 1825. 'Yet the Colonial Office', says Madgwick, 'failed to administer land policy with any certainty (R.B. Madgwick 'Immigration into Eastern Australia'). There was no uniform policy adopted to encourage economic development in a systematic and rational way. The Wakefield system found new supporters. The principle had been established that the sale of land was preferred to the old system of grants. The dual system of sales and grants had failed to encourage local (colonial) purchases. They were willing to accept grants or even 'squat' rather than purchase land. Sales to absentee landlords and investors stepped up, and as can be seen from the following table, provided extensive revenue to the British Government to promote free and sponsored migration.

6. Successful exploration promotes new interest in the Colony

A period of rapid expansion followed the change in economic policy. Wool exports by 1831 were 15 times as great as they had been only 10 years earlier (in 1821). The increase in the number of sheep led to a rapid opening of new territories for grazing. It was the search for new land with economic value that underpinned most of the explorations. Settlers and sheep-men quickly followed exploration, and growth fanned out in all directions from Sydney town.

However, exploration was not the only catalyst for growth. a. The growing determination to exclude other powers from the continent stimulated official interest in long-distance exploration by sea and by land and in the opening of new settlements. For instance, J.K. Ward in his work 'The Triumph of the Pastoral Economy 1821-1851' writes that Melville and Bathurst Islands, were annexed and settled between 1824 and 1827, whilst Westernport and Albany were settled in order to clinch British claims to the whole of Australia b. When Governor Brisbane opened the settlement at Moreton Bay in 1824, it was to establish a place for punishment of unruly convicts and a step towards further economic development, and of extending the settlements for the sake of attracting new investment

7. Colonial Failures fuel loss of Confidence

The collapse of British Investment can be traced to one or two causes, or indeed both.

I. The British crisis of 1839 reflected the availability of capital for expansion by the Australian banks of that day–The Bank of Australasia and the Union Bank. These banks, three mortgage companies and the Royal Bank went into a slump due to shortage of available funds and deferred the raising of new funds until after the crisis. Stringency in the English Capital market had a serious impact on the capital raising opportunities in the colonies.

II. The second possibility is that the sharp decline was initiated by bad news of returns in the colonies, and that its role accentuated a slump with the dire consequences experienced in 1842-43. Recovery was delayed and made more difficult as there was 'no surplus labour in the colony'

It would be dangerous to imply or decide that every slump in Australia could be explained as being caused by economic events. British investment was independent then, as it is now, and so the more valid explanation of the downturn in British investment in this period is that negative reports from the colonies disappointed and discouraged investors with capital to place.

Most facts about public finance in New South Wales lead to the conclusion that it was disappointed expectations that caused the turn down in the transfer of funds. At this same time Governor Gipps (Sir George Gipps) was being pushed by bankers and merchants to withdraw government deposits from the banks and thus this action caused a contraction in lending by the banks which in turn caused a slowdown of colonial economic activity. The attached statistics of land sales, registered mortgages and liens on wool and livestock reflects the strong downturn in the agricultural economy, which naturally flowed on to the economy as a whole.

CHAPTER 7

THE NEED FOR
MANUFACTURING

Hainsworth in his Chapter Twelve 'Dawn of Industry' from _The Sydney Traders_[71] guides us in a review of the growth of manufactures before 1825.

'Thanks to the initiative of Sydney traders, manufacturing and processing industries emerged very early and helped to transform NSW from penal settlement to colony'.

The traders supplemented government activity, often by carrying out similar activities, and sometimes launched various types of manufacturing in which the government was not concerned. It was natural that the government should play a dominant role at this early stage, for it had the responsibility of clothing, housing, feeding and working the convicts, both male and female. The government role was as the chief employer of the convicts, the chief provider of capital and of course, and the chief consumer of their output. In a limited way, the government was prepared to foster industrial enterprise, though this encouragement was haphazard, capricious and oftentimes playing favourites. The government, itself, launched brewing, salt-making, milling and basic textiles, and operated a number of crude industrial processes before allowing them to be taken

---

[71]   Hainsworth, D.R. The Sydney Traders

over by enterprising colonists on favourable terms. Privatisation was not a deliberate policy, one more so of convenience.

Sealing[72] by 1800 was dominating the trading calendar. The official return for that year showed over 118,000 skins had passed through Sydney with Simeon Lord and his fellow ex-convicts, Kable and Underwood handling over 72,000 from just one source–Antipodes Island. By 1815, the *Sydney Gazette* was reporting the sealing industry was in decline. The intense harvesting of the seals had lowered their natural numbers, but the British Government was influenced by the 'whale lobby' to raise discriminatory duties against colonial oil, seal and whale. Spermaceti oil was to bear a duty of 15s 9d per ton for British ships but £24 18s 9d if obtained by colonial ships. Duties of £8 8s a ton were imposed on Black Whale oil from the Derwent estuary. Thus through these discriminatory tariffs, colonial oil was virtually barred from London.

Cottage industries were not only the preserve of the small home-based manufacturers. Coghlan[73] points out 'those who had the enterprise and industry to devote land to gardening were amply repaid'. The broad acre crops raised were chiefly wheat and maize, with a little oats and barley, some potatoes and other vegetables.

Excellent opportunities, for fresh fruit and vegetables, were provided by the weather, the climate and the generally good soil around Sydney, but gardening was not undertaken other than by the few conscious of home grown vegetables. They were able, says Coghlan, 'to grow almost all ordinary English vegetables, all the English fruits and some fruits, such as grapes, grew in abundance. Macquarie described his garden at Parramatta as 'full of vines and fruit trees and abounding in the most excellent vegetables'

Stock-raising was given impetus when, in 1805, the two Blaxland brothers arrived in the colony, bringing a considerable amount of capital and more than a little acquaintance with husbandry of cattle. In 1810, horned cattle numbers stood at 12,442. Ten years later, when Macquarie left, the herds

---

[72] Based on Hainsworth 'The Sydney Traders Ch12 'The Dawn of Industry'
[73] Coghlan, T.A. 'Labour & Industry in Australia' (Page 117–Vol I)

numbered 102,939, so that the annual increase was at the rate of 20.5%. The numbers were carefully guarded and there was no undue slaughtering, and salt beef was still being imported in 1814. Even so, the records show that beef was cheap with a herd selling at £8 per head. Horses, says Coghlan, 'throve[74] in the settlement from the beginning although their numbers increased very slowly. In 1800 there were only 203 horses, but by 1810 the numbers had grown to 1134 and by 1821, the numbers totalled 4564.

Coghlan recognises the importance of the timber industry and writes "the export of timber became fairly considerable and in 1803, Governor King spoke of it as the only staple of the colony"–the inland forests could not be exploited because of the lack of any means of transport, and as a result 'numerous saw-pits were established on the inlets of Port Jackson, along the banks of the Hawkesbury, and later at Newcastle on the Hunter, where convicts were engaged cutting timber as well as in mining coal"

Occasionally cargoes were shipped to India, and in 1809 timber to the value of £1500 was sent to that country in part payment for a return shipment of rice. "The presence of so much valuable timber would in ordinary circumstances have led to the establishment of shipbuilding yards. Vessels were built for sealing purposes as early as 1791, but the presence of craft capable of going to sea was considered a menace to the safe-keeping of the convicts and the governor directed no boats were to be built of greater length than 14 feet". Hunter removed this restriction in 1798, and in fact encouraged the shipbuilding industry by permitting a vessel of 'thirty tons to be built to procure seal skins and oil in Bass Straits'.[75] Campbell then built a vessel of 130 tons launched in 1805[76].

There was considerable activity mostly through the *Dockyard* (attached to the Commissary) in boat-repairs, refurbishing and provisioning, but the stoppage of the fishery in 1810 was a serious blow to the industry.

---

[74] This is an editor's change–the Coghlan text states 'shrove'
[75] Coghlan, Labour & Industry Vol 1 Page 121-2
[76] Steven, Margaret 'Merchant Campbell 1769-1846'

Immigration to the colony was mostly by way of assigned servants between 1821 and 1826, but the difficulty experienced in collecting the payments for the servants made the whole notion difficult. Coghlan tells "in the matter of indentured service many employers, principally those in the country districts were willing to advance £8-10 towards the cost of each immigrant labourer obtained by them and in February 1832 Governor Bourke despatched a list of 803 labourers who might be sent out on these terms. It was on immigration at the cost of land revenue that the colonial authorities placed their confidence. They offered to set aside £10,000 from the land fund for emigration purposes; of this sum they desired that about two-thirds be devoted to promoting the emigration of unmarried women, as the proportion of men in the colony was excessive and that one-third should be used in loans for the emigration of mechanics".

After 1836, it was decided that the whole of the rapidly increasing land revenue of NSW should be devoted to immigration[77] and in 1837 over 3090 immigrants were brought to the colony of whom 2688 were sponsored through the Emigration Commissioners in London and 405 were under the bounty scheme by colonial employers.

The need for manufacturing in the colony was created by local demand for tools, materials and supplies, in large demand for meeting general construction and housing needs. Manufacturing in the colony was catered by the private sector and the government sector. The private sector was sponsored by a handful of entrepreneurs or skilled settlers, who wanted to satisfy local demand for their product by creating a 'cottage industry', due to generally limited demand and a constantly changing market. The public/government sector became involved through the commissariat operations. In order to put convicts to productive work, reverse the long lead time for purchasing urgent materials from Britain, and more fully utilise the 'free' local resources such as timber and convict labour. Barnard observes[78] 'The colony was never wholly penal like France's Devil Island, nor was it intended to be. It was, in due course, to be balanced by freed men, their children, and such other settlers, soldiers, seamen and the like who cared to take the reward for their services in land, of which

---

[77] Coghlan 'Labour & Industry in Australia–Vol I Page 178

[78] Barnard, Marjorie *A History of Australia* 1962 (Page 304)

the Crown had a superfluity. Actually, NSW suffered very little from being a penal settlement and was fortunate in that her first unpromising colonizing material was early swamped by infusions of new blood, that wool, land grants and then gold attracted free colonists. There were no foreign elements to arouse Imperial suspicion, no subject race to put what might have been considered a necessary brake on progress'. This statement by Barnard is a rewriting of history, but would be an ideal policy, if it were true. The settlement was designed to be a penal one, and every move made was designed to be about the convicts–their work, protecting them from themselves, feeding, clothing and maintaining them, providing them with tools, equipment and supplies. Laissez-faire might have been in vogue in London during the Phillip Administration but the settlement struggled whilst awaiting food and other supplies, and convicts were held tightly accountable for all their activities. Until 1823, the entire responsibility for the settlement rested on the Governor. Upon him was bestowed a power to control lawlessness, which he effectively exercised.

The diversity of manufacturing within the colony by 1821, at the end of the Macquarie Administration was far more impressive than could reasonably be expected from a former penal colony transforming itself into a free market economy. Macquarie's enthusiasm for free enterprise and 'cost saving' led to great production sponsored by the commissariat. Convict labour was considered to be without 'cost' and therefore without 'value', as was local raw materials, so much of the output of the commissariat business enterprises left without recognition of value, which well-suited Macquarie's purposes. As early as 1812, he had been sternly warned by Colonial Secretary Liverpool [79] that 'the burden of the colony of NSW upon the Mother Country has been so much increased since the period of your assumption of the government of it, that it becomes necessary that you should transmit a more satisfactory explanation of the grounds upon which the unusual expenditure has been sanctioned by you'. Liverpool admitted he had misgivings of this attack when he continued his letter to Macquarie in terms of 'I can't point out what expenses have been unnecessarily incurred, and the only ground I have for forming a judgement is by comparison of the total amount of bills by your predecessors and yourself'. Naturally enough, absolute total were progressively higher, but

---

[79]   HRA 1:7:476 Liverpool to Macquarie 4th May, 1812

in terms of bills drawn per head of convict on the store' the comparisons declined. Macquarie was actively creating an investment for the future, and at some future point the colony could easily be self-supporting and outside the need for treasury appropriations. However, in philosophical terms, why should the local revenues be used to support any form of a penal colony for Britain. Surely the free settlers could grow in conjunction with the transfer of convicts to the colony; whilst Britain supported the convicts and the colony supported its own operations. One of Macquarie's goals in having the government business enterprises so active in the colony was to quickly achieve this self-sufficiency and be out from the clutches of Whitehall. Macquarie's thinking was only half right. He was so preoccupied with the economic and fiscal arrangements in the colony that he lost sight of the overall plan. Local revenues were first raised in 1802 and were designed for 'discretionary' expenditure by the governor of the day. The reason for this loose arrangement was that the Treasury appropriated funds for specific purposes such as convict maintenance, and civil establishment salaries, but did not see the need for maintenance works, repairs, infrastructure development and the like, so the money for these essentials had to come from local sources and be reserved for deployment by the government. Whitehall soon caught onto this stream of revenue and although the Treasury officials knew it was illegal revenue, they restricted its use by withholding British funds to the amount of revenue raised within the colony. Thus in Macquarie's administration, private enterprise figured as a means of both import replacement and cost saving for the colony. Manufacturing filled the joint roles of availability of key/essential merchandise and of putting convicts to productive work.

Barnard records[80] that even the 'boys—some as young as eleven—were kept in Sydney at Carter's Barracks near Brickfield Hill and were working as a carpenter, shoemaker, stone-cutter, blacksmith, and other trades to which the boys were apprenticed. The product of their labour went into the public store, and a pool of much needed mechanics was created'. This observation is rather unique, is unsourced and does not have the ring of accuracy about it. Barnard is implying that these trades were carried out at the Barracks, which means that materials and tools were brought daily to the barracks. With carts and bodies for hauling purposes being

---

[80] Barnard, M *A History of Australia* Page 237

in very short supply, it seems unlikely that large lumps of stone or tree trunks would be hauled from Upper George Street (the Lumber Yard was at the corner of George and Bridge) all the way to Brickfields Hill for young boys to play with. The carter barracks were used for confinement and punishment, and there was little space for practicing wood craft or stone masonry. It is much more likely that the boys were released on a weekly basis, under supervision, and taken to the raw materials source–for instance the stone-yard and the Timber Yard, which were both on George Street North. This is a rare unsourced apparent contradiction by Barnard. She is probably incorrect when she states the apprentices' output went to the public store–it probably went to the Lumber Yard store–from where all building materials, supplies and tools were inventoried. The public store kept only dry goods, fresh foods or grain.

The extent of private sector manufacturing ranged from clothing, castings and carts to soap, silver-smithing, tanneries and tin-smithing. In addition government manufacturing covered an equally broad range–from nails to timber framing, bricks tiles and stone blocks, forged items and boot making.

The broad intent, because of the small local population, which by itself would not have supported such a sector, was two-fold–to replace imports and the timeframe of a year or two between ordering and receipt of goods, and to create an export market of sorts.

According to Jackson[81], the population in the colony during 1820 was only 34,000 and too small to create sufficient demand for private sector output and to establish economic development.

The early entrepreneurs and their activities raise numerous questions which to-date has not been studied in the literature. Hainsworth records[82] 'Simeon Lord cannot be described as a typical emancipist trader for his operations were too large and diverse, but he was a member of a numerous group. Another was Henry Kable, whose commercial beginnings are still more shadowy–an illiterate man transported in the first fleet, Kable was

---

[81]   R.V. Jackson *Australian Economic Development in the 19th Century*
[82]   H.R. Hainsworth *Sydney Traders* P.41

for several years a constable of Sydney and probably profitably plied with liquor the drunks he locked up'. What Hainsworth is by implication questioning, is how these two (of many) eventually became such successful traders? What was their source of start up monies? How did these emancipist traders get started? Hainsworth, later in his study concludes 'the capital they mobilised for shipbuilding and sealing in 1800 must have come from trading'[83] Other examples of early unexplained success include John Palmer and his associates, who as the third Commissary on 5/–per day, became the wealthiest man in the colony during the King Administration, and that was before his sister, Sophia, married the largest merchant in the colony, Robert Campbell. Palmer and his trading colleagues prospered in a colony whose commercial life was supposed to be monopolised by an officer clique.[84] Although the officer class is usually described by historians as having caste a large shadow in the early 1790s under Hunter, they could not stop an undertow of small dealers and emerging traders growing up around them. Rather the officers brought this about by allowing the retail trade to fall into the hands of 'ambitious and able (if uneducated) men with no gentility to lose'[85] In many cases because the wholesale market was officer controlled and these emancipist retailers wanted to continue to expand and grow, they moved into 'cottage' manufacturing–often working with the commissariat to supply finished goods or raw materials for further processing by the Lumber Yard or Female Factory (e.g. Tanned leather, scoured wool, and crushed grain). For many emerging entrepreneurs, this was the way they commenced their manufacturing activities–trader, marketer and then manufacturer. According to Hainsworth[86], Simeon Lord was typical of the early merchant traders. When a shortage of circulating notes occurred, Lord (amongst others) requested his creditor customers to liquidate their debts to him by any means possible. The result was that Lord accepted grain, (which he then put into the store on his own account), most of which he had bartered from his retail customers, payroll bills from military officers with whom he was dealing on a wholesale basis, individual 'notes or bills' payable, which were freely circulating and classed as petty banking. Lord would consolidate these bills and exchange them

---

[83] Hainsworth refers his readers, on this point, to his inserts in the ADB for Lord, Kable and Underwood Volumes 1 & 2

[84] ADB Volume 2–John Palmer (Hainsworth)

[85] Hainsworth *The Sydney Traders* Page 42

[86] Hainsworth *Sydney Traders* Page 83

for one large bill drawn by the Commissariat on the Treasury in London. This bill he would then release to his suppliers–usually visiting ship's captains, or transfer to his Indian or Macao (Hong Kong) suppliers. So obviously the greatest limitation to entrepreneurial activity in the colony was 'the medium of exchange: the lack of a mint and a Treasury, or even a private bank of issue. However with all its faults the system worked. It was the only system they had and the traders made the best use of it'.[87]

Thus private sector output was limited by government demand for food and materials.

The Jackson theory is that the sale of goods to the government store (commissariat) provided a major source of foreign exchange to the private sector because sale proceeds were made available in the form of Treasury Bills drawn on London.

Organisation of Government Business Enterprises

Under the guise of controlling the activities and rehabilitation of convicts, Macquarie decided that placing all convicts on assignment, thereby removing any financial obligation for their maintenance, a percentage could be put to work on behalf of the government. This would be accomplished in two ways. Firstly, direct convict labour, rather than the preferred contractor program, would be used for infrastructure development and the other public works program, specifically government building.

So there became a great concentration of convicts in Sydney, employed in two big workshops, the lumber-yard and the timber-yard. Both were located on George Street, together with the stone-yard (across from the lumber-yard) and the three-storey Commissary Store, wharf and Dockyard, fronting the western side of Sydney Cove. The convicts worked on a task, or piece system. In the Lumber Yard, surrounded by an 8 foot high brick wall, for security purposes, forges were used for making nail, hinges, wheel irons and other metal products. Other 'sections' were set aside around the outside walls of the factory, for boot-making, cabinet and

---

[87] Abbott & Nairn (*Growth*) Chapters 8 & 9

furniture-making, coopers for barrel making, course wool and cotton for slops and hat making. In the centre of the large factory the two saw pits were manned by up to 25 men, who cut the timber taken from the kiln after its drying process. In the timber yards, beams and floor-boards were sawn and prepared from the timber drawn from the lumber-yard. The brick and tile yard was built around a huge kiln (22 feet long by 18 feet high producing 24,000 bricks at one raking. The Stone-yard not only produced large building blocks from stone but also flagstones, hearth-stones and mantelpieces. Within the lumber-yard, was stored all the tools required within the various business enterprises as well as on each work site. Each item was recorded going out and coming in. Equally carefully, all materials–both raw material and finished product–were recorded at the clerk's office located at the main gate. The Superintendent of Convicts, Major Ovens had set a piece work productivity rate. For instance, the shoemaker's gang of about eight me, were supposed to produce a pair of shoes each day, each man from leather tanned at the government factory at Cawdor; likewise, the brass-foundry and the tailors' gang each had their own production goals; the carpenter's gang which was usually of fifty men, was made up of cabinet-makers, turners and shinglers; the bricklayers' gang was generally between five and ten men who were expected to lay 4,500 bricks each week; the Sawyers gang was usually twenty-five men. Other gangs based in the lumber yard were also sent out to garden, cut grass, dig foundations, and carry grain. The lumber yard was responsible for over 2,000 men in all.

The government business enterprises were a comprehensive and massive undertaking, and Macquarie took pride in their output and accomplishments.

Manufacturing is only part of the story included in any study of economic development of the period. Economic development drove public finance in the same way that population growth, pastoral growth and growth of decentralisation and land utilisation impacted on the source and use of public funds. Other factors to be considered include:

The commissariat established multiple stores and supplied foodstuffs and materials (at government expense) not only for convicts but for civilian and military personnel as well. In the early years, well over 50% of the entire population would have been victualled by the commissariat

The commissariat also established work centres for convicts:

The Lumber Yard,
The Timber Yard
The Dockyard
The Stone Quarry
The Boat Yard
Timber-Cutting Camps
Land Clearing Camps
The Government Farms
The Government stores

These centres employed until 1820 over 50% of the convict population.

The output of these centres was directed at Agricultural output; Livestock supply;

Import Replacement manufactures; Materials required in the Construction and building industries; Materials required in the Public Works and Infrastructure Construction program, and Transport and storage requirements of the government.

Colin White[88] in has concluded that the colonial government controlled the local economic mechanism. There were three main elements to the mechanism:

(1)The government provided the social infrastructure to mitigate risk to individuals, and further, (2) guaranteed a market, at fixed prices, for output of the private sector. This government action also provided (3) grants of free land, inexpensive credit and cheap labour with the return of any redundant labour to government service when needed.

---

[88] *Mastering Risk–Environment, Markets and Politics in Australian Economic History* Page 52

Public Works

Public Investment in public works infrastructure was a major challenge. Britain essentially saw the settlement as little more than a tent town. These inhabitants were prisoners, under guard, transported 'out of sight and out of mind' and had no need of money or coins, public buildings or fancy housing or amenities. Early governors from Phillip to Bligh kept to the minimum work and therefore expense, and by the time of Macquarie's arrival, there was a deferred maintenance and construction schedule that dumped all of the expense and workload on his Administration. Commissioner Bigge recorded for his Enquiry that 76 buildings had been completed under Macquarie, some of which were extravagant for example the Governor's *Stables*, The Rum Hospital, and the toll booths on the Parramatta Road. Bigge directed they be revamped and put to alternate (less extravagant use). Bigge made no comment on the provision of water, sewer or drainage measures made for a town with a growing population. Macquarie had drained the marshes in the present Centennial Park as the water supply for the town–and outlawed the use of the Tank Stream for animal grazing, washing, and waste sewer.

Governor Darling, as part of his structuring of a public service for the colony, established in 1826 the first Office of Inspector of Roads and Bridges, with charge over the Engineer's office. From April 1827, his title was changed to Surveyor of Roads and Bridges, and the office remained active until 1830, when in an economy drive, Sir George Murray, Secretary of State for the Colony and War Departments passed these responsibilities to the Surveyor-General. In 1832 the Colonial Architect's Department was established in order to be responsible for the planning, repair and construction of public buildings. In 1833, in another economy drive, this department was also transferred to the Surveyor-General. Later the duties of colonial engineer for superintendence over roads, bridges, wharves and quays were added to those of the Colonial Architect and all planning came under the Surveyor-General. It was this concentration of work load in such few hands that led to an increasing public investment in public works.

Another effort by Governor Darling to centralise planning and control into a new public service bureaucracy, was the establishment of the Clergy and School Lands Department in 1826. The corporation was to receive a seventh in value and extent of all the lands in each county in the colony. Out of this land the corporation was to be responsible for the payment of salaries of clergy, schoolmasters, and for the building and maintenance of churches, school and minister's residences.

Governor Darling had centralised the planning for all public works into one department–the Land's Department which in turn employed the Surveyor-General and provided for the Lands Board. This balance assisted in prioritising and funding all public works and thus brought order to the former Macquarie chaos of building as he saw fit. A by-product of this new policy was that all convicts were now on assignment and 'off the stores', and a competitive contracting arrangement was used for tendering for all public works.

An Economic Model of the Colonial Economy GDP

The pre-1861 period has long been considered[89] too risky to assemble data for creating an economic model of the times. However certain elements of such a model can be identified and used for, in the least, a good indicative assessment of the economic growth between 1788 and 1860.

A practical example of an economic model which could be adapted for the period was found in McTaggart, Findlay and Parkin *Macroeconomics*.

THE PRODUCTION APPROACH

	1820 £
Agriculture, Fishery & Forestry	
Mining	
Water, lighting & heating	
Construction	
Wholesale Trade	
Retail Trade	

---

[89] N.G. Butlin and T.A. Coghlan write of the inaccurate statistics and other data for this period.

Hotels, Cafes
Transport & Storage
Communication services
finance & insurance
Gov't admin & defence
education
health & social services
cultural & recreation
taxes on products

The rise of manufacturing was a significant part of the economic growth in the early colony. Of all the sectors, agriculture (including whaling, sealing and wool) gave the most significant results in terms of manpower used, capital invested, export returns, and GDP. In second place would be the development of local natural resources followed closely by manufacturing outcomes. These observations can be made from individual statistics of employment, exports, convict work organisation and data about immigrants and their assets. However, the more reliable statistics will come from the assembly of a model using either the production approach, or the aggregate income/expenditure approach. Both methods will be attempted and compared, but as can be seen an understanding and assessment of manufacturing is essential to either methodology.

Hainsworth in the prologue to *The Sydney Traders* writes 'To study the 'entrepreneur' is to study the central figure in modern economic history–the central figure in economics'. The years 1788 to 1821 are the seed-time of Australian government'.[90]

Although it is difficult to connect the growth of economic development in percentage of contribution terms for any one sector, we know that the more important sectors must be

1. Growth of population
2. Government immigration policy
3. Foreign capital
4. The need for Import replacement

---

[90] Hainsworth *Sydney Traders* prologue page 14

5. The need for foreign exchange through exports.

In each of these the commissariat had a role and an important government need.

The government had to grow the economy at the lowest practical cost, but offer official services which would attract growth, trade and population. This it achieved, at least through 1821, by using the commissariat as the quasi-treasury, the manager of government business enterprises, and the employer of government-sponsored convict labour.

The point here is that the economic model had to incorporate each of these 'input' factors and reflect them. Here in brief is the methodology used.

The commissariat influence over foreign exchange, imports and exports, and government-sponsored manufacturing and even over attracting foreign investment capital is without comparison, but measurable. The economic model for the period does not nor cannot parallel Butlin's measurement of post-1861 GDP, but does use basic ingredients like:

1. Computing working free population
2. Computing working convict population
3. Assuming a productivity adjustment for lower than expected convict output
4. Valuing productive labour at Coghlan suggested rates
5. Interpolating labour product to total output.
6. Comparing annual total production per head of population and per head of 'worker'
7. Estimating total output by industry and comparing this to underlying assumptions about labour output.
8. Extending the estimated GDP from 1800 to 1860 to ensure the recessions of 1810-1816, 1828-29 and 1842-45 as shown in the GDP figures were responsive to these downturns.
9. Comparing the growth of local revenues from 1801 and of trade, for the same period reflected changes to estimated GDP.
10. Announcing the adopted GDP figures for the period 1800-1860 and seeing how they blended in with the Butlin figures.

The results are assembled on a spreadsheet for each year, but a summary has been produced as an extract in order to evidence gains for each ten-year interval, and to show that the Beckett compilations and the Butlin compilations fit in with each other.

TABLE ESTIMATES OF GDP BETWEEN 1800 AND 1900

Year	GDP per head of popln	GDP per head of workforce
1801	13.61	35.1
1811	28.06	49.95
1821	33.54	59.70
1831	35.68	63.51
1841	39.66	70.60
1851	40.13	76.43
1861	46	85
1871	47	118
1877	57	139
1881	63	151
1889	67	158
1891	66	155
1900	57	132

Source: Beckett *Handbook of Colonial Statistics for period 1800-1860*
Butlin, N.G. *Investment in Australian Economic Development 1861-1900*

Certain conclusions can be reached about this table:

1. GDP in the colony grew in each ten year period because the components of that GDP grew e.g. population, manufacturing enterprises, convict numbers, exports and immigration. As the colony went through its transition from penal to free, especially a free market-based economy, so government investment in services and infrastructure also grew. Personal investment in housing increased and the individual wealth as well as the collective wealth of the colony grew. The down turn in 1900 was due to the recession in the mid-1890s, when many banks failed, unemployment increased and the previous land boom of the 1870-80s crashed, leaving many families and businesses in tough times.

However certain questions remain: This model relates to restricted sectors of the colonial economy, but only touches indirectly on important sectors such as the pastoral industry, the whaling and seal industry. These sectors are indirectly reflective of a growing export market. A more detailed model with declared sub-elements would express the importance of these natural resource or primary production industries including timber, shipping, coal, minerals as well as wool and wool by-products

There were some distractions from within the colony to Macquarie's aggressive enterprise policies. In a wave of perversion, William Charles Wentworth led an anti-Macquarie movement against local manufacturing in favour of importations.

In January of 1819, Macquarie gave permission for a group of clergy, merchants, settlers, and other gentlemen to convene a meeting in the court-room of the new General Hospital, to prepare a petition. The petition was for a redress of grievances and essentially was to try and expand rather than restrict imports into the colony. Macquarie by trying to match exports with imports (in value terms), was restricting the type of imports authorised.

Macquarie, in a despatch to Bathurst of 22nd March, 1819 notates[91] the resolution

> '1. That a regular demand exists in the colony for British manufactures of nearly all descriptions, greater than the established mercantile houses here have supplied or are likely to supply regularly.
> 2. Restrictions prevent merchants from employing ships of less three hundred and fifty tons burthen (under the *Navigation Acts)*
> 3. That this meeting requests Gov Macquarie to try and expand shipping between Britain and Australia for transporting Manufactures and colonial produce.'

The sentiments were laudable but the request baseless. The commissariat with its huge buying opportunities could have achieved the desired result. Merchants' collaborating into a buying group could have achieved the same result but the obvious solution was to encourage the local production of all imported items at a lower cost.

---

[91]   HRA1:10:52 Macquarie to Bathurst 22nd March, 1819

Macquarie made no recommendations to Bathurst, which meant that he had strictly fulfilled his role to the petitioners, and had left Bathurst with the opinion that the colonial manufacturers and merchants were ill-prepared to fight British exports

In over 300 pages of text, John Ritchie[92] reviews the submissions made in the colony to Commissioner Bigge, but does not recite any submission made by merchants or manufacturers. However in the Bigge reports, we find details of evidence submitted by Simeon Lord about his manufacturing activities. At his factory at Botany Bay, he employed between 15 and 20 convicts in the making of:

Blankets	Stockings
Wool hats	Trousers
Kangaroo hats	Glass tumblers
Seal hats,	Kettles
Possum skin hats,	Thread
Boot leather	Shirts

Between 1810 and 1820 the number of sheep trebled in the colony, and many producers were finding it more profitable to sell carcasses instead of fleeces

Local manufactured items did not entirely replace imports. Items were still imported from India and China.

From India came
Sugar
Spirits
Soap
Cotton goods

From China came
Sugar candy
Silks
Wearing apparel

---

[92] Ritchie, John *Punishment and Profit- The Bigge Commission in to NSW'*

<u>Colonial Exports</u> included
Sandalwood
Pearl shells
Bache de mar
Whale oil and meat
Seal Oil

Trade exchange, on a barter basis, was made with a number of the Pacific Islands of 'coarse cotton' and ironware, for coconut and salt pork.

Among other evidence to the Bigge Enquiry were numerous complaints by manufacturers on the limited supply of materials, the high cost of buying from government business enterprises—for instance the cloth produced by workers at the government female factory was 2/5 1/4 d per yard, whereas at Mr Kenyon's private establishment it was only 11d. The Manager of the Robert Campbell merchant business complained to Commissioner Bigge about the duties on whale and seal oil from the colony, arriving in England. He also criticised the port regulations which required captains to give 10 day's notice of intention to sail—he claimed this resulted in high wharfage charges.

Ritchie (*Punishment & Profit*) concludes that although Bigge wanted to encourage trade and certain manufacturing, he was reconciled to the fact that their promotion would not provide an adequate or proper solution to the question of convict employment, punishment and reform. [93]

Observations on Industry & Commerce in NSW

By 1820 Simeon Lord had turned the profits of fishing in the south seas and trade in the Pacific Islands into a manufactory at Botany Bay where he employed convicts and from 15 to 20 colonial youths making blankets, stockings, wool hats, kangaroo hats, seal hats, possum skin hats, all of

---

[93] Evidence of sundry manufacturers to Commissioner Bigge Enquiry)

them shoddy but cheaper than English imports of hats, boots, leather, trousers, shirts, thread, kettles and glass tumblers. [94]

The heavy influx of immigrants during the Darling Administration brought its own difficulties, especially when drought and depression closed down on the colony at the end of the 1830s. This period led onto the severe economic depression of 1842, which had been fuelled by a reduction of foreign investment, a cessation of the British speculators and absentee landlords, as well as local factors, partly sponsored by Sir George Gipps, the successor to Darling as Governor. Between 1831 and 1841, imports had increased by 518 percent to a total of over two and a half million pounds and exports by 1257 percent to a total of two million pounds.[95]

The severe drought of 1825-8 was unfairly blamed on Darling, as was the epidemic of 'whooping cough' which killed Darling's own son and of smallpox which afflicted the colony.

Between December 1831 and December 1832 325,549 gallons of spirits and 109,406 gallons of wine were imported and at least another 11,000 gallons of gin were distilled locally–all for a population of only 15,000.

As for prices, milk was 8 pence per quart, potatoes were fifteen shillings a hundredweight, beef had declined to one penny halfpenny a pound[96], mutton twopence halfpenny, veal five-pence, pork four-penny halfpenny. Fowls cost from 1/9d to 2/3d per pair, whilst butter varied from season to season between 1/–and 3/–per pound,; cheese sold at 4 pence per pound, Cape wine was 8d to ½ per pint and port was 1/45 to 2/–per quart. Respectable lodgings were a pound per week. And a horse could be hired for 10/–a day, and a gig for 15/–per day. Housing costs had risen to 530 pound for a six-roomed cottage

---

[94] An quote extracted from Clark, A History of Australia sourced by Clark from 'An account of Mr Lord's manufactures, submitted to Commissioner Bigge, 1st February 1821

[95] Barnard, Marjorie *Sydney–A story of a City'* P.18

[96] Beef during the Macquarie Administration was bought by the Commissariat at 5 pence per pound

The depression that lasted from the late 1830s to 1842 but created a slowdown in the colony until gold was discovered in 1852 caused an estimated 1638 bankruptcies. There was a glut of livestock such that sheep were selling for 6d per head. Land sales ceased and there was an oversupply of labour for the first time in 50 years. Almost a final blow to the struggling economy came with the discovery of gold in California, with estimates of 5757 houses being empty out of the 7100 houses in Sydney town.[97]

The economy in the period up to 1800 was based upon the limited trade monopolised by military men like John Macarthur as well as a steady expansion of government-financed agriculture to feed the growing number of convicts. This expansion could only continue until the colony became self-sufficient in food. Then an alternative product, of sufficient value to be exported would be required to generate the hard currency that in turn would pay for the increasing imports demanded by the growing economy. Only by developing such a staple export could the colony become economically viable and thereby partially believe the treasury of the burden of supporting it. With such a staple export attracting additional population, the colonists would also have some hope of eventually claiming the continent's wide interior.

By 1802, Governor King could report to London that seal skins were the way ahead in terms of exports. More than 100,000 skins were landed in and shipped from Sydney between 1800 and 1806, In 1804, 11 Sydney-based ships were engaged in the Bass Strait sealing trade, in addition to the large number of ships in pursuit of whaling.

By the early 1800s there were four main types of economic activity in the colony. Agriculture and grazing was making the colony almost self-sufficient in this product, and large landowners were undermining the governor's attempts to encourage yeomen farmers. Many of these large landowners also engaged in mercantile activities. A growing number of emancipated convicts became traders on their own account, with speculation in trade marked by gluts and scarcities. Many merchants also operated their own vessels, engaging in sealing and whaling. The number of whalers operating

---

[97]   Barnard Marjorie *ibid*

out of Sydney rose from 5 in 1827 to 76 in 1835. Between 1826 and 1835 the value of fishery products passing through Sydney reached £950,000. In 1849, there were 37 boats based in Hobart employing 1000 seamen.[98]

Sealing and Whaling were followed by exports of wool. Although only 29 sheep had arrived with the First Fleet, successive convict fleets added to the flocks and herds and the numbers quickly expanded by natural increase. By 1805, there were 500 horses, 4000 cattle, 5000 goats, 23000 pigs and 20000 sheep. The efforts of these large landowners, including John Macarthur resulted in a dramatic change in the export statistics, with the weight of wool being exported rising from just 167 pounds in 1811 to 175,433 pounds in 1821.[99]

By 1835, the supremacy of pastoralism was beyond dispute, with exports of fine wool dominating the trade figures. The success of the pastoral industry was at the expense of the British government's efforts to slow the invasion of the interior. The success was the result of a combination of factors–cheap land taken from the Aborigines; cheap labour in the form of convict and even cheap Aborigine labour from those able to supervise large flocks over extensive unfenced grasslands in the interior.[100]

Not surprisingly the Europeans found the same attractive places to settle, as the aborigines also found most desirable–water sources and native grasslands.

By 1850 over 4000 pastoralists with their 20 million sheep occupied 400 million hectares (1000 million acres) of inland Australia.

The growth of population contributed greatly to the rise of manufacturing and the general economic growth in the economy. NSW grew from 76845 Europeans in 1836 to 187243 in 1851. Growth in Port Phillip and South Australia was even more dramatic. By 1841 more than half the male population of NSW was colonial-born or immigrant rather than convict, while convicts and emancipists comprised just over 1/3rd of the

---

[98] Day, David *Claiming a Continent–A new History of Australia*. Pages 49,50,51
[99] Day, David *Ibid pages 52,53*
[100] Day, David *ibid* page 74

total population. However males still outnumbered females roughly two to one.

One aspect of trade is generally overlooked when it comes to identifying special and important exports. Wool exports began to sour in the early 1820s, and most historians claim wool dominates agricultural exports and that opinion clouds the real truth.

In fact from 1788 to 1828, if a reliable set of export statistics is compiled, it will be surprising if Australian-owned whaling and sealing vessels are found to be less productive than sheep in those first 49 years. The figures do exist for the next six years from 1828 and for Australia as a whole; whaling narrowly exceeds wool for that period, whilst as late as 1833 whaling is New South Wales' main export industry. However, after that time, 'wool races away, yielding in the last three years of the 1830s almost double the export value of Australia's whale products[101]

A secondary importance of this industry is that each vessel whilst in port is estimated to have spent an average of £300, not counting the sovereigns the crew spent in the inns and elsewhere.[102] Then there was the work for the dockyards. Shipbuilding was probably the largest and most dynamic colonial manufacture before 1850, and Tasmania alone built 400 vessels from small cutters to ships of 500 tons burthen that joined the England-Australia run. Blainey also observes that the reluctance to put whaling into accurate perspective in importance to the colonial economy stems from apathy towards maritime history. He claims that 'except for ship-lovers, the sea and ships are still virtually banished from written history'.[103]

Bigge referred in his third report in 1823[104] to the high level of efficiency amongst the convicts assigned to 'task work' for the government manufactures. Commissioner Bigge discovered at the close of the Macquarie period that the significance of the Government Store as a market for

---

[101] Blainey, Geoffrey *The tyranny of Distance* Page 115
[102] Coughlin, T.A. *Labour & Industry in Australia* Volume 1, Page 367
[103] Blainey *ibid* Page 116-7
[104] Commissioner Bigge's Estimate of the value of convict labour in Sydney for 1822

colonial produce and a source of foreign exchange were greater than ever. The heavy increase in the number of convicts transported after the end of the Napoleonic wars had correspondingly increased the government's demand for foodstuffs. Thus Bigge reported, had retarded the growth of export industries by encouraging the growth of agriculture–farming as opposed to grazing. 'It is possible, given other circumstances the settlers might have turned their attention to the production of other objects than those that solely depended upon the demands of the Government'[105]

Bigge also refers to the high level of skills used in the Government Business Centre–the Lumber Yard–and to the benefit the colony derived from the local public sector manufacturing.

Summary

Of the nine economic drivers within the colonial economy, the role of manufacturing had the far reaching and desirable results.

The Macquarie Administration decided to centralise and highly regulate the labour and output of the more than 50% of the convicts, who having arrived in the colony were assigned to private or government work. For those assigned to government labour, the broad range of activities required a smarter government store than had hitherto been the case. The store was to have on hand sufficient tools and materials to keep these people fully utilised in their allotted task. Those convicts assigned to land and road clearing needed grubbing tools and axes. They required hauling equipment, and food supplies. Those allocated to public building projects and public infrastructure required tools, bricks, blocks, tiles and a large array of sawn timbers.

The Governor ordered the commissariat to create a central facility for assembling and distributing these materials. Most items could have been ordered in from Britain or elsewhere in Europe. The lengthy purchasing and requisition procedures required a lead time of between fifteen months and two years. Thus Macquarie's charge to the Commissariat to employ

---

[105] Bigge, J.T. *Report on the Agriculture and Trade of NSW* 1823 Page 22

convict labour in the manufacturing locally of as many imported items as possible created an import replacement program that created employment, led to private sector entrepreneurs, and generated a program of transition in local manufacturing from the public to the private sector.

Commissioner Bigge reported on the extent of the trades utilised in the Lumber Yard and it makes an impressive list[106]. The trades carried on in this government business enterprise [in this case, the Lumber Yard] are also reported on by Major Ovens, the former Superintendent of Convicts[107]

'In the Lumber Yard are assembled all the indoor tradesmen who work in the shops such as blacksmiths, carpenters, sawyers, shoemakers, tailors etc. The workmen, carrying on their occupations under the immediate eye of the Chief Engineer are probably kept in a better state of discipline than those, who working more remote, are dependent on the good behaviour of an overseer for any work they may perform. Whatever is produced from the labour of these persons[108], which is not applied to any public work or for any supply of authorised requisitions, is placed in a large store and kept to furnish the exigencies of future occasions'.

Growth in the colonial economy came in numerous guises, such as technological progress in industry and agriculture, transport and communication; the growth of population, and the accumulation of capital; the discovery of raw materials, and the spread of economic freedom.

The rise of a manufacturing sector relied on most of these areas, especially technological gains, supply of capital, immigration of skilled trades and Macquarie's sympathetic encouragement of entrepreneurs. Although not as vital as the agricultural sector, the manufacturing sector provided substantial employment, innovation, skills training, and the basis for potential decentralisation. Most importantly, during the Macquarie

---

[106] Bigge, J.T. *Report on the Agriculture and Trade of NSW* 1823 Page 22

[107] Report by Major Ovens to Governor Brisbane on reorganisation for the Lumber Yard HRA 1:11:655-7

[108] Sawn timber for framing, roof battens, flooring, window frames, doors, nails, bolts, bellows, barrels, furniture - from Beckett *The Operations of the Commissariat of NSW 1788-1856*

Administration, the manufacturing sector supported Macquarie's transition from a penal to free market economy. As the colonial economy stabilised, it became attractive for a large number of British based industries wanting to open branch offices in the colonies to invest in small scale activities, often transferring skilled labour from Britain to underpin their colonial operations.

Local industry also helped develop local resources, both human and capital. Both coal and timber became important exports for the colony, whilst the list of other natural resources being developed for both local use and exporting grew longer and longer.

New industry required new talents and skills. So a number of adjunct industries came into being–engineering design, equipment manufacturing and equipment maintenance. Not all new equipment was imported and particularly in agricultural equipment suitable for local conditions, local manufacture and assembly was the norm rather than the exception.

Employment in the sector grew to an important level, with the number of factories in NSW increasing from 37 in 1829 to 174 in 1850[109]. Exports increased during the same period from £79,000 per annum to over £8,000,000[110]. Boatbuilding peaked in 1843 at 46 vessels for the year, although the average size halved between 1841 and 1843. There were 102 vessels registered in the colony in 1841 disbursing 12,153 tons. By 1843, this number had declined to 77 and continued to decline until the 1900s.[111]

Even as late as 1827, the Colonial Office was still very suspicious about the expenses of the convict establishment. Lord Bathurst wrote of 'the difficulty I feel in reconciling the scarcity of assignable convicts . . . . with the enormous and increasing expense with which this country is still charged'[112] Every effort to trim convict maintenance expenses or expand

---

[109] Butlin, Ginswick & Statham *The Economy before 1850* (Australians: Historical statistics–p.108)

[110] Butlin et al *ibid* - P. 109

[111] Sourced by Beckett from original data in *Australians: Historical Statistics,* Coghlan and Butlin

[112] HRA 1:8:221

the assignment system impacted on the Commissariat business operations. The Superintendent of Convicts would agree to the training of apprentices, only to find them sent of 'on assignment' whilst the best workers in the Lumber Yard were always in demand by private manufacturers, and government building workers, were constantly in demand by the private contractors.

CHAPTER 8

THE ABORIGINAL ECONOMY IN 1788[113]

Recording a model of the Aboriginal economy in 1788 would not be an approach recognised by Aborigines, for they do not appear to distinguish between economic activity and any other necessary activity. We, on the other hand, draw the distinction in order to highlight the difference the Aborigines make between necessary material support, as an economic system, and their philosophy of land care and resource management for survival.

1. The basic difference between European culture and Aboriginal culture is simple. For centuries Europeans relied upon agriculture (and therein 'farming') to feed themselves. For many thousands of years and therefore hundreds of centuries, Aboriginals did not plant crops or tend or domesticate animals or live in towns, nor possess houses worthy of the name, as we would define them. The Aboriginals were survivors by being hunters and gatherers (hunting wild animals and gathering necessary and useful natural resources). But we know now that hunters and gatherers, generally, were knowledgeable and sophisticated managers of the limited natural resources, which allowed them to live off the land with a minimum of effort. Although they appear to have possessed ample time in their busy lifestyle to enjoy a full spiritual, ceremonial

---

[113] Tony Dingle '*A Pattern of Experience: The Aboriginal Economy*' p4

and social life, their need for careful time management ensured that their food needs were always satisfied and occupied a central position in their daily life.

2. The pattern of their lives is something that we of the industrial age require an imaginative understanding to bridge the gap between the Aboriginal lifestyle and the European pretences at fulfilment.

3. Much of what grows is inedible, and many animals and plants that can be eaten flourish only in habitats that suit them. Some birds, animals and fish move over quite an extended area. Consequently the food supply of a locality typically consists of a large variety of species some of which might be available for only limited periods during a year or season.

4. Hunters and gatherers used two approaches to adapt to the ever-changing nature of the food supply.

    i. They lived in small groups thinly spread across the land. Nowhere was its density similar to agricultural or industrial societies. In fact there was never any concentration.

    ii. They moved residence regularly—not necessarily travelling very far, but moving unlike the manner of 'farmers' with a set piece of land for resource extraction.

5. Storage was a limiting factor as well. There was little point in collecting more than is needed for a day or two. They learnt the skills to only collect certain foods but to go out each day to get what they needed. Their move every couple of days was designed to harvest food close to the vicinity of the campsite. Game, which was to be hunted, became less plentiful and more wary, while convenient sources of plant food are depleted. The longer the hunters and gatherers remain in one location the more energy they must expend to feed themselves. This is a neglect of good time management and so the group must move. If people wish to minimise the need for movement it is sensible to keep the tribe size small.

6. Many groups will define their territory and move, during the course of a year, from one campsite to another within the boundaries of its territory. The timing of each move is usually governed by the time it takes to feed itself at that location and the expectation

(availability) of food and water in other locations. Since the food is largely seasonal, and often defined by gluts and shortages of specific foods, the patterns of movement are likely to be repeated year after year.

7. Another characteristic of the hunter-gatherer's economic existence is the adaptation to regularly occurring foods by regular movement and small group living. To suit this lifestyle, material possessions are kept to a minimum; people possess few clothes or furnishings, maintaining only basic (abandonable) housing and small kits of tools, weapons and water containers. In a European society, many material possessions are prized, but if movement is necessary, they become a burden. This western preoccupation with accumulating wealth by way of material goods and possessions makes no sense in the context of hunting and gathering.[114]

8. In western economic thinking, the factors of production are broken down into *land, labour & capital*. If we try to apply this concept to the Aboriginal economy, then most forms of Aboriginal production will require little capital equipment, and are speedily accomplished, and whereas hunting and collecting takes hours instead of months with western farming; simplicity of tools, housing and weapons is also a part of the plan for the Aborigines. Among the primitive people, the labour factor of production is more evenly distributed and specialisation occurs. A significant development is that everyone is trained as an alternative to physical capital, and everyone has access to the group's skills and knowledge and acquisition of this training is recognised as a transfer into adulthood.

9. The 'ownership' of land and capital is concentrated and centralised, whilst the rewards from 'production' are more equally shared in the Aboriginal economy than in the European economy.

10. Ecological management is carefully planned, since the supply of food consists mainly of edible plants and animals in the area of hunting and gathering. The measure of sustainability is not the stock of animals but the productivity of the land resources. In this scenario, people can only eat the equivalent of the annual crop of kangaroos, fruit, or roots. If they go above this level the

---

[114] Blainey, G *'Triumph of the Nomads- A Natural History of Australia'*

productive capacity of these renewable resources will be impaired and supplies in future years will be in decline. In this way natural productivity places an upper limit on how many people can be fed and this policy becomes a flexible but natural constraint on population growth. It is flexible because natural phenomena affect the levels of natural productivity. Short–and long-term climate changes such as an increase or decrease of average rainfall, the type of animals and plants will affect the amount of food available. Increased food supply could come not from 'farming' or domestication of wild animals but from increasing and aggressive resource management. Such measures can include: the attempt to develop 'storage' facilities; conversion of inedible plants to edible, by grinding and baking; the careful use of fire can change the environment and allow animals to multiply.[115]

11. Land was vital for physical survival, but was more than an economic resource: People were tied spiritually to a particular locality-this was their 'country' and 'dreaming place', a tangible link with ancestors who lived and died there. Based on an interview with an elder in the Northern Rivers (NSW) 'clan' the following association has been characterised. Each individual belonged to a family, but also to a clan or territorial (estate) group. A number of clans united by shared language, beliefs, customs and kinship ties. Each clan 'claimed' an estate within the boundaries of the larger group territory. The clan would exercise proper rights over its estate and defend it against trespass by unauthorised individual or other clans. Land could not be bought or sold, but was used, cared for and held in trust for future generations. The control was not exclusive but shared, through joint use of its resources, with others. Hunting rights could be temporarily assigned and in return similar permission extended over other estates.[116] Such complex social, spiritual and territorial arrangements ensured that everyone had access to land to sustain themselves physically and spiritually.[117]

---

115 Dingle, T. 'aboriginal Economy: Patterns of Experience' p 8
116 Bell, Dianne Daughters of the Dreaming'
117 Dingle, T. 'aboriginal Economy: Patterns of Experience' p 11

12. The hunter-gatherer diet was varied depending on the season of the year and the locality that they were temporarily occupying. In some seasons the diets may be exclusively meat or purely game (when catching migratory birds) or simply seafood (when living by the coast). The women appear to be the more reliable food providers, because their food sources were generally more plentiful and stable. Women usually sourced their food from 'gathering' whereas men were not always successful in their hunting'. Foraging was not arduous work–they usually kept within 5 kilometres from the camp and would return within four to six hours, having taken time to rest and talk. Aboriginal women would collect for a day with minimal effort since they were also the child minders. Hunters would be away for a similar time but would travel much further, particularly if there were tracks of promising game. Most hunting was carried out singly or by three or four men. This would become a co-operative effort in tracking, killing and hauling the game. Richard Lee, in surveying surviving hunting and gathering societies in 1960 concluded that "hunting was a high-risk, low-return activity whilst gathering was a low-risk, high–return activity".[118] This combination of hunting and gathering ensured a more diversified and tastier diet. It most probably ensured a more reliable food supply due to the combination of skills.

Before we examine aspects of technology and bartering in the Aboriginal economy, let me find a way of summarising the Aboriginal economy from the viewpoint of hunting and gathering. Harry Lourandos offers his reader a well-developed conclusion about the Aboriginal economy.[119]

*The hunter-gatherer economy has been viewed traditionally as basic, elementary and subsistence-based, guided by ecological factors. However, the prior distinction between 'food producers' composed of land and resource management strategies, agriculturalists, **and** food collectors, or 'hunter-gatherers' has been revised. All human societies can be considered as 'producers' in the sense that food and other commodities are appropriated by a division of labour (Sahlins*

---

[118] Lee, Richard 'What hunters do for a living' *Man the Hunter* P30
[119] Lourandos, Larry *Continent of Hunter-Gatherers–A new perspective in Australian prehistory* 1997 p.17

1974[120]*; Ingold 1980*[121]*). The hunter-gatherers 'economy' itself can be seen to operate at two main levels: (a) the domestic or local group level and (b) the wider group level.*[122]

The Aboriginal Economy In 1788

There was an economy in operation in New Holland at the time of the arrival of the first white settlers in 1788.

Professor N.G. Butlin concludes:-

Early Aborigines were the first discoverers and occupiers of the Australian continent, "the first to establish functioning societies and economies, and the first to make the large-scale adaptations required using almost every type of ecological condition in Australia. The arrival of the First Fleet did not mean merely 'contact' with Aborigines, but the destruction of Aboriginal society and populations and the transfer of their resources *to the benefit of both the new arrivals and those who remained in Britain.*[123] What 'settlement' meant in this case was the cheap acquisition of Aboriginal resources, just as it did in the Americas. In other cases, overt conquest, which led to comparatively small settlement, and provided a mechanism for imperial access to resources without such an overt asset transfer? It improved the terms of trade for the conquerors, opened up opportunities for imperial development and to some extent ameliorated the imperial process by a sharing of the benefits of such development. In the process it recognised property rights, but this option did not apply in the Americas or Australia".[124]

The Cambridge Economic History of Europe explains economic development in the industrial nations of Europe in terms of the growth of inputs of land, labour and capital, plus technology. If we extend this

[120] Sahlins, M. *'Stone Age Economics'*
[121] Ingold, T. *Hunter, Pastoralists & Ranchers'*
[122] Lourandis, H *'Continent of Hunter-Gatherers'*
[123] Butlin, N.G. *Economics of the Dreamtime—A hypothetical history* p.2 (Butlin's italics)
[124] Butlin *ibid* p.3

concept to Britain, should we not also recognise that its new acquisitions did not merely imply food but included all natural resources, such as wealth under the surface?[125]

Butlin has specialised in the statistics of the Aboriginal economy in and after 1788.

Here are some observations made by Butlin:[126] Butlin's three works each record some varying aspects, at differing times of the Aboriginal population movement between 1788 and 1850 and the Aboriginal Economy.

He approaches the Aboriginal Economy through a system of time budgeting.[127]

"On that basis, it is possible to order Aboriginal time allocation in terms of a range of categories along the lines of:

Food collection
Environment management and adaptation
Food preparation and distribution
Clothing, bedding and household utensils
Production Planning, including decisions to relocate
Travel and transport
Housing
Equipment production and maintenance
Education
Law and Order
Defence
Religious Observance
Ritual ceremonies
Art & Recreation
Entertainment.

[125] Cambridge Economic History of Europe
[126] Butlin, N.G *Our Original Aggression, Economics of the Dreamtime & Forming a Colonial Economy*
[127] Butlin, N.G *Our Original Aggression*

Such a list may, adds Butlin, could be considered common to both the white and Black society, although Aboriginals were more inclined to pooling of resources and to sharing, even though in the penal society the definition of 'convict rations' and 'board and lodging' brings the two societies closer together than first thought". [128]

Butlin models the Aboriginal populations at the time of white arrival, and suggests the NSW/Vic population was 250,000 aborigines, with a total Australian aboriginal population at one million (of which only 10,000 were located in VDL). So obviously the Qld, NT, WA & SA populations were in excess of 740,000

As with the Governors before him, instructions to Governor Darling regarding Aborigines, stressed the need to protect the natives, both "in their persons, and in the free enjoyment of their possessions".[129] The Governor had also been instructed to co-operate with Archdeacon Scott (the former Secretary to Hon. J. T. Bigge) in providing the means by which the Aborigines could be converted to Christianity and 'advanced in civilisation'. In response to Thomas Brisbane declaring martial law in Bathurst, Lord Bathurst informed Darling (Brisbane's successor) that it was his duty "when the aborigines made 'hostile incursions for the purpose of plunder' and only when 'less vigorous measures' had failed, 'to oppose force by force, and to repel such aggression in the same manner, as if they proceeded from subjects of any accredited state".[130]

Attempts by Archdeacon Scott and Bishop Broughton produced reports the need for substantial expenditure on education and general welfare reform. Darling's response was that the expense and the difficulty of finding suitably qualified people posed formidable problems. Darling admitted that his response was more to economy than to any lack of interest in aboriginal welfare. He admitted he had little understanding of their culture or way of life. 'Those who he saw in an urban setting depressed him, as the appearance of the natives about Sydney is extremely disgusting, due to the frequent and excessive use of spirits. Tribes living in

---

[128]   Butlin *Economic & the Dreamtime*
[129]   Governors despatches 1826 HRA 1:12:125
[130]   Brisbane to Bathurst 1824 HRA 1:11:409; Bathurst to Darling 1825 HRA 1:12:21

the interior were not exposed to this evil and appeared to be a much finer race'.[131] Darling was critical of the language problem and the fact that different tribes could not converse with each other.

It would appear that very few of Darling's predecessors or even his successors took the time or interest to understand the Aboriginal economy or society, as a means of making informed judgements and policies about a diminishing but still aggravating problem. Darling was largely pre-occupied with skirmishes (and massacres) between the white settlers and the Aborigines. But neither legislation nor regulation seemed to be the answer to the hostilities and deaths and anger and retaliation.

Perceptions prevailed, as a basis of policy decision-making on behalf of Aborigines. David Day claims 'Officers of the First Fleet of British invaders believed they were stepping ashore on a continent that had not felt the heel of civilised man".[132] Such perceptions of uneducated stone-age peoples unfamiliar with any white man or white man's ways, persisted until the Gipps Administration, and as a result not much got changed to improve their way of life, or their economy. Even Manning Clark perpetuated the myths and false perceptions when he introduces Volume 1 with the thought 'Civilisation did not begin in Australia until the last quarter of the eighteenth century'[133] The implications of that sentence served to justify the continued dispossession of the Aborigines who, Clark argued, had lived for 'millennia in a state of barbarism'[134]

Our conception and perception of civilisation has a European orientation to it, but the Aborigines lived with some form of deliberativeness.

Butlin is concerned with implication not motives of the Aborigine as an 'economic man'. However, the main questions we need to ask relate to:

Was Aboriginal economic behaviour rational or not?

---

[131] Fletch, Brian, *Ralph Darling: a Governor maligned*
[132] Day, David *Claiming a continent–A New History of Australia* p.3
[133] Clark, C.M.H. *A History of Australia* Vol 1
[134] Clark, *ibid*

Did the population change with production (mainly climatic) setbacks or did they adapt to known technologies or change their tastes, technology, methods of production and allocation of labour?

Butlin explains "the Aboriginal economy in Australia was established over thousands of years by the successfully arriving migrants from South-East Asia and by their locally born descendents. If we accept prevalent views of very low rates of natural increase amongst hunter-gathers, it would follow that any population build-up to occupy the entire Australian continent even within a time-span of several millennia is explainable primarily by immigration inflow It is not plausible to approach the study of the Aboriginal economy in terms of a static structure and function. The dynamism may be summed up in the proposition that Aboriginals evolved in Australia from hunter-gatherers to resource managers and 'improvers'."[135]

The Aboriginal economy is structured into many segments and activities:

- Food gathering
- Food technology
- Aboriginal culture and society (this is integral to the economic understanding & interpretation
- Inter-group associations
- Property rights in land (individual, centralised or communal)
- Marriage customs
- Property in ritual
- Economic decision-making

This aspect of the pre-history of Australia is still being written.[136]

Becker suggests that hunter-gatherers had a scarce resource, which was time and that the Aboriginal economy could be better considered in this light.[137]

---

[135] Butlin *Forming a Colonial Economy* p.56
[136] Lourandos, Harry *Continent of Hunter-Gatherers - New Perspectives in Australian Prehistory*
[137] Becker, G.S. *A Theory of the Allocation of Time'*, The Economic Journal, September 1965

Mulvaney discusses some features of their life-style. He identifies many plants and animals that were common to South-East Asia and Australia in the distant past, as well as the continuous landmass between New Guinea and Tasmania with the mainland.[138] The emergence of two large lakes, one in the Gulf of Carpentaria the other in Bass Strait, provided a large food resource of fish, fowl and habitation for native animals as well as humans. With water being a prime consideration to human and animal (food) habitation, Mulvaney concludes that 60,000 years ago both the Murray and Darling Rivers were much broader than they are today and shows the existence of the active Lake Eyre and Lake Frome in south-central Australia–conditions which deteriorated after 60,000 BP.

David Day puts it in a similar way." It could even be argued that Aborigines were more sophisticated than Europeans have proved to be in Australia. While the Aborigines lived for hundreds of centuries in Australia, changing their lifestyles in reaction to gradual changes in the environment and sometimes even shaping that environment to maximise their returns from it, just two centuries of European occupation have seen almost irreparable harm done to the environment through greed or ignorance. There has been a recent return to Aboriginal methods of land management to take care of national parks and to live successfully in arid areas".[139]

Early attempts at understanding the natives was not left only to Government officials, the churchmen in the colony were assigned the tasks of 'civilising' this race, and the Rev. J.D. Lang records:

"Their wanderings are circumscribed by certain well-defined limits, beyond which they seldom pass, except for purposes of war or festivity. In short, every tribe has its own district, the boundaries of which are well known to the natives generally . . ."[140]

Some characteristics of the Aboriginal economy in Australia

- Omnivorous diet

---

[138] Mulvaney, D.J. & Golson, J (Eds). *Aboriginal Man and Environment in Australia*

[139] Day *Claiming a continent* p.7

[140] Lang, John Dunmore *An Historical & Statistical Account of NSW* 1833

- Limited inter-group trade (usually exchange)
- A marked division of labour by gender
- Education–learning by doing
- Limited storage capacity
- Communal sharing rules
- Communal property rights
- Population control
- Complex kin relationships
- Formal non-literacy
- Limited formal government
- Recognised as 'grass farmers'
- Native animals and sea-food recognised as 'valuable'

Assembling the national income accounts of the aboriginal race 1788

The challenge was issued by N.G. Butlin to compute national income figures for the Aboriginal economy.[141]

In fact on more than one occasion Butlin wrote, "We need to establish the national income of Aborigines. Such statistics have never been collected, nor are they ever likely to be. But we need to recognise, in looking at the use of Australian resources, and in understanding how our well-being improved, that whites gained in part because blacks lost."[142]

Aborigines filled the traditional history books as in the following extract

"In 1815 the Aborigines were 'killed in great numbers, so much so as to call for proclamations against the cruelty'.[143]

But rarely, if ever, is any mention made, in those same history books, of the Aboriginal lifestyle or economic activities, and yet the Aborigines survived in great number for thousands and thousands of years, and the land became and remained their life support. How did they manage this?

---

[141] Butlin, N.G. *Forming the Colonial Economy* 1788-1856
[142] Butlin, N.G Chapter 8 'Australian National Accounts' *Australian: National Statistics* P126
[143] Mukherjee, S.K. '*Crime & Justice*' Chapter 17 *Australian: National Statistics* P126

R.M.Younger reveals (albeit *unsourced)* that Governor Macquarie "up to 1817 had been able to concentrate on the advancement of those in his charge within the framework of a comparatively compact penal establishment. He had settled numerous emancipists, the few incoming free settlers, *and even some Aborigines* on small farms, to grow the food the community needed.[144] This policy was unsuccessful in both the governor's understanding of the natives and their ability to work in this way, and the ability to regiment and anglicise the Aborigine.

McMartin reports that "the fact that only £51,800 was appropriated for native welfare during the whole of the first half-century gives a better idea of the concern that was really manifested during that period.[145]

The sources for such a study as this are scarce but a few writers have developed a theme for understanding the Aboriginal economy. An outstanding work written specifically about the Aboriginal people of the northern rivers area of NSW is 'Wollumbin' by N.C. Keats.

As can be imagined Noel Butlin seemed to enjoy this area of research and wrote a series of articles and books.[146]

Another writer of significance is D.J. Mulvaney.[147]

Altogether, a methodical and a logical approach are necessary for this study. We need to know about the population in 1788, the way of life

---

[144] Younger, R.M. *Australia and the Australians* p.178

[145] McMartin, Arthur *Public Servants and Patronage* p.211 *this is the first record that the author has seen reported of the expenditure on Aboriginal Affairs, however, the agreement for the usage of crown lands revenue assigned 15% to Aboriginal matters, and no record exists of any expenditure from this source of funds. McMartin also records that the 'Protector of aborigines and his staff amounted to 34 persons in 1842 (p.210) so there was an appropriation for this expenditure at that time.*

[146] Butlin, N.G. *Our Original Aggression: Aboriginal Populations of S.E. Australia 1788-1850; 'Contours of the Australian Economy 1788-1860'; 'Forming a Colonial Economy 1810-1850'; Economics and the Dreamtime—A Hypothetical history*

[147] Mulvaney, D.J. *The prehistory of Australia (1969)*

of the Aboriginal people and their material ways, their food gathering inclinations and their territorial means. Were Aboriginal movements meaningful for food gathering and territorial protection or for another reason?

Let me start with a summary of the population problems arising after 1788.

The Aboriginal Population 1788

Butlin reminds us "it took until 1838 for the combined colonial and aboriginal populations to reach the pre-1788 level Aboriginal level. This downturn of the Aboriginal population was triggered by three factors:

a. The massive early loss of Aborigines due to introduced diseases from the white population
b. An Aboriginal recovery and colonial expansion in the 1820s, and
c. Further Aboriginal loss and rapid colonial increase from the mid to late 1820s

Did the Aboriginal population shrink with production setbacks and expand to absorb increased productivity or were per capita gains achieved, particularly with the aid of population control? This raises the question of motivation. Did Aboriginals behave rationally or not? This could be seen as looking at Aboriginal economic behaviour through the eyes of 'economic man'—which would be a misconception, since it would imply rational behaviour. Aborigines may be seen, for example, to prefer more leisure or more ritualistic activity to more consumption goods. They may be seen as being satisfied with a limited range of ends. Neither perception entails the conclusion that they behaved 'irrationally'.[148]

The Aboriginal economy in Australia was established over thousands of years by successfully arriving immigrants, from island south-east Asia and by their locally born descendents. No modelling has been completed that would associate this migration and local net annual increase with the

---

[148]   Butlin, N.G. *Economics and the Dreamtime* p.54

population at 1788. However a back-projection method of population modelling may be valuable in this situation.[149]

Aboriginal Life-Style

It was suggested in *Economics and the Dreamtime*[150] that one might approach the Aboriginal Economy through a system of time budgeting. On this basis, it is possible to order Aboriginal time allocation in terms of a range of categories along the lines of:

• Food Collection
• Environmental management & adaptation
• Food preparation & distribution
• Clothing, bedding & household utensils
• Production planning, including decisions to relocate
• Travel and transportation
• Housing
• Equipment production and maintenance
• Education
• Law & Order
• Defence
• Religious observance
• Ritual ceremonies
• Art, and
• Recreation and entertainment

Aborigines were inclined to the pooling of resources and to sharing though the definition of 'convict rations' and even the concept of 'board & lodging' also conveys the same concepts, and thus brings the two societies closer together.

Many food items were consumed in both societies (white and native)–game meats, wild fowl, eggs, wild fruit and nuts, fish, shellfish and crustaceans. This short list illustrates a cross-cultural food transfer that accounted for

---

[149] Wrigley & Schofield *'The Population History of England 1541-1871- a reconstruction using the back-projection methodology.*
[150] Butlin, N.G. *ibid*

a large part of Aboriginal diets (even if colonists and convicts drew the line at snakes and lizards). Both sides prized animal skins and sealskins. Aboriginals took sheep and cattle meat when they could. There was Aboriginal technical superiority in the capture of game and birds and colonial superiority in production of domesticated livestock.[151] The explanation for social adjustment, and the alteration to division of labour and resource exploitation in the Aboriginal lifestyle have important implications for our perceptions of Aboriginal demography and social organisation at the time of European settlement They also have significance for the dynamics of Aboriginal economy over the past 50,000 years and for any appraisal of its structure and function.

The choices for dominant population growth are:

1. Through continuous migration and a learning-by-doing for newcomers
2. Essentially by net natural increase of a small number of ever arriving migrants with primary emphasis on the inter-generational transfer of ecological understanding and a socially managed gradual adaption to change in the environment.

The predominantly migrant source of population increase would imply the likelihood of technological transmission from Southeast Asia to the Australian continent, but would also suggest an increased conflict at arrival points between earlier and later arrivals. Therefore it is not possible to assess the Aboriginal economy in terms of a static structure and function. Economic behaviour was certainly reformed and contained by water supply conditions in central Australia and the rising seawater levels in the period 40,000 to 17000BP. Other elements of the dynamics of the Aboriginal economy in more recent times is evident from regional differences in consumption patterns, production structure, division of labour and other characteristics[152] This transition from hunter-gathers to resource manager and 'improvers', is understandable from the argument as to why Aborigines 'failed' to become 'farmers'. It is generally agreed that the

[151]   Butlin, N.G. *Forming a Colonial Economy* p.214
[152]   Keats, N.C *'Wollumbin- The Aboriginals of the Tweed Region'.*

Aboriginals achieved a large-scale alteration in the natural landscape and environment through burning and this practice evolved from 30,000BP.

Likewise many side issues affect and impact on a study of Aboriginal economic behaviour. Jones in 1977 believes that Aboriginal social structure and function are part of the consideration of economic behaviour as are inter-group associations, property rights in land, marriage customs, property in ritual and so forth.[153]

Jones also stresses the point that "in the absence of any clearly defined market, individual property rights or central direction with communal property, and with little in the way of government or overt laws, Aborigines nevertheless achieved an orderly system of economic decision-making.

Butlin concludes his chapter on the Aboriginal economy by "it was the attempt to achieve modes of satisfying many competing demands (such as food consumption, ritual, reproduction, warfare, leisure and education) that made up the problem of the Aboriginal economy, as it does the modern household. Hunting and gathering was only a small part of the total behaviour in which economic considerations were relevant."[154]

Diversity of Culture

Did Aborigines prefer foods from the land or the sea?

Did they prefer animal or plant foods?

A variety of limitations influenced local preferences. Interesting as these limitations are (for example scale fish, ritualistically-imposed constraints), they are less significant than the variety of consumption patterns across the continent: the dominance of seafood consumption in some areas, or the exploitation of grains in others, or of cycads or yams elsewhere. Some of this differentiation was linked to ecology or production practicalities. For

---

[153] Jones R. *The Fifth Continent: Problems concerning the Colonisation of Australia-* Vol 8 Annual Review of Anthropology.
[154] Butlin, N.G. *Economics and the Dreamtime* p.56

instances, root crops were scarcer in the arid inland and thus grains were more important; cycads spread across northern Australia and down the east coast; seafood were more abundant in northern Australia; waterfowl were seasonally available in south-eastern and northern Australia; freshwater fish depended on inland water sources; the concentration on wild animals was influenced by supplies of drinking water and grasslands or open woodlands.[155]

A major influence on diet was the movement of the peoples. The people of eastern Cape York appear to have followed a strongly seasonal pattern of movement. Many peoples showed quite strong preferences for certain foods and did not consume all the variety of foods available to them. On the west of the Cape, tribes appear to have been stable on the seashore for periods of six months, before moving inland for the balance of the year, and changing their diet to living off the land.

Tribe sizes influenced dietary patterns. Although the average appears to have been about 40 there were considerable variations from this mean. Smaller numbers were more prevalent in the arid areas whilst higher numbers prevailed in the 'richer' environs, where harvests were readily accessible in one or a small range of particular foods.

Storage or a limited ability to store foodstuffs was another limitation of movement and tribal numbers. Water carriers were developed in a large variety of moulds–from human skulls to wooden implements and the skins of animals.[156]

Although land was fundamental to Aboriginal culture, it was also a basic means of production. Our premise must be that the hunting and gathering way of life forms the basics of sustenance for the Aboriginal people for well over 50,000 years of existence in Australia. Of all the economic systems, which human ingenuity has devised, hunting and gathering is the most ancient and long lived and it survived longer in Australia than anywhere else in the world.[157]

---

[155] Coghlan *Wealth & Progress 1886-1887*
[156] Mulvaney *ibid*
[157] Dingle, Tony *Aboriginal economy–patterns of experience* p.2

Put into perspective, it is now widely accepted that over 2,000 generations of Aborigines have been living on this continent for those 50,000 years sustained by hunting and gathering. By comparison the two hundred years of white community is a mere infant not yet demonstrated to be durable for an extended period. The Aborigines had a deep-rooted respect for and appreciation of the ecology of the land as a means of production and regulated their existence to fit in with and be sustained by the changing climate patterns. To this we compare the current abuse and constant optimising the use of natural resources without recognising the limitations naturally imposed. It appears the Aborigines did not need 'farming' as we understand it, nor the envy of permanent food sources without challenge, but would work within the confines of the ecological system and prepare for a limited lifestyle, limited only, that is by a sustainable lifestyle rather than rampaging excesses.

CHAPTER 9

WILLIAM LITHGOW 1824-1852– A GREAT PUBLIC SERVANT

The working life of William Lithgow paralleled the most interesting period of colonial history between 1824 and 1852, from the end of the Macquarie Administration to the strains of self-government approaching fast. Born in Scotland in 1784, his life tracked closely the growth of the Colony of New South Wales, however, his contribution to the colony did not commence until his transfer from Mauritius in 1823.

As characterized by Governor Darling in 1827, Lithgow was a man with great quantities of devotion and dedication, but mostly he was 'full of zeal'.

This then, is the story of Lithgow's contribution through his work and advice to the five Governors he so ably served during 28 years in the New South Wales colonial public service. Lithgow's contribution has not been verified sufficiently by previous historians, as we will see, and in economic history terms his gift to the people of the colony was unsurpassed in 'value'.

His life was as varied as the times in which he lived. A more interesting and varied Colonial would be hard to find. A lifetime of Public Service was rare for the 1800s, but Lithgow successfully divided his time between his salaried position and numerous Boards and Committees, many of which he sat on by request of the governor of the day, as a community service. He was selected for these tasks and assignments because of his broad experience, insight and loyal government service.

His mantle was broader than that offered through Commissariat accounting, to which he devoted the first 10 years of his working life. He had risen to the position of assistant deputy-commissary of accounts in Mauritius, before turning to the arduous and demanding task of auditing the Colonial Accounts under the umbrella of the Colonial Secretary's office. This experience of dealing effectively with British Commissary and Treasury bureaucracy was invaluable in the new settlement, and his know-how was called upon frequently in the struggling colony. Although he eventually became second in command under the Colonial Secretary, his activities were never fully recognised, at least publicly. He was just another Public Servant trying to set down the financial affairs of the Colony in the format demanded by the British Treasury. By today's auditing standards Lithgow's tasks were mundane, regimented and routine; however, his title of Colonial Auditor-General may well have been too generous for his real and more exacting role was as financial advisor to the colonial governors, and the implementer of practical solutions to keeping the colony on an even economic keel. The procedures of fiscal governance were demanding and bureaucratic–vouchers, vouchers and more vouchers. Each one having to be verified, firstly for authorisation within the appropriation of public funds, and then approved for payment with supporting paper work of 'receipt of goods', matched against Purchase Orders, and finally 'passed for payment' by a supervisor, within each government department. But even that wasn't the end of the process. Lithgow, as Auditor, had to confirm the trail of paperwork, and to finitely confirm that all the paperwork was in order. Each piece had to bear the correct number of signatures, carry the correct supporting vouchers and then be authorised, appropriately, for payment. Bureaucracy was rampant, but even so we find as Lithgow carried out his onerous tasks that even he was capable of making simple arithmetic errors. The Accounts forwarded over Lithgow's signature to the British Treasury in 1825, for example, contain some arithmetic errors, but any notation of weakness in this regard was more than compensated by his insatiable contribution to other aspects of the Colony.

Lithgow was made a Magistrate in 1828, a Board member of the Female Factory in Parramatta and a Board Member of the newly created 'Board of

General Purposes' who's role, as defined and laid down by Governor Ralph Darling, was to oversee the Colonial Planning Operations on behalf of the Governor.

From May 1824 until October 1825, Lithgow held the senior post within the Commissary System of being both Assistant Commissary General and also of being in charge of the Accounting Records and Returns. A second position was created after the British Treasury released in 1826 the revised 'Recording and Reporting Procedures'. These updated guidelines for Colonial Accounting were partly in response to the relatively unprofessional (and essentially 'privatised') accounting system invoked by Macquarie and his predecessors who, from 1802 to 1821 relied on amateur 'treasurers' to collect, record, disburse and report on Colonial funding. Some responsibility for this temporary clerical assistance is due to the fact that the Colony had no Treasury. Nevertheless the two 'treasurers', being Reverend Samuel Marsden and Mr (Surgeon) Darcy Wentworth, handled all the locally raised revenue and expenditures.

After Macquarie left the Colony, Brisbane and then Darling had been instructed to install the 'Blue Book' system of recording and reporting, and so from 1822 the British Treasury received two copies of the hand compiled reports whilst the Governor kept the third copy. These records were only compiled at the end of each year and rather than assist in reducing the work load of the Colonial Secretary's office, this procedure increased it substantially, since the Blue Books were summaries taken from other summaries but then recompiled into the format required by the British Treasury. The 'Blue Book' process was a marked improvement on the Orphan Fund, the Police Fund, the Land Fund and the many other 'funds' that were really an extension of have a separate bank account for each process of government.

Lithgow fulfilled the duties of Commissary of Accounts and Colonial Auditor admirably and impressed Governor Darling to the extent that when the Governor was given approval to form an 'Executive Council', Lithgow was offered the role of 'acting' secretary to the Council. It did not take long for Lithgow to move from mere scribe to active participant and he later filled a vacancy on the Executive Council itself.

Brisbane saw the need to create the position of Auditor of government accounts, having seen first-hand the benefits of having Lithgow fill the extra role of Auditor of Commissary accounts. Brisbane thought nothing of the potential conflict of interest of the one officer acting as both accountant (preparer) and Auditor (reviewer) of Commissary accounts, nor did he see the potential for conflict by having the one officer fill the roles of commissary accountant and government auditor. Today these roles would be arms length and very independent. However Brisbane's problems were of a more practical nature than considering conflicts of interest. Brisbane found a dearth of experienced public servants in the colony and having an officer of Lithgow's experience was like a godsend. Likewise Brisbane desperately wanted and needed some 'financial' advice to assist his economic planning for the economy. Again Lithgow filled that role in terms of experience and background.

Soon, however, the dual roles of Commissary Accountant and Colonial Auditor were growing too much for one man to handle, and it was Brisbane's successor, Ralph Darling who sought the approval of The Secretary of State in London to make Lithgow a full-time Auditor (in 1825) at an increased salary. Governor Darling's salary recommendation was not accepted and Secretary of State Huskisson imposed his own limits on the Lithgow remuneration.

Even after Lithgow settled into his new restricted position (as Colonial Auditor-General) he continued to take an active role in economic analysis and future planning for the Colony, by becoming an active participant in the Governor's exclusive but unofficial 'executive council'.

Four interlinking roles (which will be explored more fully in the main text) included:

a. Lithgow working with Major Ovens, before Oven's premature death, on assessing the organisation of and work practices for the convicts. The idea for and organisation of the work gangs used at the dockyard, the Lumber Yard, the timber yard, the land clearing, road making gangs was that jointly of Ovens and Lithgow, although Ovens placed his name alone on the final report, lest it be thought by Governor Bourke that Lithgow had surplus time on his hands.

b. Working on and with the Board of the Female Work Factory to develop outputs that were worthwhile and meaningful. As a former Commissary principal, Lithgow was in a good position to gauge what could be produced within the colony by the growing 'army' of female prisoners. The numbers for the Female Factory are interesting, as the private placement of 381 of the 573 women meant that the government was denied the working output of these people, although on the other hand the government was saved the direct cost of clothing, defending the morals, housing and feeding of these women.

c. The Land Board prepared a detailed series of reports (they were authored and assembled by Lithgow) for the governor that established the role and needs of land sales, land clearing; surveying and set aside land for townships, schools, churches and the need for town planning including communications and transportation.

d. His association with the Bank of New South Wales was long and successful. Lithgow was a Director, initially representing the Government, but was re-elected in his own right, an association that lasted almost 20 years. He became a trustee of the Australian Society for Deposits and Loans. Lithgow also became an initial shareholder (nominal value 100 pound) in the Bank of Australia.

Lithgow filled his position for 19 years as a member of the Legislative Council admirably and used his participation to assist in interpreting the all-important Appropriation Bills for the benefit of the other members.

The Lithgow committee work would have brought him in touch with most, if not all, of the notable and significant members of the Colonial community. His voluntary associations and community interests including those already mentioned, as well as the Southern Cattle Association and the Railway Association and the Steam Navigation Company. These committees were then extended to the Board of Trustees of the Clergy and School Lands; the New South Wales Legislative Council; The Bank of NSW and the Savings Bank of NSW; Magistrate and J.P; followed by his nomination to the Executive Council in December 1835, and membership of the Coal Board in October 1847.

Lithgow served under five governors, one of which he also served as acting Private Secretary. He liaised with eight British Secretaries of State and five British Prime Ministers. He was threatened with termination by Sir George Gipps, who was being chastised for failing to deliver the 'Blue Books' for 5 years past the due date. Gipps blamed Lithgow; Lithgow blamed the down the line record-keepers, but in the end Lithgow delivered six years of audited annual records (the Blue Books) in less than six months.

We have yet to learn very much about his early life, except that he was born and raised in the Scotland of the late 1700s. It is most likely, that the Lithgow family home was in the Lanark district in the Clyde River region of south-central Scotland. He graduated from the University of Edinburgh as a licentiate of the Church of Scotland, but shortly after graduating chose instead to join the Commissary Operations of the British Military abroad. Another conjecture, by this author, as yet unverified, is that Lithgow was a second son, expected by tradition to enter the 'church', but as the Church of Scotland was, at that time in turmoil and undergoing major change, it is likely that young clerics were paid very little and Lithgow saw a larger benefit in a secure, government position. Scottish Home Office records do not include references to the early Lithgow family, and so we are left wondering if William was a descendent of the famous Scottish explorer from the early 1600s who bore the same name We could attribute, in yet another giant leap of imagination that Lithgow's decision to remain an unmarried loner all his life could have been due to a family tragedy before he joined the army, or possibly he had the predilection of this forebear, William Lithgow (1583-1637) to roam, adventure and travel. The British Military had headquartered their commissary operation for Europe in Edinburgh, and after two years of pounding the streets following his graduation, earning a small pittance as a stipend and feeling he was going nowhere, Lithgow decided to join the military in as non-military field as he could find. He spent the next two years in the original quartermaster's stores in Edinburgh and found he had a flair for numbers, clerical organisation and a good judgment for forward planning. The military decided, following the initial training period that his commission should be made permanent and his knowledge and instruction extended. Thus commenced a lifelong period of public service.

His first appointment was to Heligoland, a small piece of British Territory–an island in the North Sea. When the British were relieved of control over Heligoland and it was handed back to the Germans, he was transferred (July 1812) to Mauritius, still with the Commissary division of the British Military, where he rose through the ranks to become assistant commissary. He was in Mauritius at the same time as Ralph Darling, who, upon his appointment (in April 1823) as Governor of New South Wales, requested the transfer of Lithgow as Assistant Commissary-General for 'Accounts' at the same destination. Lithgow had sailed directly to Sydney, via Hobart, arriving May 1824, whilst Darling took himself and family back to England for twelve months before sailing for Sydney. Whilst in London he received two commissions–one as Governor of the colony of New South Wales and the other as Governor-in-Chief of Van Diemen's Land, with a lieutenant governor, resident in Hobart responsible for day–to-day operations. Thus Lithgow's journey into Colonial Australia began in Sydney in 1824, but he was serving Governor Brisbane until Darling arrived in 1826.

Lithgow had grown up in a Scotland that had unified in 1707 with England to form a creative and beneficial union as Great Britain, and he chose to contribute to the growth of the British Colony in New South Wales. Lithgow's participation in just about every aspect of the future government of the colony made him a potentially formidable force in Colonial public affairs, and he was an influential adviser to each successive governor of the day. Darling anticipated this potential and Lithgow was the first of a number Darling had worked with prior to 1825 who he selected to gather around him in Colonial New South Wales. This 'team' included Major Ovens, his son in law, William Dumaresq, and the other Dumaresq brother–Henry.

The post Macquarie colony was a rapidly changing place–the colony had matured remarkably since Macquarie had generated unparalleled growth in the land, through his building program and his placement of the swelling ranks of male and female convicts into productive, both private and public, work. Macquarie's encouragement of new colonial industry sustained the growing levels of British investment and speculation in the colony. Decentralisation and the need to open up new settlements including Van Diemen's Land, Port Phillip and Morton Bay continued to grow the local revenue and de-emphasise the need for British Treasury funding. However the Commissary operations grew increasingly important, as they were the sole support programs for both the convicts and the military remaining in the colony, whilst also being the defacto Treasurer until 1817.

Lithgow received at least three land grants: a rural grant of two thousand acres in the Hunter district, and a residential site in Sydney town (on the North Shore at St. Leonard's), on which he built a cottage, and a grazing property on the banks of Lake George in the Monaro Plains area of Southern N.S.W. He also held a 'grazing' licence in the then Riverina District, but in an area we know today as Gundagai. His 'run' was on the eastern bank of the Murrumbidgee River, where the township of Gundagai now stands. This property was managed on his behalf and records show that he only visited this area once in the 8 years he operated the 'lease;' but this pastoral activity made him think a great deal about the agricultural planning in the colony and its potential, and he then spent many years in the two agricultural societies that became so influential during the rise of the pastoral and squatting industries.

Lithgow retired in the Colony in 1852 on a pension of £339/3/4 per annum, and relocated from Sydney to his cottage on the rural property in the Hunter region. He retired also from the Legislative Council in 1848 (after 19 years of service), and from his position of Auditor-General in 1852. Lithgow died in 1864 (11 June) at the age of 80. Lithgow's was a remarkable career, stretching 50 years in the service of his country and leaving a legacy of contribution to the colony, and such a contribution would be difficult to ever match again. His memorials are few, other than a town that retained his name and became an established settlement in the area known originally as 'Lithgow's Valley' (the name was given by Lithgow's friend and colleague (Surveyor-General John Oxley). We learn from newspaper reports of his land-sales (first at Kissing Point and then Lithgow Valley) and of his sheep 'run' at present day Gundagai in the Monaro Region of southern New South Wales.

CHAPTER 10

THE STORY OF THE NSW COMMISSARIAT

The HRNSW contains numerous references to original records reporting the instructions on how to operate, or anecdotal reports on how the commissariat operated. In 1786, Phillip wrote[158]:

'It is planned that a quantity of provisions equal to two years consumption should be provided, which will be issued from time to time, according to the discretion of the Superintendent, guided by the proportion of food which the country and the labour of the new settlers may produce.'

He added that 'Clothing per convict was estimated to cost £2.19.6 including jackets, hats, shirts, trousers, shoes' but 'the type of clothing was not always suitable for the climate, and should be ready made rather than relying on the convicts to sew their own.' He noted that 'The *Sirius* brought seed wheat and barley and four months supply of flour for the settlement, together with a year's provisions for the ships company,' and:

'Supplies of grain or flour from England will be necessary to maintain the colony until there is sufficient local crops in store rather than 'in the ground', because of grub, fire, drought and other accidents'.

---

[158] HRNSW Vol 1 Part 2

On 9 January 1793, he noted that 'I have directed the commissary to make a purchase and have thus augmented the quantity of provisions in the colony to 7 months at the established ration.'

On 6 January 1793, Phillip recorded his opinion that the projected expense for the settlement for 1794 for the 5,500 population was £25,913. With 3,000 convicts included in the population, this translated to of £13.14.0 per head per annum, (approximately 9d. per day) and pointed out 'this sum cannot increase, but must gradually diminish'. Phillip was allowing only 1,900 persons 'on the store' or less than 40% of the population. His numbers were obviously incorrect but the cost he calculated conveniently came within the official allowance of 14d. Per head per day.

On 9 November 1794, the Colonial Office reported that 'the stock of stores of provisions and ready-made clothing should now be sufficient for the settlement for one year. With the quantity of clothing shipped in mid-1794, there would be a sufficient supply for 2,500 men and 700 women, according to the last official report of numbers.' Mr. Henry Dundas (British MP) insisted that the convicts should be made 'to wear the allotted clothing for a full year.' On 15 February 1794, the Colonial Office directed that 'Each ship was to carry supplies for the trip and for maintenance upon arrival, for convicts, soldiers and sailors. 'King, as Phillip's Deputy and Governor of Norfolk Island, recorded on the 20 July 1794, that the island had produced 'a second crop in sufficient quantity for storage for the next year.–being 11500 bushels plus 4000 reserved for seed, stock, and the producing families.' 'Stores were ordered from the Cape of Good Hope for the Sydney settlement and the hospital on 22 June 1788 to be selected by John Hunter, as captain of the *Sirius*

On 10 June 1797, Governor Hunter submitted a plan that

> '. . . were Government to establish a public store for the retail sale of a variety of articles–such as clothing, or materials for clothing, hardware, tools, sugar, soap, tea, tobacco and every article that labouring people require–supported by a reputable shopkeeper who should produce regular accounts and charge a small premium to cover these other costs, then the people would get what they wanted with ease, and at far less expense than in any other way.'

On 10 January 1798, Governor Hunter repeated his request for a public store:

> 'If my suggestion is adopted, a branch of the store should be placed on Norfolk Island. Such a store should lessen the expense of maintaining the convicts and into the store; I would also suggest the retailing of liquor and spirits, for the purpose of putting a stop to the importation of that article.'

Again on the 25 May 1798, Hunter recommended using:

> '. . . the public store as a means of controlling the high price of grain. Such a store would operate as an encouragement to industry. Without some form of price control on grain the settlers cannot live let alone provide for a family. The speculators and the monopolists all contrive to keep the settlers in a continual state of beggary and retard the progressive improvements of the colony.'

The success of Simeon Lord's colonial merchandising in 1801 proves that Hunter was on the right track with his 'public' store.

The Colonial Secretary wrote to Hunter on 3 December 1798 about the meat supply:

> '. . . when the livestock belonging to the crown, added to that of individuals, is in so flourishing a state as to supply the needs at 6d a pound or less, it is evident the Government will gain by supplying the settlement with fresh meat instead of sending salted provisions from England.'

This request was later modified to limit the store purchases for meat to those from farmer settlers.

On 2 February 1800, William Broughton, a churchman and Magistrate, was also appointed as the storekeeper at Parramatta to replace a man Hunter had sacked for fraud.

Governor King recorded his success in conserving the stores by writing that

> '. . . since I took office, I have reduced the number of fully rationed people relying on the public stores by 450. This has saved annually the amount of £10,488, using the rate of £23 per head. I have also reduced the price of wheat to 8d per bushel, pork to 6p per lb, and maize to 4s instead of 5s per bushel.'

When Hunter was recalled to England, the commissariat was left with many debts owed by settlers and he was concerned that they would be denied and he be held responsible. He wrote to the new Governor, Phillip King, and recorded:

> 'I trust it is clear that there has been no lavish waste and no improvident use of the public stores during my authority. These debts are just, even though many of the individuals may doubt their being indebted to the Government for so much. 'It appears there were doubtful debts of over £5,000 due to the store.'

In response, King made demands on the settlers and accepted grain at a higher price than usual in settlement of the debts. When news of the demands became known, it produced an unusual response from John Macarthur, who suddenly recalled that much of what he had taken from the stores, and charged against the public account, over the previous 12 months was in fact his personal responsibility and he settled with the stores on this basis.

On 7 November 1800, King re-appointed John Palmer to his former position as Commissary. Other appointments included Broughton to Norfolk Island, Deputy Chapman from Norfolk to Sydney and William Sutter as Storekeeper at Parramatta. In order to conserve grain, King reduced the ration to 13.5 lb of wheat per week.

At the time of his appointment, Palmer had been handed a set of instructions, including:

'All troops and convicts in the territory were to be properly supplied and the commissary was to keep a grain stock of 12 months supply

He was to transmit annually a list of expected consumption, and all purchases were to be made under the authority of the Governor and prices paid to be no greater than market prices

All bills of exchange must be accompanied with an affidavit of purchase countersigned by the Governor.

You will also make receipts for all payments in the presence of at least one witness–preferably a magistrate–and make three sets of all vouchers, one for the treasury, one with the accounts and one for the store use.

Keep a separate account of all items transmitted from England.

Make a survey of any stores lost or damaged–which goods are to be sold or destroyed at the Governors discretion.

Make up annually an account of all receipts and expenditures, accompanied by one set of vouchers.

You are responsible for the preservation of all stores and provisions and the employees who work for you, and to the public.'

(Signed)
Portland (Duke of Portland)

This set of notes on how the commissariat should operate was prepared by the Duke of Portland and handed to Governor-in-Chief Phillip Gidley King on 28 September 1800. They are attached for historical purposes.

A list of some of the main provisions and supplies that arrived with the First Fleet indicated the role and difficulties facing the storekeeper. In addition to foodstuffs, supposedly sufficient for the first six months, some of the provisions and supplies which were shipped with the First Fleet in 1787, were:

TABLE 1.1: SUPPLIES SENT WITH THE FIRST FLEET

700 steel spades	5448 squares of glass	50 pickaxes	30 box rulers
30 grindstones	700 axe handles	140 angers	50 hayforks
700 iron shovels	200 canvas beds	700 wooden bowls	30 pincers
330 iron pots	747,000 nail of various	700 gimlets	42 splitting wedges
700 garden hoes	sizes 63 coal	700 wooden platters	100 plain measures
6 hand-carts	buckets	504 saw files	8000 fishhooks
700 West India hoes	100 pairs of hinges	10 forges	12 brick moulds
4 timber carriages	80 carpenter's axes	300 chisels	48 dozen fishing lines
700 grubbing hoes	10 sets cooper's tools	700 clasp knives	6 harpoons
14 chains	20 shipwright's adzes	60 butcher's knives	10000 bricks
700 felling axes	40 corn-mills	500 tin-plates	12 lances
14 fishing nets	175 claw hammers	100 pairs–scissors	
700 hatchets	12 ploughs	60 padlocks	
	175 handsaws		

The complete list[159] of articles sent with the First Fleet was much longer and represented a storeman's nightmare if records of issues and returns were to be maintained. For instance, the unloading of stores and provisions for immediate use commenced on 7 February but; since the settlement held over 1,000 people, there was obviously not sufficient bedding, blankets, cooking utensils, or eating utensils for everyone[160]. The allowance of clothing for a male convict for a year was equally inadequate; although raw cloth, needles and cotton had arrived with the Fleet and female convicts could be encouraged to hand sew clothing if necessary. The records show that the total costs of all male and female convict clothing was only £4,144.

In 'Botany Bay Mirages', Alan Frost has raised the question of whether the inadequate quantity of tools and supplies was deliberate, or merely poor planning. A case can be made for improper planning rather than deliberate mismanagement. Phillip was left in sole charge of the voyage and received very little guidance, support or interest from the Secretary of State's office, the Naval Board or the commissariat division of the British Treasury.[161] It is unlikely that, after a fairly ordinary career as a naval officer, Phillip would suddenly have reverted to poor leadership. Indeed, he had commented to

---

[159] HRNSW Vol 1, Part 2 p.16

[160] The list of 'stores' and 'provisions' is found in both the HRNSW and in John Cobley 'Sydney Cove' Vol 1

[161] Alan Frost raises this possibility in 'Botany Bay Mirages' Chapter 8 'No Cheaper Mode...' as does Barnard in 'Phillip of Australia'.

the Naval Board that the vessels allotted to the Fleet were not adequate in size or number. He also questioned the short amount of time allowed for the planning process, but received no worthwhile response. Clearly, this was not regarded as a voyage of high importance compared with British naval activities in other parts of the world. So, the fact that Phillip used a great deal of judgment and commonsense, speaks volumes for his quiet confidence and determination that he was the most suitable choice as the head of this mission.

For the first storekeeper, local circumstances were such that the supplies brought from England needed to be carefully protected against theft and loss. The tools, in particular, were to be issued daily and returned each evening; however according to Marjorie Barnard, within 14 days of arriving in the colony, over one-third of the tools loaned out for chopping trees and clearing land had been lost, stolen or deliberately concealed from the storekeeper.[162] The chief cause was the unwillingness of convicts to work; removing the tools meant they were unable to chop firewood or cut timber framing for the new camp. As a way of keeping the tools in repair, Miller had set up forges on the banks of Sydney Cove and used iron and steel pieces brought out as ballast to forge new tools and replace lost items. Watkins Tench in his 'Narrative of the Expedition to Botany Bay' provides some useful insights into the conditions faced by Phillip and Miller. In November 1788 he noted: 'Temporary, wooden stores, covered with thatch or shingles into which the cargoes of all the ships have been lodged, are completed, and a hospital erected'.[163] However, the stores were not to remain as such for long as the end of one such building was converted into a temporary church for Sunday services. These frail structures were neither fire-proof nor rat-proof and the summer of 1789 saw the end to these temporary structures when Phillip designed a new, sturdier and more permanent store in a location closer to the settlement's military camp. Later in 1789, Tench recorded that 'the storehouse was finished at Rose Hill (by then renamed Parramatta). It was 100 feet by 24 feet and was built of local brick, deep red in colour, but not as durable as the Sydney product'.[164]

---

[162] Barnard 'A History of Australia' Chapter 3 'Taking Shape' p60.
[163] Flannery quotes Tench in '1788 Watkin Tench' p81
[164] Flannery ibid p127

Displaying rare frustration, Phillip wrote to Assistant Secretary of State, Phillip Stephens, in August 1790 'Leather is needed for soles for men's shoes and materials for mending them. Shoes here last but a very short time, and the want of these materials and thread to mend the clothing will render it impossible to make them serve more than half the time for which they were intended'. The following month Phillip wrote to Nepean, the Under-Secretary of State for the Colonies, and made two observations: 'I cannot help repeating that most of the tools sent out were as bad as ever' and, 'the wooden ware sent out were too small; they are called bowls and platters, but are not larger than pint basins. There was not one that would hold a quart'.[165]

Tench also described the development of the new town of Rose Hill and the buildings adjacent to the store: 'the new stone barracks is within 150 yards of the wharf, where all boats from Sydney unload. In addition there is an excellent barn, a granary, an enclosed yard to rear livestock, a commodious blacksmith's shop and a most wretched hospital, totally destitute of every convenience'.[166]

In 1790 Phillip told Nepean that the colony badly needed 'honest and intelligent settlers, and free men to act as superintendents of convicts'. Phillip also requested a new, more appropriate style of clothing for the convicts, even suggesting a form of mark to protect them from being sold. He badly needed a windmill, and requested axes, saws, combs, iron pots and 'two or three hundred iron frying pans which will be a saving of the spades'.[167] Unlike Macquarie some twenty years later, Phillip was of two minds about free enterprise in the colony. He did approve an open market, but then reverted to government importing 'specialty' items into the colony. According to Barnard, "in April 1792, Phillip established a regular market in Parramatta". It was for fish, grain, livestock, clothing and anything else that might legitimately be bought or sold. It was open to convicts. In October 1790, Phillip reported to Secretary Dundas in

---

[165] Governor Phillip to Under- Secretary Nepean HRNSW Vol 1, Part 2 p481. In terms of the departmental hierarchy, the Colonial Office had a Secretary, an Under-Secretary and then a number of Assistant-Secretaries
[166] Flannery *ibid* p 145
[167] Governor Phillip to the Rt. Hon Henry Dundas HRNSW Vol 1 Part 2 p595

London: "The commissary was obliged to purchase various articles brought out by the sailing officers of the *Pitt*, where the private property sold in this settlement amounted to upwards of £4,000, which may serve in some measure to point out what might be bought by a ship loaded wholly on account of government".[168]

During 1792, Phillip was faced with a minor mutiny. The military under the leadership of Major Grose advised Phillip that they (the military) had chartered *The Britannia* to sail to the Cape for supplies. In spite of strong protests from Phillip, the ship sailed on 24 October and thus was born the 'pernicious system of private trading by the military'.[169] Phillip wrote movingly to the Right Hon. Henry Dundas, the Secretary of State in London, of this continuous struggle to get necessities: 'The period at which the colony will supply its inhabitants with animal foods is nearly as distant at present as it was when I first landed'. He added:

> *'I beg leave to observe that all those wants which have been pointed out in my different letters still exist: for iron pots, we have been nearly as distressed as for provisions: cross cut saws, axes and the various tools for husbandry are also much wanted; many of the articles are now made here, but the demand is greater than can be supplied because of the shortage of materials; many bales of clothing have been received, but arrive rotten and so injured from the damp that they have scarcely borne washing a second time'.*[170]

TABLE 1.2: VALUE OF BILLS DRAWN BY THE NSW COMMISSARY ON THE BRITISH TREASURY[171]

Year	Amount (£)
1806	13,873
1807	31,110

---

168 Governor Phillip to the Rt. Hon Henry Dundas HRNSW Vol 1 Part 2 p.613

169 Barnard, *Phillip of Australia*, p. 126

170 Governor Phillip to the Rt. Hon Henry Dundas HRNSW Vol 1 Part 2 p.643

171 These figures are assembled from Governor Macquarie despatches found in HRA 1: vols 9 & 10

1808	23,163
1809	49,514
1810	72,600

These increases could be directly attributed to the additional population being victualled in the colony, the higher level of rations, purchases by the commissary of foodstuffs and provisions from visiting foreign vessels, and higher prices of produce in England due to the prevailing economic conditions. Secretary Liverpool was also aware of the growing local revenue being raised in the colony from import duties, which he had little control. Macquarie, on the other hand, saw this locally raised revenue as 'cream' and discretionary revenue for his personal use—not to be handed over to the Treasury in London. Liverpool made mention of the growing expenditure on public works and wanted this item to be trimmed; the civil list was growing at the same rate but his goal was to make the 'Police' and 'Orphan' funds pay for these extra persons. He directed that there be 'no increase in the civil staff' unless covered by local funding. He approved the purchase of a brig for the colonial service provided it was paid for from local funds. Macquarie could see his dream dwindling away rapidly unless he could maintain his control over the commissariat, so that he could manipulate expenditures to suit his own needs whilst keeping the majority of local revenues under his control.

Some of Liverpool's premonitions of uncontrolled expenditure may well have been caused by Macquarie, especially as the commissariat pursued a 'support' role. In 1810 Macquarie wrote to Liverpool's predecessor, Viscount Castlereagh, offering his opinion of the condition of the local commissary:

'I found the Public Stores almost destitute of dry provisions, which situation had occasioned very serious alarm for some time before my arrival. This very exhausted state of His Majesty's Stores had been very much occasioned by the last dreadful and calamitous inundation of the Hawkesbury River, which had swept away the entire crops in that fertile district—an event not infrequent, and which has repeatedly involved the inhabitants in the deepest misery and distress'.[172]

---

[172] HRA 1:X: 221

In response to this finding, Macquarie acted swiftly, adding 300 acres of grain to the government farms, importing wheat from Bengal and reducing all rations. Castlereagh had expressed doubts about the preference for government over private farms but Macquarie protested that the government herds and farming should be maintained further livestock be imported for breeding purposes. He maintained control over the colonial economy by giving notice of a bank and a local currency and an appropriation of funds for the restocking of the commissariat. He also supported the operations of the Lumber and Dock Yards.

Over the next 10 years, Macquarie commenced what Commissioner Bigge later declared to be 'excessive spending; however, it produced significant results for the economy. He was generally responsive to the needs of the traders, merchants and entrepreneurs who he considered were the drivers of the economy. As shown by his instruction of 8 July 1815, he was intent on simplifying the process of business in the colony and of making the store receipts, issued by the commissariat, a form of medium of exchange for the local settlers.[173]

Summary of Instructions for Operating the Commissariat in Colonial NSW

Phillip Gidley King arrived as Governor in 1800 and noted that, up to the time of his appointment, there had been no explicit set of instructions issued for the guidance of the Commissary, except for verbal commands from each successive governor or administrator. In October 1800 he appointed Thomas Laycock as acting Commissary to fill the vacancy between the departure of James Williamson and the return in November of John Palmer from England. King saw the need for a set of instructions for the guidance of the 'officer on whom alone the public economy of the colony rests'[174] In the same despatch King advised that on behalf of the colony, he had purchased the wine cellar from retiring Governor Hunter

---

[173] HRA 1:8:p623

[174] HRA 1:2:675 King to Secretaries of the Treasury (Governor's Despatch # 2, September 1800)

and directed the commissary to pay for it and 'receive it'. The cost was £151.11.6.

King was as good as his word and produced a set of instructions as well as transmitting annual statements of the commissariat's revenues and expenses to the Treasury–the first and last governor to do so. After King, the commissariat handled its own transmittals until 1813, when they were made to Army headquarters (quartermaster's regiment) in England for consolidation and transfer to the Treasury. According to the NSW–SRO, King's commissariat records still exist in the PRO in London, but they do not appear to be part of the AJCP records.

The Instructions of Governor King

The HRA[175] offers a complete set of the instructions of Governor King, of which the following is a summary:–

The Commissary was 'to control the receipt and issue of all stores and provisions into and from His Majesty's stores.

No articles were to be received or issued without a written order from the Governor.

Detailed store receipts were required of all 'grain or animal food' purchased or otherwise received into the store.

Accounts of expenditure were to be furnished quarterly and more often if required.

The Commissary was to plan to match ration requirement with food availability. The Governor was to be advised of any shortfall and where it would be covered from and how much it would cost.

The Commissary was 'directed to reform the irregularity that has existed in the mode hitherto followed in making payment for such articles as have

---

[175] HRA 1:2:632-6 sets out a complete copy of the instructions

been purchased from settlers for public use'. Previously promissory notes had been made out for goods received; but these notes were frequently counterfeited and hence offered little security. King proposed a system of store receipts, which were to show the quantity and nature of goods received as well as their monetary value. At convenient intervals, the Governor would draw a Bill on the British treasury, at which time a call would be made for the return of all store receipts issued to settlers.

King obviously wanted to create regularised recording & reporting for the commissary and required the commissary to present to the governor once a year the following account books for audit.

'Victualling Book'—containing names of persons who received provisions during the year.

'Clothing and Slop Expense Book'—to record issues of clothing, blankets etc.

'Book to record Receipts of Stores', provisions and clothing, from all sources; also the expense thereof, and an inventory of stores on hand at the end of each year.

'Store Purchasing Book' specifying purchases of food from settlers, noting date, quantity, application and cost, a cross-reference was to be made with store receipts issued.

'Purchasing Book', to set out the quantities and cost of stores purchased from masters of visiting vessels or 'other strangers'—again to be supported by vouchers. Method of payment is to be specified—in kind, in grain, meat or money.

'Book of Particular Expense' showing provisions and clothing issued during the year to non-convicts e.g. civil and military officers. A similar book was to be kept for issues to free settlers.

An open list of all births, deaths and absentees during the year—these details were to be supplied by the clergy in the colony.

Whenever a ship was due to sail to England a 'State of the Settlement Report' was to be prepared for despatch with the vessel. This statement was to include a current population record, the number on stores, inventory in the store and a weekly return of expenditures.

A 'Weekly Victualling and Store-issue Book' was to be kept by each remote storekeeper, and a quarterly summary sent to the Sydney store.

In many ways, the requirements imposed by Governor King were not unlike the range of statistical returns provided in 1822 by the first *Blue Book*. All of the above books and returns were to be delivered to the governor on 31 October each year, prior to their transmission to England, and a 'correct copy was to be kept in the commissariat office' as directed by the British Treasury instructions.

The British Treasury Instructions

The British Treasury must have also seen the need for a formal set of instructions to be issued to the Commissary as, in November 1800, Commissary Palmer returned with a set of instructions for his guidance.[176] These Treasury regulations are more general than those of Governor King but they were not inconsistent. The main difference was a policy change which now authorised the Commissary to draw bills without the approval of the governor, contradicting the earlier written policy that 'all bills drawn for public purposes in the settlement should be drawn by the governor and by no other person'. King's despatch to the Duke of Portland of March 1802 included a State of His Majesty's Settlements in NSW Report[177], which confirmed, essentially down to the last detail, that King's instructions were being adhered to exactly and also showed

---

[176] HRA 1:3:5 King's despatch # 3 of 10 March 1801 records Palmer delivered to him a letter from Secretary Long inclosing instructions from Treasury Commissioners for the commissary's guidance. King questioned the third article, which authorised the commissary to directly draw bills, for purchases on the public account, on the Treasury instead of going through the governor.

[177] HRA 1:3:418 details the civil establishment in the colony and the lengthy report of the administration of the commissariat department

that the commissariat was becoming of considerable importance in the colony as a market and exchange. King's order of August 1802 authorised the Commissary to sell surplus perishable stores to free settlers at a profit. The commission charged varied at first but was later fixed at 50%. Remuneration to Commissary Palmer was by a small percentage of sales, although from this he had to pay for extra bookkeeping clerks from his own pocket.

A period of instability occurred during the military administration, between the time of the Bligh rebellion and the arrival of Lachlan Macquarie. During this time, Williamson, Wiltshire, Fitz and finally Broughton replaced Palmer as successive Commissaries.

Governor Macquarie's Instructions to the Commissary

Macquarie wasted no time in commencing his investigation of the commissariat for on 31 January 1810, less than one month after his arrival in the colony, he issued a general order[178], a summary of which is as follows:

Remote storekeepers were to submit vouchers (Form #1) for requisitions on the general store in Sydney each month.
Form #2 was a return of all foodstuffs received by storekeepers weekly.
Form #3 was a copy of Store receipts for all stores received.

All requisitions for stores had to be counter-signed by the Governor's secretary.

Invoices for all store purchases were to be sent to the Governor's secretary

Statements of receipts and expenditures were be made each June and December and forwarded to the Governor's secretary.

Storekeepers were to furnish to the governor weekly summaries of receipts and issues of stores.

---

[178]   Found in SRO NC11/5

The Commissary was to keep lists of all persons victualled from the public stores.

The 'Statement of the Settlement' was to be sent with each ship sailing for England.

In February 1811, Macquarie directed that only the commissariat was to import into 'bonded store' all wines and spirits ordered for the colony, with a fee receivable of one-half gallon for every one hundred gallons measured. From 1827 the Bonded Store became part of the Customs Department. He also oversaw the removal of civil servant families from store support—only the civil servant himself could draw rations. By an order dated December 1814, the sale of articles from government stores to any private individual was disallowed, thus introducing freedom of trade—this meant the colonial government would issue permits for imported articles to be distributed amongst the settlers and created a new class of merchants.

Following the Bligh rebellion, Treasury officials in London considered the commissariat to be in need of reorganisation. Up to this time, it had been a separate colonial department under the control of the governor, paid for through the Budget appropriation process. The reform proposal was to transfer responsibility for the colony's commissariat to the Commissary-General in England, who headed sub-branch of the Treasury department. A Deputy Commissary–General was to head the colonial operation and would be subject to instructions issued from the British Commissariat. Another revision was that all deputy commissaries would now be recruited in England and the colonial governor would only have a supervising role[179]. The activities of David Allen have been discussed in Chapter 2 and do not require repeating. However, there was a source of disagreement between the D.C.G and the governor, other than over commissariat personnel and their overt dishonesty. The governor was to be concerned with changes in the methods of payment to free settlers for stores received into the commissariat. The store had been using 'store receipts' as payment and, as Butlin points out in *Foundations*[180]:

> ' . . . *because of the lack of money in the colony, the store receipts became in effect the circulating currency. However, this led to difficulties in making up accounts, since it was often quite impossible to obtain the receipts back from the settlers in order to make up quarterly or annual returns. The fact was that many settlers found that the demand in the colony for those store receipts was sufficient to make the return of them unnecessary'.*

Macquarie's attempt to solve the problem came via a government order[181], which stipulated 'all store receipts are to be brought to the D.C.G at the end of every two months. Failure to hand them in would cancel the value of the receipt'.

It was David Allen's excursion into issuing promissory notes to replace the store receipts that eventually brought about his dismissal. Macquarie's

---

[179]   HRA 1:8:126 + note 19 (p657) Bathurst to Macquarie February 1814: Note 19 records 'Prior to June 1813, the commissariat department was a distinct colonial entity under the immediate control and direction of the governor. A separate establishment was created for it and salaries were voted annually by Parliament. On 11th June 1813 David Allen arrived holding the appointment of D.C.G. He assumed control of the commissariat and a new *regime* was established. The department became a branch of the commissary-general in England, a sub-department of the treasury and officers held their appointments as part of the general English commissariat staff. The D.C.G. was head of the department generally, qualified by the local supervision of the governor of the colony. He communicated directly with his superiors in England and not through the governor as formerly. It is evident that the functions of the governor were curtailed considerably by this change

[180]   S.J. Butlin's Foundations of the Australian Monetary System 1788-1851'

[181]   SRO records NC11/5

reports[182] on the matter show that, at this time, the commissariat had branches in Sydney, Parramatta, Windsor, Liverpool, Bathurst, Hobart, Port Dalrymple and Newcastle. Allen's replacement was Drennan who arrived in January 1819 but, immediately upon his arrival, he attempted to mislead Macquarie by alleging he had also been authorised to issue promissory notes in lieu of store receipts. A subsequent Commission of Inquiry into Drennan's activities did much good for there are no further accounts of corruption during the Macquarie Administration. Drennan could not explain a debt or account for missing funds of 'upwards of £6,000'[183] Brisbane had also directed D.C.G Wemyss to transmit a detailed and;'certified' statement about Drennan to London, explaining the public accounts deficiency.

The next attempt to reorganise the stores was made by Governor Darling in August 1827, with the support of', and upon written instructions from, the Treasury. The Treasury requested:

> '... it being desirable, with a view to a more systematic arrangement of the Accounts of the Public Expenditure of the Colony, that the expenses of articles issued from the General Store, be ascertained and classified under the following three headings:

> 1. Colonial 2. Military 3. Maintenance of Convicts.

> It will be necessary that the D.C.G be furnished with separate requisitions and vouchers for each of these heads respectively.

> Under Heading 1, are to be classed all articles, issued for purposes not military or not connected with the maintenance, clothing, housing or management of convicts

> Under Heading 2, all Army, Military, hospital barrack, and quartermaster's stores and all articles for the construction or repair of buildings for the housing of the troops.

---

[182] HRA 1:10:116 'Macquarie to the Lord Commissioners of the Treasury (Pages 100 -135)

[183] HRA 1:10:629 Brisbane to Earl Bathurst 6th April 1822

Under Heading 3, all articles issued for the purpose of clothing, management or housing of convicts. This will also comprise all stores and supplies for the other penal settlements and for the use in government vessels and for agricultural establishments'.

The practical arrangement for this proposal required that[184]

' . . . *once every six months a Board comprising the Colonial Treasurer, the D.C.G, the Commissary of Accounts and the Colonial Auditor was to be convened for the purpose of transferring adjustments between the colonial treasury account and the Military Chest account and in that way reimburse the store for obligations made on behalf of the colonial administration.'*

In 1827[185], the British Government accepted that the whole expense of police, gaols, convicts and the colonial marine was to be carried by the 'Home Treasury', although the arrangement was short-lived. Ten years later, the colonial legislature claimed Britain owed its treasury over £700,000 in reimbursements for costs expended under these categories. This 1827 plan soon caused problems for the commissariat because, at this time, the use of coinage was becoming genera. The depleted military chest could not continue to draw bills for reimbursement, so the commissariat regularly 'borrowed' funds from the colonial treasury in order to save the military chest.[186] In June 1827 D.C.G Laidley was appointed to run the commissariat but, when Darling recommended that he keep an extra set of books for the information of his superiors in London, Laidley complained about being short-staffed. An enquiry showed that 'the number of clerks employed in the commissary nearly equalled the number in all civil departments put together. A number of government orders following the enquiry were aimed at improving the efficiency in the keeping of accounts in the commissariat'.[187]

---

[184] HRA 1:13:698 Minute #51 Darling to Goderich
[185] HRA 1:14:332 Darling to Huskisson August 1828
[186] HRA 1:16:658 Bourke to Goderich confirming loan of funds to D.C.G Laidley (June 1832)
[187] HRA 1.15.745 Darling to Under-Secretary Hay–September 1830; (the number of clerks employed by the D.C.G. was 40)

It appears that Darling listened to his small, select Board of General Purposes, which was in effect an advisory board to the governor. Darling issued an order (Government Order #1 of 1827) providing for the formation of a Board of Survey to examine the stores in each government department and recommend how best to integrate them with the commissariat store. Reports of the survey were prepared and submitted to William Lithgow, Auditor of Colonial Accounts. The eventual results of the survey were seen in 1836 when the British Government made further changes to the operations of the commissariat by establishing within it a branch of the British Ordnance Department. This new department was given physical custody of 'the military works and buildings' and the ordnance and other stores, as well as the buildings occupied by the convicts, and the stores and clothing required in the convict establishments.[188] The result was a commissariat very much reduced in size after January 1836. With this change the physical stores had moved entirely to the Ordnance Storekeeper's department, leaving the commissariat virtually an administrative-financial branch of the British Treasury. It was still required to transport stores and this led to the growth of a transport branch of the commissariat. Under the same minute the total responsibility for gaols, police and colonial marines transferred from the Imperial to the colonial government.

The downsizing was all part of a plan in the early 1840s to stop transporting convicts to the colony. Until 1855 the NSW commissariat continued to pay for all convict establishments, including hospital and other medical expenses for convicts, although in 1850 all barracks and military buildings were handed over to the colonial government. Britain's military responsibility to the colony continued until 1870, when all imperial forces and the remaining commissariat functions (mainly payroll) were withdrawn from the Australian colonies.[189]

---

[188] HRA 1:17:706 Treasury Minute dated 10 March 1835 attached to letter from Hon J. Stewart (H. M. Treasury) to Under Secretary Hay
[189] Australian Encyclopaedia: 'Military'

Macquarie's Reform of the Commissariat

In April 1817, Macquarie confirmed with the Earl of Bathurst that he intended to reform the operations of the commissary in the colony, in line with recommendations received from London. He advised Bathurst of new appointments to senior posts to replace officers engaged in insider trading and 'maladministration' and then went on to describe the 'old' and the 'new' systems.

> *'When the settlement was founded, the commissariat department was a distinct colonial entity in the charge of a 'commissary of stores and provisions' that was directly under the control of the governor. The first commissary was Andrew Miller, who resigned in 1790 due to ill health. After the wreck of the Sirius at Norfolk Island in March 1790, the purser, John Palmer, was appointed to succeed Miller as commissary. As the colony developed, the commissary expanded, and the staffs were increased by the appointment of assistant and deputy commissaries and storekeepers. Those officials received a colonial salary, rations and allowances. In the year 1812, it was decided to alter the system and the commissariat in the colony became a branch of the army commissariat, a sub-department of the English Treasury. The change was made immediately after the arrival of deputy commissary-general David Allen in the convict ship Fortune in June 1813'.*

Macquarie's latest change was based on his perception that the operations were presently unnecessarily large and expensive. He also observed that the commissary was now subjected to internal abuse, waste and fraud. He proposed to restore government farms and make the commissariat much more self-supportive by manufacturing more of its own produce. The commissariat was also to source as much as possible from its remaining procurement from local suppliers, thus leaving private suppliers to carry large inventories and offer purchase terms. Thus, the commissariat would not have to prepay British-based suppliers with FOB bills.

The first livestock to be removed from the government herds were transferred free of charge to eligible settlers who were encouraged to use these animals for breeding purposes. There were other procedural changes;

in 1813 responsibility for the military reverted back to the commissary rather than the civil authorities.[190] This change was part of an overall revamping of the military system and a restructuring in anticipation of economic rehabilitation which would occur after the Napoleonic Wars. The change involved separation of ordnance support services, the military commissariat and a convict commissariat into three separate operations and independent stores . . .

As if sensitive to his wavering place in history, Macquarie assembled all his official reports for the previous ten years and wrote what he called a 'synopsis' of his administration for the Earl of Bathurst. With reference to the commissary, he commented:

> 'The system I have invariably pursued in respect of the treatment and management of the convicts is to temper justice with humanity. The value of savings to the colony and the commissary by killing wild herds of cattle for meat will be over £7,000 (using 5d per lb for the valuation). The reduction in the price of fresh meat has caused great economy to the commissary. Beef supplies are growing, and the government herds prevent monopolies of individual suppliers to the commissary. A new government farm was established at Emu Plains because of the need for fresh produce from this extremely fertile tract of land. The use of convict labour in this way means that they are usefully employed and they more than repay to the government the amount of their maintenance and all of the other expenses of the Establishment. There are over 300 convicts employed there, these being those convicts who were not required for the settlers, or for the public roads and bridges or other government purposes. The principal part of the present expense of the colony is incurred in feeding, clothing and lodging the male and female convicts. Other slightly lesser expense is incurred in the support of the civil, military and marine establishments, and in victualling, for a certain period, free settlers, their families and convict labourers. The commissary carries out the planning and support for each of these groups.'

---

[190] Bathurst to Macquarie HRA 1:8: 619

Although Macquarie attempted to reduce the price of wheat delivered into store to 8 shillings per bushel, the settlers convinced him that 'the grower of grain would be a loser at that price' and he restored the price to ten shillings per bushel[191.] His earlier opinions had been influenced by Commissioner Bigge and, as a result Macquarie, changed from being a supporter of government farms to supporting the purchase of grains from the settlers.[192] However by 1820, after Bigge's departure, he again reported that 'there is no further economy in the measure of cultivating lands on account of the crown'.[193] This concern was later reiterated and confirmed by Major Ovens in his report on convict work practices for Governor Brisbane.[194] In addition to Macquarie's observations that government farms were uneconomic, Ovens concurred with his theory that the cost of convict labour used in clearing open pastoral land was not recovered by any increase in the sale price of the land. Ovens had calculated that eight convicts in a team or gang took one week to clear and burn one acre of land.[195]

The Macquarie 'Synopsis' also included an impressive list of the public buildings and works erected, and other useful improvements made in NSW at the expense of the crown from 1 January 1810 to 30 November 1821. He listed 67 items in Sydney, 20 in Parramatta, 15 at Windsor, twelve at Liverpool, and 52 in the outlying settlements of Richmond, Pitt Town, Penrith, Emu Plains, Spring Wood, Bathurst, Campbell Town, Pennant Hills, and Castle Hill.[196] He also drew attention to the impressive

---

[191] (HRA 1: X: 683 Emphasis added
[192] Commissioner Bigge was a former Chief Justice of the British West Indies and was appointed by Bathurst to complete an assessment of the government operations in NSW for the House of Commons
[193] M.H. Ellis *Lachlan Macquarie* P.124
[194] M.H. Ellis *Lachlan Macquarie* P. 132
[195] M.H. Ellis *Lachlan Macquarie* P135
[196] The Sydney and Parramatta buildings by Macquarie are listed in the last Chapter. The writer has computed the construction costs of each building by estimating the material content and the estimated length of construction time. Some estimates have been based on the Greenway notes found in the appendix to M.H. Ellis's biography of Francis Greenway, especially those relating to construction rates by various trades.

progress made in road construction, claiming 267 miles of roads around Sydney and Parramatta had been made under his direction.

In a memorial presented to Macquarie on his departure from the colony, the magistrates, clergy, merchants, landholders, free settlers and public officers wrote, 'Your Excellency's exertions for the welfare and improvement of these settlements, strongly exemplified by the rapidly increasing and growing consequence of the colony, have fully evinced the judgement of your appointment and command our gratitude and affection'.[197] They were well chosen and relevant words of appreciation from a selection of grateful settlers all of whom had benefited from Macquarie's administration, as had the entire settlement.

The governor of the day demanded statistics, statistics and more statistics. In addition to the 50-80 pages in the annual 'Blue Books', the Commissary prepared reports on inventory levels, the value and source of all purchases and rations by each group, where sent, and how many were being served.[198] From these sources it is possible to track how the commissary funds were distributed between each of the banks in the colony; we know the cost of supplies as well as the quantity of grain and meat and the value of clothing and cloth supplied. We also know the contractors for all provisions and their payments, the quantity of tools provided, military and hospital rations, bills drawn each year and details of loans flowing between the commissary, military chest, colonial treasury and the London Treasury.

---

[197] HRA 1:11:102

[198] The 'Blue Books' Reporting System commenced in 1822 and was a compilation of internal reports of revenues and expenditures and colonial statistics. The British Treasury in London prepared its format and three copies were prepared at significant clerical time and expense. One copy was sent to the Secretary of State's office in London, one was retained by the Governor in the Office of the Colonial Secretary and the third was directed to the House of Commons. Previous to the Blue Books, the three colonial funds were the Gaol (and then renamed Police) Fund, the Orphan Fund and the Colonial Fund. After 1822 other funds emerged for revenue discretionary purposes and they were fully reported in the Blue Books; such ancillary funds included the Commissary Fund, the Land Fund, and the Immigration Fund.

Between 1832 and 1842, the Military Chest was the preferred funding source for military and commissary revenue and expense. The Treasury renewed with vigour its instructions on handling funds and recording advances, loans, transfers and all expenditures. Although the working instructions provide an insight into the approved methods of operating the commissariat stores and accounts, to understand the process fully it is necessary to examine the inventory control procedures, purchasing and 'receiving into store' procedures, detailed accounting reports, ration levels established from time to time, and funding mechanisms. These topics are explored in detail in the following chapters.

CHAPTER 11

THE RISE OF
MANUFACTURING IN NSW

In 1882 Charles Lyne wrote a book about Colonial industry of the time–*The industries of NSW*. He reviewed a total of 35 articles about Colonial Industry in the last quarter of the 19th century, for industries such as Hunter Valley Farming, Lithgow Coal, and Pottery & Brick-making. This was a landmark analysis and the first and last of such studies. Subsequent studies have been more of an overview of industrialists and their activities rather than detailed studies of specific industries.

This present study is that of tracking early manufactures and their growth over time. Innovation and growth involved entrepreneurs, privatisation and a great deal of foreign investment.

For many years, Australia was essentially a primary-producing country. Manufacturing was geared largely to supplying local domestic requirements. The discovery of minerals, a growing population and military equipping created a profitable home market and led to an expansion of this sector.

Manning Clark writes (Vol 1, *A History of Australia*–P.249) 'Up to 1810 and the time of Macquarie, neither the convict stain nor clothing, lodging, or way of life distinguished the bonded (convicts) from the free workers. Nor within the free group was it possible to distinguish the ex-bond from the native-born and the free immigrant. Tradesmen were much in demand in the building trade; others (*ex land grant owners who had failed or been turned off their land)* found employment in the small industries of the colony, in the pottery, the hat-manufactory, the tannery, the brewery, or with the shoe-maker, the tailors or the tin-smiths; others took to the sea, on coastal vessels, or a ship trading with the Islands'

The last significant study of colonial manufacturing was completed by G. J. R. Linge in *Industrial* Awakening published in 1979. In 2000 it is timely that a further review be made of the earliest industry not of 1900 but of 1800.

The reasons that early governors sponsored developing industries in the early colony are various and commence with basic survival

Of course Governor King faced his own series of challenges. He began his term of office under strained relations with Hunter and, naturally, Macarthur. Macarthur wanted to boycott this new governor and his new policies of controlling the public herds and their grazing whereabouts. However, under King, the colony made great strides in new business activities. After Macarthur was transported to England for trial, King saw that whaling was the only 'staple' and envisaged great secondary industries and huge colonial profits. An export trade in coal began from Coal Harbour (Newcastle), which received government support through a large allocation of convict labour. Coal was sent to both India and the Cape . . . Some timber was exported, but did not receive a good reception at its destination. A source of cheap salt pork was found in Tahiti. Then in August 1800, King announced 'the manufacture of linen and woollen goods has begun with some success. Tuppence a pound was paid for local wool, which was woven into blankets. The raw wool was paid for by exchange of blanket material. This could well have been the start of the flourishing future wool industry.

The Naval Officer, (Harbour master) shared his revenues between the Orphan Fund and the Police Fund. This was the start of taxation in the colony and to an extent gave the colony an imprimatur of a successful colonial trading post.

Of all the early industries, it was the timber industry that was most important. After food provision, the governor's chief role was to create housing and barracks for free immigrants, convicts, and military personnel. Not until Macquarie's arrival did any significant planning for public buildings and infrastructure begin. The timber gathering and processing by its very nature was left to convict workers, and Ralph Hawkins (The timber-getters of Pennant Hills) provides a scenario of timber–gathering in the Hornsby Shire.

Governor Phillip encouraged sealing as an entrepreneurial activity and as an alternative and supplement to his policy of independent farming and Agri-production through 30 acre land grants.

1. Sealing also supported a fledgling boat-building and provedore industry and became the first export industry. Up to 1841 whaling and sealing exports were greater than wool, coal or timber.

2. New industries such as tallow, soap, tannery, linen, hats, slops, blankets were encouraged to serve a local market (some of these were government-sponsored e.g. linen, clothing, distillery), but Macquarie saw the limitations of the size of the local market to manufacturing industries; he also saw the convict labour as a means of creating output with minimal if not competitive costs, especially where local raw materials were involved. He then built a public works program around his output until the output itself created a catalyst for new manufactures.

3. The Lumber Yard and its associated operations, in employing over 3,000 convicts had the opportunity for using any skilled labour arriving in the colony, and for making a wide-range of items in local demand, and which were encouraged as being import replacers.

4. His decision to privatise many established L/Y operations created a grass roots manufacturing industry, which although it may have been assumed by private entrepreneurs, would have been a lot longer in arriving. Entrepreneurial encouragement by Macquarie also over-rode any endeavours by Macquarie to have monopoly operations in the Lumber Yard.

5. Thus the LUMBER YARD. was the real catalyst for growth of a manufacturing sector, mostly because of the positive policies of Macquarie and the heads of the commissariat

Thus the direct link between the commissariat L/Y and the rise of manufacturing!!

Upon his arrival, Bligh was appalled by the conditions of the colony and told Windham back in London (HRA 1:6:26) that much needed to be improved in the colony. He also wrote that of his being convinced that the immediate economic future lay in the encouragement of agriculture rather than in the development of commerce (for example the development of the wool trade) or the Bass Strait and overseas trade, for they were extremely trifling (HRA 1:6:121).

Clarke records (A History of Australia, Vol 1, P.331)

> 'by 1820 Simeon Lord had turned the profits of marriage, fishing in the south seas and trade in the Pacific Islands into a manufactory at Botany Bay where he employed convicts and from 15 to 20 colonial boys making blankets, stockings, wool hats, kangaroo hats, seal Hats, possum skin hats, all shoddy but cheaper than the imported English hats, boot leather, trousers, shirts, thread, kettles and glass tumblers. The bulk of the wool grown in NSW was shipped direct by the growers to England, and Lord was the exception to the principle that the settlers should use their great natural advantages of grass and climate to grow food and wool and import the other goods they needed'.

Bigge reported glowingly about the future prospects for grazing and agriculture but also recorded a downside to the growth in the agricultural economy; 'between 1810 and 1820, the numbers of sheep trebled, and some settlers were finding it more profitable to sell the fleeces rather than the carcasses (J.T. Bigge: Agriculture & Trade Report–p16-18)

The Macquarie legacy was described by the retiring governor during the handing-over ceremony with Governor Brisbane. 'I found the colony in a state of rapid deterioration: threatened with famine, discord and party spirit prevailing, and the public buildings in a state of decay. I left it a very different place: the face of the country was greatly improved; agriculture flourishing, manufactories had been established and commerce revived;

roads and bridges built and inhabitants opulent and happy'. (HRA 1:12:331)

This same principle of comparative advantage was considered carefully by the Commissariat and the Macquarie Administration before the decision to expand the numerous government business enterprises which were responsible for employing convict labour was implemented and became fully operational. The colony, it was decided, needed a manufacturing and industrial base to work in conjunction with the agricultural enterprises, and to supply the government with its public works materials from local sources, rather than rely on imports from Britain.

It was a source of great delight to Macquarie that he had brought about such change, and what a difference in approach and attitude between the two governors. In fact, although Phillip, Hunter and King could have contributed little more than they did towards trade, commerce and industrial development, it was the Macquarie pro-entrepreneurial policies that brought about such great progress in both industrial and economic development

Ralph Hawkins in '*The Convict Timber-getters of Pennant Hills*' writes

> "*The Chief Engineer's department enquired after the trades of convicts after arrival and kept the most useful of them in Government employ. The Engineer's department systematised the labour of the convicts, classifying men according to their trades and instructed those unskilled and young enough or willing enough in a suitable trade. The Lumber Yard in Sydney was the centre of industrial operations in the colony. Here men practiced both timber and metal trades, preparing useful products for the government. A number of outlying gangs prepared raw materials for the public works programme. The brick maker's gang worked At Brickfield Hill, the Shell gang gathered oyster shells for lime from the Aboriginal middens along the foreshore of the harbour and the Lane Cove River. The quarry gang prepared the stone, while further afield in the woods to the north-west of Sydney at Pennant Hills was the Timber-getting gang. This latter gang was a gang of men chosen for their skills and not a gang of men under*

secondary punishment. These men were mostly drawn straight from the arriving ships and worked shorter hours than most other convicts. They were of sufficient confidence to go on strike in 1819. Macquarie needed their services and they returned to work after only 3 weeks."

In the listing of key events, certain sectors of the secondary industry economy have been selected for a time-line of progress. There are reasons for specific industries being selected.

A brief outline of events before 1810 draws attention to a number of circumstances that are of fundamental importance to an understanding of early industrial development:

i. There was a general shortage of labour
ii. Circumstances combined to prevent real income and output from small settlers from rising
iii. monopoly position of military officers buying incoming provisions from visiting ships and retailing at exorbitant prices and profits
iv. most small farmers had neither the knowledge nor the capital to improve their farming techniques or to buy stock and equipment
v. the need to take people off the store
vi. the arrival of only a few free migrants
vii. large increase in arriving convicts

References Used and Literary Review

Of particular note is that the following literature is made up of economic history writings and general history. No other economic historian has made anything of the link between the operations of the commissariat and the rise of a manufacturing sector in the colony.

This link assumes that the commissariat business enterprises under the Macquarie Administration commenced the initial manufactory before transferring operations from the public to the private sector where practical, and then allowing competition to develop, in further satisfaction of the mechanism of a market economy. This process was under the overall encouragement of free enterprise by Macquarie, and was designed to

create a support sector for the already strong agri-business sector, to attract
free skilled labour to the colony and to attract investment to the colonial
economy as well as being an import replacement facility. Manufacturing in
the Lumber Yard was intended to satisfy an artificial government market
whilst transference to the private sector

1. HRA
2. HRNSW
3. Coghlan (x 3)
4. Butlin (x 2)
5. Steven
6. Blayney
7. Linge
8. Lyne
9. Hainsworth
10. Abbott & Nairn
11. Maloney: History of Australia
12. Clark: History of Australia
13. Barnard: History of Australia
14. Hawkins: The Timber-getters of Pennant Hills
15. Hainsworth: 'In search of a staple–the Sydney Sandalwood trade
    1804-09'
16. Abbott, G.C. 'Staple theory and Australian economic growth
    1788-1820'

These Key Events are set down by industry group as a means of
demonstrating the surprising amount of originality within the economy
and the potential for men of education with a flair for innovation and
access to capital. They are later sorted onto a time-scale.

A. Fishing & Whaling

1. **Sealing in Bass Strait** (1797) **commenced**
2. **Boat building** for hunting seals (1798)
3. By 1804 11 privately owned sloops were engaged in Bass Strait
   sealing

4. Between 1800 and 1806, over 100,000 seal skins landed in Sydney
5. **Whaling began** (1802)
6. **Boat building** for hunting whales
7. By 1830, 17 ships operated from Sydney, and by 1835, 76
8. Whaling stations established in NSW (1830), Victoria (1831) and S.A.(1837)
9. In 1830, NSW exported £60,000 worth of whaling & sealing products with wool at £35,000. By 1835, wool had overtaken fishery products. By 1841 whale oil exports peaked at £150,000 p.a.; by 1850, this had declined to £28,000. The decline was accelerated by the gold rushes which caused a shortage of labour for the whaling ships. In 1851, the whaling stations in Mosman's Cove closed. By 1853, exports from NSW had fallen to £16,000
10. By 1841 there were 41 bay-whaling stations in Tasmania. In the 1840s, over 400 vessels were built in VDL boat-yards

B. Timber

1. 1788 First Fleet cuts Sydney Cove timbers as clearing of land for initial settlement.
2. Earliest tree trunks not dried and when used *in situ* warped, twisted and bowsed.
3. Phillip sent out scouts to seek better quality timber and came across the Pennant Hills Timber-getting area.
4. Government Farms

   i. Within the commissariat, responsibility was allocated for the supervision of convicts undertaking government work. Even after London had directed cost cutting for convict maintenance a certain number of convicts were kept for government service, and during the King, Bligh and Macquarie Administrations government farms were established in 5 rural locations, not only to provide fresh fruit vegetables and meat for use within the colony but to manage the labour and output of over 500 convicts.

C. Manufacturing

1. 1788 First bricks used for building (Darling Harbour, Brickfield Hill, St. Peters, Granville, Gore Hill, Rosehill
2. Pottery works produced plates, jars, clay pipes (1788). By 1804 several other pottery works were operating
3. 1789–first vessel built for ferrying passengers between Parramatta and Sydney
4. 1795–Sydney's first windmill had been imported and erected on Observatory Hill
5. 1795–First ale brewed at Parramatta
6. 1796–Naval Dockyard established in Sydney Cove
7. 1799–Government broom factory opened with 1 man making 6 dozen brooms each week
8. 1800 Linen manufacturing on the Hawkesbury from locally grown flax
9. 1800 House of Industry, the women's section of Parramatta Gaol and later, the Female Factory made linen and other clothing items (hats, slops, blankets)
10. 1815 Steam powered flour mill
11. 1820 Local paper mill supplying all material for publishing *Sydney Gazette*
12. 1820 carriage and harness making in Sydney
13. 1824 Sugar made from local cane for first time
14. By 1838, NSW had 2 distilleries, 7 breweries, 12 tanneries, 5 brass and iron foundries, 77 flour mills and single factories producing salt, hats, tobacco and other goods
15. In 1839, Australian Sugar Company formed in NSW

C. Mining

1. 1797 Coal found on banks of Hunter River
2. 1801 All coal and timber declared by Governor King to be property of the Crown
3. 1801 Robert Campbell shipped coal to Calcutta and Cape of Good Hope

4. 1823 Commissioner Bigge recommended Newcastle coalfields be privatised
5. 1824 AAC company opens up 1 million acres
6. 1839 Gold discovered but kept quiet
7. 1841 Silver-lead ore discovered in Adelaide and 10 ton exported to Britain
8. 1846 Tin discovered in S.A.

D. Agri-Business

1. 1788 First Fleet arrived with livestock, seeds and young plants. However, the small cattle herd and sheep mostly died; only 2 horses survived more than 2 years
2. Phillip established a 3.6 ha farm where the Botanical Gardens now stand.
3. 1789 First Government farm commenced at Rose Hill. James Ruse received one acre at Rose Hill for wheat /grain experimenting.
4. 1791 The Ruse grant was increased shortly to 30 acres.
5. 1791 First tobacco grown
6. 1792 Planting of citrus trees along Parramatta River
7. 1795 Horses imported and by 1810 there were 1134 horses in NSW
8. 1797 NSW held about 2500 sheep
9. 1797 Governor Hunter reported the first planting of grape vines; by 1802 12,000 vines had been planted around Parramatta. Original cuttings had arrived with First Fleet
10. 1807 Samuel Marsden took first cask of cross-bred wool to England for testing.
11. 1813 First crossing of Blue Mountains
12. 1816 Botanic Gardens in Sydney developed
13. 1816 First wheat grown near Bathurst
14. 1820 First dairy industry established in Illawarra district

E. Exports & Trade (202,152,177,186,221)

1. 1790 The *Sirius* under John Hunter (Phillips' intended successor), returned with a cargo of flour, seed wheat and barley, and a year's provisions. Phillip had despatched the ship to acquire rations for the colony as the second fleet had been delayed and the colony was starving. The brig *Supply* was also despatched to Batavia for a supply of rice and other provisions

2. 1792 Army officers traded in goods from visiting vessels–a pattern which was to last for many years. Dutch and Indian vessels brought further supplies for trading and officers realised huge profits. Further plans were made for ships from Cape Town, Batavia and India to bring other tradable items. Strong trading links developed between Sydney and Batavia.

3. 1798–The Commissariat's first commercial purchase of grain from local farmers–1500 bushels of wheat were purchased from Hawkesbury farms.

4. 1798 The first boiling works was opened on Cape Barren Island, where they collected over 12500 seal skins and 3000 litres of seal oil for export to China

5. 1801 Robert Campbell exported 100 tons of Hunter Coal to Calcutta and 100 tons to Cape of Good Hope.

6. Although colonial trade in sealing, whaling, sandalwood and trepang (sea slug) was well underway by 1806, export was still hindered by the British Navigation *Acts* and the East India Company monopoly.

7. In 1810, Wentworth, Riley and Blaxall signed a contract to build a new main hospital in the settlement in exchange for a monopoly on import of spirits

8. 1812, first wheat purchased by NSW from VDL

9. 1813, Scarcity forced corn prices up from 5/–a bushel to 15/–per bushel. And wheat from 6/3 to £1/8/-

10. 1814, nearly 15,000 kg of wool was exported

F. Newspapers

1. 1795 A wooden-screw press, brought with the first fleet, was used to print the first official directive by Gov. Hunter
2. 1803. First newspaper (*Sydney Gazette*) founded by Gov. King mainly for government orders and proclamations. The weekly was edited by ex-convict, George Howe.
3. 1824 The weekly *Australian* first appeared owned by W. C. Wentworth and Robert Wardell. It was published without a licence. It was printed until 1848
4. 1826. The *Monitor* was first published by E. S. Hall, who became an antagonist of Governor Darling and spent numerous times in gaol.

G. Banking

1. 1811 Macquarie considers the need for banking upon his arrival, but is directed by the Secretary of State not to proceed
2. 1817 Macquarie issues banking licence for a private investment group to start the *Bank of NSW*.
3. Bigge determines the licence is illegal but recommends the continuation of the enterprise provided directors and stockholders assume all liability for deposits. No responsibility is to fall to the Government. The licence is ratified. and
4. The Bank of Australia commences in 1826

H. Roads and Bridges

1. 1788 Governor Phillip prepared the first town plan
2. 1788 First wooden log bridge built over the tank stream
3. 1794 Timber bridge built over the Parramatta River at Parramatta
4. 1810 Macquarie introduced a toll and turnpike system for major arterial roads from Sydney
5. 1811 Engineer John O'Hearne built a stone bridge over the tank stream

6. 1813 A large span bridge built over Hawkesbury at Windsor–65 metres long
7. 1814 Old South Head Road built and Sydney–Liverpool road built
8. 1815 Road down Bulli pass built to Wollongong
9. 1818 Oxley charted what is now the Oxley Highway to Port Macquarie
10. 1826 Great North Road commenced
11. 1830 Sydney–Goulburn Road surveyed
12. 1835 Track linking Sydney–Melbourne completed

Timescale of Manufactures

1788   1. 1788 First Fleet cuts Sydney Cove timbers as clearing of land for initial settlement.

1788   2. Earliest tree trunks not dried and when used *in situ* warped, twisted and bowsed.

1788   3. Phillip sent out scouts to seek better quality timber and came across the Pennant Hills Timber-getting area.

1788   1. 1788 First bricks used for building (Darling Harbour, Brickfield Hill, St. Peters, Granville, Gore Hill, Rosehill

1788   2. Pottery works produced plates, jars, clay pipes (1788). By 1804 several other pottery works were operating

1788   1. 1788 First Fleet arrived with livestock, seeds and young plants. However, the small cattle herd and sheep mostly died; only 2 horses survived more than 2 years

1788   2. Phillip established a 3.6 ha farm where the Botanical Gardens now stand.

1789   3. 1789–first vessel built for ferrying passengers between Parramatta and Sydney

1789   3. 1789 First Government farm commenced at Rose Hill. James Ruse received one acre at Rose Hill for wheat /grain experimenting.

1790   1. 1790 The *Sirius* under John Hunter (Phillips' intended successor), returned with a cargo of flour, seed wheat and barley, and a year's provisions. Phillip had despatched the ship to acquire rations for the colony as the second fleet had been delayed and the colony was starving. The brig *Supply* was also despatched to Batavia for a supply of rice and other provisions

1791   4. 1791 The Ruse grant was increased shortly to 30 acres.

1791   5. 1791 First tobacco grown

1792   6. 1792 Planting of citrus trees along Parramatta River

1792   2. 1792 Army officers traded in goods from visiting vessels–a pattern which was to last for many years. Dutch and Indian vessels brought further supplies for trading and officers realised huge profits. Further plans were made for ships from Cape Town, Batavia and India to bring other tradable items. Strong trading links developed between Sydney and Batavia.

1795   4. 1795–Sydney's first windmill had been imported and erected on Observatory Hill

1795   5. 1795–First ale brewed at Parramatta

1795   7. 1795 Horses imported and by 1810 there were 1134 horses in NSW

1795   1. 1795 A wooden-screw press, brought with the first fleet, was used to print the first official directive by Gov. Hunter

1796   6. 1796–Naval Dockyard established in Sydney Cove

1797   **1. Sealing in Bass Strait** (1797)

1797   1. 1797 Coal found on banks of Hunter River

1797   8. 1797 NSW held about 2500 sheep

1797   9. 1797 Governor Hunter reported the first planting of grape vines; by 1802 12,000 vines had been planted around Parramatta. Original cuttings had arrived with First Fleet

1798   **2. Boat building** for hunting seals

1798   3. 1798–The Commissariat's first commercial purchase of grain from local farmers–1500 bushels of wheat were purchased from Hawkesbury farms.

1798   4. 1798 The first boiling works was opened on Cape Barren Island, where they collected over 12500 seal skins and 3000 litres of seal oil for export to China

1799   7. 1799–Government broom factory opened with 1 man making 6 dozen brooms each week

1800   8. 1800 Linen manufacturing on the Hawkesbury from locally grown flax

1800   9. 1800 House of Industry, the women's section of Parramatta Gaol and later, the Female Factory made linen and other clothing items (hats, slops, blankets)

1801   2. 1801 All coal and timber declared by Governor King to be property of the Crown

1801   3. 1801 Robert Campbell shipped coal to Calcutta and Cape of Good Hope

1801   5. 1801 Robert Campbell exported 100 tons of Hunter Coal to Calcutta and 100 tons to Cape of Good Hope.

1801   6. Although colonial trade in sealing, whaling, sandalwood and trepang (sea slug) was well underway by 1806, export was still hindered by the British Navigation *Acts* and the East India Company monopoly.

1802   **5. Whaling** (1802)

1803   **6. Boat building** for hunting whales

1803   2. 1803. First newspaper (*Sydney Gazette*) founded by Gov. King mainly for government orders and proclamations. The weekly was edited by ex-convict, George Howe.

1804   . By 1804 11 privately owned sloops were engaged in Bass Strait sealing

1806   4. Between 1800 and 1806, over 100,000 seal skins landed in Sydney

1807   10. 1807 Samuel Marsden took first cask of cross-bred wool to England for testing.

1810 7. In 1810, Wentworth, Riley and Blaxall signed a contract to build a new main hospital in the settlement in exchange for a monopoly on import of spirits

1812 8. 1812, first wheat purchased by NSW from VDL

1813 11. 1813 First crossing of Blue Mountains

1813 9. 1813, Scarcity forced corn prices up from 5/–a bushel to 15/–per bushel. And wheat from 6/3 to £1/8/-

1814 10. 1814, nearly 15,000 kg of wool was exported

1815 10. 1815 Steam powered flour mill

1816 12. 1816 Botanic Gardens in Sydney developed

1816 13. 1816 First wheat grown near Bathurst

1820 11. 1820 Local paper mill supplying all material for publishing *Sydney Gazette*

1820 12. 1820 carriage and harness making in Sydney

1820 14. 1820 First dairy industry established in Illawarra district

1823 14. 1823 Commissioner Bigge recommended Newcastle coalfields be privatised

1824 13. 1824 Sugar made from local cane for first time

1824 5. 1824 AAC company opens up 1 million acres

1824 3. 1824 The weekly *Australian* first appeared owned by W. C. Wentworth and Robert Wardell. It was published without a licence. It was printed until 1848

1826 4. 1826. The *Monitor* was first published by E. S. Hall, who became an antagonist of Governor Darling and spent numerous times in gaol.

1830 7. By 1830, 17 ships operated from Sydney, and by 1835, 76

1830 . In 1830, NSW exported £60,000 worth of whaling & sealing products with wool at £35,000. By 1835, wool had overtaken fishery products. By 1841 whale oil exports peaked at £150,000 p.a.; by 1850, this had declined to £28,000. The decline was accelerated by the gold rushes which caused a shortage of labour for the whaling ships. In 1851, the whaling stations in Mosman's Cove closed. By 1853, exports from NSW had fallen to £16,000

1831 Whaling stations established in NSW (1830), Victoria (1831) and S.A.(1837)

1838 14. By 1838, NSW had 2 distilleries, 7 breweries, 12 tanneries, 5 brass and iron foundries, 77 flour mills and single factories producing salt, hats, tobacco and other goods

1839 15. In 1839, Australian Sugar Company formed in NSW

1839 6. 1839 Gold discovered but kept quiet

1841 10. By 1841 there were 41 bay-whaling stations in Tasmania. In the 1840s, over 400 vessels were built in VDL boat-yards

1841 7. 1841 Silver-lead ore discovered in Adelaide and 10 ton exported to Britain

1846 8. 1846 Tin discovered in S.A.

CHAPTER 12

GOVERNMENT BUSINESS ENTERPRISES IN NSW 1802-1835

Government business enterprises commenced from close to day one of the settlement in 1788. We can define them as government operated, financially supported and for the direct benefit of the colony as opposed to an export facility. The very first public enterprise was that of farming to raise food, supervise the few head of livestock that had arrived alive in the colony. \Public farming kept the colony alive for the first few years before private farming based on selective land grants commenced.

The role of the commissariat in government economic planning

The commissariat had two key roles. It was an important economic driver and acted as a quasi-treasury to the colony for the first 30 years, until the B of NSW opened in 1817.

Detailing the Enterprises

The main enterprises commenced with the need for food production but shortly after moved onto the need for construction work, building materials and an export staple.

Introducing the Colonial Economy

The colonial economy was destined to grow in response to increasing population, the development of an infrastructure to underpin the colonial growth and living standards and the need for import replacing activities, in addition to the goal of creating an export market

Convict management

With few free settlers to fill the role of supervisors, and the military abdicating their duties in this respect, the job of convict supervision was left to the best behaved convicts. This was a generally unsatisfactory position. The most prominent principal convict managers were Majors Druitt and Ovens, who were the first the reform convict work practices and set goals and plan targets for the convict workers.

Manufacturing in the commissariat

From the public business enterprises and the necessity of finding export staples, a secondary industry grew in the colony. Invention really was the mother of necessity. A secondary industry commenced in export replacement areas and spread to those areas of continuing need, such as agricultural equipment as that primary industry got underway, then onto manufacturing on behalf of British industries wanting to have a presence in the colony.

Operating and managing the government farms and the public enterprises

There was continual growth in the public farming and manufacturing areas for two reasons. The number of convicts arriving in the colony increased each month, so there were more mouths to feed, and more men to put into productive work. So output increased naturally but then so did the public works program, that kept the business enterprises operating, and then diversity of manufacturing commenced which meant more technical production and output. Much of this flowed to the private sector having been first established in the Lumber Yard.

Accounting and Finance in the public enterprises

The commissariat system after 1822 attracted many convict clerical assistants, so the bookkeeping indulgences were endless. Sadly few of these records survive, but we know that orders from government departments for supplies and the public works department for materials were prepare, whilst the commissariat and lumber yard used issue dockets to account for supplies transferred. The main accounting was not the number of inventory items made or issued in the commissariat but the money it was spending. Bills drawn by the commissariat supposedly reflected the amount of value going through the commissariat as opposed to the raw materials used the convict output or the value of materials issued on account of public works.

Measuring the economic impact of the enterprises on the economy

This will be the most difficult chapter to prepare. We will have to assess the GDP annually for the colony from 1800, and try and indicate what part was generated by the business enterprises. This will have to be done on an industry by industry basis to estimate the items of output the number of convicts in use for each item of manufacture and compare it with the gross GDP. The problem with this methodology is that most items produced by the commissariat enterprises had no value due to the convicts having no value as labourers and raw materials have no assigned value, thus convict output had no value.

INTRODUCTION TO GOVERNMENT BUSINESS ENTERPRISES

From its commencement in 1788, the aim of the Colony of New South Wales was self-sufficiency even though it had been set up to solve the problem of Britain's overcrowded prisons. By 1823, the British Government had decided that it would limit its direct expenditure to the transportation of the convicts and their supplies while in transit; the Colonial Administrators would be responsible for the convicts' security, food, clothing and accommodation in the Colony. Furthermore, proceeds from the sale of Crown land were to be the exclusive reserve of the British authorities rather than the colonists. The Governors were therefore forced to look for ways in which the Colony could help to support itself through working the convicts to create food, minerals (e.g. coal production), roads, housing and public buildings. Other convicts were assigned to landowners on a fully-maintained basis, thus saving the British Treasury a great deal of money.

This policy of maintenance of convicts by the Government created the need for an accounting by the Colony to the British Parliament. This led to the appointment in 1824 of a Financial Controller/Colonial Accountant to prepare monthly and annual despatches to the British Colonial Secretary. Following self-government in 1856, the procedures changed as the Colony became fully responsible for its own economic planning and fiscal management.

A Brief Overview of the Government Store

The first storekeeper arrived with Governor Phillip and the First Fleet. Andrew Miller had been appointed whilst the Fleet was preparing to sail, initially to take responsibility for the loading and recording of requisitioned stores. Upon arrival in Sydney Cove, Miller's first task was to erect a stores tent, secure it as far as possible, and commence unloading from the ships the stores that would be required during the first few weeks. These stores and provisions included such items as tents, pots and cooking utensils, blankets, hospital equipment and supplies and tools for clearing the land and erecting tents. Little was known about local conditions and Phillip's plan to have a wooden storehouse built within a few weeks could not be accomplished. He had tried to anticipate a wide range of obstacles and challenges, but encountering a difficult landscape and understanding characteristics of the local forestry proved the most difficult of all. In their various reports, Cook, Banks and Matra all praised the local timbers after only a cursory evaluation but, with no expertise amongst his crew or the convict population, Phillip's task of clearing timber and using it for construction was almost impossible.[199]

Upon their arrival, Phillip relied on Miller to operate the most basic of stores and without burdening him with limiting rations as he anticipated that the second Fleet store ships would be carrying provisions for the next full year. Miller's biggest task was the security of the provisions; the remaining items were then to be unloaded so that the ships could return to naval service. Phillip later prepared a rationing program for Miller so that the provisions would last six months, the time Phillip thought the Second Fleet was behind his own.

The stress of establishing the commissary for the new settlement and acting as private secretary to the governor eventually broke Miller's health and he wanted to return home. However, he was not to see his home again; he died during the sea voyage back to England.

Miller's successor, John Palmer, had sailed as purser aboard Phillip's flagship, *Sirius*. He had joined the Navy at the age of nine and participated in a series of voyages to many parts of the world, including North America where he married into a wealthy colonial family. After the founding of the colony, and with the expectation that he would soon return to England, Palmer sailed with the *Sirius* to the Cape Colony and Batavia on a mission to purchase food for the struggling, and hungry, colony of NSW. Whilst shipping provisions from Sydney to Norfolk Island, the ship struck an

---

[199] Cook & Banks had written positively (and subsequently amended by Beaglehole) about the lush landscape to be found at Botany Bay, and James Matra (another Cook crewman) extended this interest in local timber to its use as a trade item between the colony & Britain, when Matra submitted his recommendation of the use of the new land as a penal settlement. Refer also Beckett: 'Reasons for the Colony' in *British Colonial Investment in the Colony 1788-1856*.

uncharted submerged rock just southeast of the Island and sunk. Palmer was saved, but the *Sirius* and its cargo was lost and Phillip found a new posting for Palmer in Sydney, replacing Miller as chief store-keeper. It was a further seven years before Palmer sailed for England, but he soon returned to the colony with his wife and sister, Sophia. The Palmer family became financially secure with a magnificent walled estate, carved from the rocky terrain of Woolloomooloo Bay, just east of Farm Cove. Sophia was to shortly marry Robert Campbell thus forming a most strategic alliance between the colony's first successful trading house (Campbell & Co, the chief supplier of stores to the colony) and the chief procurer of provisions for the colonial store (John Palmer).[200]

Governor Phillip was active in most facets of the initial colonial administration, especially the planning for the new settlement and the difficult challenge of feeding the people. He found the soil conditions around Sydney Cove were unsuitable for vegetables, grain and fruit. The vegetable patches located in the Governor's Domain failed to provide the produce desired, and Phillip was constantly looking for new, more fertile, locations. Travelling up what was to become known as the Parramatta River; he located more fertile soil, and what appeared to be a suitable clay reserve, on the south bank of the River; he named the area Rose Hill. Phillip planned a new settlement at the head of the river which he named Parramatta. Phillip recorded that, 'the soil is more suitable for cultivation than the hungry sand covering the hills near Sydney'[201.] It was imperative to grow food as quickly as possible and Parramatta offered the additional advantages of a constant supply of fresh water and a means of transporting food by boat rather than having to build building a road.

During the Palmer administration of the stores, new settlements had to be served in addition to Norfolk Island established in 1789. Settlements were developed and serviced by branch stores in areas such as Hobart (1802), Port Dalrymple (later Launceston, 1802), Liverpool (1803), Hawkesbury (Windsor, 1802) and Bathurst (1814). The role of the main store in Sydney was constantly changing as was its location. All the stores

---

[200] Refer: Margaret Steven '*Merchant Campbell1769-1846*' and Beckett '*John Palmer—Commissary*'

[201] HRNSW Vol 1, Part 2 p469 (Despatch by Governor Phillip to Hon W. Grenville)

required personnel and organisation as well as a good supply of clerical assistance and many of these roles were set-aside for trusted convicts and ticket-of-leave men. The reason for the use of convicts in a sensitive and secure area of government was straightforward. As Butlin has established, the cost of convict labour was a charge against the English Treasury and not included in the appropriation to the colony, so the use of convicts as workers for the government kept government civil salaries understated and artificially low. It was Commissioner Bigge who reviewed the workforce and, observing the number of convicts employed within government and thus civil service ranks, became aware of the understatement of costs in the colony. Butlin adds, 'as public employees, a great deal of convict labour was engaged on farming and public infrastructure construction and thus avoided being charged as a direct cost to the colony. It was more convenient, however, to transfer them into the labour market.'

Butlin described the functions of the Commissariat in the following terms.

'The (British) Treasury described the commissary as one that 'keeps in the stores and issues provisions, fuel and light for the use of the service abroad'. Such a formal description fails to capture many of the crucial features of the Australian Commissariats and their subsidiaries. In addition the commissary in NSW became a source of foreign exchange and of local instruments of exchange. They were, at once, banks and credit agencies, and a springboard for banking enterprises. They were also the instruments for encouraging and reallocating productive activity for regulating staple prices and subsidies to such an extent that they have been perceived as 'staple markets'. The commissary also became the means for making supplementary allowances to officials, for compensating persons for performing public services for which no British appropriation existed or for totally funding some other public services. Through rations distribution, they effectively paid workers engaged in convict gangs on public infrastructure. [202]

---

[202]   Butlin, N.G.' What a way to run an Empire, Fiscally' p52

That the commissariat operations reflected the changing needs within the colony is evidenced by its regular reorganisation. Until Macquarie's arrival, there had been stability in the organisation structure and only two commissaries had been appointed: the basic operations of victualling convicts and selected settlers had remained constant, as had the provision of tools and equipment to convict work parties. Under Macquarie, the expansion of services provided by the commissariat had grown disproportionately and into relatively uncharted areas. He recognised the need for banking and financial services in the colony but, when his proposal for a chartered bank was rejected, he imposed that role on the commissariat. Likewise, the growing intake of convicts into the colony led to vast organisational limitations on government, and thus these tasks were assigned to the commissariat.

The demand on the commissariat was always significant and varied according to the number of convicts arriving in the colony, which in turn depended on the military and economic circumstances prevailing in Britain and Europe. On 1 February 1793, only five years after the First Fleet arrived in Botany Bay, Britain was at war with France, the Napoleonic Wars that dragged on until 1815. There were several important consequences: the attention of the British Government was distracted [18] away from the affairs of an insignificant and distant colony (Botany Bay); transportation of convicts more difficult and less necessary; the flow of free immigrants to the colony was reduced even further; and it enabled a small group of elite military officers stationed in the colony to create a monopoly position. In spite of the *Navigation Acts,* the war in Europe provided an excuse to develop trade between the British colony and the American colonies, although it was one-sided in favour of the American shippers.

Heavy economic commitments to the war in Europe and a downturn in the British economy from 1810-1815 led to constant pressure from the British Government to reduce expenditure in the colony. The Colonial Office in London thought this could be partly accomplished by moving people 'off the store' and reducing expenditures on public works. Both of these alternatives affected commissary operations. Apart from foodstuffs, the commissary mainly bought timber for building, leather for boots and shoes, wool (hair) for blankets and supplies such as barley for brewing beer.

The commissariat received supplies from four general sources: imports, government farms and workshops, civil and military officers and private individuals. In some matters, the commissary strongly supported private enterprise–for instance the area under grain on government farms never rose above 10% of the total farmed land in the settlement and by 1808 this was insignificant[19]. Similarly, government cattle numbers, notwithstanding the lost herd later found in the Cow Pastures at Camden, represented a decreasing proportion of total cattle numbers in the colony, falling from 70% in 1800 to 12% in 1814, whilst government sheep numbers fell from 10% to 2% of those in the colony in the same period.

The third Bigge Report provides an important insight into Commissariat activities. Commissioner John Thomas Bigge, a former Chief Justice of the West Indies colony of Jamaica, was appointed by Lord Bathurst to visit the Colony and assess progress and to evaluate the growing expenditures of Governor Macquarie. The instruction to Commissioner Bigge read in part: 'you will inquire into the courts of justice, the judicial establishments and the police regulations of the colony[203]. You will also turn your attention to the question of education and religious instruction. The agricultural and commercial interests of the colony will further require your attentive consideration. With respect to them you will report to me their actual state and the means by which they can be promoted.' Bathurst added:

I would more particularly refer to the authority, which the governor has hitherto exercised, of fixing the prices of staple commodities in the market, and of selecting the individuals, which shall be permitted to supply meat to the government stores. With respect to these regulations, you will investigate how far their repeal is likely to lead to any general inconvenience, or to any public loss. I am aware that when the colony was first established the necessity of husbanding the scanty means of supply and of regulating its issue, might justify an interference on behalf of the government; but now that the quantity of land in cultivation is so much increased, and the number of cultivators enlarged, I confess I have great reason to

---

[203] The first two paragraphs of Earl Bathurst's letter of 6th January 1819 to J.T. Bigge have been summarised for purposes of expediency
The full instructions from Bathurst to Bigge and the correspondence from Bathurst to Sidmouth are printed

doubt the expediency of these regulations; at the same time I feel unwilling to recommend so material an alteration without some examination on the spot as to its probable effects.

A second letter of the same date and also from Earl Bathurst directed J.T. Bigge to consider the suitability of Sydney town as the main recipient of convicts and the opportunity of:

'forming on other parts of the coasts, or in the interior of the country, distinct establishments exclusively for the reception and proper employment of the convicts, who may hereafter be sent out. From such a measure, it is obvious that many advantages must result. It would effectively separate the convict from the free population, and the labour of forming a new settlement would afford constant means of employment, including that of a severe description. By forming more than one of such separate establishments, the means of classifying the offenders, according to the degree of crime, could be facilitated. But on the other hand, you will have to consider, what would in the first instance, be the expense of the measures, and what may be the probable annual charge which may result from their adoption.'

Earl Bathurst, in a separate note [2046] to Viscount Sidmouth dated April 1817, set out his concerns of the mixing of convicts with free settlers and the problems resulting from ever increasing numbers of convicts being transported [205]. He wrote:

'Another evil resulting from the increased number (of convicts transported), is the great difficulty of subjecting any of the convicts to constant superintendence, either during the hours of work or relaxation; and the necessity of leaving a large proportion of them to the care of providing their own lodgings during the night, from the inadequacy of public buildings allotted to their reception, forms one of the most formidable objections to the current system.

---

[204]   *with the third report by Bigge to Westminster, as presented to the House of Commons in February 1823*

[205]   Ritchie, John *Punishment and Profit*

I intend to place the settlement on a footing that shall render it possible to enforce strict discipline, regular labour and constant superintendence, or the system of unlimited transportation to New South Wales must be abandoned. I propose the appointment of commissioners with full powers to investigate all the complaints which have been made, both with respect to the treatment of the convicts and the general administration of the government'.

In his instructions to Commissioner Bigge, Bathurst had recognised the impact of over-regulation and enforced pricing of goods sold to the government stores. However, the commissariat (or Government store) relied on imports for its grain and meat supplies and, until 1800, to a lesser extent on the private sector. From 1804, grain was in reasonable supply, except in periods of drought, floods and disease, and was grown mainly by the small settlers. Cattle and sheep raising tended to be in the hands of the military and civil officers and other settlers with larger holdings. The government set basic prices for commodity purchases by the Stores, but these were often exceeded because of the general shortage of labour[206]. The governor set fixed prices for the commissariat for grain but the settlers found they had to sell at lower rates to influential middlemen, who then obtained the fixed price. This group had influence over what supplies the stores would buy and from whom. According to Linge [207,] a similar clique 'was able to buy up ships' cargoes and resell them at ten times the price and more' After 1800 Governor King tried to break the monopoly position of these groups (mainly officers) but his efforts brought only temporary relief to small settlers, many of whom were in debt.

The difficulty of changing the role and activities of small farmers was that the vast majority was ex-convicts with little literacy and certainly neither the knowledge nor capital to improve their farming techniques or buy stock and equipment. In Van Diemen's Land, Lt-Governor Sorrell lent small operators a bull or ram from the government herds and flocks for breeding purposes in an endeavour to improve the herd and provide some small assistance so these operators could acquire breeding livestock. Such

---

[206] Fletcher, B.H 'The Development of Small-scale farming in NSW under Governor Hunter' JPRAHS, 50 pp 1-8
[207] G. J.R. Linge 'Industrial Awakening'

arrangements was not extended to or followed in the colony of NSW although Samuel Marsden, a leading practitioner of flock improvement in the colony, did loan some special rams to neighbours and parishioners around Parramatta. The record shows Governor Darling loaned 'cows' to small farmers although this was a strange way of increasing the private herds rather than the public herds.

Commissioner Bigge[208] reported:

> 'Clerks in the Commissariat department generally consist of persons who have been convicts, and also of persons who are still in that position, but who have received tickets of leave. They receive pay, differing in amounts from 1s 6d to 5s per day, and 'lodging' money; they likewise receive the full ration, and a weekly allowance of spirits. A system must be installed that reduces the perpetual temptation to plunder from the necessary exposure of public property. It is for this reason recommended that public rations of bread should be baked by contract (at a potential savings of 1/6th of the flour used); Private contracts (let under the tender process) to supply the hospitals with bread, meat and vegetables have proven to be of advantage to those establishments; both changes result in considerable savings to government'.

The report confirms that in 1820, those victualled in NSW numbered 5,135 to whom 7,027 rations were issued daily (some convicts were on 1½ regular ration because they were considered to be in heavy manual labour). In total, the numbers victualled, including military and civil officers, rose from 8,716 in August 1820 to 9,326 in December 1820. Bigge reported 'I see no reason for not applying the former rule by which the rations of those officers whose salaries exceeded £90 per annum were taken away. I recommend that they be taken off the stores and a compensating amount be paid to them from the Colonial Police Fund.'[209]

The British Government constantly reminded colonial governors of the growing cost of running the colony and the need to take people 'off the

---

[208] Bigge, J.T. Report # 3 Agriculture & Trade in NSW (1823)- p.132
[209] Bigge, J.T. Report # 3 Agriculture & Trade in NSW (1823)- p.149

stores'. During 1800-1803 more than 2000 convicts were transported, adding to the number dependent on the store: there was also a significant increase in the number of small farms allotted, mainly to the growing number of convicts whose sentences had expired. At that time, a small 30-acre land grant, achieved at least three benefits for the new owners: they generally improved his social status (and therefore their mindset towards crime and property ownership); they were taken off the stores and told to be self-sufficient; and they became eligible to sell produce to the store thus becoming an important cog in the colony's food chain.[210]

In his 'Working Paper', Butlin offers some interesting numbers with respect to the growth in farming activity, for the period 1800-1810. 'Excluding the holdings of civil and military officers, the number of farms grew from 400 in 1800 to 600 in 1804 and 700 in 1807. Thus, even though grain production had reached a reasonably satisfactory level by 1804 and 40 new farms were coming into production each year; the number of mouths to feed was increasing by only a few hundred annually at this time. However, meat remained scarce. Cattle were preferred to sheep because they were less prone to attack by wild dogs, thrived better in the wet and humid climate and were more suitable for salting down; whereas in 1801 the ratio was 6 to 1 in favour of sheep, by 1809 the ration was reduced to only 3 to 1'[11] The 'Epitome of the Official History of NSW' suggests the numbers of livestock in 1800 was 1,044 cattle and 6,124 sheep; in 1810 the number had increased to 12,442 cattle and 25,888 sheep; by 1821 cattle numbers had grown to 102,939 and sheep to 290,158[211].

This series of events before 1810 set the foundation for the future direction of the pastoral industry in the colony. Although there were troubling but isolated incidences of military officer domination of trade and profiteering, the colonial economy was growing and settling into a pattern of life suitable for self-sufficiency and growing independence and local governance. From 1811 to 1815, the pattern changed and turned into a commercial depression in the colony, brought about by a number of internal and

---

[210] Butlin, N.G 'What a way to run an Empire, fiscally' (Working Papers in Economic History (ANU)

[211] 'An Epitome of the Official History of NSW' compiled from the Official and Parliamentary Records of the Colony in 1883, under the direction of the Government Printer, Thomas Richards.

external factors. 'Sealing vessels were having to sail further to find grounds not already picked bare by Colonial, British and American gangs, and in 1810, news reached Sydney that the British Government had imposed a duty of £20 per ton on oil caught in the Colonial waters.'[212] Further, in England the price for sealskins fell from 30/-to between 3/-and 8/-. Between 1810 and 1812 the British economy suffered a downturn and the financial troubles, brought on by a long drawn-out war in Europe, were soon transmitted to NSW. Indian and English merchant houses called up debts and refused to underwrite further speculations and the British Government pressed the colonial administration to further reduce running costs [213]. Locally, the Commissariat's venture into money operations helped intensify the shortage of money in the settlement and, to add to these distractions; in 1813 local duties were imposed on sandalwood, sperm oil, skins and timber, whether intended for home consumption or export. The English Government weighed in with another cost cutting exercise by reducing the military numbers in the colony from 1600 in 1813 to 900 in 1815. Steven concludes that by 1815, 'Sydney's commerce had almost totally collapsed'[214.] She also suggests that one side benefit of the commercial downturn was that, because individuals and partnerships could no longer see easy openings in trade, commerce, land and livestock, they may have turned their attention to industrial activity, establishing a profitable base for further local production of manufactured items and import-replacement industries.[215]

In summary, one of the supplies carried by Governor Phillip on the First Fleet was a 'forge'. Such an item would have been considered necessary to make or shape a metal object by heating and hammering e.g. for use by farriers and vets, but for the First Fleeters' there were no horses and very little metal objects, so Phillip must have had a repair use in mind for broken axes, adzes, hammers etc. However, the forges were to come in handy later during the Phillip administration when, first Phillip then Hunter and finally King required small metal items specifically adapted

---

[212] Linge 'Industrial Awakening' *op cit*

[213] To these circumstances, Briggs and Jordan, writing the 'Economic History of England' adds the Malthus observations on a rising population (8% between 1808 and 1812) and the effects of the industrial revolution.

[214] M. Steven 'Merchant Campbell 1869-1846' p.136

[215] Steven *ibid* p.142

to colonial conditions. The local environment was much harsher than originally anticipated by Phillip when ordering supplies for the first voyage, and few items adapted well to the new surroundings. Thus it was time thought King to put the forges to good use. Ordering new supplies took at least twelve months before receipt, and the quality, of even the most expensive items was inadequate, so the decision was made to save time, to be in receipt of suitable items by making them locally. Obviously there were side benefits–'no direct cost' and thus a saving of foreign exchange; developing a local secondary industry and developing local skills.

This was the beginning of the network of government-owned and sponsored industries, other than public farming. The novel concept of government owned and operated farms, (as opposed to full privatisation) had been a bi-product of necessity undertaken by Phillip. Without public farming of grain, vegetables livestock and fruit trees, private settlers would not have been able to support the settlement's needs for many years. However it was not long before having gotten the basics of food production for the settlement, Phillip commenced the privatising approach, by making land grants to suitably enterprising emancipists and military officers who wanted an alternative to trading in speculative cargoes. Thus the scenario became one of a *directed economy*, the acceptance of prisoners as unpaid but supported labour, and the usage of that labour to underpin private and public farming. But farming also needed access to roads and public infrastructure, so some of the convict labour had to be set aside to make roads (really cart tracks, build barracks, build a water supply system and develop a system of public buildings as hospitals, churches, commissariat store and wharves, bulkheads around Sydney Cove, gardens etc. All this need stretched the usage of the few prison labourers, and Hunter appealed for further transfers.

A small settlement, struggling to feed itself, receiving significant number of prisoners, and being watched for every penny it spends, and therefore struggling to find an export commodity. Such an export can't be manufactured, but instead must be a primary or basic industry. Meat is not exportable, nor grain, since both are in limited supply, but natural resources are a possibility. The items that come to mind are timber and coal. These are always in demand in Britain, and Britain is the only available export market. Fisheries are explored but a local market exists for fish; however, seals are a multiple product source and their by-products of skins and oil are much in demand. Finally a staple capable of being exported from the settlement–an industry that is not too labour intensive and capable of employing a number of skills and of being associated with other industries. The shipbuilding and provisioning industries are young and in need of support. Visiting ships will also be supportive of these two industries. The commissariat can't get involved in these commercial type businesses, other than by providing financial services in the absence of a treasury. What the commissariat needs is some basic routine industry that is capable of employing a growing number of convicts and of producing a relevant product for the settlement. If the commissariat can't directly contribute to generating export income, it can contribute in another important way and that is to save on import expenditures, and that is exactly what operation is available. Instead of importing many standard items, why not produce them locally. If man hours were valued, and if raw materials were priced, then these items may well be more expensive that their importation, but the system does not work this way. In the mind of the British Treasury officials who make the rules, prison labour is not costed nor is extracted resources priced. So if other needs are identified, such as timber frames for housing, doors, windows, trusses for roofs, etc, then by matching supply and demand, the commissariat can meet production needs of all types of building products. This in turn will require a great deal of labour, up-skilling of many trades, a lot of supervision but most of all, a public works program can be got underway for little cost.

CHAPTER 13

INTRODUCTION TO THE PUBLIC FINANCE & THE REPORTING SYSTEM IN THE COLONY

BACKGROUND TO THE COLONIAL ACCOUNTING

Colonial Origins of Public Accounts

One goal of the Governor of the Colony of New South Wales in 1788 was to achieve self-sufficiency for the colony even though it was a penal Colony. By 1823, the British Government had taken the approach it would be limiting its direct expenditure to the transportation of the convicts and they're travelling food and supplies. The Colonial Administrators would be responsible for the convict's security, food, clothing and accommodation in the Colony. The proceeds from the sale of Crown land were to be the exclusive reserve of the British authorities, and not that of the colonists. The Governors commenced working the convicts for creating food, minerals (e.g. coal production), roads, housing and public buildings, and generally paying their own way. By 1796, other convicts had been assigned to landowners on a fully maintained basis, thus saving the British Treasury a great deal of money.

Such policy, of the Government maintenance of convicts, created the need for an accounting by the Colony to the British Parliament with the appointment of a Treasurer acting as a Financial Controller, who could prepare monthly and annual despatches to the British Colonial Secretary. Following self-government in 1856, the procedures changed, as the Colony became fully responsible for their own economic planning and fiscal management.

Colonial Accounting in New South Wales

The Colony went through two stages before adopting the standards recommended in the 1823 'Blue Book', which replaced the 'gaol' and orphan funds. These two phases were the Gaol and Orphan Funds pre-1810, and the Macquarie promoted Police and Orphan Funds of 1811-1821, which results were published quarterly in the Sydney Gazette. The 'gaol' fund was a record of funds raised by a surcharge on the citizens of Sydney town, as a means to complete the construction of the Sydney 'gaol'. The voluntary collections fell far short of the funds needed and a part-completed gaol required official support. Customs duties were imposed on imports, and the gaol was completed with Government monies, the fund was renamed the police fund. The orphan Fund started in 1802 accepted as its revenue the customs duties on spirits and tobacco and was later (1810) named the Orphan School Fund with the intention of creating a fund to erect the first school building in Sydney town. The advisory Legislative Council were appointed in 1823, and the first Appropriation Act was passed in 1832, even though, in the interim, the Governors were passing 'messages' of the financial condition of the Colony to the members of the Council.

Upon self-government in 1855, the government accounting procedures were again revised, since the Colony was now fully responsible for all its fiscal matters.

About this time, gold was discovered and license fees, duties on exports of gold and duties on the domestic conversion of gold were applied and helped fill the Treasury coffers.

This was a major step forward in Government economic planning. A limited deficit budgeting commenced at this time. Deficits were short term and recovered usually within 5 years, although the Colonial debt, mainly to overseas bondholders was kept very much in check after the surge of investment in railways and telegraph services.

The formal Federation debates commencing in 1888 were based around the role and adjustment to individual Colonial tariffs, their discussion in the Finance Committee of the National Debates, and their incorporation into the final Constitution of 1901. These trends from 1856 are to be discussed and analysed

Federation installed a new system within the structure of the new Commonwealth Treasury whilst the States revised their reduced revenue collection procedures and accounted for the grants (return of surplus) of revenue from the Commonwealth.

Federation brought further changes to the raising of revenues, whilst the largest expenditure of the Commonwealth became the return of centrally collected funds to the States. The advent of the Commonwealth Treasury improved once again the quality of recording keeping and brought into being the first Commonwealth estimates and National budgets. By 1901, the public finance mechanism had grown from a colonial exercise by appointed settlers to a fully charged Government instrumentality.

From the earliest records (HRNSW), certain conclusions can be drawn, and these can be set out as follows:

a. There was a wide range of duties and taxes imposed on the early settlers, especially on alcoholic beverages. The general rate of duty on spirits was 10 shillings per gallon, and on wine it was 9 pence per gallon. On tobacco the rate was 6 pence per pound, while timber attracted a rate of one shilling per solid foot. General Cargo attracted an ad valorem duty at a flat 5% rate.

b. There were also licenses and tolls. Hawker's Licenses sold for 20 pound, and it cost a settler 2 pence (tuppence) to go from Sydney town to the settlement of Parramatta. A country settler (in the Hawkesbury) paid One penny to cross the Nepean River Bridge at Windsor.

c. References to crown land sales were recorded in the 1825 'Blue Book', and based on the decree by George 3rd in a Proclamation on 25th March, 1825, that there was to be imposed a new charge on crown lands at the rate of One shilling for every 50 acres, to commence 5 years after the date of the original grant. To that date all crown lands had been disposed of by way of grants, and this rent was a form of back door compensation to the crown. In the official grant documents, the receiver of the land grant was given notice that further costs may attach at some future time to the land, and it was this opportunity that provided the Crown to raise this 'rent' charge on the land in 1825.

d. There was to be a Land-holders fee of Fifteen shillings per 100 acres of crown land reserved for each three years for free settlers, followed by a two shilling fee per 100 hundred acres redeemable after twenty years from purchase.

e. On the 18th May 1825, the 'rent' was changed, by order of Governor Sir Thomas Brisbane, to a flat rate of 5% of the estimated value of the grants, without purchase (as opposed to purchased land), to commence 7 years from the date of grant. 'Rents' on any 2nd and subsequent grants were payable immediately, without the benefit of the 7 years grace period.

f. The Table of Land Grants between 1789 and 1850 shows the substantial number of acres granted to settlers and we can conclude that the revenue sourced from 'rents' on Crown land grants could build into a considerable sum for the Crown in the future.

g. By Proclamation, also dated 18th May 1825, George III authorised the sale of crown lands at the rate of 10 shillings per acre, to a maximum of 4,000 acres per individual or a maximum of 5,000 acres per family. Payment was by way of a 10% deposit and four equal quarterly instalments.

h. The title pages to the 1822 'Blue Book' are entitled 'Abstract of the Net Revenue and Expenditure of the Colony of New South Wales for the Year 1822', which indicates (and as the detailed records also reflect) that all Colonial revenue and expenses were consolidated in the 'Blue Book'.

i. The Table of Civil List Salaries for 1792-1793 sets out the Governor's Salary at One Thousand Pounds. But in the 1822 statement of expenditures on the Civil Salaries, the Governor's Salary had increased to Two Thousand Pounds. By 1856 the

Governor's establishment was costing 15,000 pounds per annum.

j. In fact, the total of Civil List salaries in 1792 was only 4,726.0.0 pounds, but by 1822 the total had increased to 9,828.15.0 pounds, due to both individual salary increases as well as more people being placed on the Civil List.

k. The official 'Observations upon revenue for the Colony in 1828' (written by the Colonial Treasurer of New South Wales) makes an interesting point. It observes that the 'net colonial income' of the year 1828, as actually collected, is exclusive of sums in aid of revenue, which cannot be viewed in the character of income. This item is further defined as 'the proceeds of the labour of convicts, and establishments connected with them, being applied to the reduction of the amount of parliamentary grants for their maintenance'. In subsequent reports, 'receipts in aid of revenue' included items such as—'sale of Crown livestock; sale of government farms produce; sale of clothing and cloth made at the Female Factory at Parramatta; sale of wheat, sugar, molasses and tobacco produced by the convicts at new settlements such as Port Macquarie.

l. The total quantity of alcohol imported into and thus consumed in the Colony, even in 1828, and with a population in 1828 of only 37,000 people, of which adult numbers would be less than 25,000, was 162,167 gallons of spirits and 15,000 gallons of Colonial distilled spirits (distillation from sugar was prohibited in 1828, however, the high price of grain and the higher taxing of locally manufactured spirits became a natural deterrent). A final observation was made in the 'Blue Book' compilation of 1829 that the only duties imposed on spirits in that year was upon spirits imported directly from H. M. Plantations in the West Indies. So the British authorities received a double benefit in trading and duties.

m. The quantity of dutiable tobacco in 1828 was 136,748 pounds (compared to 91,893 pounds in 1825). The Government experimented with locally grown tobacco at establishments in Emu Plains and Port Macquarie with the result being 51,306 pounds produced. So the total consumption of tobacco in 1828 was over 4 Lb. Per head of adult population.

n. Shipping companies also paid lighthouse charges, along with wharfage. The growth of shipping, into the Port of Sydney, was so great that it meant that by 1828, the revenue from lighthouse dues, harbour dues and wharfage was over 4,000 pound.

o. In 1828, the postage of letters attracted fees, for the first time, and the official Postmaster collected 598 pounds for general revenue. This revenue grew rapidly so that by 1832 the amount of postage collected was 200 pound. Each colony imposed its own postage and printed its own stamps until Federation.

The commencement of sales of both crown lands and crown timbers increased general revenues to the extent that in 1828, the amounts realised were:

Sale of Crown Lands 5004.19.2
Sales of Cedar cut on crown land 744.15.11
Sales of other Timber 9365.11.4

The Governor imposed a fee of one halfpenny per foot for all cedar cut on crown lands. The 'Blue Book' makes the further observation that this charge 'has checked bushrangers and other lawless depredators by depriving them of ready means of subsistence by the absence of all restraint from cutting Cedar upon unallocated lands'. q. There was a major improvement in record keeping and reporting after self-government in 1855. The "Financial Statements of the Colonial Treasurers of New South Wales from Responsible Government in 1855 to 1881" provide a detailed accounting mechanism for recording classifications and compilation of budgets and reporting to the Authorities. They contain 'explanatory memoranda of the financial system of New South Wales, and of the rise, progress and present condition of the public revenue'.

The interest in this period (from 1822 to 1881) is that these records, of the 'Blue Book' and the printed Financial Statements of 1881, provide the first identification of the items included in the revenue and expenditures for the Colony. This historical data is relevant to understanding the social conditions in the Colony, the application of duties, tariffs, tolls and fees which embraced the essential revenue of a Colony that was designed to be self-sufficient and which was being given minimal economic support by the British Government, even though the opportunity cost of housing 'prisoners' in the Colony was a fraction of the cost of housing them in England.

Colonial Accounting in Victoria

The new settlement of Port Phillip adopted the standards set out in the Governor George Gipps Report on Government Accounting and Reporting after 1836 Public Finance following separation from New South Wales to form the Colony of Victoria. The Blue Book was more accurately kept in the new settlement (than in the colony of New South Wales) and full records are available concerning the commencement of the settlement and leading to the separation from New South Wales.

TABLE A

NEW SOUTH WALES PUBLIC FINANCE
ORPHAN, GAOL & POLICE FUNDS 1802-1821
REVENUE

Year	Opng Balances	Customs	Total	Works Outlay
1802	490			
1803	5,200			
1804				
1805	3,100			
1806	1,900			
1807	1,200			
1808				
1809				
1810	1,384	3,272	2,194	
1811	769	7,872	10,939	2,965
1812	5,016	5,579	13,494	3,259
1813	4,502	5,228	14,621	4,426
1814	6,016	4,529	13,325	4,993
1815	1,681	13,197	17,994	6,350
1816	3,327	11,200	17,782	5,582

1817	5453	16,125	24,706	7,048
1818	9363	17,739	31,008	6,219
1819	18900	22,579	42,968	17,131
1820	10725	27,891	44,507	14,700

Commentary on Table A

In 1876, the Colonial Financial Officer (the Treasurer–James Thomson), acting for the Colonial Secretary of New South Wales, wrote, in a report to the Imperial Government that "From the foundation of the Colony in 1788 to 1824, the records of local revenue and expenditure are too imperfect to render them of much value for statistical purpose, or for comparison with subsequent years."

However these figures, from Table A above, have been collated in the 'Historical Records of Australia–Statistics' from reports by the Colonial Governor to the British authorities and go someway to telling a story. The claim made by historian N. G. Butlin in his introduction to the Historical Records of Australia series–'The economy before 1850'–"that the British Colonial Office spent millions of pounds to start up the Colony"–does not seem to be verifiable. In fact exactly the opposite.

The British expected their colonies to pay their way

We know that the British authorities had the choice of building new prisons in Britain and housing, feeding, guarding and clothing these prisoners, or relocate them to a 'penal colony'. The previous penal colony in America was no longer available because of the American Wars of Independence and the British were no longer welcome there. The recommendation of Sir Joseph Banks, after his voyage to the southern oceans with Captain James Cook, was to use the land and resources available in the newly charted East Coast of 'Australia'. The favourable opportunity cost of this arrangement was enormous. Britain was fighting wars in a number of areas and had numerous Colonies to administer, and one more Colony; supposedly rich in potential rewards and able to be converted to self-sufficiency was most attractive. So, the opportunity cost was became one form of savings.

By 1824 the convicts were also paying their way (in opportunity cost terms) by removing coal from the ground in the Maitland area and using it for heating purposes. No value was ever placed on this work, or on the use of convicts as builders of roads, housing, barracks, storage sheds, port wharves, churches and government buildings. It would appear that the convicts earned their keep whilst the Colony paid its own way very quickly. The 'Blue Book' of 1828 states that there was revenue from the sale of convict produce such as 'coal, wheat, sugar, molasses and tobacco' but the value of convict labour was to remain unreported. Historians should recognise the value of the convict work as well as the opportunity cost of having transported the prisoners offshore, when an assessment is made of the 'investment' made, and the benefits gained by Britain in the new Colony of New South Wales.

The original estimate of direct gains by the British authorities from the original and continuing investment in the Colony of New South Wales was based on 5 (five) identifiable and quantifiable events, even though the convicts were assigned jobs on the basis of 'full keep'.

1. The opportunity cost of housing, feeding and guarding the convicts in the Colony compared with the cost of doing the same thing in Britain.

The original estimates, in this category, were based on an estimated differential of ten pound per head–an arbitrary assessment of the differential cost.

However recent and more reliable information has come to hand which gives further validity to a number of 20 pound per head per annum, compared with the original 10 pound per head per annum.

A letter to Under Secretary Nepean dated 23rd August 1783, from James Maria Matra of Shropshire and London assists us in this regard.

It was Matra, who first analysed the opportunity of using the new Colony as a Penal Colony; only his estimates were incorrect and ill founded. He had advised the Government that it would cost less than 3,000 pound to establish the Colony initially, plus transportation cost at 15 pound per head and annual maintenance of 20 pound per head.

In fact the transportation was contracted for the second fleet at 13 pound 5 shillings per head and Colonial revenues from 1802 offset annual maintenance.

However, Matra made a significant statement in his letter to Nepean, when he pointed out that the prisoners housed, fed and guarded on the rotting hulks on the Thames River were being contracted for in the annual amount of 26.15.10 per head per annum. He also writes that 'the charge to the public for these convicts has been increasing for the last 7 or 8 years' (Historical Records of NSW–Vol 1 Part 2 Page 7)

Adopting this alternative cost (of 26.75 pound) as a base for comparison purposes, it means that the benefit to Britain of the Colony over a twenty-year period increased from 140,000,000 pound to 180,000,000 pound. This calculation assesses the Ground 1 benefit at 84,000,000 pound.

2. Benefit to Britain on Ground Two is put at 70, 000,000 pound (again over a 20-year period) which places the value of a convict's labour at 35 pound per annum. Matra had assessed the value of labour of the Hulk prisoners at 35. 85 pound.
3. The valuation of convict labour in the new Colony should reflect the convicts not only used on building sites, but also on road, bridge and wharf construction. This would add (based on 35 pound per annum) a further 21,000,000-pound.
4. The Molesworth Committee (A House of Commons Committee investigating transportation) concluded that "the surplus food production by the convicts would feed the Military people and this, over a period of 10 years, would save 7,000,000 pound for the British Treasury.
5. The benefits of fringe benefit grants of land to the Military etc can be estimated (based on One pound per acre) at over 5,000,000 before 1810.
6. We learn from Governor King's Report to Earl Camden (which due to a change of office holder, should have been addressed to

Viscount Castlereagh as Colonial Secretary) dated 15th March 1806 that the Convicts engaged in widely diverse work. The Report itself is entitled

"Public Labour of Convicts maintained by the Crown at Sydney, Parramatta, Hawkesbury, Toongabbie and Castle Hill, for the year 1805

Cultivation–Gathering, husking and shelling maize from 200 acres sowed last year–Breaking up ground and planting 1230 acres of wheat, 100 acre of Barley, 250 acres of Maize, 14 acres of Flax, and 3 acres of potatoes–Hoeing the above maize and threshing wheat.

Stock–Taking care of Government stock as herdsmen, watchmen etc

Buildings–

- At Sydney: Building and constructing of stone, a citadel, a stone house, a brick dwelling for the Judge Advocate, a commodious brick house for the main guard, a brick printing office
- At Parramatta: Alterations at the Brewery, a brick house as clergyman's residence
- At Hawkesbury: completing a public school
- A Gaol House with offices, at the expense of the Colony
- Boat and Ship Builders: refitting vessels and building row boats
- Wheel and Millwrights: making and repairing carts

Manufacturing: sawing, preparing and manufacturing hemp, flax and wool, bricks and tiles

Road Gangs: repairing roads, and building new roads

Other Gangs: loading and unloading boats"

(Historical Records of NSW–Vol 6 P43)

Thus the total benefits from these six (6) items of direct gain to the British comes to well over 174 million pound, and this is compared to Professor N. G. Butlin's proposal that the British 'invested' 5.6 million.

However, one item of direct cash cost born by the British was the transportation of the prisoners to the Colony, their initial food and general well being. Although the British chartered the whole boat, some of the expense was offset by authorising private passengers, 'free settlers' to travel in the same fleet. A second saving was the authorities had approved 'back-loading' by these vessels of tea from China.

Only limited stores and provisions, tools and implements were sent with Captain Arthur Phillip, the appointed first Governor, and his efforts to delay the fleet until additional tools were ready was met with an order to 'commence the trip forthwith'. This turned out to be a mistake as the new Colony could only rely on minimal farming practices to grow a supply of vegetables and without the tools to scratch the land, remove the trees and vegetation, little progress was made. A potential big cost to the fledgling Colony.

i.   The 'Blue Book' accounting records as maintained by Governor Macquarie from 1822 includes a reference to 'net revenue and expenses' which suggests an offset of all revenues against all expenses, and would include as revenue certain convict maintenance charges, to be reimbursed by the British Treasury. Such reimbursement was accounted for and reported only once—in 1825, when it is recorded as a 'receipt in aid of revenue' that an amount of 16,617 pound 'the amount of the parliamentary grant for the charge of defraying the civil establishment'. Prior to and since that date, there are only reports of payments and outgoings to the civil establishment, military and other personnel, without offset from reimbursement.

ii. Other notations in 1825 include revenues from rentals of government assets (Government outsourcing and privatisation obviously started back in 1825) such as;

iii. Ferries 1584 pound

Toll gates 6554
Gardens 1835
Mill 1749
Canteen 910
Church pews 1296

The hire of 32 convict 'mechanics' raised 6853.27 pound

Slaughtering dues contributed 975.54 whilst duty on colonial distillation reaped 4901.30 pound.

The biggest revenue earners were duty on imported spirits (178,434 pound) and duty on imported Tobacco (21,817 pound)

i.   Even in 1822 the Colony was showing a small operating surplus. This surplus grew through 1828 until, other than for transportation of convicts to the Colony; the charges on account of the British Treasury were less than One Hundred Thousand pounds for protecting, feeding and housing nearly 5,000 fully maintained convicts. Against this cost, the charge for housing, feeding and guarding this same number of prisoners in Britain would have been substantially higher, since in addition to the 5,000 gully maintained convicts there were a further 20,000 being paid for by free settlers and used as supervised labour. Britain surely had found a cheap source of penal servitude for at least 25,000 of its former prisoners, and found a very worthwhile alternative to the American Colonies as a destination for its prisoners.

j.   Revenue from Crown Land sales and rents was used to offset Civil (Crown) salaries and expenses.

j.   It is probably incorrect, at this stage; to say that it cost Britain nothing or at best, very little, to establish and maintain the Colony, but it can be said that from 1822 the costs were limited to maintaining fewer and fewer convicts. But from these convicts great value in terms of agricultural produce, coal and other minerals was derived. Just in terms of coal for lighting, heating and power, the cost to the government of purchasing these items would have been substantial. The 'Blue Book' reflects the use of the coal as a cost rather than a gain as would be the accounting standard today.

k.   A final conclusion could be given that there are much more known records available for this period (the first One Hundred Years) than the author originally thought. The reproduction of the 'Blue Book' by the State Archives Office is a major step forward in understanding the economic challenges faced by settlers and convicts in the early Colony. The sourcing of material from the Blue Book unveils the financial statements and conditions of these early years. It is still considered that finance records of the period 1788 to 1822 are not re-constructible, but the author feels that a deep search through the microfilms forming the Joint Copying Project will provide information on the two Colonial operating funds of the period–the 'Police Fund and the Orphan Fund'. This is a challenge for another time.

An interesting observation is found in_'The Constitutional History of Australia' by W. G. McMinn (1979), referring to the post 1855 financial arrangements. On P 33 he records "Subject to the need for a vice-regal message, accepting that any locally (Australian Colony) initiated legislation of a money bill nature requires The Sovereign's ratification, the New South Wales Legislative Council was to have a general right to appropriate revenue from taxation, except for an amount of 81,600 pounds, the expenditure of which was to be in accordance with 'three schedules' to the Act; 33,000 pound for the salaries of those on the civil list e.g. Governor et al, the superintendent of Port Phillip and its judges and for the expenses of administering justice; 18,600 pound for the chief civil officers and their departments, for pensions and expenses of the council; and 30,000 pound for the maintenance of public worship.

The Sale of Waste Land Act of 1828 raised the minimum reserve price of crown land to one pound per acre, except that large remote areas might be sold at a lower price, and established a formula for the use of the land revenue; fifty percent was to be spent on immigration, the rest was to be expended by the Governor in accordance with British Government directives from time to time. The Governor was to continue to have power to issue depasturing licences and to make regulations for the use and occupancy of unsold lands, but the existence of the Sale of Waste Lands Act placed an important restriction on the colony by implying a prohibition against the Legislative Council legislating on these matters. The first directive on how the Governor was to spend a portion of the fund, enjoined the Governor to spend a proportion on Aboriginal protection and another on the roads; he was left free to hand any surplus over to the Council for appropriation; but it was made clear that the whole of the fifty percent was to be considered as an emergency reserve if the Council proved difficult". McMinn sheds some further light on the Crown Lands mystery but there still remains the question of whether, year after year, these funds were fully used or just included as a contribution to general revenue. It would appear that somewhere there is a firm directive from the British Treasury that the revenues from Crown Lands sale were to be used to 'offset' British costs of maintaining the Colony. The 'Blue Book' is evidence that as general revenues, these funds were already being used to pay for the costs of feeding, clothing, housing convicts, and we know they were specifically used to pay for 'sponsored immigrants', aboriginal 'protection', and now roads. The costs of the military establishment were charged against general revenues so in the quite large 'pot', nearly all Colonial expenditures were subsidised or offset by revenues from the Sale of Crown Land. Britain put its hand in the till only, it seems, to pay for the shipping and supplies costs of getting their prisoners to the Colony. After 1828, we know that convict production–both agricultural and mineral–went a long way to paying their expenses, so perhaps the British Treasury did in fact get off very lightly indeed, especially for the benefits it derived.

The vexing question of Crown Lands revenues still remains. It is apparent from the 'Blue Book' notations that this revenue was 'reserved' for specific allocation by the Crown and remained in the Colony as an offset against British Government fiscal obligations (e.g. Civil List salaries) until self-government in 1855. A relevant quotation from the 1887 Financial Statements of the Colonial Treasurer of New South Wales follows:

"Prior to the passing of the Constitution Act, the Territorial Revenues of the Colony belonged to the Crown, but upon that coming into operation in 1855, they were placed at the disposal of the local Parliament, and together with the taxes, imposts, rates and duties were formed into one fund, under the title of the Consolidated Revenue Fund. In lieu of the Crown Revenues thus given up to the Colony, an annual Civil List of 64,300 pound was made payable to Her Majesty out of the Consolidated Revenues of the Colony." What this means is that the British Treasury allowed the offset of all direct British payments made on account of the Colony against revenues raised by the sale, rent or lease of Crown lands. A theory promoted by the writer but hitherto before unable to be officially verified.

CHAPTER 14

GOVERNANCE OF PUBLIC FINANCE

Included in the appendix to the 'Financial Statements of 1887' is the record (by the Colonial Treasurer–James Thomson) that:

"The Financial System of the Colony of New South Wales is regulated chiefly by the Constitution Act of 1855 and the Audit Act of 1870, and in matters relating to Trust Funds and Loans by special Appropriation Acts of the local legislature.

The Imperial Act granting a constitution to the Colony of New South Wales was assented to on 16th July 1855, and became effective on the 24th November 1855. This Act provides for a Legislative Council (Upper House) and a Legislative Assembly. The Upper House members were to be nominated by the Governor, while the Lower House members were to be elected by inhabitants of the Colony.

"Prior to the passing of the Constitution Act, the territorial revenues of the Colony belonged to the Crown, but on that Act coming into operation in 1855, these revenues were all placed at the disposal of the local Parliament, and together with the taxes, imposts, rates and duties, were formed into one fund, under the title of the Consolidated Revenue Fund. In lieu of the Crown Revenues thus given up to the Colony, an annual Civil List of 64,300 pounds was made payable to Her Majesty out of the consolidated revenues of the Colony.

The Constitution Act also provides that the legislature of the Colony shall have power to make laws for regulating the sale, letting, disposal, and occupation of the wastelands of the Crown within the Colony; and also for imposing taxes and levying customs duties. All Money Bills must, in the first place, be recommended to the Legislative Assembly by message from the Governor, and no part of the Public Revenue can be issued except on warrants bearing the Governor's signature, and directed to the Treasurer of the Colony.

The Audit Act of 1870 was passed to regulate the receipt, custody and issue of public monies, and to provide for the audit of the Public Accounts. The Treasury is the Department entrusted with the collection and disbursement of the revenues and other public monies of the Colony. It is under the control and general management of the Treasurer and Secretary for Finance and Trade. The permanent head of the Department is responsible to the Minister for the efficient conduct of its business.

The revenue of the Colony is now to be classed under the following general headings:

1. Taxation
2. Land Revenue
3. Receipts for services rendered
4. Miscellaneous receipts

The main elements of these four categories items consist of:

a. Taxation
   1. Customs duties
   2. Excise duties
   3. Duty on gold exported
   4. Trade licenses

b. Land Revenue
   1. Proceeds from land auctions
   2. Sales of improved lands
   3. Rents and assessments on pastoral runs
   4. Quit rents

5. Leases of mining lands
6. Miner's rights

c. Services receipts, include:
1. Railway & telegraph revenue
2. Money orders
3. Mint charges
4. Gold escort fees
5. Pilotage & harbour fees
6. Registration of cattle brands
7. Other fees of office

d. Miscellaneous
1. Rents
2. Fines
3. Sale of government property,
4. Interest on bank deposits
5. Other general revenues

The revenue and expenditure of the Colony is increasing year by year in proportion to the prosperity of the people and the increase of population. This is naturally to be expected for as new lands are taken up and outlying districts occupied, demands upon the government for all those services which tend to promote the well-being of a community are constantly being made; and although these services when granted create an additional expenditure, there generally follows an augmentation of the revenue both from the sale and occupation of the waste lands of the Colony, and the larger consumption of dutiable articles"

When responsible government was established in 1855, the revenue amounted to 973,178 pounds (or 3.51 pound per head) and the population was then 277,000. In 1875, exactly twenty years after the introduction of responsible government, the population had increased to 606,000 and the revenue to 4,121,996 (or 6.80 pound per head)."

From the Government Gazette of 2nd January 1879, this condensed statement is taken:

REVENUE, 1878

Taxation Customs Duties	44,220
Duty on gold	6,898
Licenses	109,851

Land Revenues

Sales	1,915,466
Other	410,254
Services	1,183,582
Miscellaneous	172,907

TOTAL REVENUES for 1878 4,991,919 pound

An interesting observation on latter day government finance and government involvement in entrepreneurial activities is made by Trevor Sykes in his book, 'The Bold Riders' 1994–Chapter 14, Page 438:

"The Savings Bank of South Australia was formed in 1848 and the State Bank of South Australia was formed in 1896. By 1984 they had led stolidly blameless lives for 136 and 988 years respectively. In 1984 they merged to form a new, larger State Bank of South Australia.

The chairman of Hooker Corporation, Sir Keith Campbell, headed the Campbell Committee, set up by Federal Treasurer, John Howard, in 1979. The Committee delivered its report in March 1981. The Report recommended deregulation of the financial system, a part of a worldwide trend, leading to deregulation in the federal sphere in 1984 by Paul Keating. The Campbell Report recommended that, once the banking system had been deregulated to make it more competitive, there would cease to be any justification, on efficiency grounds, for continued government ownership of banks, so that if government banks were to remain, should be no more fettered or subject to government interference than private sector institutions undertaking similar activities."

The State Savings Bank of South Australia foundered and failed in 1989, only 5 years after deregulation and 140 years after its opening.

GOVERNANCE OF PUBLIC FINANCE IN THE COLONY
GENERAL OBSERVATIONS

On the origin and nature of the New South Wales Colonial Revenue:–

"The Revenues collected within the Colony of New South Wales, from its establishment until the commencement of the administration of Governor Macquarie in 1810, were raised in support of the 'Gaol' and 'Orphan'Funds respectively. The Revenue thus levied for, and appropriated to the Gaol Fund consisted of a Duty of 1s. per gallon on Spirits, 6d per gallon on wine, 3d per gallon on beer, together with a wharfage duty of 6d on each cask or package landed. These duties appear to have been first established upon the authority of Governor John Hunter R.N. during his administration in 1795-1800 and were the earliest sources of local revenue in the Colony.

The Revenue raised for the Orphan Fund was derived from fees on the entry and clearance of Vessels, and for permits to land and remove spirits–both first levied in 1800; from licenses to retail liquor and from a duty of 1.5% on goods sold by auction (first collected in 1801); from a duty of 5% ad valorem on all articles imported, the produce of countries to the eastward of the Cape of Good Hope (first imposed in 1802); from fines levied by the Courts and Magistrates; from fees from grants of lands and leases, and quit rents on crown lands (Quit rents ceased in 1805). Other than quit rents and crown land fees, all revenues were levied upon Colonial authority.

The following is revenue raised in 1805 (James Thomson reports that the records from 1805 to 1810 are 'imperfect')

1805 Revenues in Gaol and Orphan Funds:

Duties on Spirits 1569.11.3 Fees on Vessels, licenses 595.13.7 Ad valorem duty 531.10.3

Fines by courts 86.5.8

Revenue raised in 1805 2783.0.9

In 1810, Governor Macquarie changed the designation of these two funds to 'Police Fund' and Orphan School Fund. The designated revenues were split 3:1 into each fund. The Act 3 Geo IV c.96 of 1822 gave further powers of taxation to the Governor.

UNDERSTANDING THE PUBLIC ACCOUNTS OF 1810-1818

In preparation for understanding the Public Accounts of the Colony as printed by the Sydney Gazette between 28th August, 1810 and the 28th November 1818, and published under the authority of the Governor (Lachlan Macquarie), we must understand firstly the nature of the two Treasurers.

The Orphan Fund, whose official nomenclature is 'The Female Orphan Institution Fund' (a successor by name–change to the Orphan & School Fund) was administered by the Reverend Samuel Marsden, an Anglican churchman, who, as an official (principal) chaplain was on the Civil List for receiving an annual stipend or salary, as well as being the principal trustee and administrator of the Orphanage, the rector of St. John's Church, Parramatta, livestock trader, a marriage celebrant, a large land and livestock owner and a pastoralist, as well as self-appointed moral censor of the Colony. Marsden was also a magistrate at Parramatta–'the hanging preacher'.

That a conflict of interest is perceived is acceptable but the nature of the accounting process allowed the distinct possibility of misappropriation of funds. For instance the orphan fund was designated as being used for the operation of the Female Orphanage within an existing building in Sydney town, with a larger building to be constructed at Parramatta. However, we find that the orphanage farm sold produce in the amount of less than 1,000 pound during seven years. Marsden also 'sold' the labour or services of orphans for 310 pound during that period, and deposited that cash as revenue to the fund, instead of either dropping fees from people having to place children in the orphanage (usually 3 pound per head) or giving the money (or its equivalent in goods) to the Orphans themselves. The governor shared the import duties between the two funds so that the Orphan Fund received 17,649 pound and the Police Fund received 77,600 in funds or bills receivable during this period.

But Marsden acted with impunity in expending over 1,000 pound on expenses, repairs and improvements to St. John's church. At least this amount was recorded.

The frightening thought is that some of the higher, unexplained expenditures could well have been going into the Marsden personal fund and assisting with the expenses of operating his 4,000 head herd of sheep and cattle or of paying farm expenses for his 4,500 acres. The small 30-acre farm attached to the Orphanage cost 1,268 pound to run for seven years so it is reasonable to expect that Marsden's broad acres were costing a goodly amount to operate. His stipend of 150 pound per annum would not have stretched to paying farm expenses, especially with a wife and 5 children, 5 servants and 10 'assigned' convicts. He eventually became the largest sheep owner before 1819.

Without proper authorisation, the new orphanage building had cost 4,000 pound to construct. The original estimate to Macquarie (HRNSW) was 500 pound. This is just another example of Macquarie's extravagance, which could not be reined in, not even by Lord Bathurst. It demonstrates the deviousness that Marsden could show when he craved something badly enough.

It is questionable, as well, that the 45 orphans housed in the original buildings could consume a monthly average food bill, for meat (of 70 pound) or of flour (of over 50 pound). With meat selling at about or below 6d per lb, the supposed quantity of meat was unmanageable, in infants. It is possible that during the period, the butcher was being paid for extra sheep on the hoof going to the Marsden farm. The amount of firewood purchased was 278 pound, regardless of the available wood on the orphanage farm and the surplus labour available to the farm. Shoes and clothing, in the amount of 600 pound during the period from 1825, for the orphans suggests frequent new clothing items, whilst the monthly 'donation' to the orphanage matron of 5 pound made her the highest paid female in the Colony.

There were five 'charity' schools operating until Macquarie decided to bring them under the umbrella of the governor, leave the administration to Marsden but now using paid and supervised teachers and other staff. These schools paid over 2,000 pound in salaries to its staff plus a further 187-pound in school supplies, books during the period.

Darcy Wentworth's fiduciary responsibilities, as Treasurer of the Police Fund were marginally better but this is mainly due to his handling over 120,000 pound during his eight years as Treasurer. His areas of revenue raising were hotel and spirit licences, road tolls (mainly Sydney to Parramatta), auction and marketing licences, and the bulk of import duties.

Wentworth also had ample opportunity to salt some revenues away to his own use, although in the main his financial statements did not contain too many arithmetic errors. His main areas of expenditure were repair work and new work on the many streets and roads within the Sydney and Parramatta areas.

Wentworth was the Treasurer of the Police Fund as well as a Police Magistrate for the town, and the 'Commissioner' of Police, it was not surprising to find that all of his repair work was carried out by soldiers and police officers. The recapturing of escaped convicts was paid for handsomely and Wentworth again made most of these payments to police officers and soldiers. It may be questioned whether they were being paid more to guard to convicts or to re-catch them, after they escaped. So, if 'trading' was not the military people's forte, Wentworth remunerated them well with extra pay for services and assistance from within his bailiwick. Road repairs and minor new construction came to over 15,000 pound whilst new wharves came to 2,000 pound. His largest single item was for salaries to those many people not on the civil list. This amounted to over 53,000 pound during the period

For full details of revenue and expenditure of these two funds between 1810 and 1821, refer to the appropriate table of statistics, in the appendix.

The Funds available to Wentworth and the Governor from the Police Fund, at the end of 1818 was nearly 17,000 pound. Macquarie directed in 1818 that this amount be placed on deposit in the new Bank of New South Wales.

Macquarie's policies of improving the Colonial operations did work, as can be seen from the 'investment', from Wentworth's account, in new buildings and other contract work of over 25,000 pound.

In terms of revenue, the Colony increased its costs of living by over 173,000 pound in just 7 years. In terms of pounds per head per year, it is estimated that amount is equivalent to an impost of nearly two pound per head per year of additional duty, tolls, fees etc.

That Macquarie's successor, Sir Thomas Brisbane, as well as Commissioner Bigge, demanded full, proper and regularised accounting of all revenue and expenditures is reflected in the transfer to the 'Blue Book' system in 1822 and the appointment of a full-time salaried financial officer, for the Colony, in the same year.

THE ROLE OF THE COMMISSARY

(In The Operations of the Colonial Government)

Planning for a Commissary for the new Penal Colony was well under-way by the 1795, and was to be operated and managed along the lines of a naval purser's office. The Commissary was to be responsible for all purchasing, storage, payment and distribution of goods. Its purpose was to provision the convicts, civil employees, the military personnel, and their families.

However for a new colony, which had decided not to adopt a currency, the Commissaries role was made especially challenging. A currency is the traditional means of exchange. There would be no buildings initially available and only convict labour to work the stores in Sydney, Parramatta and the Hawkesbury area–'always unreliable and untrustworthy', said John Palmer the third Commissary.

The first supply ships arrived with the rest of the first fleet on the 26th January 1788 in Port Jackson. The unloading of bare essentials, such as tents and a few tools and minimal food was completed that day, but the balance of the supplies would be left aboard the Sirius and the Golden Grove until a storehouse was available.

Every carpenter available was busy with the building of barracks for the soldiers and military personnel, followed by a facility for the Governor and only then a storehouse. But first the land had to be cleared of trees and timber cut for the first makeshift buildings.

The first Commissary, Andrew Miller, had been handpicked by Governor Arthur Phillip, based on Phillip's past experience with Miller (as a seaman), rather than Miller's experience as a Commissary chief. Phillip had provided detailed instructions of how he wanted the operation performed. Phillip, in turn, had been given his instructions by the Lords of the Admiralty and the Colonial Secretary, and the most important of these were the overall goals:

- Keep the cost per head per day for supplies as low as possible
- Keep the number of fully victualled persons as low as possible
- Establish the Colony to be self-supporting as quickly as possible
- Put the convicts out to work to earn their keep (although this was a new and untried policy)
- Assign convicts to non-government masters on a full support basis (again, this policy was untried and untested–but one strongly supported by Phillip)

Phillip had transported the first One thousand convicts and military without loss of life or loss of property. He had brought the first animals for breeding into the Colony, all healthy and was assigning duties by the 28th January 1788 (2 days after arrival in Port Jackson or Sydney Harbour) for the general unloading of the animals, convicts and material supplies ready to commence his Colonial operations.

Convicts were set to clearing the ground for vegetable plantings and building sites.

Phillip decided that instead of relying on stores transported on an irregular basis from Britain, that he would commence a planting program to provide fresh vegetables and grain; fresh meat, fish and game and make it a happy colony in which to live and work. He did not plan, nor was prepared for the harsh climate and the periodic droughts and flooding rains, or the unhappy natives.

His goal of victualling the whole Colony for less than 14p per day was going to be difficult, but he could do it if some level of self–support could be accomplished. He had brought quantities of seed for planting, but his fears were that northern hemisphere soils and climate would be very different from local 'New Holland' conditions and his crops would fail or yields would be minimal. His first corn crop, however, returned his planting twenty times over (HRNSW), and he was pleased and hopeful of the future returns being plentiful. In fact, he wrote to the Lord Commissioners stating that 'this Colony will become the greatest investment ever made by the British'.

Phillip planned for other possible ways to reduce costs; such as reducing imports, commence an export trade, establish settlers on farming ground, establish remote settlements establish jobs and trades and build the necessities and Phillip thus went about his work, putting these plans into practice. He assumed, incorrectly, that the convicts and the military shared his enthusiasm and commitment to hard work.

However, his experiment with tobacco planting, and grains, other than corn and wheat, and even sugar was encouragingly successful.

He planned for another new settlement at the head of the harbour, near fresh water, and with boat access at high tide. Rose Hill, soon to become Parramatta, was to be established with convict and military quarters, a church, and some emancipist settlers. To this end he released convicts for good conduct, who were willing to marry, and provided them grants of good land, usually 30 acres, and an admonition to become self contained and sell their surplus to the Commissariat store. He did allow the emancipists to retain access to the Government store for a period of two years. He would, in the future, exchange settler's grain for Government–owned cows, to enable a breeding program to commence and further expand the likelihood of a successful colony.

His building and construction priorities changed. He saw the priority need for a hospital building, especially since he had a surgeon in his midst, and some of his convicts had been speared and even killed by the natives. So the barracks were completed and then the hospital and finally the storehouse were ready by early April 1789. Phillip wrote in his journal that 'the timber has one very bad quality, which puts us to great inconvenience; I mean the large gum tree, which warps and splits in such a manner, when used green, to which necessity obliges us, that a storehouse boarded up in this wood is rendered useless' (HRNSW)

David Collins, a military Lieutenant and Phillip's Private Secretary, wrote on the 5th April, 1788, 'As the winter of this hemisphere is approaching, it becomes absolutely necessary to expedite the buildings intended for the detachment, so, every carpenter that could be procured amongst the convicts was sent to assist, since as many as could be released from the transports were employed working on the hospital and storehouses.'

Collins recorded on the following day, the 6th April, 1788 'worship was moved indoors as divine service was performed in the new storehouse. One hundred feet by twenty-five feet were the dimensions of the building, constructed with great strength and covered in with thatching. But we were always mindful of fire since no other materials could be found and we became mindful of accidental fire.'

Obviously, the hospital was finished, the storehouse was complete, some female convict huts had been completed and the military barracks were well under way. Phillip's plan was now in full swing.

This first and temporary storehouse was built somewhere around the Sydney cove (at the top end of High Street, now George Street), where a landing wharf had been constructed and where the camp was getting into working order. Subsequently permanent storehouses were built nearer the hospital, using roof tiles instead of thatching, and connected from the landing area to the hospital past the storehouses via a convict constructed 'road'.

Andrew Miller, the first Commissary, grew sick and frail (during 1788), in the service of Phillip and asked to be returned to England. He died on route but was replaced as Commissary by his former assistant, Zachariah Clark, who had come from England originally as agent to Mr Richards the shipping contractor.

Collins reported on the 12th April, 1788 that the 'issuing of provisions, was in future, under Mr Clark, to be once a week.'

Lieutenant John Hunter, soon to be Lieutenant Governor of Norfolk Island, recorded in his diary for 5th September 1788, that 'because of some failed crops, rotting food, and a plague of rats in the storehouse, that the colony would need more stores and provisions than any Pacific island could supply, and he would dispatch the Sirius to the Cape of Good Hope, in order to purchase such quantity of provisions as she might be capable of taking on board; and that she should be made as light as possible for that purpose. In consequence, eight guns and their carriages were removed together with 24 rounds of shot for each gun, 20 barrels of powder, a spare anchor and various other articles. These were all put on shore at Sydney Cove. I was also directed to leave the long boat behind for use by the Colony. The master of the Golden Grove store-ship was also ordered to get ready for sea to take supplies, convicts and some military personnel to Norfolk Island.'

Phillip was obviously panicking about the shortage of supplies and the empty storehouse. The proposed settlements at Rose Hill and Norfolk Island and a ship to the Cape had almost emptied the first settlement at Sydney Cove, of people as well as provisions.

A number of storehouses had been established. The first, a temporary one at the Cove, now the permanent one near the hospital on the first Sydney town street—High Street (now George Street), the lumber yard store, the military detachment store and the naval store. Clarke was nominally in charge of all stores but was also assigned other duties with the Governor, and with the hope of cutting rations even further by only opening the regular store once each week, was obviously in charge of only empty buildings.

In October, 1788, Warwick Tench observed, in his diary that 'we have now been here over half a year and are becoming acclimatised, even if we lack the shelters thought necessary. Since our disembarkation in January, the effort everyone has made was to put the public stores into a state of shelter and security and to erect habitations for the hospital, convicts and ourselves. We are eager to escape from tents, where only a fold of canvas was between us and the hot beams of the summer sun and the chilling blasts of the winter wind from the south. Under wretched covers of thatch lay our provisions and stores, exposed to destruction from every flash of lightning and every spark of fire. A few of the female convicts had got into huts but almost all of the officers and all the men, were still in tents.'

In February 1789, the only free immigrant, James Smith, who had procured a passage from England on the Lady Penrhyn was placed in charge of the new storehouse at Rose Hill and was also sworn in as a peace officer, or special constable. Claiming to be a 'practical farmer', Phillip gave him a number of convicts to assist him in exercising his abilities. This was the first trial of the assigned convict system.

On the 18th March 1789, Collins recorded the first major theft of stores and provisions from the secured commissary. There were seven of the military, convicted of theft, undertaken over a period of some weeks, robbing the store of liquor and large quantities of provisions. Phillip made an example of these men, but to little avail, as later that same year another six soldiers were convicted and hung for doing exactly the same thing.

The Economic Role of the Commissary

Over time Phillip increased and improved the operations of the Commissary and planned to offset the effect of having no currency in the Colony by creating a barter economy. To aid in this plan, Phillip arranged that all goods received into the Commissary would be recognised and accepted by 'store receipts'. Payment for goods arriving by ship or purchases made from other ports and brought to Sydney town was done via official 'bills' drawn for payment upon presentation on the British Treasury.

By 1790 store receipts and the related official government bills formed the basis of the currency in the colony. The settlers would lodge their grain, wool, or meat with the store and receive an official receipt in exchange.

The receipt stated the recipient's name, type and quantity of goods and the price paid. Because they were backed by the Government, the receipts became an increasingly popular instrument of exchange. They could be transferred between parties in payment for a debt, exchanged amongst settlers in the course of trade and for products from the Government stores, redeemed for the equivalent in coin and banknotes, and through the commissariat, exchanged for government bills drawn on the English Treasury". Eventually when colonial banks became established, store receipts and government bills were accepted as deposits. In these early days, a store receipt was as good as cash and for many people, a lot more convenient." (Encyclopaedia of Australia)

The Final Volume (# 7) of Historical Records of Victoria (Vol 7–Public Finance) sets out some background of what was happening in New South Wales whilst Victoria was still part of the Port Phillip colony.

"New South Wales was one of only three of the Empire's colonies established at the expense of British taxpayers. Most British colonies were begun by trading companies or settlement associations, and were expected to be self-sufficient. The British Government was usually prepared to provide a civil administration and military protection, but wherever possible, these were to be funded from local sources. The commissariat was responsible for many of the early financial arrangements in New South Wales. From the beginning, practices had been highly unsatisfactory and allowed much corruption. The first fleet brought with it in 1788 only the most meagre of supplies of coin. This shortage of a circulating currency became increasingly acute. In the short term, the government used promissory notes, government store receipts, treasury bills, spirits and shipments of coins of various denominations and currencies to which varying values were assigned. All were part of a volatile and unstable money market."

Britain had, prior to the first fleet invoked its right to tax its dependencies. The loss in the 1770s of its valuable American colonies, the previous dumping ground for convicts, was directly attributable to these taxes. The Napoleonic Wars (1793-1815) almost beggared Britain, and ruthless experiments with new taxes and duties were tried in a desperate effort to meet national debts. Income tax was introduced in 1798, modified in 1805 and 1807 but discontinued in 1816. The unpopularity of direct taxation resulted in wider nets of indirect taxation, such as customs duties. The New South Wales experiment echoed some of these developments. But it became Governor Gipps' opinion (1838-46) that nowhere else was so large a revenue raised from so small a population." And this opinion is borne out by the official Treasury reports of the time (refer attached Statistics).

Marjorie Barnard in her fine work–'A History of Australia' (P327) reflects on the early workings of the commissary and the financial dealings it accommodated.

"The commissariat had charge under the Governor of all stores and provisions. It acquired locally produced supplies, but the importation of food, clothing and other necessities from overseas was the responsibility of the home office, or in emergency, of the governor.

The commissariat was the colony's store and it also became the financial centre of the colony, where all transactions were by barter or note of hand. The only note in which there could be universal faith was that issued by the commissary as a receipt for goods received into the store. This department was the quasi-treasury, so that when a colonial treasury was set up, the commissary remained for provisioning of the convicts and only withered away at the end of transportation. Large sums could only be paid by the commissary's notes, for these alone had credit behind them, and they had to be eventually redeemed by bills on the treasury."

R. M. Younger in his work 'Australia & The Australians–' writes (P78) "The only market for produce was the government store in the various farming districts, run by the commissariat under the ultimate control of the superintendent of public works. The governor fixed the price of grain, and it was left to the storekeepers to decide whose grain should be bought and who's refused. David Collins, former secretary to Governor Phillip wrote of this operation:

'The delivery of grain into the public storehouses when open for that purpose was so completely monopolised that the settlers had but few opportunities of getting full value for their crops. The ordinary settler found himself thrust out from the granary by a man whose greater opulence created greater influence. He was then driven by necessity to dispose of his grain at less than half its value. He was forced to sell it to the very man who had first driven him away and now whose influence was the only available way to get the grain into the public store.'

Such incident evidenced a fundamental weakness in the economy. Farming had to be expanded so that the community could become self-supporting; but since the demand was in fact small and inelastic, and since there was no export, a glut or a shortage could easily occur. Because of strictly limited demand the wheat acreage could not be expanded too greatly, yet when two bad years occurred, there were dangerous shortages, and the colony had to revert to imports.

The commissary store continued to be the centre of the colony's economy. A great number of the population were still victualled from the store; these included the military and civil list people and their families, together with settlers receiving land grants, whether expirees or free, for the first two years on the farm. And convicts unassigned or working for the government. The requirement that the military officers clothe, feed and house assigned convicts was not strictly enforced and so in 1800 Hunter's record must show that 75% of the population was victualled by the government."

The anomaly was that by 1813 a few Sydney merchants were exporting, even though the NSW Corps still dominated local business. Exporting had begun in 1801 with Simon Lord, selling coal, whale oil and seal-skins to the American boats visiting Sydney for the purpose of two-way trade; they brought moderately priced cargo for general sale as well as provisions and supplies for the commissary. Campbell, the biggest trader got around the British support of the East India Company having a trade monopoly with China by using French or American ships. Campbell had built a warehouse in 1800 supplying wine, spirits, sugar, tea, coffee and tobacco and a wide range of household articles However Campbell was additionally soon selling livestock, grain and merchandise to the commissary and private buyers, with the government spending several thousand pounds with his firm each year. He then entered the whaling and sealing trade and sent a trial shipment of each to England. This caused a dispute between the East India company on one side (pushing for exclusion), Sir Joseph Banks on the other (encouraging freedom of trade) and Simeon Lord, whose cargo had now been seized in Britain as contraband."

One of the charges made to Justice Bigge when he was sent to Australia to investigate and report on the Macquarie governorship, was to review the cost of operating the colony in terms of its original charter. It was of great concern to Lord Bathurst that the British Treasury in 1820 was still paying so much of the colonial operations.

So Bigge reviewed and commented on the high number of persons still victualled from the government store as late as 1823. An extract from his third report (dated January 1823) into 'The Nature of the Expenditure in the Colony' sets out his observations.

He writes that in 1821 the Civil list salaries amounted to 8,474.17.6 but those paid from local revenues, being the 'Police Fund'_amounted to 9,824.05.0. So it is confirmed that within 22 years of the Colony being established, it was substantially on course to paying its own way. In fact Bigge writes, that "some of the salaries included in the parliamentary estimate (the Civil List) have not been drawn in this, or in some of the preceding years but have been defrayed by the police fund of NSW, including two government school masters, six superintendents and the clerk to the judge advocate, all amounting to 500 pound.

The clerks in the commissariat generally consist of persons who have been convicts and also of persons who are still in that condition (being ticket-of-leave individuals). They are paid variously from 18d to 60 d per day, plus lodging money. They also receive the full ration. And a weekly allowance of spirits. Bigge recommended that to reduce the fraud on the commissary, along with the high cost to the public purse, that (a) all bread is baked by a variety of contractors in lieu of convicts, and (b) that contracts for the supply of hospitals with bread, meat and vegetables be also let. He likewise recommended that all meat to the King's stores be furnished by contract from the settlers at the price of 5d per lb. He reports that the number of provisioned convicts is constantly changing. For instance, the total number of people provisioned from the Sydney store on 30th December, 1820, was 9326, of which only 5135 were convicts unassigned."

Author's Note: As can be seen from the following table, the number of victualled convicts (and others) is surprisingly high, especially at the end of the last two periods (1810 & 1820). The Governor's were directed to assign convicts to settlers or military officers for assistance with farming operations; the intention was for the colony to supply its own provisions and stores. The settlers and officers were directed to house, clothe and feed all assigned convicts and take them off the public stores. However, by virtue of being in a special position in the colony, most civil list persons and military were still being supported by the public stores. Even emancipists or free settlers that carried out special duties (e.g. police constables) became entitled to support from the stores.

Number of people on Rations (number victualled from public store) between 1795 and 1820 were:

1795	1,775
1793	1,682
1799	1,832
1800	3,545
1804	2,647
1810	5,772
1820	9,326

(compiled from individual records in vols 1-7 HRNSW)

As Bigge's concluded "some rations were issued in higher allowance than decreed because of extra work or hard labour.

Government owned livestock is held at the Cow Pastures, Parramatta and Emu Plains. These facilities are operated by a Superintendent and 3 overseers, all paid by the police fund. In addition 75 convicts are employed as stockmen and general labourers. All these people in total draw 122 daily rations from the public stores. The cost of daily rations were estimated by Bigge at 4s 8d or 56 pound per annum, or nearly 4 (four) times the targeted cost.

There were also 451 head of wild cattle which had over the previous year run off from the holding areas, but were recovered in 1820 and used for public meat supply. In total, with slaughtered sheep and cattle from government herds, over 237,000 lb of fresh meat was supplied at a savings of 5,000 pound to the government. This still left 6,000 animals in the government herd, but the settlers were increasing their pressure on the Governor to buy only meat from the settlers and not use government herds for slaughtering.

Of the total colonial expenditure in 1820 of 189,008 pound, the cost of rations for troops, civil list and convicts amounted to 143,370 pound or 75% of the total expenditure. Bigge did report that the general expense of erecting buildings in the Macquarie years in the colony of New South Wales is lessened by the use of convict labour and locally found timbers and locally made bricks, tiles and stone. He suggested that the cost of local funds used for buildings would be better spent on clothing, and feeding the convicts and taking them off the public stores.

Reviewing the Official Records on the Commissary

The HRNSW contains numerous references to original records reporting the instructions on how to operate, or the anecdotal reports on how the commissariat operated.

Phillip wrote that 'It is planned that a quantity of provisions equal to two years consumption should be provided (written 1786), which will be issued from time to time, according to the discretion of the Superintendent, guided by the proportion of food which the country and the labour of the new settlers may produce.'

'Clothing per convict was estimated to cost 2.19.6 including jackets, hats, shirts, trousers, shoes'. Phillip further wrote that 'the type of clothing was not always suitable for the climate, and should be ready made rather than relying on the convicts to sew their own.'

He noted that 'The Sirius brought seed wheat and barley and four months supply of flour for the settlement, together with a year's provisions for the ships company,' and, 'Supplies of grain or flour from England will be necessary to maintain the colony until there is sufficient local crops in store rather than 'in the ground', because of grub, fire, drought and other accidents.' and 'I have directed the commissary to make a purchase (9th January, 1793) and have thus augmented the quantity of provisions in the colony to 7 months at the established ration.'

On 6th January 1793, Phillip recorded his opinion that the expense for the settlement projected for 1794 was 25913 pound for 5,500 people. With 3000 convicts this cost translated into a per head cost per annum of 13.14.0, (or approx. 9p per day) which he pointed out 'this sum cannot increase, but must gradually diminish.' This converted within the officially targeted allowance of 14p per head per day.

'Whitehall reported on 9th November 1794 that the stock of stores of provisions and ready-made clothing should now be sufficient for the settlement for one year.

With the quantity of clothing shipped in mid-1794, there would be a sufficient supply for 2,500 men and 700 women, according to the last official report of numbers.' Mr. Henry Dundas (British MP) insisted that the convicts should be made to wear the clothing for a full year.'

The Colonial Office insisted that 'Each ship was to carry supplies for the trip and for maintenance upon arrival, for both convicts soldiers and sailors.' (15th February, 1794)

King, as Governor of Norfolk Island on the 20th July 1794, recorded that the island had produced a second crop in sufficient quantity for storage for the next year.–being 11500 bushels + 4000 reserved for seed, stock, and the producing families.'

'Stores were ordered from the Cape of Good Hope for the settlement and the hospital on 22nd June, 1788 to be selected by John Hunter, as captain of the Sirius.

Governor Hunter submitted a plan on 10th June, 1797 saying that "were Government to establish a public store for the retail sale of a variety of articles–such as clothing, or materials for clothing, hardware, tools, sugar, soap, tea, tobacco and every article that labouring people require–supported by a reputable shopkeeper who should produce regular accounts and charge a small premium to cover these other costs, then the people would get what they wanted with ease, and at far less expense than in any other way."

Governor Hunter repeated his request for a public store on 10th January, 1798 "If my suggestion is adopted, a branch of the store should be placed on Norfolk Island. Such a store should lessen the expense of maintaining the convicts and the store; I would also suggest the retailing of liquor and spirits, for the purpose of putting a stop to the importation of that article."

Again on the 25th May, 1798 Hunter recommended "the public store as a means of controlling the high price of grain. Such a store would operate as an encouragement to industry. Without some form of price control on grain the settlers cannot live let alone provide for a family. The speculators and the monopolists all contrive to keep the settlers in a continual state of beggary and retard the progressive improvements of the colony." The success of Simon Lord's colonial merchandising in 1801 evidences that Hunter was on the right track with his 'public' store.

The Colonial Secretary wrote to Hunter in 3rd December, 1798 about the meat supply "when the livestock belonging to the crown, added to that of individuals, is in so flourishing a state as to supply the needs at 6d a pound or less, it is evident the Government will gain by supplying the settlement with fresh meat instead of sending salted provisions from England. This request was later modified to limit the store purchases for meat to those from farm settlers.

On 2nd February, 1800, William Broughton, a Churchman and Magistrate was also appointed to be the storekeeper at Parramatta to replace a man sacked by Hunter for fraud.

Governor King recorded his success in conserving the stores by writing that "since I took office, I have reduced the full rationed people relying on the public stores by 450. This has saved annually the amount of 10488 pound using the rate of 23 pound per head. I have also reduced the price of wheat to 8d per bushel, pork to 6p per lb, maize to 4s instead of 5s per bushel."

When Hunter was recalled to England, the Commissary was left with many debts owing by settlers. Hunter was concerned that these would be denied and he be held responsible. He wrote to the new Governor, King, 'I trust it is clear that there has been no lavish waste and no improvident use of the public stores during my authority. These debts are just, even though many of the individuals may doubt their being indebted to the Government for so much. It appears there were doubtful debts of over 5,000 pound due to the store.

In response King made demand on the settlers and accepted grain at a higher price than usual in settlement of the debt. When the public demands became known it also produced an unusual response from John Macarthur, who suddenly recalled that much of what he had taken from the stores, and charged against the public account, over the previous twelve months was in fact his personal responsibility and he settled with the stores on this basis.

King appointed a new head of the store on 7th November, 1800–A Mr Palmer. Other appointments included Broughton to Norfolk Island and Deputy Chapman from Norfolk to Sydney and William Sutter as Storekeeper at Parramatta.

In order to conserve grain, King reduced the ration to 13.5 lb of wheat per week per person.

Palmer, at the time of his appointment had been handed a set of instructions, which included the instruction that:

a. all troops and convicts in the territory were to be properly supplied and a stock of 12 months supplies to be kept at the store.
b. transmit annually a list of expected consumption.
c. purchases were to be made under the authority of the Governor and prices paid to be no greater than market prices
d. all bills of exchange must be accompanied with an affidavit of purchase countersigned by the Governor
e. you will make receipts for all payments in the presence of at least one witness—preferably a magistrate—and make three sets of all

vouchers, one for the treasury, one with the accounts and one for the store use.

f. keep a separate account of all items transmitted from England.

g. make a survey of any stores lost or damaged–which goods are to be sold or destroyed at the Governors discretion.

h. Make up annually an account of all receipts and expenditures, accompanied by one set of vouchers.

i. You are responsible for the preservation of all stores and provisions and the employees who work for you, and to the public.

A set of notes on how the commissary should operate was prepared by the Duke of Portland and handed to Governor-in Chief Phillip Gidley King on 28th September 1800. These notes are attached for historical purposes.

OFFICIAL INSTRUCTIONS FOR THE COMMISSARY– 28th September, 1800

Instructions to the Commissary by Captain Philip Gidley King, Governor-in-Chief, &c., in and over His Majesty's territory of New South Wales and its Dependencies, 28th September, 1800.

In consequence of my instructions, you are hereby required to conform to the following directions for your conduct:-

1st. You are to be present yourself as much as possible, and control the receipt and issue of all stores and provisions into and from His Majesty's stores; and as you are answerable for the conduct of those under you and about the different stores, if you should have any cause to be dissatisfied with their conduct in discharge of their duty you are to report the same to me, when a proper notice will be taken thereof.

2nd. You are not to receive or issue any articles whatever, either public or purchased, into or from the stores, but by a written order from me, delivering me an account thereof, on the receipt or issue having taken place, taking care to comply with all such general orders as I may judge necessary respecting your department.

3rd. When any grain or animal food raised by those at government work, or received from England or elsewhere, is delivered into your charge, you are to furnish me with a particular receipt for it, specifying the place and person you received it from, charging yourself with it as provisions received for the public use, and to observe the same with respect to all stores belonging to the Crown, and to deliver the quarterly accounts of the expenditure and the remains thereof, or oftener, if required.

4th. When there is not a sufficiency of grain and animal food raised by the convicts at public labour for the use of those necessarily maintained by the Crown, and that it becomes necessary to purchase the deficit required from the settlers, you are to give me an account of the quantity that may be absolutely necessary weekly, or at a stated period, but not to require more gain at a time than can be kept from the weevil. After my approval thereof, and the price at which such articles are to be purchased is fixed, you are to give public notice thereof, and open a list at the different settlements for the insertion of those persons' names who can spare any quantities of the articles required from the reserve necessary for seed and their own use; such persons being freemen, possessed of ground are known cultivators, are to be regularly entered on the list in preference to any other description of persons, as they offer themselves, and their required produce to be received in the stores without any preference or partiality. The grain thus purchased is to be measured at such times as I may direct in front of the storehouse, and from thence lodged in the store in the presence of a superintendent and another creditable person. When the receipt is ended for the day, a return thereof it to be made the next morning to me, specifying the person's name and quality from whom it is received, the superintendent and other witnesses attesting the same, one or both of whom are to sign their names to the witness column in the voucher when payment is made.

5th Being particularly directed to reform the irregularity that has existed in the mode hitherto followed in making payment for such articles as have been purchased from the inhabitants for the public use, the persons who take your printed receipts, audited by me, for their respective produce being lodged in the stores, may transfer them from one to another for their accommodation; all such receipts to be called in as often as I may judge proper, when payment will be made by me of all outstanding receipts by a bill on His Majesty's Treasury for the amount of such receipts as may be in the hands of individuals, such bills not to be drawn for less than (Pounds) 100, and the vouchers in support thereof to be verified by liquidating your receipts in rotation. And whenever such payments are made you are to take care that five complete sets of vouchers with their documents, agreeable to the annexed form, be prepared to be signed before me at the time of payment being made, which I am directed to control and superintend.

6th. When it is absolutely necessary for any stores, clothing or provisions being purchased from masters of ships, or other strangers, after the price is regulated by two proper persons on the part of Government, and the same on the part of the proprietors, the Commissary will be ordered to receive such articles into the stores in the presence of two respectable witnesses, who are to sign the vouchers, two of which are to be delivered to me, with the proprietor's receipt for the payment, witnessed by two other respectable persons.

7th. As I am directed to forward my account current, made up to the 10th of October annually, with the Right Honourable the Lords Commissioners of His Majesty's Treasury, to the Inspector General of Public Accounts, under cover to His Majesty's Principal Secretary of State for the Home Department, you are therefore not to fail in delivering to me, on or before the 10th day of October, for my inspection and auditing, the following books and papers in support of your account current with the Lords Commissioners of His Majesty's Treasury, together with the surgeon's account of the expenditure of stores and necessaries received from you, in order that those accounts may be sent with mine by the first opportunity after the above date, viz.:-

First—A census book, containing each man, woman, and child's name that has received any provisions from the stores during the year, distinguishing those in the different rations.

Second—A clothing and slop expense book, for those supported by the Crown, expressing as above.

Third—A book specifying the receipts of stores, provisions, and clothing from England or elsewhere, belonging to the Crown, also the quarterly expense thereof, and remains at the time of making up the public accounts, which is to be distinctly stated and carried over the next year's account, as a charge.

Fourth–A book of the particular expense, and the application of the above described provisions and clothing issued by you during the year, to those supported by the Corn, also another book stating the expense and application of the above described stores issued by you for the use of the public, and signed relatively by the superintendent, overseer, or other person to whom they have been delivered.

Fifth.–A store purchasing book, specifying the different quantities of grain and animal food bought from settlers, &c., noting the time of purchase, quantity and application thereof, with a reference to the proper vouchers in support of the receipt and payment, which documents are to be annexed to this book.

Sixth._ A similar book to the above, specifying the different quantities of stores, &c., purchased from masters of ships, or other strangers, verified by proper vouchers, &c., as last above, to which book you are to annex the general expenditure thereof and remains at the time of making up the public accounts, which is to be distinctly stated; and carried over to the next year's account as a charge. At the end of this book you are to insert whether such articles have been paid for in grain, meat, or money, and to debit yourself accordingly, either in your account current of cash, or store account, and to charge yourself in the same manner with any other payment made to you on behalf of the Crown.

Seventh.–A list of all births, deaths, and absentees during the year.

You are not to fail (on peril of being subject to an exchequer process) in delivering me for my examination all the above books and papers, with every other explanatory document, on the thirty-first day of October, annually, which accounts you are to attest before me previous to my transmitting them to England and you carefully to preserve correct copies thereof, in case of any accident happening to those sent to England. You are to keep an open list in your office, containing the names of each class of people in the colony, according to the form you are provided with, in which you are to make regular entries and discharges as they occur.

Eighth.–Exclusive of the above papers, when any ship is going from hence to England, you are to furnish me with a general return of the inhabitants, according to the annexed form, also a return of the expenditure and remains of Government stock.

Ninth.–The issue of provisions is to be attended by a superintendent, or principal overseer, and a non-commissioned officer, for the purpose of detecting and reporting any improper proceedings; but no report will be attended to that is not made on the day of the issue. A weekly victual and store-issue book are to be kept at each store by the person who has charge of it. No person whatever is to be put on or off the store but by a written note from me or by a note from the person who has the superintendence of the district where the stores are. The master carpenter, and every other description of persons that has charge of the workmen supplied with materials from the different stores for the public use, as well as such individuals as are allowed to receive that indulgence, are to apply for the orders on Monday mornings, and to give receipts for the same to the Commissary, delivery an account of the expense thereof to me weekly. By this regulation, the necessity of persons frequenting the stores on the intermediate days between stores and victual issue will be prevented, and the stores properly appropriated. The different storekeepers are to deliver you a weekly return of their expenditure and remains, keeping the same ready for my inspection when required, and you are to furnish me with a quarterly return of Government stock, charging yourself with any that may be killed and issued as a ration, accounting for it under the head of provisions raised by those at public labour. And as it is necessary the Deputy-Commissaries and storekeepers at detached places should be supplied with regular directions how they are to conduct themselves, you are to furnish them with such parts of these Regulations as relate to their duty, and you are to direct them to deliver their returns and receipts to me, if I should be on the spot, or to the officer who has the direction of the public concerns in the district where they are stationed.

GORDON BECKETT

Philip Gidley King

In addition to the above instructions, the Commissary will give directions to the Deputy-Commissary and storekeeper to obey all such directions as they may from time to time receive from the Reverend Mr Marsden, at Parramatta, and Charles Grimes, Esq., at Hawkesbury, reporting to him all such orders on the day they send their weekly returns.

THE WORKING OF THE FUNDS 1800-1810

There were numerous 'funds' probably supported by accounts with the Bank of New South Wales from 1818, when the surplus balance of the Orphan Fund was ordered to be placed on deposit with the Bank of New South Wales. This was followed by the Military Chest, the Land Fund, the Commissariat Fund and many others, all of which were probably raised to simplify accounting recording and reporting–a Bank account can be used to greatly simplify accounting records.

a. The Police Fund is intended to cover the expense of all items relating to the goal and police, and replaces the gaol fund but is entirely distinct from the female orphan fund. (from a dispatch by Governor Macquarie 31.03.1810 and effective 1st April, 1810
b. ¾ ths of all the duties and customs collected in the port and Town of Sydney are to be paid into the Police Fund. The remaining 1/4th to be paid to the Orphan Fund, which will be necessary to defray the expenses of that institution.
c. Liquor Licenses to be paid to the Police Fund. D'Arcy Wentworth to be Treasurer of Police Fund. Quarterly accounts for both funds to be completed inspected and published.
d. The naval officer, previously responsible for collecting customs and duties to settle his accounts by the 31st May, 1810
e. John Palmer to close up and settle all accounts for the commissary and pass over control to his deputy William Broughton until Palmer's return from England
f. Samuel Marsden to be treasurer of the orphan fund

On 30th April, 1810, Macquarie wrote to Castlereagh concerning the two funds

Previously all duties and customs collections have been allocated to the Gaol and Orphan Funds. I have revised this practice in favour of sharing the collections between the Police–¾ ths.–and Female Orphan Fund 1/4th.

From the Police Fund is to be defrayed the expense of the jail and police establishments, the erection of wharves, quays, bridges and making/ repairing of roads. The second fund is to cover establishment of the orphanage and other charity schools.

The Second Period 1810-20

Timothy Coghlan in 'Wealth & Progress 1900-01' (P837) writes about the Land Fund

> *"When in 1831 it was decided to abolish the system of free land grants, and to dispose of the public estate by auction in lieu of private tender, it was also decided that the proceeds of land sales should be paid into what was called the Land Fund, from which were to be paid the charges incidental to the introduction of immigrants; and it was from the inability of the Land Fund to meet these charges that the public debt of NSW first had its rise. From 1831 to 1834 the Land Fund was sufficient, but in 1841 the engagements for immigration purposes were so heavy that it became necessary to supplement the fund in some way and it was decided to borrow against the security of the Land Revenue. On 28th December 1841 a debenture loan of 49,000 pound was offered in the colony through the Sydney Gazette, the first loan raised in any colony.*

Sundry Funds 1864

From "The Epitome of History of NSW" P409, the Government Printer reports that:

"The deficiency for 1864 was 407,626.7.11 of which, the sum of 357,408 had been already paid with funds borrowed from accounts as follows:

- Treasury Bills   30,948.1.11
- 1865 revenue   98,714.10.8
- Bank of NSW   83,333.14.8
- Oriental Bank, London   20,818.14.9
- Lodgements   92,238.16.4
- Church & School Fund   19,658.09.7
- Civil Service Super Fund   1,429.7.10
- Scab in Sheep Fund   10,267.2.10

It can be concluded from the above statement by the NSW Treasurer of 1864, that these funds were established as 'collectives' or depositories of segregated receipts and a means of trying to simplify an accounting, recording and reporting system. It is probable that the Church & School Fund, was operated by The Church & School Lands Corporation (under the Act of 1834; 'to provide for the maintenance of the police and gaol establishments of the colony, the surplus of the land revenue (land fund) and of the other casual Crown revenues had been placed at the disposal of the Council.

ON THE TRACK OF THE MANY COLONIAL FUNDS

From 1802, the first date that the Colony of New South Wales attempted to manage some of its fiscal destiny by recording certain transactions in the Colony, in the Orphan Fund or the Gaol Fund.

The Crown did not put its hand out for a share of colonial revenues until 1822, but as early as 1802, the colony applied duties and customs to imported items, as a means of raising necessary revenue to provide a small amount of independence to the Governor's operations. The first year's revenue of 900 pound did not amount to much but it was the start of something big. That revenue grew quickly to reach over 100,000 by 1829 and over 1 million pound by 1854.

The Goal & Orphan Funds were shortly replaced by the Female Orphan and Police Funds sponsored by Governor Macquarie in 1810.

Later, during the 'Blue Book' period, the number of funds grew. From 1802 and the Orphan & Gaols Funds, the colonial revenue was distributed eventually through the Female Orphan & Police Funds, the 'Military Chest' Fund, The Land Fund, the Colonial Fund, and the Commissary Fund. Each with a unique role and purpose.

From an accounting viewpoint, the matter of allocating certain revenues must have caused some confusion. Thus the 'parliamentary grant to reimburse the local expenditure on the convicts' was handled by placing the revenue in a new category–"Receipts in Aid of Revenue". This was soon changed to the heading of "Revenue of the Crown".

A BANK ACCOUNT BY ANY OTHER NAME?

The Colony was initially operated through a series of 'funds' which were simply a bank account by another name. For the first 32 years of the colonial administration, there was no 'treasury'; and so that fact, along with the administration of watching over a mere penal colony, a treasury was neither demanded nor necessary. But times changed. There became a demand for immigration of free people, of both families and single women; there were the demands of the traders for a means of purchasing their wares and paying for them via an acceptable means of exchange; and then the dereliction of duty by the Marine Corps led to officer's influencing, if not controlling much of the economy of the colony, especially the Commissariat. A Treasury became essential and the first token Treasury came with the local recording of colonial revenue from customs duties and tariffs, tolls and rents. There were a number of such funds going back to 1802. The Colonial Treasury commenced in 1822 under the auspices of the Colonial Secretary and until 1827 the Colonial Treasury was the sole source of deposits of revenue and the source of expenditures. In 1827 we find the first mention of the 'Military Chest'. It is safe to assume that the successor to the Military Chest was the Land Fund whose functions, not unlike the military chest were to pool the 'revenue of the crown' raised in the colony from the sale of its 'waste 'or crown lands. We will consider the role and function of the Military Chest momentarily, but first there were a number of funds between 1802 and 1855 including:

* The Goal Fund 1802-1809
* The British Treasury 1788-1835
* The Commissariat Fund 1822-1850
* The Orphan Fund 1802-1822
* The Police Fund 1810-1822
* The Blue Book Period 1822-1857
* The Military Chest
* The Land Fund
* The Colonial Fund
* Scab on Sheep Fund
* Church & School Fund
* Civil Service Super Fund

Because these funds have never been discussed or identified in any texts, this work has been designed to uncover and discuss two of the many funds mentioned above and trace their use and activity.

It would appear from the use of these minor funds that a new accounting procedure was under-way. A simple and inexpensive recording and reporting mechanism could be maintained with a fair degree of accuracy, if separate bank accounts were used for each collection point, or each source of revenue was identified by a separate account, into which these funds could be deposited.

UNDERSTANDING THE FUNDS

a. THE MILITARY CHEST

With a name as romantic as 'the military chest', this story may be expected to unfold as a historic novel, but the 'military chest' was the first fund identified following the initiation of the 'Blue Book' period being the first formal accounts transmitted to England from the birth of the colony in 1788.

The First Period 1800-1810

Historical Records of New South Wales records that Lieutenant-Governor King wrote to The Rev'd Richard Johnson 'and others' (these others included William Balmain, John Harris, Samuel Marsden and Mrs Paterson, the wife of Major George Paterson–all being the preferred committee to oversee the proposed orphanage in Sydney) on 7ᵗʰ August, 1800, and reported that he had (without proper authorisation) 'made a conditional purchase of Captain Kent's dwelling house. Offices and ground, in this town for the reception and education of orphans, the number of whom, are 398 out of the 958 children accounted for at the general muster.

There were already funds available to commence the project. As King writes 'I am informed by Mr Johnson that a sum of money and some property arising from former subscriptions for the use of the orphans, and fines, remains in his hands which he will deliver to Mr Marsden, who I have requested to act as Treasurer, to the establishment I am forming.

In relation to the operation of the orphanage, King recorded that 'as this house will not hold more than 100 children, it is my intention to make an addition to the back of it which will allow for greater numbers. Planks for bedsteads is now sawing, to be paid for out of the money in hand. Another building will be commenced in Parramatta to house 200 orphans and will be paid for out of the funds for this establishment.

The accounts produced by Mr Johnson in early September 1800 showed a balance due to the Orphanage of 114.16.0 pound, plus some articles of cloth and spirits (304 gallons of brandy) taken in settlement of fines; plus repayment of a loan to the Orphans fund by Mr Balmain of 200.10.9d.

In late September 1800, Marsden informed the Committee that 196 pounds has been subscribed since the beginning of that month of which he has received 60.18.6, plus repayment of the loan to the public jail of 200.10.9.

The first licence fee of 5 guineas was received, in all totalling 517.1.9 plus the cloth and brandy on hand.

On 11th October, 1800 Marsden informed his Committee that the sum of 55.9.11 had been subscribed since the last meeting of which 17.6.0 had been paid. The amount of subscriptions paid to date was 572.11.8. Marsden also advised that the cost of building the new building in Parramatta may be as high as 2,000 pounds.

King 'ordered' in the Sydney Gazette of 10th October, 1800 the fees on entries of ships, bonds, permits, certificates and assessments to be levied by the naval officer and clerk/assessor and which revenue was to be accepted by the Orphan Fund. Further revenue for the Fund was announced by King in late October, being port fees on visiting vessels.

The Commissary fund, being in operation at this time was due monies from departing settlers, and King decided to delay the sailing of the 'Buffalo' until debts due to the commissary of 2166 pound were collected.

King also announced that by removing 450 full rationed persons from the commissary list, he would save the Government over 10,488 pound per year at 23 pound per head per annum.

After a series of bad storms on 4th, 5th, and 6th June 1799 had layed flat the old wooden jail, Governor Hunter met with the settlers and proposed a new jail to be built at the expense of the colonists by voluntary subscription. He wrote to the Duke of Portland on July 10, 1799 that 'The prison I have proposed is large and substantial, built of stone and which we have abundance of fit use for it' The gaol fund was set into operation in July 1799 with 'the expense of the building being defrayed by the inhabitants of the colony. When in January 1800, Hunter was still dissatisfied with the progress being made in the construction, in no small part the responsibility of the lower than anticipated subscriptions, he directed that a levy or toll of sixpence per bushel of wheat be collected at the public store on deliveries King reported in August 1801 that the gaol was completed and the cost was 3,954 pound–it included separate sections for debtors and six strong and secure cells for condemned felons. To complete construction, the public stores or commissary provided the iron as required

The Second Period 1810-1821

Our story starts with Governor Macquarie in 1810 who, having decided that the accounting records for the colony (contained in the early gaol and Orphan Funds from 1800-1810) were, in effect, in a shambles, and did not properly reflect the fiscal condition of the colony, allocated certain local revenues to firstly the gaol fund and other revenue to the Orphan fund, each of which was to have a non-government or public citizen Trustee and Treasurer. The treasurer for the Orphan Fund was the Reverend Samuel Marsden. Marsden was known and feared for his despotic ways, and we find from his records of the fund, as reproduced in the Sydney Gazette each quarter from 1811 to 1821 that certain unusual practices were undertaken with the accounts.

D'Arcy Wentworth, the Treasurer for the Gaol Fund from 1810, which was then renamed the 'Police' Fund, also took substantial liberties and bestowed fiscal favours upon many fellow officers of the Military Corps, and supported many of the non-trading military men with road repair work, which may or may not have ever been completed at least to any acceptable quality, since month after month the same men received rather large sums for road repairs, bridge and wharf repairs.

The Third Period 1822-1838

The successor to these early privately run funds was the British Government introduction of a standard recording and reporting format called the 'Blue Books' because they were, in fact, bound in blue covers.

A search of the "List of Colonial Office Records" preserved in the Public Records Office, published by HM Stationery Office, 1911, suggests that there was no Blue Book compiled prior to 1822 nor for the year 1824. The volumes continued to be compiled until 1855 in a set of four copies; two being sent to the Colonial Office, one went to the Governor and the other to the Colonial Secretary, and from 1855 to 1857 an additional copy was placed before the Legislative Assembly (after self-government). The volumes continued to be compiled after 1857 until 1870 but were then printed instead of being written out by hand and contain much less information, usually only the returns of the Civil and Ecclesiastical Establishments.

The Blue Books were compiled retrospectively from groups of returns sent out from the Colonial Secretary's Office, which were filled in by the various officials, and then sent back to the Office.

The first reference to the 'Military Chest' was in the 1828 'Blue Books' where we find, as one item of Revenue:

- 'The amount of Revenue & Receipts derived from local resources of the colony', together with a 'Loan from the Military Chest'
- This first 'loan' from the military chest was in the amount of 5,000.00 pound. It was obviously a short-term loan, because there is a reference to the "Balance in the Colonial Treasury on the 31ˢᵗ December, 1828, applicable to the service of the year 1829 being 11722.09.5 ½ *."

A further footnote attempts to clarify this item.

"*This Balance includes the sum of 5,000 pound, a loan which has been repaid into the Military Chest since the 31ˢᵗ December, 1828.'

The Blue Books for the year 1828 make for interesting analysis.

a. In spite of the final accounts being certified by Alex. McLeay, as Colonial Secretary, there is a substantial arithmetic error in the statements. We can track this error by accepting the opening balance in the colonial treasury as of 1ˢᵗ January, 1828; the closing balance on the 31ˢᵗ December 1828; both balances were represented by cash deposits in the Bank of New South Wales and the total receipts and disbursements recorded and added.

opening balance	3,862.16.8 ¾.
total receipts	226,191.16.7 ¾.
Total expenditure	214,469.07.2 ¼.
Closing balance	11,722.09.5 ½.
Difference	2,962.16.8 ¾.

This is an error in addition in the items of expenditure, or else, an error of transposition from one set of records to the next set.

THE REVENUE OF THE CROWN
OR THE FIRST LAND FUND

b. We note that in the following year, 1829 that a notation on the 'Receipts in Aid of Revenue' is that these deposits have been paid into the Military Chest. These deposits include:

- Consignment of specie (transfer of coinage from Britain to the Colony)
- proceeds of bills drawn by the Deputy Commissary
- proceeds of sale of stores sent from England

Sale of:

- crown stock (livestock)
- coals ex Newcastle
- wheat from Bathurst
- sugar & molasses grown at Port Macquarie
- the Schooner 'Alligator'
- sundry stores & articles
- miscellaneous receipts

A special notation on the accounts is made for 'receipts in aid of revenue (i.e. revenue of the crown) which are exclusive of the value of colonial produce delivered to the commissariat from the convict agricultural establishments'

In subsequent years, this statement is modified because sale of produce from the Government farms is listed, but the notation is modified to say that the value of convict labour (other than labour for hire) is excluded

MILITARY FUND–ITEMS OF REVENUE & OUTGOINGS

proceeds of bills
proceeds of sale of stores
Sale of crown livestock
:coal
:wheat
:sugar & molasses
:sundry stores

civil establishment
convict establishment
military establishment
retired army pay
retired military pensions

a. The Military Chest usually made payments in the following categories:

- civil establishment
- convict establishment
- military establishment
- retired army pay & pensions

b. The main revenue and expenditures were deposited into and paid out of the 'Colonial Treasury'. The first reference to the balance in the Military chest is found in 1828, but the first reference to a balance in the Colonial Treasury is not found until 1829. From those dates, the closing balance at the end of each year is identified until 1831 when there are headings such as "Paid into the Colonial Treasury" "Defrayed from the Colonial Treasury"; "Paid into the Military Chest", "Defrayed from the Military Chest", providing the means of tracking balances in each account.

c. In 1829, the disbursements on account of miscellaneous civil services states "total disbursements out of the military chest, in aid of the civil establishment of the colony"

d. In 1834, the 'Receipts in aid of Revenue' used each year, was changed to 'Revenue of the Crown'. The items included remained the same, viz. proceeds of land sales, quit rents, fees on delivery of deeds and leased land revenue. These revenues were claimed by the British Treasury for dedication to their exclusive use to offset treasury expenditure on items such as the civil list, the military and interim commissary expenditure on public stores for improvements, until the Commissary Fund was properly established in 1833.

e. Back in 1826, for the first and only time, there was an entry for the British "parliamentary grant for the charges of defraying the civil establishment of the colony for the year 1826". The amount involved is 8,283.15.0; however the financial statements show the full civil establishment as costing 62,554.18.2 ½. The British Government must have decided that the cost of supporting the full civil establishment was too expensive and that it would only contribute to the salary of selected personnel. The details as listed in the 1826 statement do not allow us to decipher how the 8,283 pound is made up; We can only assume that the Governor, the chief justice, and possibly the chief medical officer are covered. The reason we cannot identify the amount is that individual salaries were no longer being shown in the records, but rather the Governor and his establishment received a grant of 4933.06.5 ¾, whilst the judicial establishment receive a grant of 13,462.02.8 1/4.

f. The reference above to the 'notes' incorporated into each statement to the effect that 'the total is exclusive of the value of articles of colonial produce delivered to the commissariat from the convict agricultural establishment' stood until 1825 when the military chest received and deposited receipts from "the sale of articles of colonial produce delivered to the commissariat from the several convict agricultural establishments and coal mines". The first ever recognition that the production of convict labour should be shown as a 'crown receipt'.

g. The 1826 Financial Statements from the 'Blue Book' of that year record the consignment of specie as being 50,000.09.0 pound. Butlin "Foundations of the Australian Monetary System" refers to the copper coins sent to the colony at the instigation of Governor King in 1805, together with a second consignment in 1806 to Governor Hunter. Hunter recommended that the coins be circulated at "a greater value . . . . than their intrinsic worth."

h. Butlin suggests that the progress of government finance in the colony goes along these lines:

• the earliest coins arrive in the pockets of the first Fleeters

- Phillip's Bills & Dollars–bills on the English Treasury & Spanish dollars
- The 'Rum' Currency and Barter
- Promissory Notes–personally pledged
- Commissary's Store receipts and Bills of Exchange
- Paymaster's Bills & Notes–Copper coins of 1805
- Legal Tender & Colonial Currency
- 'Holey' dollars
- Macquarie's Bank & exchange rates

Butlin concluded that, between 1788 and 1803, the 'Colony had no treasury', but this omission was not to last long. The earliest funds were controlled out of England with even the colonial commissary operating purely on a barter system for the first fifteen years. The first colonial accounting was commenced in 1802 (through the Goal & Orphan Funds) with revenue amounting to 900 pound. The Colonial Fund commenced with the 'Blue Books'. The Land Fund according to the 'Australians: Historical Statistics' opened in 1833, although the 1833 financial statements do show the balance at the end of the year, in the Military Chest was 22,719 pound. It is logical, subject to further verification, that the Land Fund was the successor to the Military Chest; the main evidence being that, in 1834, the 'Receipts in Aid of Revenue' was changed to 'Revenue of the Crown' and included the proceeds from the sale of crown (waste) land, and other crown assets of the colony.

The names of the various funds changed at different times between 1802 and 1834, including:

- Gaol Fund
- Orphan Fund
- Police Fund
- Orphan School Fund
- 'Blue Books' & The Colonial Fund
- Military Chest
- Commissary Fund
- The Colonial Fund
- Land Fund

This was the story of how the Military Chest which became, during the Blue Book era, the holder of large balances in the Colony; became the main lender to an malnourished colonial treasury; and the beneficiary of the 'profitable' commissariat trading and discounting of bills drawn on the English Treasury. Its successor was termed the Land Fund, but we have little official recognition of this fund, other than what we learn from some of the economic historians.

The second THE LAND FUND

The military chest, as an account style for the colonial treasury was identified in the financial statements contained in the 'Blue Books', and we can readily identify the revenues credited to that account as well as the expenditures charged against the military chest.

However the Land Fund is without mention in the 'Blue Books' at least through the end of 1838, and the origin of this nomenclature must be accepted as 'untraceable' without proper basic evidence. We know only of its existence in firstly, the Australians: Historical Statistics P112, and then its mention in the works of economic historian, S.J. Butlin:

We find the following table in Historical Statistics of NSW

NEW SOUTH WALES PUBLIC FINANCE

LAND FUND (ACCOUNT ACTIVITIES) 1833-1850

	REVENUE '000				EXPENDITURE '000		
Year	Land	Other	Total		Immign	Other	Total
1833	**	26.1	0.1	26.2	9.0	17.2	26.2
1834	48.2	42.9	60.8		7.9	52.9	60.8
1835	88.9	121.3	131.9		10.7	121.2	131.9
1836	131.4	121.1	263.3		11.8	251.5	263.3
1837	123.6	202.6	254.9		44.4	210.5	254.9
1838	120.2	185.8	353.8		108.0	245.8	353.8

1839	160.8	148.8	321.8	158.3	163.5	321.8
1840	325.3	283.6	480.0	148.0	332.0	480.0
1841	105.8	21.4	386.5	331.6	54.9	386.5
1842	44.1	51.7	117.2	112.0	19.7	131.7
1843	29.3	49.3	56.5	11.6	44.9	56.5
1844	16.9	126.0	127.5	69.0	58.5	127.5
1845	38.0	131.0	127.9	20.0	107.9	127.9
1846	38.8	153.5	146.5	1.2	145.3	146.5
1847	51.7	109.7	212.3	1.0	232.6	233.6
1848	51.7	109.7	212.3	113.8	98.5	212.3
1849	109.0	237.4	296.0	138.5	157.5	296.0
1850	158.5	104.8	373.1	166.2	206.9	373.1

** Receipts in aid of Revenue (i.e. paid into military chest–no record of land sales)

This table extracted from Historical Statistics can only be verified by reference back to the Blue Book Financial statements for those years, provided we make a generous assumption.

That assumption must be as follows:

a. If the 'military chest' is accepted as a predecessor to the 'Land Fund' then its purpose must have been essentially the same. The military chest took its revenue from the proceeds of sale of crown lands, sale of stores sent from England, sale of produce from the Convict Establishments and sale of crown livestock. In other words, only material items possessed by the crown; and that is most probably why the notations on the Blue Books changed from 'Receipts in Aid of Revenue' to 'Revenue of the Crown'. This important change occurred in the 1834 financial statements.

b. Obviously the Land Fund was so designated either officially or by Australian Economic Historians to be the account into which official 'crown' revenue is deposited and from which crown reserved expenditures are drawn. The crown reserved its use of portion of the funds for conveying selected immigrants into the country, and for (15%) aboriginal welfare. We will return to the official sanctioning of these funds later.

c. S.J. Butlin in his masterwork "Foundations of the Australian Monetary System 1788-1851" makes several passing references to the 'Land Fund' without fully identifying its source or use.

Butlin writes that "in February 1838, William Rucker, a Melbourne storekeeper, announced the opening of a Derwent Bank agency, to 'receive deposits and discount bills and orders for account and under the responsibility of the Derwent Bank Company in Hobart. He fixed the discount rate at 20%, letting it be known that Hobart rates would apply when a court was established in which debts might be recovered. Attempts were made, with what success it is not clear, to secure the accounts of the Customs Officer and of the Land Fund for the agency. But the agency met with considerable difficulty."

In 1846 there was a squabble between Stuart Donaldson, NSW Treasurer, Murray MHR and Dr. Bland MLC as to where certain colonial debentures were to be funded. Donaldson wanted the subscription to come from the public; Murray thought the Trust and Loan Bank should do the funding, but "Dr Bland wanted the loans to come from the Land Fund"

"Because of its late settlement and mining boom, land purchase in South Australia was heavy in the late 'forties and the local accumulations in the Land Fund were more than the local commissariat required. The practice developed, with English blessing, that any surplus in the Fund was paid to the commissariat which shipped the specie to other colonial commissariats in need, especially that in New Zealand, the amount being credited to the colony's account with the Land and Emigration Commissioners in London"

Grey, in South Australia, decided to use, contrary to official directions from London, to use any bank he chose for Government business, and he used the Bank of South Australia. Being contrary to official direction, this action permitted a penalty. The Land Fund, which was a transient deposit remitted to England for immigration payments, was divided between the Bank of Australasia and the Bank of South Australia, but all other government business was given to the Australasia."

"In 1851, the SA Treasury decided to require banks to hold cash at least equal to the government deposit, and to insist on this for the Land Fund."

Some of these references through doubt on the strict governmental use of the Land Fund. Other quotes come from 'Historical Records of Victoria–Volume 7'

"It was Lord John Russell's opinion in 1840 that the general revenue ought to provide for the general expenditure, leaving the Land Fund, apart from 15 percent to be used for expenditure on Aborigines, free for immigration purposes as originally intended"

A. Coghlan in his extensive work "Labour & Industry in Australia "helps place some of these matters in relation to sale of crown land & immigration into perspective.

It was upon emigration from England at the cost of the land revenue that the colonial authorities finally placed their confidence. They offered in 1822 to set aside 10,000 pound from the Land Fund for emigration purposes; of this sum they desired that about two-thirds should be devoted to promoting the emigration of unmarried women, as the proportion of men in the colony was excessive, and that about one-third should be used in loans for the emigration of mechanics. The colonial office objected vigorously but the British Treasury agreed to the proposal with the proviso that no further sum should be expended upon immigration until the money received from the sale of land had reached 10,000 pound.

"It had been Edward Gibbon Wakefield's philosophy that the idea of land disposition in the colonies was adopted . . . . If the land was sold, the proceeds of the sale might aptly be applied to transferring labour from Britain to the colony without which labour the land would be of very little value. In 1831 the English Government resolved to alter the land system of Australia with the view of throwing open the country more freely to settlement, and thereby increasing immigration. In the first four months of 1832, 103 mechanics reached the colony but were disappointed to find pay rates considerably less than those promised in England. The female emigrants all found ready employment, chiefly as domestic servants.

Considering its resources, the colony went into the immigration business in a big way. The estimated expenditure of 1838 was 120,000 pound of which 80,000 pound was spent in chartering 26 ships, and 40,000 expended on bounty immigrants. With the overall success of the program it was decided that the whole of the rapidly increasing land revenue of New South Wales should be devoted to immigration and in 1837. 3093 immigrants arrived of whom 2688 were sponsored and 405 arrived under the bounty regulation of the colonial government.

CHAPTER 15

THE SECOND PERIOD 1811-1822

The Macquarie years are the most special period–they were dynamic in every respect–economically, socially and politically. After the years of torment during the Bligh era, Macquarie was like a breath of fresh air, arriving in the colony. His role was an important one, and he brought with him, not only a new regiment which would further assist in ridding the colony of the vestiges of the 'Rum Corp' and all it stood for, but the hopes and aspirations of the British Government for Macquarie to complete the transition and transformation of the heavily subsidised colonial operations but the possibility of the colony feeding the British manufacturers with resources of raw materials and grow into a recipient of British manufacture. Wakefield foresaw the British Treasury reaping rich harvests from the sale of pastoral land, whilst the free traders saw the colony as an opportunity for being the outlet for British machinery and in so many ways, the branch office for British manufacturers.

A.T. Yarwood states that Marsden's name once again came to the fore during the early Macquarie years. He writes in 'Marsden of Parramatta'

"During the first few years the relations between Marsden and Macquarie deteriorated steadily, for Macquarie identified him as the leader of wealthy colonists who opposed his policies of self-interested and unworthy motives. Involved in the dispute was Macquarie's vision of the colony as a place where convicts had the chance, on proven good behaviour of regaining freedom and aspiring to social recognition and even official positions.

We will set down some of the major economic highlights of the Macquarie era–those very special 11 years between 1810 and 1821. Obviously the one highlight not to be overlooked is the massive contribution to the economy and the future of the colony made by his building program.

Macquarie told Bigge, in a very understated way that he decided the colony could justify a major building program because it would lift the tenor of the colony, lift the spirits of the residents, set the tone for future generations, use local materials (timber, bricks and tiles, lime and, mortar–all of these items were made by convict labour) and use an ex-convict as designer / supervisor (Francis Greenway). The equivalent value of the labour, using 3/–per day as a base rate is 500,000 pound, whilst the value of materials is approx 420,000 pound. Although Bigge agreed that it was a good use of convict labour, and the results cost very little in cash terms to the British Treasury, the benefits were enormous to the morale and the social well-being of the settlers–they were given a boost that might not have come in ordinary circumstances for another few generations, in fact not until the discovery of gold sand the resulting gold rush.

Macquarie began his administration with a goodly amount of economic passion. He talked about establishing a bank. He discussed with his senior officials the expansion of private enterprise and expansion of local industry. Immigration of free settlers was not high on his list of things to do, since he considered the economy needed lots of attention. In this area Macquarie made good progress. The naval boatyard was carrying out building and repair work. The sealing and whaling industry had established a viable export business and was bringing a regular supply of goods and supplies into the colony with every foreign boat that arrived. Blaxland advertised his locally grown salt for sale at 2p per pound. Thus, in addition to the milling operations, boat building, clothing and boot manufactures; the colony could boast a salt manufacturer.

It is only when things are starting to go right that the Government wanted to make change. The second committee on Transportation recommended in 1812 that fewer ticket-of-leave convicts be created. This would affect the commissary operations as well as expanding the cost of maintaining convicts on government rather than assigning them to private 'masters' and taking their clothing, feeding and housing costs off the government.

1812 also saw a second credit/liquidity crisis due to credit withdrawal by British investors.

The next major event with long-term ramifications was the crossing of the Mountain range (the Blue Mountains) that was boxing in the pastoral and farming prospects of the colony. In 1813, Blaxland, Lawson and W.C. Wentworth proudly advised Governor Macquarie that they had found a way across the mountains and witnessed the open panorama on the other side.

Locally, another drought in 1813 created a scarcity of corn and wheat and drove prices higher. Wool was catching on both at home and abroad. The significance of the crossing of the mountain range west of Sydney can be seen in the record quantity of wool being grown and thus the number of sheep running in the colony. In 1814 the Female factory at Parramatta used over 35,000 pound of wool, rising to 40,000 pound by 1818. In the same year the colony exported 30,000 pound of wool to Britain. Macquarie sent Surveyor-General Oxley and Mitchell to mark the route taken across the mountain and explore the open land on the west side of the range. After the 'explorers' returned Macquarie determined to establish Bathurst as the first plains settlement. Wool exported to England was not only a boon to the colony; it raised revenue for Britain as well. Britain decided to impose a duty on wool. Before 1819, the rate of duty was 6p per pound; during 1819 the rate was halved to 3p. During 1819 a new industry was introduced to the colony. In spite of the tariff, the woollen mills could not buy enough colonial wool and asked the British Government to do whatever it could to lift production.

Local industry demonstrated the capacity for innovation which resulted in productivity gains as reflected in total output increases without accompanying increases in labour input. This gain in productivity led to a mini 'business' boom. New settlements were still in demand and a penal settlement was established at Port Macquarie on the north-coast of New South Wales. For every door that opens another closes. Having supported the concept and operation of private enterprise and having encouraged new industry as well as a favourable setting for progress in the colony, Macquarie was confronted with his adversary Commissioner Bigge recommending the privatising of the coalfields. Consolidation in the pastoral expansion meant that in 1821, 80 owners controlled 60% of all land in the colony. Another sign of the times arose from the coal-mines being placed into private hands. The first free labour was used in the coal-mines in 1821. Settlement was now taking place along the south-coast of the New South Wales colony.

The paper used for the *Sydney Gazette* was now locally produced

The credit squeeze of 1812 was the first time economic hardship or stress had reached the colony since 1788 and was the first occasion that the withdrawal of British investment scrambled the comparative gains being made steadily in the colony. Of course, Macquarie tried to counter the effects of the credit squeeze by encouraging trade, creating the atmosphere for entrepreneurs and encouraged local business to establish and grow. This was an unusual credit squeeze and an even more unusual impact on the new and fledgling economy. Since there was little employment, as we know it today, there was little unemployment created as a result of the downturn. The main impact in the colonial economy was in the level of confidence. After the Bligh years and the constant warring between the governor and the military, Macquarie went out of his way to keep the military in its place. Having come to the colony as head of his own regiment he expected and received strong and loyal support and little distraction from the military officers. As a way of reversing the troubled mindset of the population away from the turbulent Bligh years, Macquarie commenced his four-fold program of

- A building program of fine buildings that would make the people proud
- A local revenue raising program that would provide a significant amount of discretionary revenue to support his local and almost all unapproved activities
- A social revolution whereby convicts who had served their time and returned to the regular community were welcomed into society and seated at his table. Simeon Lord was even appointed a Magistrate by Macquarie much to the consternation of leading citizens including Rev'd Samuel Marsden
- Encouraging free enterprise and new businesses privately capitalised and operated.

The withholding and withdrawal of investment capital had only marginal impact. Mostly the traders lessened their level of speculation, which slowed the introduction of new supplies and stocks of new goods into the colony. The export trade still continued but prices sat their destination were lower and in spite of lower wholesale prices demand was reduced in Britain. For once the Keynesian laws of supply and demand did not work.

Governor Brisbane arrived in 1821 to replace Macquarie who had returned to Britain and his home in Scotland.

CHAPTER 16

FINANCIAL STATEMENTS FOR THE
FIRST PERIOD–1800-1810

A reader may ask, why 1800 and why 1810. As we saw in the first chapter of this study on the rise of public finance and public accounting in the colony, 1802 was the first attempt to record either income or expenditure in the colony. The British Treasury had for the years between 1788 and 1801 recorded all of the expenditure in equipping and moving the first and second fleet, and for the provisioning and victualling the colony for this same period. However, with the necessary, but loose, mechanism of drawing Bills on the Treasury for most purchases, there is a great deal of doubt in the mind of Butlin, Shann and even Clark, that the published figures of the period are accurate.

For this study we are relying on the source documents–the hand-written documents prepared by Reverend Samuel Marsden and Asst Surgeon Darcy Wentworth, 'audited' by the Lieutenant Governors each quarter and then published for all settlers to read in the *Sydney Gazette*.

In a splendid work, edited by James Thomson in 1881, the resources of the Sydney Morning Herald were used (since the Hansard transcription service had not yet commenced in the New South Wales Legislative Chambers) to assemble the Treasurers statements between 1855 (the First Parliament) and November 1881 (the Tenth Parliament).

Thomson wrote in the Preface "Some years ago it was considered desirable that all the Financial Statements made since the inauguration of Responsible Government should be collated and printed for future reference, and for distribution amongst the Public Libraries, Schools of Arts and other literary institutions of the colony. The task of editing these Statements was entrusted to me, I presume, of the experience, which I had acquired, during a long course of years, of the financial affairs of the colony, and the practical knowledge which I possessed of its public accounts generally. Until recently (when Hansard commenced a reporting service in 1880) no authorised copy of any of the Financial Statements (by the Colonial Treasurers) was in existence, so that in the discharge of the duty imposed upon me I had to carefully revise the reports that were given of them in the *Sydney Morning herald*, which I found extremely accurate. In revising these statements I had to compare the Herald's figures with the published printed documents,–a labour which necessarily involved much trouble and occupied a considerable amount of time.

I have placed, as an Appendix to the Financial Statements, a memorandum explanatory of the financial system of New South Wales and an account of the rise, progress and present condition of the public revenue, as it is considered they may be found useful to those who take an interest in the financial affairs of the colony. I prepared these two papers in 1876 and 1879 for the information of the Imperial Government, who had it in contemplation at the time to publish some kind of official work on the defences, financial resources, and general condition of the several Australian colonies."

Why 1810? This was the year during which Lachlan Macquarie arrived in the colony, as the successor to William Bligh, whose failure to govern for all residents led to a slackness and sickness in the colony, which would take many pains from Macquarie to make better and allow the deep wounds to heal. Macquarie reformed the Commissary operation firstly, then 'reformed' the public finance and the public reporting of the colony, but tightening up the currency movement, creating a bank to assist both the traders and the colonial merchants, and 'regularising' the accounting mechanism of the 'Orphan Fund' and the 'Police Fund'.

The period between 1802 and 1810 was highlighted by a change of governor (King to Bligh) in 1806. This date marked a social decline in the colony, with Macarthur turning into a bitter enemy of the governor, followed by a re-alignment of the NSW Corps allegiances away from the governor and towards the rampant self-serving individually profitable trading activities of the military officers.

The colonial economy had been running in freefall. Little government support, a touch of entrepreneurial activity and a few governor declarations that urged the emancipists onto a self-supporting 30 acres and off the general stores. By the end of the King era, he could account for only 180,246 pounds in 'value' of assets as a 'credit against expenses'.

- The value of grain and supplies in the commissary stores of about 62,000 pound
- The value of buildings completed by King, could only account for 6,500 pound
- The value of public livestock owned by the governor would amount to 112,000 pound

The contribution of King to the colonial economy was little (especially when compared to Macquarie). He was not even the able administrator that Phillip had encountered in the time prior to 1792, and other than a few social welfare titbits, King managed to let the colony run without much interference by government. Many more persons were dependent on the government store in 1806 than when King accepted his appointment in 1800. Hunter had led the social decay during his years of 1795 and 1800, but much of his era was spent undoing the damage completed by the interim administrators (between Phillip and Hunter)–Captain Grose (upgraded from Lieutenant Governor for two years, and then Captain Paterson, acting as Lieutenant governor for the next year. These three years allowed the military officers to become dominant in the colony and run things on their own terms–the assignment of the convicts; the run-away trade in spirits; the use of spirits as the means of exchange; the absolute domination of the military in buying shiploads of goods for re-sale. It took the shipment of Macquarie's own regiment to the colony and the withdrawal of the NSW Corps to finally put a stop to the military occupation of spirits and trade. Bligh saw the problem but appeared powerless to intervene.

H.V.Evatt describes these years well in his 'Rum Rebellion'. In a forward to the 1938 edition, Hartley Grattan (a Carnegie Scholar 1937-38), and an American who became enamoured with Australian History wrote" the law can become a weapon in the social struggle and the courts a battleground of opposing class interests on which justice is weighed in favour of one side. This is in response to Justice Evatt's assertion that 'the Courts were the true forum of the little colony . . . . there was no legislature, no avowed political association or party, no theatre and no independent press' but the major social issues are generally apt to be subverted to the interest of the dominant class in the community." This class struggle pitted Bligh against Macarthur even though the English Government's economic plan for the colony envisaged the strong establishment of a small-holding peasantry in the country, the bulk of the peasants in any future of the colony then visible would be limited to time expired and emancipated convicts. Grattan suggests this economic plan was merely the projection on virgin Australia of an economic pattern being disrupted by the industrial revolution, which plan was destroyed after Phillip's departure from Sydney by the military officers.

The military, in the period between Phillip and Hunter, manipulated their own plan into full operation. They wanted a trading monopoly which was a combined with land holding on an extensive scale along with the ruthless exploitation of convict labour. Rum became the established medium of exchange and it was monopolised to raise its price, whilst consumption was pushed to the limit, thus allowing the monopolists to make huge profits. The defence of the system became the Rum Rebellion' of 1808-09. The struggle over the rum traffic was merely symptomatic of a deeper issue. The small landholders only existed to be exploited until economically exhausted and then removed through inevitable bankruptcy.

Grattan records in his Forward that "since the officers held, in their hands, the military power, as well as such minimum civil as had been developed, whilst the Courts held the supreme economic power, the combined power made them masters of the community. They directed it in a fashion that benefited themselves, but allowed for no progress". The 'brains' of the system was John Macarthur though he was far from being the sole initiator, beneficiary or protagonist. These monopolists broke three governors–Hunter, King, through complete lack of scruple and set a pattern for any successor, even though Bligh had been instruction to break up the monopoly and return the small landholders to the place in the community originally planned for them. Setting about his orders, Bligh quickly fell afoul of Macarthur and his associates

Macarthur came through this relatively unscathed, especially in latter-day public opinion, and his legacy, as muted through John Thomas Bigge in 1822 was to create a third economic program of foreseeing a broad acre pastoral industry, utilising the free labour of the convicts, but repaying the costs of the colony afforded by the British Treasury through the export of raw wool and the resulting strengthening of the woollen industry in England.

A review of significant events will show that the 'Rum Rebellion' was not the only big event that affected the colony.

When Phillip arrived in the colony in 1788 and established the penal settlement, he came with the authority to raise taxes. This was part of his instructions dated 2nd April 1787.

"Our will and pleasure is that all public monies which shall be raised be issued out of warrant from you and disposed of by you for the support of the government and for such other purpose as shall be entirely directed and not otherwise".

Phillip had been instructed to create a local commissary (he was provided with a commissary officer) in order to acquire, stock and furnish supplies within the colony to victual convicts, the military and the 40 military wives and families that had arrived with the Fleet. The commissary thus became the heart of the local economy for at least the first 20 years of settlement. The commissary was responsible for planning the rations required for the number of persons to be provisioned, based on the governor's decision on individual rations. The role of the commissary was to purchase supplies from visiting ships or, when available, local suppliers and pay a bill of exchange drawn on the British Treasury. This system provided the supplies needed but promoted great inaccuracies in the recording area, and thus, according to N.G. Butlin, the figures from the British Treasury for the tooling and victualling of the colony during the first few years are questionable and likely inaccurate. Phillip had been authorised to draw a bill at the Cape on route with the First Fleet, in order to purchase fresh supplies for the remainder of the voyage. It would have taken many months for this bill to be presented in London, and so, even if accurate, it is unlikely that the expenditures via bills presented would have reflected the correct time period.

There were many items that became short in the first few years and since there were no local persons to provide a source of supply, the governor stepped in and provided the labour within a government-inspired operation. The governor created his own vegetable patch and orchard in the 'governor's domain' and on 'Garden Island'. The governor organised a 'government farm' for watching over the livestock that had arrived and to grow grain that appeared to do well in the colony. It was to take a convict experienced in English style farming to cross grain strains and achieve a suitable local strain of wheat, barley, corn and maize. Clothing had become a major difficulty, with convicts going around in an advanced state of undress and shoeless. The answer was to establish a clothing factory in which the female convicts could be utilised. This answer would also segregate the male and female convicts as already the fear of growing numbers of illegitimate children running around the colony occupied the governor's mind. Children meant education, as well as extra mouths to feed and this was a penal colony with growing numbers of convicts expected. Phillip's planning for the colony had not included social or political matters. He had not anticipated free settlers, other than military or civil officers needing to retire and wanting to remain in the colony. Phillip himself had planned only to return to England at the end of his official term.

There were many opportunities for small business in the colony. For a start, very quickly it became apparent that the tools and equipment supplied with the First fleet were neither entirely suitable or in sufficient quantity. The felling axes were of little use against the standard trees in need of clearing around Sydney Cove and the Rose Hill settlements, and naturally, each new 30-acre farmer required a set of tools if he was to clear his land and become a farmer supplying produce to the commissary. But the second most important need was that of transportation. Since there were no working horses there was no need for carts, but there was an urgent need for boats for fishing and movement of people and goods between Sydney and Rose Hill. It took until 1790 for the first locally made boat to be ready to cover the Sydney-Rose Hill (Parramatta) link.

The first mill assembled on Observatory Hill could only grind 6 bushels of wheat each day. Mills were to play an important role in the colony and from just one operating mill in 1795, the number grew rapidly so that by 1848, there were 220 operating mills of which 79 were steam powered, and the remainder were horse, wind or human driven. Mills accounted for over 50% of total industry by the middle of the 19th century.

New industry was to be the mainstay of the fledgling colonial economy. The growth of industry was slow but creative and ranged from road making and road repairs to boat building, whale and seal hunting to a broad range of farming–vineyards, brooms, clothing and linen (from locally grown flax).

Other developments that created work for convicts and a trading and export opportunity were the discovery of coal. Newcastle became a convict centre as well as the main provider of coal for export to South America, England and Calcutta. The discovery of seals in Bass Strait gave encouragement to a large sealing industry, which led to a dramatic growth of the local boat-building industry. Exporting commenced in 1800 with the first shipment of sandalwood, wheat and pork. Obviously trading was expected to grow and become quite important to the colony, because Governor King built the first Customs House on the edge of Sydney Cove.

Funding for the first twelve years of the colony had come from the British Treasury but keeping in mind that the colony was instructed to become self-sufficient as quickly as possible, and also that the governor had been given taxing powers, King decided to impose tariffs on spirits, wine and beer in 1800 to complete the new Sydney Gaol that could not be completed by subscription as originally planned by Hunter.

Thus, by 1800, the colony was finding a sense of direction. King was not the right man for the times and there was more neglect during the Bligh times until Macquarie arrived with enthusiasm and a resolve to build the colony into the giant economy that was expected by the British Treasury.

One of the last acts of Phillip before he left the colony for his home in Britain was to proclaim the hours of work to be adopted by the convict labourers.

Phillip set "from sunup to sundown, with a break of 2 ½ ours during the day". When food was particularly in short supply, Phillip had expected that the finishing hour would be 3 o'clock in the afternoon, which would allow time, before dark, to tend to a vegetable patch or such food sources (livestock) that was being set aside for nutrition apart from foodstuffs supplied by the Commissary.

Hunter era was unremarkable for any positive gains in the colony. He claimed at one time that the Combination act in Britain of 1799 would restrict economic activity in the colony, but this piece of legislation intended by Westminster to stop formation of unions and prohibit strikes, was of little, if any, interest to colonial settlers, who went on their own way building homes, farming, trading, protecting what little they had and being subjugated to the military officers. The only relief or release would come from orderly organisation of the convict work gangs but since the military decided it was not their role to supervise convicts the work supervision was left to independent supervisors, but mostly to other convicts. The system did not work well, at least until Macquarie came to the colony.

Both Hunter and King arrived in the colony with instructions from the British Government to break the trade monopoly by the military, but reform was slow to gain any foothold at all. Even King sought relief from the military activists. King decided to rebuild the government herd of livestock, which was a noble enough plan and designed to provide food in the event of another severe drought and food shortage, but in order to implement his plan, he purchased cattle from the very military officers who were rorting the system and King paid far in excess of their real worth. Lackadaisical supervision of both cattle and convicts saw the cattle escape and until near the end of the Macquarie years, build into a substantial herd worth a goodly sum to the settlers when finally recaptured.

King did introduce a ticket of leave system for the convicts who were in good stead with the military, their direct supervisors, the commissary, and the law. It was King's way of removing convicts who could be trusted to be good colonial citizens from the commissary ration list.

King's other contribution was to foreshadow the usefulness to the colony of a local vineyard, and upon receiving two Napoleonic War prisoners in 1801 put them to work in establishing a wine industry for the colony.

The Hunter River area received a boost when it was found that locally grown flax could be used to produce linen. It was not the best quality but the governor thought it could be of great interest to the English government. In this way King recognised the conflict he was in the middle of. He was the British representative in the colony, was paid (rather handsomely as it turns out) by the British Government from the Civil List, but was usually respected and befriended by the settlers to whom he felt a moral and ethical, if not a legal responsibility. In the event of a conflict between the colony and the crown whose side would he choose?

The flax exercise should have been beneficial to both sides, but King knew in his heart that the local product was not of a high quality and would not be accepted by the British public or the British manufacturers. Likewise in declaring in 1801 that all coal and mineral reserves in the colony were the property of the Crown, he knew that only lackadaisical convict labour would be used to extract, load and work the coal removed from the Newcastle coal–fields. King was a free enterprise man under his gubernatorial cloak and invited Robert Campbell (from India) to set up a warehouse and trading post in the colony.

Campbell brought immediate gain and benefit to the colony by shipping a load of colonial coal from Newcastle to Calcutta.

The British encouraged free enterprise in other ways. The English government was going through one of its phases of privatisation. After the second fleet was thought to be much more expensive that Matra had projected, the Colonial Office decided to ship via contractors future prisoners to the penal colony, for a fixed fee. Competition brought a high price for the privately transported prisoners. Savings were encouraged by the contracts on the ship's captains by cutting food (both quantity and quality), limiting appropriate clothing, eliminating exercise and generally creating deplorable conditions for the prisoners, not least being the overcrowding. As a result the death rate of prisoners between England and Botany Bay was nearly 50% in the third fleet. The Government was only mildly offended by the charges of unlawfulness by Wilberforce and his ilk. But the resolve was to make failure to deliver healthy humans instead of human misery hurt the contractor's pocket. Surgeons were included on each shipping manifest with a bonus of 10/6 for each convict landed in healthy condition and a bonus of 50 pound to the ship's captain for assisting the surgeon to land healthy convicts. The problem may not have been solved but was made much better by these incentives.

With the sealing industry showing great promise, the whaling industry was given new strength mostly by the arrival of American whalers into Sydney Harbour. The local industry got underway in 1802 with 7 ships operating from Port Jackson. The Bass Strait area was using half of the 22 ships operating by 1803. The others were successfully operating in New Zealand and South Australian waters.

The colony by this time was moving through turbulent times. The settlements were mostly rural in nature and relied mainly on produce grown with the assistance of assigned convicts. By governor regulation these assigned persons were to be fed, housed, clothed and generally maintained by the 'master'. This was not an inexpensive program for the masters, especially where smallholdings were involved. King ordered that the commissary purchase all produce from these landholders and set a minimum price at which wheat and other grains would be purchased. In this way the landowners could be seen to receive adequate compensation to meet their obligations to their convict workers. As the colony grew demand for 'luxury' items as well as a broader range of staples also grew and this attracted a growing number of 'speculative' ships into the port of Sydney. A price war developed between the traders, the military and those wanting to participate in the purchasing of imported goods. Governor King, having set the original tariff collections on only spirits, wine and beer, decided to impose a 5% ad valorem duty on all imports in 1802. This immediately created a steady revenue stream that needed accounting for. King assumed that this was discretionary income available to him to dispense, as he considered fair and not as an offset to what the British Treasury was providing to the colony.

King had identified a growing social problem as the one where street children were in large numbers, and decided to do something about it. King formed the female Orphan Committee, with the object of housing, feeding, clothing and educating these children until they could be put into service in the colony. The committee included the Reverend Samuel Marsden who had really been instrumental in recognising the problem and finding a partial solution. King appointed Marsden the Treasurer of the committee and decided to use certain Treasury funds to buy the house of the departing Lieutenant Kent, who made it known that he (Kent), had the finest residence in Sydney. Kent was leaving the colony to return to England and take up another posting and he negotiated with the governor for the government to buy his house at 'valuation'. The valuation was based on a replacement cost, whether or not another house like Kent's would ever be built again and the valuation came to 1,700 pound. Kent received his money via a bill drawn on the British Treasury, which King prayed would be accepted by the Treasury. The bill was negotiated and the Female Orphanage got a residence for about 80 waifs off the streets, although a revenue-raising plan came about when Marsden accepted destitute children from single fathers for a lump sum of 5 pound. It was not as though Marsden or the Orphan Committee were short of revenue. With the growth tax imposed by King, the amount of revenue raised by the Harbour Master from imported goods, especially the alcohol trade, Marsden was constantly looking for ways to spend his money.

King sent Lt-Governor David Collins off to open a settlement at Port Phillip but Collins decided that the Mornington Peninsula was not an ideal place to commence a colony and crossed the strait and selected Hobart instead. Van Diemen's Land had been settled first in 1803, just as the *Sydney Gazette* newspaper was being founded by King as a means of keeping the settlers informed. He would make many proclamations to the free settlers as well as advertising that certain convicts had gone bush. The scourge of the importation of spirits could not be handled but King decided that 32,000 litres of rum brought to the colony from Bengal by Campbell should be returned and he accepted no counsel to the contrary although Marsden led a group to announce how great noble and strong the governor was becoming. It was at this time, with minimum imports transferring from the colony into Britain that the British Government decided to impose a tariff on all colonial imports. Sealskins had yielded either to the colony or to the British merchants over 100,000 skins between 1800 and 1806. This could be considered an ecological disaster or a trading triumph, depending on one's viewpoint, but then the British Government cashed in on the colonial 'success' by imposing this levy on all imports.

In the colony, prices were heavily influenced by local conditions including droughts and floods, and English economic conditions all affected events in the colony. The drought of 1804 for instance affected the wheat crop and thus the price of wheat within the colony. King decided to increase to price the Commissary would purchase private farm grain but even so the shortages were reflected in the price of bread. A settler could buy a loaf of bread for 4p or barter it with 2 ½ pound of wheat.

By 1805 Macarthur could see the writing on the wall for his days as a military officer and accepted his grant of land available to all military who intended to settle in the colony and opened his estate at the Cowpastures, probably the best grazing land within the 1805 limits of the colony.

King's next contribution to the social needs of the convicts was to proclaim a 56-hour workweek for all assignees in return for bed and breakfast, tobacco and tea. The convict rations from the commissary would meet their needs for lunch and dinner.

The first free settlers were wealthy Britons who were enticed into relocating by the offer of free land grants, convict labour to work the land and an allocation of government livestock. The Blaxland brothers responded to this enticement in 1805. In that same year the first colonial built whaler was launched so that greater local participation could be realised.

Pressure on the colony was coming not only from outside the territory but inside as well. We have accounted for King's sudden interest in the growing orphan numbers in Sydney town, but the cause of the problem raises concerns as to the type of society the colony could develop into. Two measures offer some indication of the underlying movement.

- In 1805, there were 1400 women in the colony but there were only 360 married couples
- Of the 1800 children, under 18, over half were illegitimate
- The crime rate in the colony was by 1807, 8 times the rate in England.

The 1806 drought made the wheat crop fail, and the grain became scarce. The price of wheat rose from 1/1/–to 3/14/–per bushel and the price of bread rose 12 fold from 4p to 4/–per loaf. The new governor, sent to replace Phillip Gidley King arrived in Sydney. Tales of the Bounty mutiny and its remarkable voyage of skill and endurance had foreshadowed William Bligh's arrival across the Pacific. Having outlined the many events, which both curtailed and encouraged the colonial economy, it is time to review the impact on the financial situation brought about by these economic conditions.

N.G. Butlin reports in *Forming a Colonial Economy*

"British decision makers were far from consistent in their attitudes to fiscal obligations to and from the colonists. All governors to 1821 left with at least his fiscal reputation tarnished. Intermittent and at times irascible and condemnatory intervention in colonial expenditures reflected, in part, British ignorance and suspicion. In fact, complex colonial fiscs operated almost from the beginning of the settlement. By 1830, local revenues were offsetting expenditures for everything except convict and defence functions.

"The transfer of prisoners was, from a colonial Australia view, a capital transfer, even if, from a British perspective, the human capital involve had a negative vale. Britain was determined to constrain the British contribution to the colonial operations and to narrow the range of support. It sought ways of ever reducing, to the British taxpayer, the per capita costs of prisoners landed in the colony and to limit the total budgetary costs of sustaining colonies. One way, they decided to achieve this was through auditing public accounts and criticising local behaviour. Other ways was the adoption of a policy of private development of the country, and make the country no longer dependent essentially on convict transfers. A second they decided would be to encourage the emergence of a freed society from a freed population. Thus part of the funds could be diverted from the convict population to the funding of public activity.

"The question remains is the extent to which the colonists could be encouraged to enter the colony and how much of the burden could they bear".

A study of the types of public and private British Investment in the colony is the subject of another exercise, but it can be said here that a wonderful model could be constructed of the formation of a colonial economy.

Consider the inputs: British investment of capital and goods, the transfer of industry–the branch office in the colony, the use of the colony as a source of raw materials–the colonial garden, ripe for the picking. British ships transferring people and goods.

Consider the restraints of population to adopt and utilise the investment

Consider the ultimate limitations of human personality–the convicts forced to labour, when their colleagues back 'home' were lounging in a prison cell. Why should they work in exchange for a limited freedom?

If all this sounds farfetched let us consider the role of free trade and its benefits to Britain.

This is a piece by Sir T. H. Farrer (Bart) from his 1887 book 'Free *Trade versus Fair Trade*'. The notation on the front-piece of the book shows the Cobden Club emblem with the words 'free trade, peace, goodwill among nations'. We will discuss Cobden a little later when we review the work of the Federation Senator Edward Pulsford–another outspoken supporter and devotee of the Cobden philosophy, and free trade and open immigration.

"The amount of English capital constantly employed abroad in private trade and in permanent investments, including Stock Exchange securities, private advances, property owned abroad by Englishmen, British shipping, British-owned cargoes, and other British earnings abroad, has been estimated by competent statisticians as being between 1,500 and 2,000 million pounds, and is constantly increasing. Taking the lower figure, the interest or profit upon it, at 5 per cent, would be 75 million pounds, and at the higher figure it would be 100 million pound."

Farrer then equates this income figure to the spread of imports over exports and finds that the two compare. But then he argues there is the question of freights. "A very large proportion of the trade of the United Kingdom is carried in English ships, and these ships carry a large proportion of the trade of other countries not coming to England. This shipping is, in fact, an export of highly-skilled English labour and capital which does not appear in the export returns of the 19th century, and considering that it includes not only the interest on capital but also wages, provisions, coal, port expenses, repairs, depreciation and insurance; and that the value of English shipping employed in the foreign trade is estimated at more than 100 million pound per annum, the amount to be added to our exports on account of English shipping, must be very large". But he goes further, "add to this the value of ships built for foreigners amounting to over 70,000 ton per annum, worth together several millions, and all these outgoings, with the profits, must either return to this country in the shape of imports, or be invested abroad–I believe 50 million pound is too low an estimate of the amount of unseen exports. In addition there are the commissions and other charges to agents in this country, connected with the carriage of goods from country to country, but each of these items do not appear in the statistics of exports. I can only assume that we are investing large amounts of our savings in the colonies, such as Australia".

The Farrer argument in favour of 'free trade' then turns to the 'fair trade' objections to foreign investments.

Farrer writes "When we point to the indebtedness of foreign colonies to England as one reason for the excess of imports, they tell us that we have been paying for our imports by the return to us of foreign securities; and at the same time they complain bitterly that, instead of spending our money at home, our rich men are constantly investing their money abroad, and thus robbing English labour of its rights here"

But we know that is not the whole story.

If England investors remit capital to the colonies, it is not only in the form of cash (which would come from savings) but it is more often in the form of capital goods. England sends iron; the shipbuilders who make the ships that carry the goods, and the sailors who navigate them. When they reach the colonies, what happens then? They return with grain, or coal, or wool, or timber, and that makes those commodities cheaper in England. The investor receives the interest or profits on that capital invested which would generally be greater than what could have been earned if the capital had been invested in England. Now that return can be spent on luxury goods, invested locally or re-invested overseas to commence the whole cycle again. That return will be employed in setting to work English labour, earn a return and so on.

It remains true that on the whole, based on the Farrer argument, the transfer of English capital from an English industry that does not pay to a colonial industry which does pay, is no loss to England generally, and causes no diminution in the employment of English labour. There are at least two drawbacks to colonial investment by a maritime power; one, in the event of a war, the returns would be open to greater risk, and two; the investors can more easily evade taxation by the English Government.

Obviously since 1886, when Farrer constructed this argument, the world has changed, investment opportunities have changed, England has fallen from its pinnacle as a world power and international commercial leader and the improved collection of statistics now recognises movements of goods and investments on both current account and capital account. But the concept helped put the Australian colony on the map and attracted enormous amounts of private capital into the colony to make it grow and prosper.

Farrer concludes his argument with this observation.

"The desire to make profitable investments, however valuable economically is not the only motive which governs rich men; it's the love of natural beauty; interest in farming and the outdoor life; personal and local attachments; all of which are quite sure to maintain a much larger expenditure on English land than would be dictated by a desire for gain. Let these other motives have their way, as these investors still contribute to the welfare of the toilers and spinners who produce the goods, and make a good return that in the end makes England wealthier"

If Farrer really believes his wholesome argument, then the theory of developing a colony economy as espoused by the British Government took on great validity, and if it had been followed through fully, the colony may have developed faster and been self-sufficient long before 1830, but on the other hand, it may or would have emulated the British economy much more than it did.

A closer examination should be made of the original intention of 'local' revenue raising. Phillip's instructions had included the right to raise local 'taxation', however Butlin, in *Forming a Colonial Economy* writes that

"At least as early as 1892, Phillip had sought approval for introducing indirect taxation. The British officials approved the raising of charges but not as 'revenue' for disposition by the governor. It took until 1896 for such charges to be put into operation, when Hunter imposed a charge on access to imports, not a duty on the goods themselves".

Hunter's action, writes Butlin appears devious when put into the context that the British reserved the sole right to raise revenue from duties, tolls, and licences.

Again, in the context of the British policy to make the colony self-sufficient and self-regulated, it does not make sense to have firstly included in the official instructions to Phillip the right, if not the obligation to raise local revenues, to then impose restrictions on the governor by limiting the area, range and amount of taxes, but by 1800 King was raising duties and tariffs, with any restriction on amount, disposition or accounting. Butlin may, himself, have misinterpreted the role and intent of the local efforts and the British policy.

Far from being able to privatise development in the colony and rely on private development, the British Government had to take account of the recommendations of the Select Parliamentary Committee on Transportation, which reported in 1810 on the need, and benefits of continuing with transportation of prisoners to the colony. This policy would continue to provide workers and population for the colonial economy, since by the time the Committee reported, less than 33% of the population were convicts at this date.

On the other hand, four statistics provided to the Committee should have persuaded the Committee to terminate transportation

- The cost of convict maintenance rose to a high of 120 pound per convict per annum. This had risen from the previous average of less than 32 pound
- Marsden took the first wool for weaving to England and received a very positive reception
- The Commissary was able to buy fresh beef and mutton from farmers for rations, and replace salted imports
- The port duties in 1810 had risen to 8,000 pound annually and were making a good contribution towards local discretionary revenue for the governors.

The colony was finally finding its feet. A solid base had been set, one from which Macquarie could build and use a building program with investment opportunities relying on free enterprise. The economy was on the move.

The financial statements for the colony during this period come to us via the *Sydney Gazette* each quarter. The newspaper published the quarterly statements of the Orphan Fund and the Police Fund (the successor by name change) to the Hunter-sponsored Gaol Fund.

CHAPTER 17

THE THIRD PERIOD 1823-1840

These are the years leading up to the great recession of 1842. The foundations of the causes of the recession lay in the British influence on and over the colonial economy.

Naturally 50 years from the founding of the first penal settlement produced more than just one recession, although the term of the day referred to the economic collapse as being a depression. Gipps, as governor of the senior colony, found it difficult to ascribe more than partial blame on the British situation, but modern economic historians including Brian Fitzpatrick, Noel Butlin and A.G.L. Shaw place much if not most of the blame on the withdrawal of British Investment from the colony. The depression of 1842 was a follow-on event from the hiccup of 1827. The credit squeeze of 1812 was the first time economic hardship or stress had reached the colony since 1788 and was the first occasion that the withdrawal of British investment scrambled the comparative gains being made steadily in the colony. Of course, Macquarie tried to counter the effects of the credit squeeze by encouraging trade, creating the atmosphere for entrepreneurs and encouraged local business to establish and grow.

Brisbane's arrival in the colony in 1821, marked the end of the successful Macquarie years, and reduced the growth of activity in the colony to a more normal level.

Factors Affecting British Investment in the Colony

A number of factors affected the level of capital investment into the colony–many were ill informed and relied on delayed newspaper reports on activity in the various settlements.

a. The offer of assisted migration
b. The failing economic conditions in Britain
c. Economic expansion for the pastoral industry due to successful exploration in the colony
d. The settlement at Port Phillip and the eventual separation of Victoria from New South Wales would promote great investment opportunities
e. The rise of the squattocracy
f. The crash of 1827-28 in the colony shakes British Investors
g. The Bigge's' Report of 1823 breathed new life into capital formation especially with Macarthur sponsoring the float of the Australian Agricultural Company
h. Further along, the good credit rating of the colonies (and there being no defaults on loans) encouraged larger investments and loans into the colonies
i. Shortage of Labour in the colony and the offer of land grants to new settlers became a useful carrot to attract small settlers bringing their own capital by way of cash or goods or livestock with them.
j. Two other steps had important consequences, one in the colony and the other in Britain. In 1827 Governor Darling began to issue grazing licenses to pastoralists, and the terms were set at 2/6d per hundred acres, with liability to quit on one month's notice. From this movement grew, writes Mad wick in Immigration into Eastern Australia, the squatting movement and the great pastoral expansion, and the idea of the earlier Governors that the colony of New South Wales should be a colony of farmers was thus abandoned. The concurrent event was the floating of the Australian Agricultural Company in London. Development by the AAC and by the free settlers brought increasing prosperity. Exports tripled between 1826 and 1831.
k. There is a connection between availability of factors of production and the level of investment. In the early days of the colony,

labour was present—bad labour, convict labour, but still labour. The governors had demanded settlers with capital to employ that labour and develop the land. They proposed to limit land grants in proportion to the means of the settler. Governor Darling declared (HRA ser 1, vol 8) that 'when I am satisfied of the character, respectability and means of the applicant settler in a rural area, he will receive the necessary authority to select a grant of land, proportionate in extent to the means he possesses.

Under Macquarie the colony had boomed with new buildings, new settlements, new investment and lots of convicts. Under Brisbane the needs for economic consolidation and new infrastructure would be addressed, together with an appeal for free settlers.

Some significant events took place during the Brisbane guardianship

- The British were intent on accessing every available trading opportunity with the colony, and formed in Scotland *The Australia Company*
- A road was built to connect the Windsor settlement to the new settlement at Maitland. This decision opened up the Hunter River district to new farming opportunities
- The responsibility for convicts was transferred from the Superintendent of Convicts to the Colonial Secretary, although this move was to be reversed within the next decade
- The first documented discovery of gold was made. It was hushed in the colony lest convicts run off to find their fortunes
- In Bigge's third and final report, he recommended extra colonial import duties and less British duty on imported timber and tanning bark

The most significant event of all was the confidence placed in Bigge's favourable opinion of the potential of the colonial economy by the London Investment community and the resulting subscription of one million pound for the Australian Agricultural Company. The subscription was accompanied by a grant of one million acres of land around Port Stephens and the allocation of 5,000 convicts, but also brought inflation to livestock prices and availability throughout the colony.

J.F. Campbell wrote about the first decade of the Australian Agricultural Company 1824-1834 in the proceedings of the 1923 RAHS.

"Soon after Commissioner Bigge's report of 1823 became available for public information, several enterprising men concerted with a view to acquire sheep-runs in the interior of this colony, for the production of fine wool.

The success which attended the efforts of John Macarthur and a few other New South Wales pastoralists, in the breeding and rearing of fine wool sheep and stock generally, as verified by Bigge, gave the incentive and led to the inauguration of proceedings which resulted in the formation of the Australian Agricultural Company.

The first formal meeting of the promoters took place at Lincoln's Inn, London, (at the offices of John Macarthur, junior).

Earl Bathurst, advised Governor Brisbane in 1824 that . . . .

His Majesty has been pleased to approve the formation of the Company, from the impression that it affords every reasonable prospect of securing to that part of His Majesty's dominions the essential advantage of the immediate introduction of large capital, and of agricultural skill, as well as the ultimate benefit of the increase of fine wool as a valuable commodity for export.

The chief proposals of the company are:

   i.   The company would be incorporated by Act of Parliament or Letters Patent.
   ii.   The capital of the company was to be 1 million pound sterling divided into 10,000 shares of 100 pound each
   iii.   A grant of land of one million acres to be made to the company
   iv.   That no rival joint stock company to be established in the colony for the next twenty years
   v.   That agents of the company would select the situation or the land grants.

vi. The shepherds and labourers would consist of 1,400 convicts, thereby lessening the maintenance of such convicts by an estimated 30,800 pound or 22 pound/per head/ per annum

The Royal Charter of 1824 forming the company provided for payment of quit-rents over a period of twenty years, or the redemption of the same by paying the capital sum of 20 times the amount of the rent so to be redeemed. These quit-rents were to be waived if the full number of convicts were maintained for a period of five years. No land was to be sold during the five-year period from the date of the grant".

Being important that the investment be seen to have the support of strong leaders in Britain, and democratic governance, the company operated with

- A Governor
- 25 directors
- 365 stockholders (proprietors)

Leading stockholders included

- Robert Campbell
- Chief Justice Forbes
- Son of Governor King
- Rev'd Samuel Marsden
- John Macarthur
- Each Macarthur son, John jr, Hannibal, James, Charles, Scott & William John Oxley, the Colonial-Surveyor had recommended the area of Port Stephens as an eligible spot for the land grant. The local directors inspected and approved the site but John Macarthur was extremely critical of the selection, the management plan and the extravagance of the first buildings.

This venture was the first major investment into the colony and set the scene for later developments. In 1825 the Van Diemen's Land Company was chartered by the British Parliament and granted land on the northwest corner of the territory.

Both the A.A. Coy and the VDL Coy still operate today after nearly 180 years of continuous operation, a record beaten only by the operation of the Hudson Bay Company in Canada.

Sir Timothy Coghlan was the colonial statistician whilst he was involved in preparing the series 'The Wealth and Progress of New South Wales 1900-01'. He was later appointed as Agent-General in London before compiling the 4-volume set of 'Labour and Industry in Australia'.

A review of the Coghlan account of Public Finance includes references to

- Loan expenditure
- Government Services
- Public Debt
- Colonial Debt Rating
- Land Grants versus Sales
- Treasury bills
- Assets of New South Wales
- Private Finance

The Coghlan theory on each of these points will now be given analysis.

I. Loan Expenditure

The Loan Account was not established until 1853, although the system of raising money by loans commenced as early as 1842. The first ten loans of the colony were raised on the security of the Territorial Revenue, which fund was the proceeds of Land sales and used for the benefit of assisted immigration. Prior to 1842, capital expenditure was made from normal revenue and no differentiation was made between expenditure on capital account and expenditure on current account. All funds flow into and from Consolidated Revenue. From 1853, after the securing of funds through the Loan Account, all proceeds of loans were paid into Consolidated Revenue fund, without being separated into specific capital or current account allocations. So those funds that were raised for specific capital projects had to rely on available surpluses in Consolidated Revenue if the project was to proceed and be fully funded.

The use to which loan funds were generally put was capital works such that the citizens of the settlements would have running water, sewerage, tramways, and telegraphic services. docks, roads and bridges, public works and buildings, fortifications and military works, immigration, public instruction and school buildings, lighthouses and improvements to harbours and rivers.

Coghlan states that 'a vigorous works policy was usually the order of the day'. This, put simply, meant that 'the opportunity engendered the desire, and the open purses of the investors tempted the colonies to undue borrowing and lavish expenditure'. It is Coghlan's opinion that 'the plethora of money has been harmful in many ways, but is most apparent in the construction of a few branch railways in outlying and sparsely-settled districts which do not even pay their working expenses, with the consequence that interest on loan capital has to be paid out of general revenue. Overall, it will be found that the proceeds of loans have been well expended.' The attached loan expenditure table reflects the growing debt per inhabitant. The table shows two interesting facts a. The annual loan expenditure per inhabitant varies from 18/9d to 4/4/-, and b. The accumulated debt per inhabitant grew, in twenty years, from 17/0/6d to 44/17/6d

ii. Public Borrowing and Public Debt

It was after 1831, when the system of free land grants was abolished, and the auction system of land disposal was introduced, that it was decided to pay these auction proceeds into the Land Fund. It was from this fund that that charges relating to the assistance for migrants was to be paid. From 1831 to 1841, this fund was adequate, but in 1841 the fund was insufficient and it was decided to borrow on the security of the Land Revenue. Thus on the 28th December 1841, a notice was placed in the Gazette to the effect that 49,000 pound was to be raised by way of a debenture loan with interest at 5.25%. This was the start of public debt in the colony, and the first ever raised by Australian Government. A further 10 loans between 1842 and 1850 quickly followed, amounting in total to 705,200 pound, the proceeds of which were allocated exclusively to furthering immigration.

At 1850, when responsible government was underway, the public debt was 1,000,800 pound. Of this amount, 640,500 had been raised on the security of land revenue. The balance of 360,300 pound was raised on the security of general revenue.

Of the total, railways accounted for 474,000, water and sewerage 82,900, public works 21,000 and immigration was 423,000. Of the total 1,000,800 only 47,500 was redeemed out of general revenue, the balance being rolled-over into new loans.

The Public Debt balances for this period are shown on the attached table

Nothing quite engenders confidence in an investor like the thought of a new bank opening for business.

Less than three months after his arrival in the colony, Macquarie foreshadowed his plan for a bank on the South African model, as a 'remedy' to 'be speedily applied to this growing evil' of private promissory notes. With some exaggeration he explained that there was 'no other circulating medium in this colony than the notes of hand of private individuals' which, as he said, had 'already been productive of infinite frauds, abuses and litigation'. He accordingly announced his intention to' strongly recommend the adoption here of the same system of banking and circulating medium as is now so successfully and beneficially pursued at the Cape of Good Hope'.

By June 1810 Macquarie had developed his plan for 'The New South Wales Loan Bank' as a government institution 'as nearly as possible on the same system and principles as the Government Loan Bank at the Cape of Good Hope'. There, he explained the government issued notes by way of loan on the security of mortgages at 6 per cent per annum. He also pointed out that in England the government borrowed on exchequer bills at 5 %, so that the Cape was 11% better off. 'It appears to me' was his conclusion, 'the most perfect model in all its parts that could be possibly adopted here' By October 1810, he was willing to accept any alternative form of bank which Liverpool (Secretary for the Colonies) might believe to be 'better calculated to effect the desired object'.

Obviously a Bank would form the foundation for a monetary policy in the colony, and stop the use of Commissary receipt (store receipts) as an exchange mechanism, promote a currency and an official exchange rate for traders and cease to rely on bills drawn on the British Treasury to pay for goods and services.

3. The British Scene

Circumstances in Britain contributed greatly to the climate of 'greener pastures' over the seas.

Conditions were never more favourable for emigration than they were during the 1830s. The decade had opened with rioting in the agricultural districts in the south of England. This was followed by the upheavals of the Reform Bill of 1832, the Factory Act of 1833 and the Corn Laws, which kept wages low and unemployment high. The Poor Law of 1834 withdrew assistance from the poor and re-introduced the workhouse. The Irish rebellion was creating both upheaval and poverty

These conditions were met by the enthusiastic reports coming from Australia of the progress being made in agriculture, commerce and the pastoral industry. The assistance granted to emigrants as a result of Edward Gibbon Wakefield's reforms made possible the emigration of people who had previously been prevented by the expense. It is almost certain that free passage would not have been a sufficient enticement if conditions in Britain had not been unfavourable. It is significant that years of small migration coincided with good conditions in England accompanied by unfavourable reports from the colony.

4. Creating Opportunities in the Colony

Availability of land and labour to yield profit on invested capital is the constant decisive condition and test of material prosperity in any community, and becomes the keystone of an economy as well as defining its national identity.

British Government policy for the Australian colonies was formulated and modified from time to time. Policies for the export of British capital and the supply of labour (both convict and free) were adjusted according to British industrial and demographic and other social situations, as well as the capability and capacity of the various colonial settlements top contribute to solving British problems.

By the 1820s there was official encouragement of British Investment in Australia by adopting policies for large land grants to persons of capital and for the sale of land and assignment of convict labour to those investors. Then followed the reversal of the policy of setting up ex-convicts on small 30 acre plots as small proprietors. The hardship demanded by this policy usually meant these convicts and families remained on the commissary list for support (food and clothing) at a continuing cost to the government. It was much cheaper to assign these convicts to men of property and capital who would support them fully—clothe, house and feed them.

We can ask, what led directly to the crash of 1827? a. Firstly, the float of the Australian Agricultural Company raised a large amount of capital, mostly from the City of London investment community, and this contributed to speculation and 'sheep and cattle mania instantly seized on all ranks and classes of the inhabitants' (written by Rev'd John Dunmore Lang) 'and brought many families to poverty and ruin'. b.When capital imports cease, the wherewithal to speculate vanished; speculation perforce stopped; inflated prices fell to a more normal level, and wrote E.O. Shann in Economic History of Australia 'because those formerly too optimistic were now too despairing, and people had to sell goods at any price in order to get money; men who had bought at high prices were ruined, and perforce their creditors fell with them'. c.In 1842, it was the same. The influx of capital from oversees, pastoral extension, and large-scale immigration, caused much speculation. The banks, competing for business, advanced too much credit. Loans were made on the security of land and livestock, which later became almost worthless; too much discounting was done for merchants (Gipps, HRA Vol 23) In the huge central district on the western slopes, along the Murrumbidgee and the Riverina; the squatters triumphed, as was inevitable. He had the financial resources to buy his run—especially after the long period of drought. Four million acres of crown land was sold for nearly 2.5 million pound. The confidence of British investors was waning. A crisis in the Argentine and the near failure of the large clearinghouse of Barings' made them cautious. Stories of rural and industrial strife in the colony were not inducements to invest: and wood and metal prices were still falling Loan applications being raised in London were under-subscribed, at the same time; the banks were increasingly reluctant to lend money for land development, which was so often unsound.

5. Assisted Migration

The dual policy of selling land to people with sufficient capital to cultivate it, and keeping a careful check on the number of free grants was adopted after 1825. 'Yet the Colonial Office', says Madgwick, 'failed to administer land policy with any certainty (R.B. Madgwick 'Immigration into Eastern Australia'). There was no uniform policy adopted to encourage economic development in a systematic and rational way. The Wakefield system found new supporters. The principle had been established that the sale of land was preferred to the old system of grants. The dual system of sales and grants had failed to encourage local (colonial) purchases. They were willing to accept grants or even 'squat' rather than purchase land. Sales to absentee landlords and investors stepped up, and as can be seen from the following table, provided extensive revenue to the British Government to promote free and sponsored migration.

6. Successful exploration promotes new interest in the Colony

A period of rapid expansion followed the change in economic policy. Wool exports by 1831 were 15 times as great as they had been only 10 years earlier (in 1821). The increase in the number of sheep led to a rapid opening of new territories for grazing. It was the search for new land with economic value that underpinned most of the explorations. Settlers and sheep-men quickly followed exploration, and growth fanned out in all directions from Sydney town.

However, exploration was not the only catalyst for growth. a. The growing determination to exclude other powers from the continent stimulated official interest in long-distance exploration by sea and by land and in the opening of new settlements. For instance, J.M. Ward in his work 'The Triumph of the Pastoral Economy 1821-1851' writes that Melville and Bathurst Islands, were annexed and settled between 1824 and 1827, whilst Westernport and Albany were settled in order to clinch British claims to the whole of Australia b. When Governor Brisbane opened the settlement at Moreton Bay in 1824; it was to establish a place for punishment of unruly convicts and a step towards further economic development, and of extending the settlements for the sake of attracting new investment

7. Colonial Failures fuel loss of Confidence

The collapse of British Investment can be traced to one or two causes, or indeed both.

I.   The British crisis of 1839 reflected the availability of capital for expansion by the Australian banks of that day–The Bank of Australasia and the Union Bank. These banks, three mortgage companies and the Royal Bank went into a slump due to shortage of available funds and deferred the raising of new funds until after the crisis. Stringency in the English Capital market had a serious impact on the capital raising opportunities in the colonies.

II. The second possibility is that the sharp decline was initiated by bad news of returns in the colonies, and that its role accentuated a slump with the dire consequences experienced in 1842-43. Recovery was delayed and made more difficult as there was 'no surplus labour in the colony'

It would be dangerous to imply or decide that every slump in Australia could be explained as being caused by economic events. British investment was independent then, as it is now, and so the more valid explanation of the downturn in British investment in this period is that negative reports from the colonies disappointed and discouraged investors with capital to place.

Most facts about public finance in New South Wales lead to the conclusion that it was disappointed expectations that caused the turn down in the transfer of funds. At this same time Governor Gipps (Sir George Gipps) was being pushed by bankers and merchants to withdraw government deposits from the banks and thus this action caused a contraction in lending by the banks which in turn caused a slowdown of colonial economic activity. The attached statistics of land sales, registered mortgages and liens on wool and livestock reflects the strong downturn in the agricultural economy, which naturally flowed on to the economy as a whole. ii. Government Services

Sources of Revenue for each colony was generally classified under four (4) headings–taxation, land revenue, receipts for government services rendered and miscellaneous revenue. Prior to 1850, the 'Blue Books' were compiled annually for circulation to the Colonial Office in London, the Colonial Governor, Colonial Treasurer and Legislative Council. After self-government a new system of public accounting was introduced which reflected the four headings mentioned above. Annual comparisons are best made on a per inhabitant basis, and whilst 'taxation' remained fairly constant at a rate per head of 1/17/6d to 2/4/2d, land revenue and government services ranged widely. Land revenue grew from 1/9/7d per head to 2/6/0d; government services naturally grew from 1/11/11d to 3/15/1d, obviously reflecting the growing demands for government to provide all manner of assistance to the settlers and growing population. Services included:

Railways
Tramways
Postage
Telegraphs
Money orders
Water supply
Sewerage
Public school fees
Pilotage and harbour fees
Mint fees

Coghlan confirms that 'the income derived by the government from services, has, been steadily increasing; this is only what would naturally be expected in a growing community, but income per head has been fairly well sustained, holding in a 12 year period from 3/9/11d to 3/17/11d.

This result is in spite of the fact that the railway system rarely made a 'profit' with earnings generally being around 3.81%, with the average interest payable being 3.61%. As the revenue from services naturally depends upon the amount of production, the rate per inhabitant will not only cease to increase, but will ultimately decline.'

Government services were supposedly being conducted on commercial principles; except that in the case of providing most services, receipts are less than expenditure meaning that these services were generally subsidized from general revenue. The gap appears to have increased exponentially year after year.

CHAPTER 18

THE FOURTH PERIOD 1841-1855

Two interesting discoveries emerge from an analysis of British Investment in to the Colony 1800-1850. We have noted above that T.A. Coghlan, that doyenne of all things statistical, especially in relation to the colony, states very strongly and without qualification that 'the private capital invested in the colony prior to 1871 was 16 million pound.

Coghlan provides no supporting evidence to substantiate this statement, but having broken the actual verifiable figures down into components, that Coghlan figure sounds quite plausible. This writer's estimates of private capital invested in the colony between 1800 and 1850 are 14,388,000 pound. The components include Government borrowings overseas; immigrant's capital; foreigner's investment, and I have included the amount of land mortgages recorded under the Deeds Registration Act of 1843. Although land mortgages after 1843 would normally have been recorded, there was provision in the Act for re-registration of earlier mortgages and many lenders, both private and corporate, took advantage of ratifying their previous lien rights. Since my figures relate to the period to 1850, it is more than likely that between 1851 and 1870, a further 1.7 million pound was invested privately. So Coghlan is essentially. Correct.

However it is the N.G. Butlin assumptions that trouble me, and I would like to restate an earlier conclusion that the British accepted an excellent return on their investment in the colony, and this is really what the opening of the colony was all about.

The Table of British Public Investment in the colony shows from the inception of the colony, through to self-government, the British 'invested' nearly 70 million pound in capital works or their equivalent. What this means is that I have included the cost of shipping and transporting the convicts to the colony and the cost of food and provisioning. Professor Butlin, at one point, refers to the level of British investment for this same period as being 74 million, but the components are not described. However, it is a not unreasonable figure to work with. It includes the early grants to the colony from the British Treasury; it includes the transportation of the convicts and their food en route; it includes the treasury bills drawn by the colony on the British Treasury for materials and contract labour, purchases from trading ships coming into the Harbour; it concludes payments made for civil list and military salaries, and it includes the verified public works expenditure. Each of these figures has been drawn from the 'Joint Copying Project of Historical documents' and 'historical statistics'.

The essential point of this assembly of public investment is to put into perspective the original investment by the British Treasury and compare it with the level of 'return' the British, as a whole, were to receive.

So, before we assemble the figures into a table of investment and return, let's review again the elements of what constitutes a 'return'.

Each of the elements of the return, and we might even say the expected return, for it was James Matra's submission to the British Government that first identified that the colony would be self-supporting within two years of commencing and provide advantages to Britain. It was Arthur Phillip in a letter to Lord Sydney in July 1788 who wrote ' . . . nor do I doubt but that this country will prove the most valuable acquisition Great Britain ever made . . . .'

The elements of this 'opportunity cost' include: a. The opportunity cost of housing, feeding and guarding prisoners in England. This is set at the rate of 20 pound per head per annum, but does not take into account any offset for work undertaken by prisoners. b. The use of convict labour for construction work on colonial buildings. This is set at 35 pound per annum for 2/3rds of the convicts (Macquarie employed about 70% of the male convicts in this way. c. The balance of the male convicts were used on road construction, wharves, barracks etc and had an equivalent value, net of support payments, of 35 pound per annum (The James Matra letter of October 1784 stated that the contract price for maintaining prisoners on the hulks was 26/15/0 per annum). In the early years, we can also include in this figure, the convict labour used for land clearing, farming and food production, and the convict labour used for maintaining the supply of building materials, timber, bricks, tiles etc d. The Molesworth Committee concluded in their Report to the House of Commons that there were significant savings in food costs for these convicts e. Another benefit to the British by way of opportunity cost is the value of the land grants to the Military officers by way of fringe benefits as civil payments. On average, the land had a value of 1 pound per acre and we know that land grants were in the order of 5228015 acres f. An as yet economically unquantifiable gain to British industry was the value of the import wool trade, and the export purchases of tobacco and spirits for the colony. In addition timber, coal, whale oil, skins and fur were all important imports by British Industry, and assisted Britain by making them less reliant on Europe. g. It is assumed that the private investment received a return on capital equivalent to an interest and super profit.

So out Summary Table can now be assembled

TABLE BRITISH INVESTMENT & RETURNS FROM THE COLONY OF NSW

Public Investment

Treasury grants	23741000
Convict transport/food	6051550
Treasury Bills	5384584
Civil List	888858
Military	9629170
Commissary	8134000
Public Works	1265000
Total Public Investment	69,482,162

Benefits & Gains to the British

Opportunity Costs–	a.	84000000
Convict labour–	b	70000000
Convict labour–	c	21000000
Food savings–	d	7000000
Land grants–	e	5228015
Total estimated Returns		180228015

CHAPTER 19

THE FIRST POST-SELF GOVERNMENT FINANCIAL STATEMENT–1856

The first financial statement of a Treasurer to the New South Wales Parliament following self-government was that made by the Honourable Stuart Alexander Donaldson on 6ᵗʰ November 1856 to the new Legislative Assembly.

(This extract is taken from the Sydney Morning Herald of 7ᵗʰ November, 1856.)

In the LEGISLATIVE ASSEMBLY of *Friday, 6 November 1856.*

FINANCIAL STATEMENT of the COLONY

Mr Donaldson said: Sir, I am sincerely glad that in taking the course which I am now permitted to pursue, I am not proceeding contrary to the ruling of, or in any disrespect to, the honourable the Speaker of this House. The honourable Member, who sits at the head of the benches opposite, has spoken of the way in which this important matter has been introduced by the present Government, but I can only tell him that so far as the substantial part of the matter is concerned, we have taken the constitutional course. The financial affairs of the country must, in any instance, be indicated by the Governor himself, by message to this House. The difference between the course adopted by the late Ministry and the present is that the late Ministry sent down a message from the Governor, in which the whole matter of the Ways and Means and the Supplies were included; while the present Ministry have adopted that constitutional plan recommended by the Opposition, of separating these matters. I hope the House will bear with me while I now proceed to make that financial statement of the affairs of the country which has been so long promised; and I also hope hon. Members will bear with me if I am compelled to trespass on the patience at some length, which, from the severe cold I labour under, will render my full exposition of the subject matter of some difficulty to myself. In making this statement of the financial affairs of the country, it will be my desire, as far as possible to exhibit not only the debit but also the credit side of the account. To show distinctly our present financial condition, how that condition was brought about, its historical antecedents, the policy which has led to it, and the principles on which we propose to proceed—in short, to exhibit, as fully as I possibly can, the position of our financial affairs, and to bring before the House, as fully as possible, the steps the present Ministry are prepared to take in regard to them. It may not be uninteresting if I commence my observations with a short synopsis of the financial history of the colony for some years bygone. You must remember we are now entering on a new sphere—which our financial arrangements, both of expenditure and income, are in future to be regulated by ourselves alone. Hat for the first time we are to run on our own legs, and it may not therefore be unapt that in order to guide our policy for the future, we should proceed to some review of the past. I shall therefore turn to a period of 20 years ago, and in a cycle of 20 years, in a young country like this, all must be well aware of the great changes in the position of the community—social, moral, and political—which must infallibly take place. It will not be necessary to me to detain the House with all the figures in detail to afford the House the information, which I now wish to supply. Fortunately, we have an intelligent and well-regulated Press—the influence of which will, I doubt not, enable the statements I am about to make to be put fully before the public. Well, Sir, I find that in the year 1836 the revenue of the colony was £340,533 the expenditure £287,376; in 1837, revenue £353,785, expenditure £398,496; in 1838 revenue £334,079, expenditure £463,161; in 1839 revenue £427,368 expenditure £567,966, in 1840, revenue £682,473, expenditure £561,023; in 1841, revenue £497,302, expenditure £756,580; in 1842 revenue £428, 730, expenditure £503,913; in 1843, revenue £350,891, expenditure £369,489; in 1844, revenue £386,617, expenditure £345,583; in 1845, revenue £436,920, expenditure £314,368; in 1846, revenue £346,481, expenditure £305,730, in 1847, revenue £369,259, expenditure £413,073; in 1848, revenue

£396,862, expenditure £460,430; in 1849, revenue £575,692, expenditure £516,633; in 1850, revenue £633,711, expenditure £567,165; in 1851, revenue £486, 698, expenditure £444,108; in 1852, revenue £682,137, expenditure £600,322; in 1853, revenue £987,476, expenditure £682,621; in 1854, revenue £1,239,147, expenditure £1,136,568; in 1855, revenue £1,660,710, expenditure £1,657,024–making a total of revenue through the twenty years, £11,616,879, and of expenditure £11,369,540. If the House will take the average of these returns, they will find that the expenditure and revenue of the country for the last twenty years has a little exceeded £500,000 per annum. It is impossible for any man to read these returns without being struck with the enormous increase of the revenue and expenditure, particularly when it is considered that since the separation of New South Wales from the powerful and productive province of Victoria, the then joint revenues of the colony have been nearly doubled. That must prove to any man, theorize as he may, a progression in the resources of the country most marvellous–a progress that would appear to be absolutely chimerical, but which nevertheless is an absolute fact. In further explaining the present financial position of the country, I shall allude to the exports and imports, and in doing this I shall not take so long a period, but commence from the year 1839.

In the year 1839 the imports of the whole colony, Port Phillip included, amounted to £2,236,371, and the exports to £948,776. A period of seventeen years passed away, and what do we find to have been the result of the enterprise of the community?–Its eager grasp at the advantages, which the productive resources of these colonies held out to them. Why, they found that the increase in commercial enterprise had changed them from a mere province to almost the financial position of an empire.

In 1855 the imports to New South Wales were £4,668,525, while the exports were £2,884,130. The imports to Victoria, which I cannot but regard as one with us, as a great constituent of this Australian colony, were £11,568,904 the exports £13,469,194,–making a total of imports of £16,237,429, and of exports of £16,353,324.

These figures, I think, are sufficient to show the rapidly increasing importance of our commerce and of our social and political growth, while under the political guardianship of the empire to which we are proud to belong. But we are now to start on a new career; for the first time we have to run on our own legs, to guide our own footsteps, through all the intricacies of finance. I fear not for any retrograde movement of this country, and have such faith in her resources that I believe that the rate of progression in wealth, power, and importance, under her own Government, for the next twenty years, will compare with the twenty years that are just gone by. I believe that the same almost miraculous amount of progression of the year 1876 over the year 1856 will equal that of the year 1856 over the year 1836.

With such hopes, with such prospects, with such aspirations as these, who, Sir, can refrain from pride, mingled with awe, in taking charge of this infant Hercules?—And in no respect can this progression be influenced more than by the successful regulation of the finances of the country. I have now gone over the details of the revenue and expenditure, and of the exports and imports of the country for some years past, and it may be interesting on many accounts that I should now afford the House some statement in detail of its present indebtedness, and the causes from which that indebtedness arose. It is necessary that the different purposes for which these loans were incurred should be separately stated. I will now read the return which I hold in my hand, showing the debt of the Colony of New South Wales, the year in which the different loans were contracted, and the purposes for which the money was raised:—

	18 Vic., No. 35	1855	21,000	
Public Works	18 Vic., No. 35		269,700	
	19 Vic., Nos 38 and 40	1856	290,000	
		1854	10,000	
Sydney Waterworks		1855	18,000	
		1856	87,400	**115,400**
		1854	10,000	
Sydney Sewerage		1855	44,900	
		1856	123,400	**178,300**
	TOTAL			**£2,087,700**

I must state in passing that these services properly pay their share of the interest on the debt contracted. I have said that I think it will be the duty of every Finance Minister to treat this debt under different heads and view them from different points. The debt incurred, for immigration for instance, does not stand on the same footing as the debt incurred for the construction of railroads, and the debts for railways and public works stand in a very different position to those incurred for any other purpose whatsoever. As I shall, however, have to allude to this matter when a proposition which will probably be brought before the House by the Government shortly, for the raising of revenue, is under consideration, I do no more than allude to it to-day in a passing way, in order that honourable gentlemen may be somewhat prepared for its discussion.

In connection with the tabular statement just read, I will read another, also intensely interesting, now that we are likely on the threshold of making great outlays on public works–more especially those for internal communication. I find from a statement I have in my hand of expenditure for works and buildings (exclusive of those provided for by loan) from 1836 to 1855, that for the last twenty years a very large portion of the public works of this colony,–larger perhaps than honourable Members who have not paid much attention to the matter have been accustomed to think–has been paid for out of the revenues of the colony from year to year. I think this statement is valuable. Our prospects are now growing clearer and clearer, and it is evident that the cost of our public works of former years, though large in amount, have been trifling to what we must look for in future. In the year 1836 the whole amount, as will be seen from the tabular statement, was only £8,621. One could almost smile at the triviality of such a sum when we consider that it is not nearly so much as one month's interest of our present debt. The following is the statement to which I refer:–

Statement of Expenditure for Works and Buildings (exclusive of those provided by loan), from 1836 to 1855 inclusive.

Year	Amount		
1836	£8,621	0	7
1837	22,851	12	3
1838	63,937	18	7
1839	58,877	15	9
1840	49,703	2	11
1841	37,527	6	2
1842	33,195	19	0

1843	25,494	8	3
1844	22,262	8	8
1845	15,943	4	8
1846	17,070	0	1
1847	41,595	6	10
1848	32,013	18	1
1849	25,992	0	11
1850	16,163	15	7
1851	14,117	8	10
1852	17,823	6	5
1853	44,596	1	0
1854	101,878	14	8
1855	82,314	14	1
Total	**731,980**	**3**	**4**

The progress of the colony did not appear to attract the attention of the Government until 1854, when it took a sudden jump from £44,596 1s 0d to £101,878 14s 8d; and in 1855 to £82,314 14s. 1d. The total expenditure according to this statement during the last twenty years has therefore been nearly £732,000 without one farthing for roads. This, I think, is an interesting paper, especially as it has a bearing on the prospects of the colony in reference to public works for the time to come. With these preliminary observations, I now feel called upon to state to the House what is the actual financial condition of this colony at the present moment. I am sorry it should fall to my lot—but at the same time, as a public man, I have no right to expect that my path will be strewn with roses, or that I am to enter upon my duties as Finance Minister of this colony with nothing but that calculated to felicitate me.

I am sorry to begin my career as a public man with a state of affairs certainly not agreeable either to myself or to the country. It is no use, however, to conceal from the House that fact that in bygone years—I will not lay the blame on any individual or on any body of individuals, owing to the mode of Government, the propositions made by the Executive Government, as it were, added to the proposals of honourable Members representing constituencies, and owing to the weakness of the then Government when they could not carry their financial schemes—although they were bound by the necessities of the day to give way to the pressure for money—the expenditure had exceeded the income until it had left the colony in a bad state.

I am sorry I differ totally with my honourable friend opposite—if he will allow me to use such an expression to one so hostile as the late Finance Minister. I do not know what attention he may have paid to the particular department of which he was the head, but he stated—and statement coming ex cathedra are considered to have some weight—that the debt was about £30,000 (Mr Campbell: £40,000 or £50,000.) The honourable gentleman says £40,000 or £50,000; he has jumped up some 50 per cent, but even now he falls far short. I am afraid he had a pair of diminishing spectacles on when he turned his attention to the matter, if he could not see that the debt was much larger in amount. I have taken great pains to go through this matter, assisted by a gentleman whose able head and ready hand were at my disposal, and I am astonished to hear the honourable gentleman opposite make such a statement, whether he really had charge of the department of which he was ostensibly the head or not. The deficit at the end of 1855, estimated in the most fair and reasonable way, cannot fall short of £120,000 exclusive of the Supplementary Estimates before the House. That would be about a true statement, and I neither wish to conceal that fact, nor the difficulty with which I am encompassed. That deficit I must explain has not accrued during the year 1855-6; it is an accumulated debt since 1854. I have drawn up an account which, availing myself of the Press; I shall possibly be able to give to honourable members before it is laid upon the table of the House formally. This account of the estimated revenue and expenditure shows how the deficit arose. The revenue is enormously deficient of what was anticipated. I do not blame the late Government for this. They propounded a financial scheme objectionable to me, as a Member and also, I believe, objectionable to a majority of the House. I speak of the Government, which existed previously to the inauguration of Responsible Government. Whether they based their conclusions on the financial scheme they withdrew, or upon the result of the ways and means I cannot say. I am sorry to say all the calculations made fall far short of the truth. Their estimates were larger than had been realised.

It is a principle now acknowledged that if you have a tariff calculated to raise a certain revenue, and were to put 10% more upon it, it by no means follows that there would be 10% more revenue.

The fiscal scheme of the late Council was bad and there were other circumstances, which pressed upon the country. A reaction took place after the over-stimulated trade of 1853 and 1854–a reaction which it did not require a prophet to foretell. The Customhouse revenue fell short at the beginning of 1856. The late Government was also exposed to another difficulty. Some hon. Gentlemen who represented constituencies pressed the Government for a large expenditure, which was granted, with the expectation of support. I was not in the ranks of those who pressed the Government for a large expenditure while I refused to supplement their revenue. I felt it my duty to withhold from the Executive Government any extravagant expenditure for fear of an improper expenditure being expected afterwards.

I can recollect that even up to the close of the last session as much as £8,000.00s were forced from them by this pressure from the representatives. The balance sheet for 1856 has been drawn in a tabular form and is as follows:

On the expenditure side of the account there is the deficit on the 1st January 1855, £65,225. 17s 5d, and the late Government told us fairly enough that there would be a large deficit for us to commence with, though they estimated it at only £40,000 or £50,000, not being very much less than the actual amount. Then the appropriations voted in 1855, for the year 1866, amounted to £1,174,029; but we have been able, owing to some of the votes not being required for the services–such as the votes for the Artillery, and the steamer "Torch" about which so much had been said, and for other matters not necessary to particularize, to save out of this £57,000; thus leaving on £1,117,029 of appropriations to be met. Then follow the Supplementary Estimate of 30,689 14s 2d every farthing of which will be wanted: sums chargeable on loan, £4,181; for sewerage £22,235; and for water works, £82,023 6s 8d; making a total of £1,321,383. On the other side, to meet this expenditure, we have made an estimate as nearly as we can of the revenue for the current year. This we are able to make as accurate as will be necessary for all purposes, seeing that we have the actual receipts for the last ten months past; and that we can make with something like a certainty an estimate for the other two months; this we have set down at £1,060,000; and I will here say, that for some of the figures I have used I am indebted to the late Ministry, and although I have not been able altogether to agree with them, yet I own they have helped me very materially in my task. Then followed amounts to be raised by loan, viz., for public works and buildings, £4,181; for sewerage £22,235; and for water works £82,023; being the exact amounts charged on the other side; thus showing an estimated deficiency at the end of 1856 of £152,942. This deficiency will include the £65,225 deficiency on the 1ˢᵗ January 1856 and the supplementary estimate for the year.

Having now brought you to the end of 1856, I propose to carry you to the end of 1857, in order that we may take a view of what our position will then be. Taking the deficit remaining as I have just shown on the 1ˢᵗ January 1857, we have £152,944 as the first item to be provided for. I then estimate the expenditure of the year at £1,060,914; and it is a curious coincidence that the expenditure estimated for 1857 should be precisely the sum at which the revenue of the preceding year had been estimated. My colleagues and I have gone very carefully over both our Estimates of Expenditure and Ways and Means.

I therefore trust that whatever opinion may be entertained of our scheme as a whole, honourable Members opposite will not have it in their power to accuse us of rashness, seeing that we have computed no more for the future than we have received in the past. Then comes the following items:—Interest and special appropriations, £127,500; chargeable on loans, £563,200; sewerage, £60,932; water works, £103,935. This, it will be seen, would leave a deficit of nearly £150,000; but we propose to wipe off this in a way that I shall explain more in detail to the House later in my speech, when I hope to be able to make honourable Members confess that we are justified in the proposal we make, which is that the money should be raised on loan, by terminable annuities, and in a manner that I shall, by-and-by, proceed to explain. Taking this sum then to the credit side of the account, there would be an apparent credit balance of £14,749. This, no doubt, is not a very large amount for them to trade upon, and might be thought to be drawing the revenue and expenditure rather finely together. But then honourable Members opposite must remember that we propose no new taxation, we do not suggest any additional burden on the people; and if we can manage what we propose, it will be something worth remembering that we, the first responsible Ministry of New South Wales, though starting with a heavy load of debt upon our shoulders, had manager after the first year of our office to make la carte blanche; and that in the next year we could start with a clear balance, and that tough in debt we had nothing to do but to go steadily ahead and work it off. There is every hope that we shall go on improving, as I have shown we have hitherto done; and in proof of this

I need but point to the revenue for the last ten months. When I held office with my honourable friend the Member for Stanley Boroughs as Treasurer, the amount of Customs' revenue received during the first six months was most disheartening, but since the month of June the unfavourable anticipations that were then justified have become entirely out of place, for our Customs; revenue has increased from that time in a most remarkable degree, but latterly more particularly; and I have only to hope that it will go on so increasing. No doubt a great deal of the falling off at the beginning of the year owed its origin to the uncertainty that mercantile men felt, and the unsettlement, as I may say, of the commercial mind, at the expected ministerial changes, and when alterations to the tariff had been counted on.

We all know how much this is the case, and that until the financial statement is made in England, by the Chancellor of the Exchequer public interest is excited, and the mercantile world remains in a state of uncertainty until the changes proposed are ascertained. In the Customs department this sensitiveness is always more particularly felt than in any other.

There are two things that are most sensitive, particularly of the acts of a Government—the public credit and the Customs revenue; the latter is more especially so, and if at all tampered with will never be a good one.

Although I am aware that there are great temptations now to interfere with the Tariff, because we could readily tax articles of luxury which are yet also articles of ever day consumption, and must have been tempted to take advantage of it,

CHAPTER 20

CONCLUSIONS AND SUMMARY

CONCLUSIONS

As a general conclusion to this work, a number of observations should be made by way of summary, on matters such as:

- Management of The Police & Orphan Funds
- The Consequences of transportation
- The Gains & Benefits by the British from Transportation
- Fiscal Management during the 'Blue Book' Period
- Other Financial Observations
- Observations on Crown Land Transactions
- Making Improvements in the Public Accounts

A. Management of the Police & Orphan Funds 1810-1822

Marsden and Wentworth were the official recorders of transactions in these two accounts, and as Treasurers of the respective funds, their appointment created the potential for major conflict of interest situations.

It is interesting to muse how a Reverend gentleman (Samuel Marsden—was the appointed trustee of the Female Orphanage as well as a Magistrate in Parramatta) who was paid from the Civil List at the rate of 150.0.0 pound per annum, could afford to operate 4,500 acres of pasture land and build up a flock of 3,500 sheep in a time-frame of less than twenty years.

Even allowing that the land came about from grants, the sheep had to be purchased from the market place or the Governor's flocks and although the convict labour assigned to him was unpaid, they had to be kept, with huts, food and clothing furnished.

We might also ask why the monthly meat bill for the orphanage ran to over 60 pound (whilst the Baker's account averaged over 76 pound per month). Even though the Orphanage owned and operated a farm and the farm regularly sold livestock 'on the hoof', the Orphanage for Young Females then bought back dressed meat from the same butcher.

Marsden was also entitled, on behalf of the orphanage to draw rations from the commissary, especially grain.

For its annual sale of livestock in 1811-1812, Marsden received, on behalf of the orphanage, only 127 pound, but from the same source purchased over 700 pound of dressed meat (which at the going rate of 6d per Lb comes to 25,000 lb of meat each year).

The means were easy to share the spoils between those that could help him gain wealth and reach his target of becoming a large landowner and successful grazier. Marsden housed only female orphans aged from under 5 to 14. On an average month, Marsden paid the butcher over 60 pound, being for an average of 2,500 lb of meat. By the 30th September 1818, Marsden held 3,033 (pound) in the Orphanage account, and on average disbursed 550 pound each month from that account. The only 'admonishment' that Macquarie made (if one can imply from a regulatory change, an act of admonition). Macquarie, at this time, chose to modify the basis of the Orphanage Fund revenue and deleted an item by redirecting that revenue to the Police Fund. He also reduced the percentage of customs duty received by the orphanage from ¼ to 1/8th. Even so, the orphanage Fund built up a substantial balance, which was deposited in 1818 into the newly formed Bank of New South Wales.

Macquarie made no objection to Marsden misdirecting funds from the orphan fund to repairing St. John's Church in July 1811 to the extent of 56 pound, nor to paying the Matron of the Orphanage a monthly stipend of 5 pound (he recorded the payments as 'donations') when the going rate would have been only 1 pound per month, nor of paying 4.5.0 for a bonnet for his wife from the fund. Marsden was married with 5 young children to raise, and because he was a magistrate, he was entitled to draw on the government stores, in spite of his obvious pastoral (agricultural) wealth.

Wentworth too had his questionable methods. He built up large surpluses of cash and bills receivable rather than spend funds on road, bridge or wharf construction; he expended large amounts through the military for 'repairs' to the streets of Sydney and other questionable contracts, never commented on by Macquarie. Wentworth was also the town Magistrate, responsible for fines which were an important source of revenue to the Police Fund. Two items of regular expenditure open to abuse, and which appear to be inordinately high were purchase of firewood and oil and payment for the capture of absconding convicts. The Military personnel were fleecing the Government stores, operating the barter system in the Colony and were obviously getting even more ample rewards in cash from Wentworth. What we can't find any certainty of is who gave directions to D'Arcy Wentworth to make all these payments. It can only have been the Colonial Secretary or the Governor himself.

This raises questions of the 'arms length' treatment of revenues and expenditures, generally, in the Colony.

Events that shaped the Colony

There were a number of events that influenced the course of the early economy and impacted on the extent and rate of economic growth have been selected and outlined. The list of events is not extensive but indicative of sometimes obscure events which have impacted on economic growth e.g. education.

Although it may be suggested that the Report by Commissioner Bigge did not largely influence the Colonial economy, it must be stated that his recommendations to continue with the new Bank of New South Wales, which had been chartered incorrectly by Governor Macquarie, moved the economy along, as did his support for the continuation of the transportation of convicts to the Colony. His lack of support for land grants and early release of convicts may have slowed the economic growth until the consequences of his recommendation that the sale of Crown land be made, is considered. The revenue from customs duties, licenses, tolls and fines was considerable and kept the economy afloat, even if it was being badly managed, until 1810 and the arrival of Macquarie.

Other events tended to feed on each other and gather momentum by cross-pollination. Exploration across the mountains and uncovering the mystery of the rivers opened up huge pastoral areas of first class grazing land, especially that of the Bathurst Plains and fostered the growth of the sheep and wool industries. The continued growth of the pastoral industries all through the 1800s was eclipsed as the prime exporting commodity only upon the 'official' discovery of gold. The discovery of gold also filled the Colonial coffers and set into motion the most remarkable of events that of expanding the rail system across the Colony and to the other Colonies—a line was developed all the way from Adelaide to Brisbane. Instead of relying on sea transport, (the very reason that the major cities were located on harbours and bays), the cities were now to be connected by rail. The senior colony of New South Wales could now diversify its population, move livestock and produce from Ballina to Albury, Broken Hill to Parramatta. The most powerful benefit of the advent of the rail system is the most simplistic one. The Colonial labour-force learned how to engineer bridges (the Hawkesbury); how to construct gradients (crossing the Blue Mountains); lay track at record rates and lowest costs in the world; and engineer the iron horses themselves for local conditions. This new knowledge led directly to the growth of the large engineering shops and the likes of business adventurers such as Thomas Mort, whose remarkable drive, ingenuity and entrepreneurial ability led to the Mort Dry Dock & Engineering complex in Balmain, NSW Fresh Food & Ice, in Sydney and Lithgow, the Bodalla Cheese & Milk factory, relying on refrigeration, together with abattoirs, for the first time, in remote locations rather than in Sydney town.

We cannot overlook the value of education to a largely illiterate economy. Literacy rose by 1835 from 55% to 97% of the adult (15 yrs +) population. The placement of schools and churches throughout the Colony was responsible for this remarkable achievement.

There may well be more 'special events ', other than those discussed but it seems that these interlinking events boosted the Colonial economy in a remarkable way:

- the crown land policy and reform
- the growth of education
- the Report by Commissioner Bigge
- exploration
- pastoral expansion
- the expansion of the rail system
- the Fiscal impact of Federation
- Commonwealth-State Financial Relations

B. The Consequences of Transportation:

The next conclusion must be to record some of the Consequences of Transportation to the Colony of New South Wales. It was during the time that convicts provided the principal source of labour for government purposes and private enterprise, that the consequences of transportation appeared to be measurable. One of the indirect consequences was the 'opportunity' cost to both Britain and the Colony of the transportation program. The Molesworth Committee in 1838, believing that their definitive opinion on the value of transported labour could only justify its continuation stated that transportation was an obstacle to continued economic growth. Some twelve years later, An advocate of transportation, (Archibald Atchison–Crime and Transportation) produced figures to show that just the opposite was true.–Transportation had been of great value to the Colony.

A consequence first raised by Samuel Marsden was that adult convicts were beyond re-training but that the young people needed education. A further social consequence was that the transfer of so many male convicts led, by 1841, to 'a dearth of females', a situation named as alarming by Ralph Mansfield 'Analytical view of the census of 1841 in New South Wales'.

Governor Phillip was the first to publicly recognise that the nature of the penal settlement required a 'peculiar form of government', but one of the goals of Commissioner Bigge was to review the legal side of Colonial administration and report on changes needed for the administration of justice. Bigge did make such a report and the recommendations were immediately adopted by Macquarie.

The Molesworth Committee report into transportation concluded that "Some persons contend that the pecuniary interests of the penal Colony require the continuation of transportation; that as the extraordinary commercial prosperity of these colonies was occasioned by the constant supply of convict labour, if that supply be cut off the colonies would be ruined, from great wealth be reduced to great poverty; and that this change in the fortune of inhabitants, especially if it were sudden, would necessarily produce the worst moral effects upon their character, and still further demoralise the already demoralised.

"The extraordinary wealth of these colonies was occasioned by the regular and increasing supply of convict labourers. The convicts were assigned to settlers as slaves, they were forced to work in combination, and raised more produce than they could consume; for this surplus produce Government provided a market, by maintaining military and convict establishments, which have cost this country above 7,000,000 pound of the public money.

"Labour is in short supply whilst capital has amazingly increased. The flocks of sheep are double the size they ought to be; a vast number perish for want of care; labour must be furnished from sources, other than convicts, if the colonies are to continue to flourish"

C. Analysing the Benefits to the United Kingdom

Although the more significant consequences of transportation of British convicts to the Colony of New South Wales may have been both economic and social, the general benefits of transportation of British convicts out of the United Kingdom are economic.

The essential question becomes–Would the United Kingdom have pursued a Colonial expansion policy if there had not been a need to transfer convicts from the Americas elsewhere?

The answer is of course, a simple–'yes'. The trade, defence and colonisation policies, in place, and under discussion, made territorial acquisition essential. The British Navy needed supplies of masts and spars to maintain its fleet in sailing condition. The British Trade tsars wanted to see further expansion, after a successful entrance into the Caribbean area, and the eyes of the East India Company wanted to spread further across the Asian region. Terra Australis–the great south land–was an obvious desire.

Therefore, it is fair to say that the gains to Britain were enormous in economic terms, especially in terms of the opportunity cost in dealing with the housing, feeding and guarding of the great surge of prisoners between 1750 and 1850.

Some of the direct advantages to Britain include:

a. The build-up of trade by the East-India Company
b. The advantage of a secure, in-house, supply of raw wool, to keep the spinning mills occupied
c. the opportunity cost of housing, feeding and guarding prisoners
d. The use of convict labour in the new Colony

- land clearing, farming, food production
- for road construction
- public wharves
- barracks
- Public Buildings
- for Materials supply e.g. brick & tile production.
- as unpaid day labour for the pastoral & agricultural industry

e. We can assume that Land grants, in the Colony, to men on the military and civil list was a form of 'fringe benefits' and should be quantified as an alternative to paid remuneration for these people.

f.   Even land grants to emancipists were used as an incentive to increase food production.

g.   We can quantify items C, D, E and F into a 'value of direct gain to the British economy of nearly 140,000,000 pound (refer details in the attached), compared with the publicly recorded expenditure on transportation, supplies, and military personnel of 5,600,000 pound, between 1788 and 1822.

The extent of the benefits depends on the pound value attached to the opportunity cost of a prisoner housed in Britain. James Matra wrote in 1784 that the contract cost of a prisoner maintained on the Thames River hulks was 26.75 pound, probably significantly less than cost of prisoners housed in the London prisons especially Ludgate, which was probably costing close to 40.0.0 pound per head per annum. So if we assume an opportunity cost of 20 pounds in lieu of the 10 pound, our benefit rises to 180 million pound from 130 million.

The purposes of trying to quantify these benefits are to challenge to traditional concept that 'the British invested millions of pounds in the Colony of New South Wales'.

It is obviously only the case, that the British Treasury invested millions when the outlay is shown and by not accounting for the on-going benefits for over fifty years, and indeed for two hundred years. It is still arguable that the Continent of Australia is, in Captain Arthur Phillip's words 'the best investment Britain will ever make'.

What the accounts don't tell us but in hindsight we could see happening is that the short-sighted English arrogance and limited social understanding was heading in a definite direction. They had no alternative plans for the placement of convicts after the loss of the American Colonies, except the earlier consideration of Africa, which idea was scotched before Botany Bay became so attractive, but there was a move, not long after the penal colony had been commenced that the transportation program was not going to work. We noted previously the negative observations in the Molesworth Report of 1828, however, John Howard, in 1770 wrote a serious report on 'The State of the Prisons in England and Wales' and noted:

"the general prevalence and spread of wickedness in prisons, and abroad by the discharged prisoners will now be as easily accounted for, as the propagation of disease. It is often said, 'A prisoner pays no debts;' I am sure, it may be added, that a prison mend no morals. Sir John Fielding observes that . . . . 'a criminal discharged by the court will generally, by the next sessions, after the execution of his comrades, become the head of a gang of his own raising'. Improved, no doubt, in skill, by the company he kept in gaol: petty offenders who are committed to prison, not to hard labour, but in idleness and wicked company or are sent to county gaols, generally grow desperate, and come out fitted for any villainy."

We can conclude that this view held a lot of sway with Pitt, the Prime Minister of the day. So, this view along with the projected cost of transportation and establishing the Colony, suggested that strong opposition would be prevalent within the Commons to stop the transportation program very quickly.

That funds were short in the British Treasury is suggested by a number of events, especially the pressure on each Governor, to trim costs. It took the appointment of the Chief Justice of Jamaica, John Thomas Bigge, sent to Sydney to review progress in the Colony, to muzzle the extravagances of Macquarie, because he took little interest in the pleadings and persuasion of Colonial Secretary Bathurst, who was concerned about the expense of new exploration, the expense of the new settlements in Newcastle and elsewhere. The substantial 'investment' in new buildings as well as the new roads and bridges in this vast and empty land as well as the early emancipation, conditional discharges and early release that were being handed out to many of the convicts, along with land grants.

Further support for cutting the high cost of the transportation program was forthcoming from the Report by the Select Committee on Finance released to the Commons on 26th June, 1798.

"For the first twelve years of the transportation program, 5,858 convicts were transported at a cost of 1,037,230.6.7 ¾. This worked out at the extraordinary cost of 177 pound per head for naval expenses, supplies, civil salaries, military costs and establishment costs.

That this figure was inflated or padded by the British Treasury officials is without doubt, as the naval cost portion of the total charge of 1,037,230 pound was 166,341 or 29 pound per head. The contracted cost for the second fleet onward was less than 12 pound per head for convicts loaded in England, rather than the number unloaded in Sydney or elsewhere. This cost cutting exercise was the biggest contributor to the high loss of convict lives on route from London to Australia in the second and third fleet and was substantially due to the treatment received by the convicts from their handlers, the contractors, (whose sole goal was to complete the run at a profit) whereas Phillip lost no convicts or passengers, or military personnel during his long trip.

The Select Committee on Finance thought obliquely about the problems of making the Colony too attractive. They concluded" The more thriving the setting, the less terrible the threat. It may lose its terrors altogether, especially if by money or other means, servitude be avoidable." The original estimate of total cost, including transportation was 30 pound per head. This estimate was accompanied by a Government projection that within the first four years, 10,000 convicts would be shipped for this 30 pound per head rather than the 5,800 convicts shipped over twelve years at 177 pound per head. The Peel Plan of 1828 which had compared the original estimates with the actual results also concluded that 'should the authorities succeed in sending home to Britain the expected surplus produce, for which at the moment the Government are indebted to Powers which it would be their policy to suppress, they would effect a national good which time could not erase from the annals of British History.'

Thus the real argument was not one of not punishing the prisoners sufficiently or of releasing them before full redemption could be guaranteed, but of the cost to the British Treasury. No official in that day considered or noted the opportunity costs or the other benefits accruing to the Government, as has been analysed above.

D. Fiscal Management during the 'Blue Book' period.

The 'Blue Book' was kept by the Colonial Secretary as a record of all financial transactions affecting the Colony, and was reported annually to the British Colonial Office and the House of Commons Committee on Colonies.

The' Blue Book' was written in meticulous copperplate writing (until 1828), and contains detailed records and notes relating to the items of revenue and expenditure of the Colony in the years from 1822 to 1857. The records for the Year 1824 are missing and could not therefore be examined. In 1827, the records were recorded in a printed form, and can be reviewed in the photocopies in the Appendix to this Report. The handwriting makes it virtually impossible to photocopy the handwritten text. However, a copy of selected pages from the printed text of 1827 is attached as Exhibit A. These printed notes also include guidelines for recording and reporting items of revenue and expenditure. The reports were obviously made to conform to standard British Treasury recording methods and to comply with the then known parliamentary reports by the British Treasurer.

From the Exhibit, certain conclusions can be drawn, and these can be set out as follows:

a. There was a wide range of duties and taxes imposed on the early settlers, especially on alcoholic beverages. The general rate of duty on spirits was 10 shillings per gallon, and on wine it was 9 pence per gallon. On tobacco the rate was 6 pence per pound, while timber attracted a rate of one shilling per solid foot. General Cargo attracted duty at a flat 5% ad valorem rate.

b. There were also licenses and tolls. A Hawkers Licenses sold for 20 pound, and it cost a settler 2 pence (tuppence) to go from Sydney town to Parramatta town. A country settler (in the Hawkesbury) paid One penny to cross the Nepean River Bridge at Windsor.

c. References to crown land sales were recorded in the 1825 'Blue Book', and as set out in the decree by George 3rd in a Proclamation on 25th March, 1825, that a new 'rent' was to be imposed on crown lands at the rate of One shilling for every 50 acres, to commence 5 years after the date of the original grant. To-date all crown lands had been disposed of by way of grants, and this rent was a form of back door and back-dated compensation to the crown. In the official grant documents, the receiver of the land grant was given notice that further costs may attach at some future time to the land, and it was this opportunity that provided the Crown to raise this 'rent' charge on the land in 1828.

d. There was to be a Land-holders fee of Fifteen shillings per 100 acres of crown land reserved for each three years for free settlers, followed by a two shilling fee per 100 hundred acres redeemable after twenty years from purchase.

e. On the 18th May, 1825, the 'rent' was changed, by order of Governor Macquarie, to a flat rate of 5% of the estimated value of the grants, without purchase(as opposed to purchased land), to commence 7 years from the date of grant. 'Rents' on any 2nd and subsequent grants were payable immediately, without the benefit of the 7 years grace period.

f. The table of Land Grants (1789-1850) shows the number of acres granted to settlers and the conclusion can be drawn that this revenue source of 'rents' on Corn Land grants could build into as considerable sum for the Crown.

g. By Proclamation, also dated 18th May, 1825, George III authorised the sale of crown lands at the rate of 10 shillings per acre, to a maximum of 4,000 acres per individual or a maximum of 5,000 acres per family. Payment was by way of a 10% deposit and six equal half-yearly instalments.

h. The title pages to the 1822 'Blue Book' are entitled 'Abstract of the Net Revenue and Expenditure of the Colony of New South Wales for the Year 1822', which indicates (and as the detailed records also reflect) that all Colonial revenue and expenses were being accounted for in the 'Blue Book'. It is immediately recognisable that the Table of British Financial Costs in the Colony is incomplete and misleading in that the outgoing expenditures do not reflect any offset revenues which would provide a true net expenditure. The official Table thus overstates the expenditure by the British Treasury on the Colony.

i. The table on Civil List Salaries for 1792-1793) sets out the Governor's Salary at One Thousand Pounds. But in the 1822 statement of expenditures on the Civil Salaries, the Governor's Salary had increased to Two Thousand Pounds. By 1856 the Governor's salary had increased to 15,000 pounds.

j. In fact, the total of Civil List salaries in 1792 was only 4,726.0.0 pounds, but by 1822 the total had increased to 9,828.15.0 pounds, due to both individual salary increases as well as more people being placed on the Civil List.

k. The official 'Observations upon revenue for the Colony in 1828' (written by the Colonial Treasurer of New South Wales) makes an interesting point. It observes that the 'net colonial income' of the year 1828, as actually collected, is exclusive of sums 'in aid of revenue', i.e. items which cannot be viewed in the character of income. This item is further defined as 'the proceeds of the labour of convicts, and establishments connected with them, being applied to the reduction of the amount of parliamentary grants for their maintenance'. Thus it took 30 years for the Colonial Government to officially recognise the contribution of convict labour in the Colony.

l. The total quantity of alcohol imported and thus consumed in the Colony, even in 1828, and with only a population in 1820 of only 26, 000 people, of which adult numbers would be less than 15,000, was 162,167 gallons of spirits plus 15,000 gallons of Colonial distilled spirits (distillation from sugar was prohibited in 1828, but the high price of grain and the higher taxing of local manufactured spirits became a natural deterrent). In 1829, the only duties imposed on spirits in that year were upon spirits imported directly from H. M. Plantations in the West Indies. So the British authorities received double benefit by both international trading and local duties.

m. The quantity of dutiable tobacco in 1828 was 136,748 pounds (compared to 91,893 pounds in 1825). The Government experimented with locally grown tobacco at establishments in Emu Plains and Port Macquarie with the result being 51,306 pounds produced in 1830.

n. By 1827 shipping companies were also paying light house charges, along with wharfage.

o. In 1828, the postage of letters attracted fees, for the first time, and the official Postmaster collected 598 pounds for general revenue.

p. The commencement of sales of both crown lands and crown timbers increased general revenues to the extent that in 1828, the amounts realised were:

Sales of Crown Lands 5004.19.2
Sales of Cedar cut on crown lands 744.15.11
Sales of other Timber 9365.11.4

The Governor imposed a fee of One halfpenny per foot for all cedar cut on crown lands. The 'Blue Book' makes the further observation that this charge 'has checked bushrangers and other lawless depredators by depriving them of ready means of subsistence by the absence of all restraint from cutting Cedar upon unallocated lands'.

In 1810, Governor Macquarie changed the designation of these two funds to 'Police Fund' and Orphan School Fund. The designated revenues were split 3:1 into each fund. The Act 3 Geo IV c.96 of 1822 gave further powers of taxation to the Governor.

E. Other Financial Observations

The analysis of Accounts extracted from the 'Blue Books' of 1822 through 1828 allows a number of conclusions to be drawn.

a. The initial claim by the author that the cost to the British Treasury of establishing and operating the Colony, was NOT the millions of pounds claimed by other historians, is now borne out by detailed examination. The accounting records as maintained by Governor Macquarie from 1810 leads to a statement of 'net revenue and expenses' which purports to offset all revenues against all expenses, and includes as revenue certain convict maintenance charges. Even in 1822 the Colony was showing a small operating surplus. This surplus grew through 1828 until, other than for transportation of convicts to the Colony; the charges on account of the British Treasury were less than One Hundred Thousand pounds for protecting, feeding and housing nearly 5,000 fully maintained convicts. Against this cost, the charge for housing, feeding and guarding this same number of prisoners in Britain would have been substantially higher, since in addition to the 5,000 gully maintained convicts there were a further 20,000 being paid for by free settlers and used as supervised labour. Britain surely had found a cheap source of penal servitude for at least 25,000 of its former prisoners, and found a very worthwhile alternative to the American Colonies as a destination for its prisoners.

b. Revenue from Crown Land sales and rents was used to offset Civil (Crown) salaries and expenses.

c. It is probably incorrect, at this stage, to say that it cost Britain nothing or at best, very little, to establish and maintain the Colony, but it can be said that from 1822 the costs were limited to maintaining fewer and fewer convicts. But from these convicts great value in terms of agricultural produce, coal and other minerals was derived. Just in terms of coal for lighting, heating and power, the cost to the government of purchasing these items would have been substantial. The 'Blue Book' reflects the use of the coal as a cost rather than a gain as would be the accounting standard today.

d. A final conclusion could be given that there are much more known records available for this period (1788-1899) than the author originally thought. The reproduction and regional distribution of the 'Blue Book' by the State Archives Office on microfiche is a major step forward in understanding the economic challenges faced by settlers and convicts in the early Colony. The sourcing of material from the Blue Book unveils the financial statements and conditions of these early years. It is still considered that finance records of the period 1788 to 1822 are not re-constructible, but the author feels that a deep search through the microfilms forming the Joint Copying Project will provide additional information on the two Colonial operating funds of the period–the 'Police Fund and the Orphan Fund'.

e. An interesting observation is found in 'The Constitutional History of Australia' by W. G. McMinn (1979).

P 33 records "Subject to the need for a vice-regal message, accepting that any locally (Australian Colony) initiated legislation of a money bill nature requires The

Sovereign's ratification, the New South Wales Legislative Council was to have a general right to appropriate revenue from taxation, except for an amount of 81,600 pounds, the expenditure of which was to be in accordance with

'three schedules' to the Act; being 33,000 pound for the salaries of those on the civil list e.g. Governor et al, the superintendent of Port Phillip and its judges and for the expenses of administering justice; 18,600 pound for the chief civil officers and their departments, for pensions and expenses of the council; and 30,000 pound for the maintenance of public worship."

Land and casual revenues were also reserved.

The Sale of Waste Land Act of 1832 raised the minimum reserve price of crown land to one pound per acre, except that large remote areas might be sold at a lower price, and established a formula for the use of the land revenue; fifty percent was to be spent on immigration, the rest was to be expended by the Governor in accordance with British Government directives from time to time. The Governor was to continue to have power to issue depasturing licences and to make regulations for the use and occupancy of unsold lands, but the existence of the Sale of Waste Lands Act placed an important restriction on the colony by implying a prohibition against the Legislative Council legislating on these matters. The first directive on how the Governor was to spend a portion of the fund, enjoined the Governor to spend a proportion on Aboriginal protection and another on the roads; he was left free to hand any surplus over to the Council for appropriation; but it was made clear that the whole of the fifty percent was to be considered as 'an emergency reserve if the Council proved difficult'. McMinn sheds some further light on the Crown Lands mystery but there still remains the question of whether, year after year, these funds were fully used or whether they were just included as a contribution to general revenue. It would appear that somewhere there is a firm directive from the British Treasury that the revenues from Crown Lands sale were to be used to 'offset' British costs of maintaining the Colony. The 'Blue Book' is evidence that as general revenues, these funds were already being used to pay for the costs of feeding, clothing, housing convicts, and we know they were specifically used to pay for 'sponsored immigrants', aboriginal 'protection', and now roads. The costs of the military establishment were charged against general revenues so in the quite large 'pot', nearly all Colonial expenditures were subsidised or offset by revenues from the Sale of Crown Land. Britain put its hand in the till only; it seems, to pay for the shipping and supplies costs of getting their prisoners to the Colony. After 1828, we know that convict production–both agricultural and mineral–went a long way to paying their expenses, so perhaps the British Treasury did in fact get off very lightly indeed, especially for the benefits it derived.

The vexing question of Crown Lands revenues still remains. It is apparent from the 'Blue Book' notations that this revenue was 'reserved' for specific allocation by the Crown and remained in the Colony as an offset against British Government fiscal obligations (e.g. Civil List salaries) until self-government in 1855. A relevant quotation from the 1887 Financial Statements of the Colonial Treasurer of New South Wales assists in clarifying the use of the revenues:

"Prior to the passing of the Constitution Act, the Territorial Revenues of the Colony belonged to the Crown, but upon that Act coming into operation in 1855, they were placed at the disposal of the local Parliament, and together with the taxes, imposts, rates and duties were formed into one fund, under the title of the Consolidated Revenue Fund. In lieu of the Crown Revenues thus given up to the Colony, an annual Civil List of 64,300 pound was made payable to Her Majesty out of the Consolidated Revenues of the Colony." What this means is that the British Treasury allowed the offset of all direct British payments made on account of the Colony against revenues raised by the sale, rent or lease of Crown lands.

G. Observations on Crown Land Transactions

There was a major improvement in record keeping and reporting after self-government in 1855. The "Financial Statements of the Colonial Treasurers of New South Wales from Responsible Government in 1855 to 1881" provide a detailed accounting mechanism for recording classifications, and compilation of budgets and reporting to the Authorities. They contain 'explanatory memoranda of the financial system of New South Wales, and of the rise, progress and present condition of the public revenue'.

The interest in this period (from 1822 to 1881) is that these records, firstly of the 'Blue Book' period and then of the printed Financial Statements to 1881, provide the first detailed identification of the items included in the revenue and expenditures for the Colony and the appropriation and approval process. This historical data is relevant to understanding the social conditions in the Colony, the application of duties, tariffs, tolls and fees which embraced the essential revenue of a Colony that was designed to be self-sufficient and which was being given minimal economic support by the British Government, even though the opportunity cost of housing 'prisoners' in the Colony was a fraction of the cost of housing them in England.

Governance of Public Finance

The appendix to the 'Financial Statements of 1887' (refer Appendix this work) records that:

"The Financial System of the Colony of New South Wales is regulated chiefly by the Constitution Act of 1855 and the Audit Act of 1870, and in matters relating to Trust Funds and Loans by special Appropriation Acts of the local legislature.

The Imperial Act granting a constitution to the Colony of New South Wales was assented to on 16th July, 1855, and became effective on the 24th November 1855. This Act provides for a Legislative Council (Upper House) and a Legislative Assembly. The Upper House members were to be nominated by the Governor, while the Lower House members were to be elected by inhabitants of the Colony.

We know that the first official empowerment of the Legislative Council to impose 'taxes' by way of customs duties was in 1823, but the payment (commenced in 1788) by the British Government of Civil salaried officials remained until 1853. So before the 1853 self-government, the British authorities maintained a civil list of officials who were paid for by the Crown.

The British Treasury directed revenues from crown land sales and rents from squatters' and pastoralists' leases (imposed from 1853) are used to meet local expenses and running costs, as well as Civil List Salaries.

The reserve sale price of crown land had been originally set at 50 pence per acre in 1833, but by 1839 it rose to 12 shillings an acre and shortly thereafter (1842) it rose to one pound per acre, and it is likely, based on the revenues from Crown Lands and the annual surplus recorded in the Colonial 'Blue Books', that the British Treasury made a surplus on its Colonial possession of Australia.

To draw this conclusion, a number of premises were made:

a. The British Government lists its Civil payments to the key officials of the Colony e.g. Governor, Attorney-, Surveyor-General, Chief Justice etc, but makes no mention of revenue collected from the Colony.

a. The three related Acts (59 Geo III c.114; 2 Geo IV. c.8 and 3 Geo IV. c.96) give the Colonial Governor the power to impose local taxes in the shape of Customs Duties on spirits, tobacco etc from about 1823,

b. The Legislative Council of 1851 adopted a Select Committee Report protesting that the more recent 'constitutional' Acts (13 & 14 Vic c.59) did not place the control of all revenue and taxation from the Colony in the hands of the legislature. The key omitted and thus missing elements–in the eyes of the Council–were the control of waste lands (i.e. Crown lands–specifically excluded by Act 9 Geo IV c.83) and revenue from mining operations.

c. The discovery of gold and the burgeoning wealth of the Colony prompted the Legislative Council in 1852 to seek the British Government's acceptance of an offset arrangement whereby the Colony of New South Wales would accept responsibility for all civil (i.e. official) salaries, provided the British Government surrendered all Colonial revenues to the discretion (under a proposed new constitution) of the Legislature.

d. The British authorities accepted Colonial funds, raised from the earliest sale and lease of Crown Land to be used for the funding of 'free immigration' to the Colony.

e. The concurrent Napoleonic wars being undertaken by the British, as well as the ongoing American War of Independence placed a substantial burden on the public purse, and the British Treasury was seeking every opportunity to limit, defray or offset expenses relating to the Colony in the Great South Land.

The conclusion should be (by implication), that the British Government had, (all during the period from 1788 to 1852) been in control of crown land (wasteland) revenues, as well as the revenue from mining. It was thus some portion of the crown land revenue that was used to pay the transportation charges for the first 'free' immigrants from Britain, until, some three years afterwards, numerous Colonial merchants supported and underwrote the transportation costs of 'free' settlers and guaranteed them jobs on arrival.

(a.) The Crown Land charges rose from 5 shillings in 1833 to 12 shillings in 1839 and then 1 pound in 1842. This revenue was used to defray Civil expenditures in the Colony, by being retained in the Colony and the Governor directed its use, on behalf of the Crown, for the payment of salaries to officials on the Civil list, to Military personnel, for government expenses in day to day running of the Colony, and it would take a mere accounting or book-keeping entry to offset such revenue and expenses.

We know from the public record (Wealth & Progress in NSW–1887) that revenue from Taxation in 1886 amounted to over two million pounds. This was largely customs duties on wines, spirits, coffee, tea and sundry other imported items such as rice and dried fruits. Stamps and license fee raised a further almost five hundred thousand pounds making the total Taxation revenue a sum of 2,611,835 pounds for 1886.

TABLE REVENUES FROM TAXATION 1886

Colony	Rail	Water etc	Immign	Other	Total '000
NSW	31380	4122	569	10573	46646
Vic	29282	5638	0	2706	37627
Qld	15374	221	2621	7623	25840
SA	11374	3321	0	5739	20435
WA	824	.05310	0	541	1371
Tas	.0173	0	.0235	4609	5019

TABLE B REVENUE FROM SALE AND OCCUPATION OF CROWN LAND 1871-1886

1871	197978	1879	1632024
1872	840453	1882	2914394
1873	1137914	1884	1753345
1875	2020629	1885	1876452
1876	2773003	1886	1643955

The research undertaken in writing this paper has led the writer to draw certain conclusions, all of which reflect on the early economic progress of the Colony.

1. The British authorities were ignorant of the radically different nature of the climate, soils and natural environment of the new colony;
2. There was no sound planning to develop agriculture, and provide the basics of self-supported living for the early population;
3. Basic farming equipment and building tools were not supplied in sufficient quantities, nor training or guidance provided by experienced persons;
4. The members of the New South Wales Corps were more interested in pursuing their own interests than in supervising the convicts and promoting self sufficiency;
5. There was no system of proper supervision and training of convicts, leading to low levels of productivity; Governor Phillip had, on numerous occasions requested professional supervisors for the convicts but was repeatedly ignored.

6. The discovery of Gold was kept secret whilst convict transfers were still being undertaken, lest the 'dream' of great wealth became stronger than the requirement to work out a penal service.

7. Despite the lack of basic necessities and poor motivation of most of the population, the enterprise of a small number of individuals, both convict and 'free immigrant' provided a catalyst for the progress and prosperity of all.

8. Needless to say, in hindsight, progress to self sufficiency could have been hastened and much suffering avoided, if appropriate planning and economic encouragement had been provided.

9. The discovery of large tracts of good grazing land and its associated export development of wool, and the discovery of large gold deposits rapidly boosted the fortunes of the Colony, but the driving force and critical factor was the motivation, energy and determination of the early entrepreneurs, acting initially and mainly in their own interest, but inevitably taking the bulk of the Colony with them in the progress towards prosperity.

After 1828, we know that convict production–both agricultural and mineral–went a long way to paying their expenses, so perhaps the British Treasury did in fact get off very lightly indeed, especially for the benefits it derived.

Another question arises after analysing the pre-Federation period. How did the Colony build up a debt to the Mother Country of 159 million pound?–This figure was quoted in 1893 at the Corowa Federation Conference by A.J. Peacock MLA (Mildura). Peacock was later to become the Minister for Lands in the first Government of 1900, and was knighted for his contribution to the Federation Movement. The answer is that Peacock quoted this figure in error and in truth the sum of 159 million pound is the total indebtedness by the Colonies to bond-holders in the City of London. This was a Colonial obligation at attractive interest rates and due over an extended period of time.

Interpreting the Public Accounts

The purpose of this work has been accomplished—the purpose being that of identifying and analysing public financial statements from 1800-1899. A niche was identified and one worthy of filling. That there could be an interest in relating and understanding the economic fundamentals of the Colony onto Federation is not surprising but a study of the early Government financial reporting can unleash an understanding of so much information relating to the social economic and political progress of the early settlers. What was the progress of the early social infrastructure? The hospital, the roads, the water supply, the sewerage disposal; the growth of industries—retail, pastoral, mineral, timber, whaling and sealing; citrus? What was the progress of education? The health and the nutritional state of the nation? Were the settlers housed properly? Did the settlers enjoy the benefits of travel, telegraph, refrigeration and other results of the ongoing industrial revolution? What did their entertainment consist of; what were the working conditions?

The government accounting and reporting system answered all these questions, and more. So, if the aim of the Government accounts was to analyse the condition of the Colony and inform its people, then the system worked well. We learnt where the revenue of the Colony was derived from, and the advent and then taxation in the Colony. We learnt where all that revenue was expended, and the resulting measurable standard of living achieved by the settlers. Government accounting was the official measure of the performance of the Colonial administrators for the British Colonial Office in London.

Interpreting the Direct and Measurable Gain to the British Authorities from the Colony of New South Wales.

The original estimate of direct gains by the British authorities from the original and continuing investment in the Colony of New South Wales was based on 5 (five) identifiable and quantifiable events

1. The opportunity cost of housing, feeding and guarding the convicts in the Colony compared with the cost of doing the same thing in Britain.

The original estimates, in this category, were based on an estimated differential of ten pound per head–an arbitrary assessment of the differential cost.

However recent and more reliable information has come to hand which gives further validity to a number of 20 pound per head per annum, compared with the original 10 pound per head per annum.

A letter to Under Secretary Nepean dated 23rd August, 1783, from James Maria Matra of Shropshire and London assists us in this regard.

It was Matra who first analysed the opportunity of using the new Colony as a Penal Colony, only his estimates were incorrect and ill-founded. He had advised the Government that it would cost less than 3,000 pound to establish the Colony initially, plus transportation cost at 15 pound per head and annual maintenance of 20 pound per head.

In fact the transportation was contracted for the second fleet at 13 pound 5 shillings per head and annual maintenance was offset by Colonial revenues from 1802.

However, Matra made a significant statement in his letter to Nepean, when he pointed out that the prisoners housed, fed and guarded on the rotting hulks on the Thames River were being contracted for in the annual amount of 26.15.10 per head per annum. He also writes that 'the charge to the publick fore these convicts has been increasing for the last 7 or 8 years' (Historical Records of NSW–Vol 1 Part 2 Page 7)

Adopting this cost as a base for comparison purposes, it means that the benefit to Britain of the Colony increased from 140,000,000 pound to 180,000,000 pound. This benefit assesses the Ground 1 benefit at 84,000,000 pound.

2. Benefit to Britain on Ground Two (2) is put at 70, 000,000 pound which places the value of a convicts labour at 35 pound per annum. Matra had assessed the value of labour of the Hulk prisoners at 35. 85 pound.

3. The valuation of convict labour in the new Colony should reflect the convicts not only used on building sites, but also on road, bridge and wharf construction. This would add (based on 35 pound per annum) a further 21,000,000 pound.

4. The Molesworth Committee (A House of Commons Committee investigating transportation), concluded that the surplus food production by the convicts would feed the Military people and this, over a period of 10 years, would save 7,000,000 pound for the British Treasury.

5. The benefits of fringe benefit grants of land to the Military etc can be estimated (based on One pound per acre) at over 5,000,000 before 1810.

6. We learn from Governor King's Report to Earl Camden (which due to a change of office holder, should have been addressed to Viscount Castlereagh as Colonial Secretary) dated 15th March, 1806 that the Convicts engaged in widely diverse work. The Report itself (Enclosure #2) is entitled "Public Labour of Convicts maintained by the Crown at Sydney, Parramatta, Hawkesbury, Toongabbie and Castle Hill, for the year 1805

Cultivation–Gathering, husking and shelling maize from 200 acres sowed last year–Breaking up ground and planting 1230 acres of wheat, 100 acre of Barley, 250 acres of Maize, 14 acres of Flax, and 3 acres of potatoes–Hoeing the above maize and threshing wheat.

Stock–Taking care of Government stock as herdsmen, watchmen etc

Buildings–

- At Sydney: Building and constructing of stone, a citadel, a stone house, a brick dwelling for the Judge Advocate, a commodious brick house for the main guard, a brick printing office
- At Parramatta: Alterations at the Brewery, a brick house as clergyman's residence
- At Hawkesbury: completing a public school
- A Gaol House with offices, at the expense of the Colony
- Boat and Ship Builders: refitting vessels and building row boats
- Wheel and Millwrights: making and repairing carts

Manufacturing: sawing, preparing and manufacturing hemp, flax and wool, bricks and tiles

Road Gangs: repairing roads, and building new roads

Other Gangs: loading and unloading boats"

(Historical Records of NSW–Vol 6 P43)

Thus the total benefits from these six (6) items of direct gain to the British comes to well over 174 million pound, and this is compared to Professor N. G. Butlin's proposal that the British 'invested' 5.6 million.

Historical Records of NSW Vol 1 Part 2

THE OPINIONS OF CAPTAIN ARTHUR PHILLIP
AS GOVERNOR OF THE COLONY OF NSW

HRNSW VOLS 1-7

a.   (P7)–Cost of Convicts (-J.M. Matra Letter)

- The estimate to create a settlement there (in Africa) amounted to 9865 pound, and the annual charge for each convict would be 15.14.0. The Government pays annually to the Contractor for each convict employed on the hulks 26.15.10
- the 1,000 felons is currently costing over 20,000 per annum

b   (P10)–The plan by Sir George Young as presented to Lord Sydney included a list of benefits for Britain. These included:

- the geographical position
- trade with South America
- the commercial position
- variety of climate and productions
- facilities for trade
- tropical products
- flax

- commercial centre
- metals of every kind
- settlers from China
- The American Loyalists
- Felons
- expense
- number of ships required
- guard-ship
- exploring ship
- cheap transportation
- back-loading

c. (P32) Estimates of Expense for equipment & supplies
d. (P67) Phillip's Commission

- "our will and our pleasure is that all public monies which shall be raised be issued out by warrant from you and disposed of by you for the support of the Government or for such other purpose as shall be particularly directed and not otherwise"
- "we do likewise give and grant unto you full power and authority to agree for such lands, tenements as shall be in our power to dispose of and them to grant to any person upon such terms and under such moderate quit rents services to be thereupon reserved . . . ."

e. (P87) Economy

- "you shall use every proper degree of economy and be careful that the commissary so transmit an account of the issues to our Treasury, from time to time . . . ."

f. (P91) Emancipation and land grants

- "you have full power and authority to emancipate and discharge from servitude any of the convicts under your superintendence who shall be deserving of such favour"
- "You may issue your warrant to make full and careful surveys of land and may pass grants to any of the convicts emancipated

e.g. to every male 30 acres, and if married, a further 20 acres more."

g.   (P146) Bricklayers Wanted

- In at least two despatches–those of 9th July, 1788 to Lord Sydney and that of 28th September 1788 to U/Secretary Nepean, Governor Phillip drew the British attention to the severe shortage of carpenters and bricklayers in the Colony.

As a general conclusion to this work, a number of observations should be made by way of summary, on matters such as:

- Management of The Police & Orphan Funds
- The Consequences of transportation
- The Gains & Benefits by the British from Transportation
- Fiscal Management during the 'Blue Book' Period
- Other Financial Observations
- Observations on Crown Land Transactions
- Making Improvements in the Public Accounts

A. Management of the Police & Orphan Funds 1810-1822

Marsden and Wentworth were the official recorders of transactions in these two accounts, and as Treasurers of the respective funds, their appointment created the potential for major conflict of interest situations.

It is interesting to muse how a Reverend gentleman (Samuel Marsden–was the appointed trustee of the Female Orphanage as well as a Magistrate in Parramatta) who was paid from the Civil List at the rate of 150.0.0 pound per annum, could afford to operate 4,500 acres of pasture land and build up a flock of 3,500 sheep in a time-frame of less than twenty years. Even allowing that the land came about from grants, the sheep had to be purchased from the market place or the Governor's flocks and although the convict labour assigned to him was unpaid, they had to be kept, with huts, food and clothing furnished.

We might also ask why the monthly meat bill for the orphanage ran to over 60 pound (whilst the Baker's account averaged over 76 pound per month). Even though the Orphanage owned and operated a farm and the farm regularly sold livestock 'on the hoof', the Orphanage for Young Females then bought back dressed meat from the same butcher.

Marsden was also entitled, on behalf of the orphanage to draw rations from the commissary, especially grain.

For its annual sale of livestock in 1811-1812, Marsden received, on behalf of the orphanage, only 127 pound, but from the same source purchased over 700 pound of dressed meat (which at the going rate of ad per Lb comes to 25,000 lb of meat each year).

The means were easy to share the spoils between those that could help him gain wealth and reach his target of becoming a large landowner and successful grazier. Marsden housed only female orphans aged from under 5 to 14. On an average month, Marsden paid the butcher over 60 pound, being for an average of 2,500 lb of meat. By the 30th September 1818, Marsden held 3,033 (pound) in the Orphanage account, and on average disbursed 550 pounds each month from that account. The only 'admonishment' that Macquarie made (if one can imply from a regulatory change, an act of admonition). Macquarie, at this time, chose to modify the basis of the Orphanage Fund revenue and deleted an item by redirecting that revenue to the Police Fund. He also reduced the percentage of customs duty received by the orphanage from ¼ to 1/8th. Even so, the orphanage Fund built up a substantial balance, which was deposited in 1818 into the newly formed Bank of New South Wales.

Macquarie made no objection to Marsden misdirecting funds from the orphan fund to repairing St. John's Church in July 1811 to the extent of 56 pound, nor to paying the Matron of the Orphanage a monthly stipend of 5 pound (he recorded the payments as 'donations') when the going rate would have been only 1 pound per month, nor of paying 4.5.0 for a bonnet for his wife from the fund. Marsden was married with 5 young children to raise, and because he was a magistrate, he was entitled to draw on the government stores, in spite of his obvious pastoral (agricultural) wealth

Wentworth too had his questionable methods. He built up large surpluses of cash and bills receivable rather than spend funds on road, bridge or wharf construction; he expended large amounts through the military for 'repairs' to the streets of Sydney and other questionable contracts, never commented on by Macquarie. Wentworth was also the town Magistrate, responsible for fines, which were an important source of revenue to the Police Fund. Two items of regular expenditure open to abuse, and which appear to be inordinately high were purchase of firewood and oil and payment for the capture of absconding convicts. The Military personnel were fleecing the Government stores, operating the barter system in the Colony and were obviously getting even more ample rewards in cash from Wentworth. What we can't find any certainty of is who gave directions to Darcy Wentworth to make all these payments. It can only have been the Colonial Secretary or the Governor himself.

This raises questions of the 'arms length' treatment of revenues and expenditures, generally, in the Colony.

Events that shaped the Colony

There were a number of events that influenced the course of the early economy and impacted on the extent and rate of economic growth have been selected and outlined. The list of events is not extensive but indicative of sometimes-obscure events, which have impacted on economic growth e.g. education.

Although it may be suggested that the Report by Commissioner Bigge did not largely influence the Colonial economy, it must be stated that his recommendations to continue with the new Bank of New South Wales, which had been chartered incorrectly by Governor Macquarie, moved the economy along, as did his support for the continuation of the transportation of convicts to the Colony. His lack of support for land grants and early release of convicts may have slowed the economic growth until the consequences of his recommendation that the sale of Crown land be made, is considered. The revenue from customs duties, licenses, tolls and fines was considerable and kept the economy afloat, even if it was being badly managed, until 1810 and the arrival of Macquarie.

Other events tended to feed on each other and gather momentum by cross-pollination. Exploration across the mountains and uncovering the mystery of the rivers opened up huge pastoral areas of first class grazing land, especially that of the Bathurst Plains and fostered the growth of the sheep and wool industries. The continued growth of the pastoral industries all through the 1800s was eclipsed as the prime-exporting commodity only upon the 'official' discovery of gold. The discovery of gold also filled the Colonial coffers and set into motion the most remarkable of events that of expanding the rail system across the Colony and to the other Colonies—a line was developed all the way from Adelaide to Brisbane. Instead of relying on sea transport, (the very reason that the major cities were located on harbours and bays), the cities were now to be connected by rail. The senior colony of New South Wales could now diversify its population, move livestock and produce from Ballina to Albury, Broken Hill to Parramatta. The most powerful benefit of the advent of the rail system is the most simplistic one. The Colonial labour-force learned how to engineer bridges (the Hawkesbury); how to construct gradients (crossing the Blue Mountains); lay track at record rates and lowest costs in the world; and engineer the iron horses themselves for local conditions. This new knowledge led directly to the growth of the large engineering shops and the likes of business adventurers such as Thomas Mort, whose remarkable drive, ingenuity and entrepreneurial ability led to the Mort Dry Dock & Engineering complex in Balmain, NSW Fresh Food & Ice, in Sydney and Lithgow, the Bodalla Cheese & Milk factory, relying on refrigeration, together with abattoirs, for the first time, in remote locations rather than in Sydney town.

We cannot overlook the value of education to a largely illiterate economy. Literacy rose by 1835 from 55% to 97% of the adult (15 yrs +) population. The placement of schools and churches throughout the Colony was responsible for this remarkable achievement.

There may well be more 'special events ', other than those discussed but it seems that these interlinking events boosted the Colonial economy in a remarkable way:

- The crown land policy and reform
- The growth of education

- The Report by Commissioner Bigge
- Exploration
- Pastoral expansion
- The expansion of the rail system
- The Fiscal impact of Federation
- Commonwealth-State Financial Relations

B. The Consequences of Transportation

The next conclusion must be to record some of the Consequences of Transportation to the Colony of New South Wales. It was during the time that convicts provided the principal source of labour for government purposes and private enterprise, that the consequences of transportation appeared to be measurable. One of the indirect consequences was the 'opportunity' cost to both Britain and the Colony of the transportation program. The Molesworth Committee in 1838, believing that their definitive opinion on the value of transported labour could only justify its continuation stated that transportation was an obstacle to continued economic growth. Some twelve years later, an advocate of transportation, (Archibald Atchison–Crime and Transportation) produced figures to show that just the opposite was true.–Transportation had been of great value to the Colony.

A consequence first raised by Samuel Marsden was that adult convicts were beyond re-training but that the young people needed education. A further social consequence was that the transfer of so many male convicts led, by 1841, to 'a dearth of females', a situation named as alarming by Ralph Mansfield 'Analytical view of the census of 1841 in New South Wales'.

Governor Phillip was the first to publicly recognise that the nature of the penal settlement required a 'peculiar form of government', but one of the goals of Commissioner Bigge was to review the legal side of Colonial administration and report on changes needed for the administration of justice. Bigge did make such a report and the recommendations were immediately adopted by Macquarie.

The Molesworth Committee report into transportation concluded that "Some persons contend that the pecuniary interests of the penal Colony require the continuation of transportation; that as the extraordinary commercial prosperity of these colonies was occasioned by the constant supply of convict labour, if that supply be cut off the colonies would be ruined, from great wealth be reduced to great poverty; and that this change in the fortune of inhabitants, especially if it were sudden, would necessarily produce the worst moral effects upon their character, and still further demoralise the already demoralised.

"The extraordinary wealth of these colonies was occasioned by the regular and increasing supply of convict labourers. The convicts were assigned to settlers as slaves, they were forced to work in combination, and raised more produce than they could consume; for this surplus produce Government provided a market, by maintaining military and convict establishments, which have cost this country above 7,000,000 pound of the public money.

"Labour is in short supply whilst capital has amazingly increased. The flocks of sheep are double the size they ought to be; a vast number perish for want of care; labour must be furnished from sources, other than convicts, if the colonies are to continue to flourish"

C. Analysing the Benefits to the United Kingdom

Although the more significant consequences of transportation of British convicts to the Colony of New South Wales may have been both economic and social, the general benefits of transportation of British convicts out of the United Kingdom are economic.

The essential question becomes—Would the United Kingdom have pursued a Colonial expansion policy if there had not been a need to transfer convicts from the Americas elsewhere?

The answer is of course, a simple—'yes'. The trade, defence and colonisation policies, in place, and under discussion, made territorial acquisition essential. The British Navy needed supplies of masts and spars to maintain its fleet in sailing condition. The British Trade tsars wanted to see further expansion, after a successful entrance into the Caribbean area, and the eyes of the East India Company wanted to spread further across the Asian region. Terra Australis–the great southland–was an obvious desire.

Therefore, it is fair to say that the gains to Britain were enormous in economic terms, especially in terms of the opportunity cost in dealing with the housing, feeding and guarding of the great surge of prisoners between 1750 and 1850.

Some of the direct advantages to Britain include:

a. The build-up of trade by the East-India Company
b. The advantage of a secure, in-house, supply of raw wool, to keep the spinning mills occupied
c. The opportunity cost of housing, feeding and guarding prisoners
d. The use of convict labour in the new Colony

- Land clearing, farming, food production
- For road construction
- Public wharves
- Barracks
- Public Buildings
- For Materials supply e.g. brick & tile production.
- As unpaid day labour for the pastoral & agricultural industry

e. We can assume that Land grants, in the Colony, to men on the military and civil list was a form of 'fringe benefits' and should be quantified as an alternative to paid remuneration for these people.
f. Even land grants to emancipists were used as an incentive to increase food production.
g. We can quantify items C, D, E and F into a 'value of direct gain to the British economy of nearly 140,000,000 pound (refer details in the attached), compared with the publicly recorded expenditure on transportation, supplies, and military personnel of 5,600,000 pound, between 1788 and 1822.

The extent of the benefits depends on the pound value attached to the opportunity cost of a prisoner housed in Britain. James Matra wrote in 1784 that the contract cost of a prisoner maintained on the Thames River hulks was 26.75 pound, probably significantly less than cost of prisoners housed in the London prisons especially Ludgate, which was probably costing close to 40.0.0 pound per head per annum. So if we assume an opportunity cost of 20 pounds in lieu of the 10 pound, our benefit rises to 180 million pound from 130 million.

The purposes of trying to quantify these benefits are to challenge to traditional concept that 'the British invested millions of pounds in the Colony of New South Wales'.

It is obviously only the case, that the British Treasury invested millions when the outlay is shown and by not accounting for the ongoing benefits for over fifty years, and indeed for two hundred years. It is still arguable that the Continent of Australia is, in Captain Arthur Phillip's words 'the best investment Britain will ever make'.

What the accounts don't tell us but in hindsight we could see happening is that the short-sighted English arrogance and limited social understanding was heading in a definite direction. They had no alternative plans for the placement of convicts after the loss of the American Colonies, except the earlier consideration of Africa, which idea was scotched before Botany Bay became so attractive, but there was a move, not long after the penal colony had been commenced that the transportation program was not going to work. We noted previously the negative observations in the Molesworth Report of 1828, however, John Howard, in 1770 wrote a serious report on 'The State of the Prisons in England and Wales' and noted:

"The general prevalence and spread of wickedness in prisons, and abroad by the discharged prisoners will now be as easily accounted for, as the propagation of disease. It is often said, 'A prisoner pays no debts;' I am sure, it may be added, and that a prison mend no morals. Sir John Fielding observes that . . . . 'a criminal discharged by the court will generally, by the next sessions, after the execution of his comrades, become the head of a gang of his own raising'. Improved, no doubt, in skill, by the company he kept in gaol: petty offenders who are committed to prison, not to hard labour, but in idleness and wicked company or are sent to county gaols, generally grow desperate, and come out fitted for any villainy."

We can conclude that this view held a lot of sway with Pitt, the Prime Minister of the day. So, this view along with the projected cost of transportation and establishing the Colony, suggested that strong opposition would be prevalent within the Commons to stop the transportation program very quickly.

That funds were short in the British Treasury is suggested by a number of events, especially the pressure on each Governor, to trim costs. It took the appointment of the Chief Justice of Jamaica, John Thomas Bigge, sent to Sydney to review progress in the Colony, to muzzle the extravagances of Macquarie, because he took little interest in the pleadings and persuasion of Colonial Secretary Bathurst, who was concerned about the expense of new exploration, the expense of the new settlements in Newcastle and elsewhere. The substantial 'investment' in new buildings as well as the new roads and bridges in this vast and empty land as well as the early emancipation, conditional discharges and early release that were being handed out to many of the convicts, along with land grants.

Further support for cutting the high cost of the transportation program was forthcoming from the Report by the Select Committee on Finance released to the Commons on 26th June 1798.

"For the first twelve years of the transportation program, 5,858 convicts were transported at a cost of 1,037,230.6.7 ¾. This worked out at the extraordinary cost of 177 pound per head for naval expenses, supplies, civil salaries, military costs and establishment costs.

That this figure was inflated or padded by the British Treasury officials is without doubt, as the naval cost portion of the total charge of 1,037,230 pound was 166,341 or 29 pound per head. The contracted cost for the second fleet onward was less than 12 pound per head for convicts loaded in England, rather than the number unloaded in Sydney or elsewhere. This cost cutting exercise was the biggest contributor to the high loss of convict lives on route from London to Australia in the second and third fleet and was substantially due to the treatment received by the convicts from their handlers, the contractors, (whose sole goal was to complete the run at a profit) whereas Phillip lost no convicts or passengers, or military personnel during his long trip.

The Select Committee on Finance thought obliquely about the problems of making the Colony too attractive. They concluded" The more thriving the setting, the less terrible the threat. It may lose its terrors altogether, especially if by money or other means, servitude be avoidable." The original estimate of total cost, including transportation was 30 pound per head. This estimate was accompanied by a Government projection that within the first four years, 10,000 convicts would be shipped for this 30 pound per head rather than the 5,800 convicts shipped over twelve years at 177 pound per head. The Peel Plan of 1828 which had compared the original estimates with the actual results also concluded that 'should the authorities succeed in sending home to Britain the expected surplus produce, for which at the moment the Government are indebted to Powers which it would be their policy to suppress, they would effect a national good which time could not erase from the annals of British History.'

Thus the real argument was not one of not punishing the prisoners sufficiently or of releasing them before full redemption could be guaranteed, but of the cost to the British Treasury. No official in that day considered or noted the opportunity costs or the other benefits accruing to the Government, as has been analysed above.

D. Fiscal Management during the 'Blue Book' period.

The 'Blue Book' was kept by the Colonial Secretary as a record of all financial transactions affecting the Colony, and was reported annually to the British Colonial Office and the House of Commons Committee on Colonies.

The' Blue Book' was written in meticulous copperplate writing (until 1828), and contains detailed records and notes relating to the items of revenue and expenditure of the Colony in the years from 1822 to 1857. The records for the Year 1824 are missing and could not therefore be examined. In 1827, the records were recorded in a printed form, and can be reviewed in the photocopies in the Appendix to this Report. The handwriting makes it virtually impossible to photocopy the handwritten text. However, a copy of selected pages from the printed text of 1827 is attached as Exhibit A. These printed notes also include guidelines for recording and reporting items of revenue and expenditure. The reports were obviously made to conform to standard British Treasury recording methods and to comply with the then known parliamentary reports by the British Treasurer.

From the Exhibit, certain conclusions can be drawn, and these can be set out as follows:

a. There was a wide range of duties and taxes imposed on the early settlers, especially on alcoholic beverages. The general rate of duty on spirits was 10 shillings per gallon, and on wine it was 9 pence per gallon. On tobacco the rate was 6 pence per pound, while timber attracted a rate of one shilling per solid foot. General Cargo attracted duty at a flat 5% ad valorem rate.

b. There were also licenses and tolls. A Hawkers Licenses sold for 20 pound, and it cost a settler 2 pence (tuppence) to go from Sydney town to Parramatta town. A country settler (in the Hawkesbury) paid One penny to cross the Nepean River Bridge at Windsor.

c. References to crown land sales were recorded in the 1825 'Blue Book', and as set out in the decree by George 3rd in a Proclamation on 25th March, 1825, that a new 'rent' was to be imposed on crown lands at the rate of One shilling for every 50 acres, to commence 5 years after the date of the original grant. To-date all crown lands had been disposed of by way of grants, and this rent was a form of back door and back-dated compensation to the crown. In the official grant documents, the receiver of the land grant was given notice that further costs may attach at some future time to the land, and it was this opportunity that provided the Crown to raise this 'rent' charge on the land in 1828.

d. There was to be a Land-holders fee of Fifteen shillings per 100 acres of crown land reserved for each three years for free settlers, followed by a two shilling fee per 100 hundred acres redeemable after twenty years from purchase.

e. On the 18th May 1825, the 'rent' was changed, by order of Governor Macquarie, to a flat rate of 5% of the estimated value of the grants, without purchase (as opposed to purchased land), to commence 7 years from the date of grant. 'Rents' on any 2nd and subsequent grants were payable immediately, without the benefit of the 7 years grace period.

f. The table of Land Grants (1789-1850) shows the number of acres granted to settlers and the conclusion can be drawn that this revenue source of 'rents' on Corn Land grants could build into as considerable sum for the Crown.

g By Proclamation, also dated 18th May 1825, George III authorised the sale of crown lands at the rate of 10 shillings per acre, to a maximum of 4,000 acres per individual or a maximum of 5,000 acres per family. Payment was by way of a 10% deposit and six equal half-yearly instalments.

h. The title pages to the 1822 'Blue Book' are entitled 'Abstract of the Net Revenue and Expenditure of the Colony of New South Wales for the Year 1822', which indicates (and as the detailed records also reflect) that all Colonial revenue and expenses were being accounted for in the 'Blue Book'. It is immediately recognisable that the Table of British Financial Costs in the Colony is incomplete and misleading in that the outgoing expenditures do not reflect any offset revenues which would provide a true net expenditure. The official Table thus overstates the expenditure by the British Treasury on the Colony.

i. The table on Civil List Salaries for 1792-1793) sets out the Governor's Salary at One Thousand Pounds. But in the 1822 statement of expenditures on the Civil Salaries, the Governor's Salary had increased to Two Thousand Pounds. By 1856 the Governor's salary had increased to 15,000 pounds.

j. In fact, the total of Civil List salaries in 1792 was only 4,726.0.0 pounds, but by 1822 the total had increased to 9,828.15.0 pounds, due to both individual salary increases as well as more people being placed on the Civil List.

k. The official 'Observations upon revenue for the Colony in 1828' (written by the Colonial Treasurer of New South Wales) makes an interesting point. It observes that the 'net colonial income' of the year 1828, as actually collected, is exclusive of sums 'in aid of revenue', i.e. items which cannot be viewed in the character of income. This item is further defined as 'the proceeds of the labour of convicts, and establishments connected with them, being applied to the reduction of the amount of parliamentary grants for their maintenance'. Thus it took 30 years for the Colonial Government to officially recognise the contribution of convict labour in the Colony.

l. The total quantity of alcohol imported and thus consumed in the Colony, even in 1828, and with only a population in 1820 of only 26, 000 people, of which adult numbers would be less than 15,000, was 162,167 gallons of spirits plus 15,000 gallons of Colonial distilled spirits (distillation from sugar was prohibited in 1828, but the high price of grain and the higher taxing of local manufactured spirits became a natural deterrent). In 1829, the only duties imposed on spirits in that year were upon spirits imported directly from H. M. Plantations in the West Indies. So the British authorities received double benefit by both international trading and local duties.

m. The quantity of dutiable tobacco in 1828 was 136,748 pounds (compared to 91,893 pounds in 1825). The Government experimented with locally grown tobacco at establishments in Emu Plains and Port Macquarie with the result being 51,306 pounds produced in 1830.

n. By 1827 shipping companies were also paying lighthouse charges, along with wharfage.

o. In 1828, the postage of letters attracted fees, for the first time, and the official Postmaster collected 598 pounds for general revenue.

p. The commencement of sales of both crown lands and crown timbers

Increased general revenues to the extent that in 1828, the amounts realised were:

Sales of Crown Lands 5004.19.2
Sales of Cedar cut on crown lands 744.15.11
Sales of other Timber 9365.11.4

The Governor imposed a fee of one halfpenny per foot for all cedar cut on crown lands. The 'Blue Book' makes the further observation that this charge 'has checked bushrangers and other lawless depredators by depriving them of ready means of subsistence by the absence of all restraint from cutting Cedar upon unallocated lands'.

In 1810, Governor Macquarie changed the designation of these two funds to 'Police Fund' and Orphan School Fund. The designated revenues were split 3:1 into each fund. The Act 3 Geo IV c.96 of 1822 gave further powers of taxation to the Governor.

E. Other Financial Observations

The analysis of Accounts extracted from the 'Blue Books' of 1822 through 1828 allows a number of conclusions to be drawn.

a. The initial claim by the author that the cost to the British Treasury of establishing and operating the Colony was NOT the millions of pounds claimed by other historians are now borne out by detailed examination. The accounting records as maintained by Governor Macquarie from 1810 leads to a statement of 'net revenue and expenses' which purports to offset all revenues against all expenses, and includes as revenue certain convict maintenance charges. Even in 1822 the Colony was showing a small operating surplus. This surplus grew through 1828 until, other than for transportation of convicts to the Colony; the charges on account of the British Treasury were less than One Hundred Thousand pounds for protecting, feeding and housing nearly 5,000 fully maintained convicts. Against this cost, the charge for housing, feeding and guarding this same number of prisoners in Britain would have been substantially higher, since in addition to the 5,000 gully maintained convicts there were a further 20,000 being paid for by free settlers and used as supervised labour. Britain surely had found a cheap source of penal servitude for at least 25,000 of its former prisoners, and found a very worthwhile alternative to the American Colonies as a destination for its prisoners.

b. Revenue from Crown Land sales and rents was used to offset Civil (Crown) salaries and expenses.

d. It is probably incorrect, at this stage, to say that it cost Britain nothing or at best, very little, to establish and maintain the Colony, but it can be said that from 1822 the costs were limited to maintaining fewer and fewer convicts. But from these convicts great value in terms of agricultural produce, coal and other minerals was derived. Just in terms of coal for lighting, heating and power, the cost to the government of purchasing these items would have been substantial. The 'Blue Book' reflects the use of the coal as a cost rather than a gain as would be the accounting standard today.

d. A final conclusion could be given that there are much more known records available for this period (1788-1899) than the author originally thought. The reproduction and regional distribution of the 'Blue Book' by the State Archives Office on microfiche is a major step forward in understanding the economic challenges faced by settlers and convicts in the early Colony. The sourcing of material from the Blue Book unveils the financial statements and conditions of these early years. It is still considered that finance records of the period 1788 to 1822 are not re-constructible, but the author feels that a deep search through the microfilms forming the Joint Copying Project will provide additional information on the two Colonial operating funds of the period–the 'Police Fund and the Orphan Fund'.

e. An interesting observation is found in 'The Constitutional History of Australia' by W. G. McMinn (1979).

P 33 records 'Subject to the need for a vice-regal message, accepting that any locally Australian Colony) initiated legislation of a money bill nature requires the Sovereign's ratification, the New South Wales Legislative Council was to Have a general right to appropriate revenue from taxation, except for an Amount of 81,600 pounds, the expenditure of which was to be in accordance with 'Three schedules' to the Act; being 33,000 pound for the salaries of those on the Civil list e.g. Governor et al, the superintendent of Port Phillip and its judges.

And for the expenses of administering justice 18,600 pound for the chief

Civil officers and their departments, for pensions and expenses of the council;

And 30,000 pound for the maintenance of public worship."

Land and casual revenues were also reserved.

The Sale of Waste Land Act of 1832 raised the minimum reserve price of crown land to one pound per acre, except that large remote areas might be sold at a lower price, and established a formula for the use of the land revenue; fifty percent was to be spent on immigration, the rest was to be expended by the Governor in accordance with British Government directives from time to time. The Governor was to continue to have power to issue depasturing licences and to make regulations for the use and occupancy of unsold lands, but the existence of the Sale of Waste Lands Act placed an important restriction on the colony by implying a prohibition against the Legislative Council legislating on these matters. The first directive on how the Governor was to spend a portion of the fund, enjoined the Governor to spend a proportion on Aboriginal protection and another on the roads; he was left free to hand any surplus over to the Council for appropriation; but it was made clear that the whole of the fifty percent was to be considered as 'an emergency reserve if the Council proved difficult'. McMinn sheds some further light on the Crown Lands mystery but there still remains the question of whether, year after year, these funds were fully used or whether they were just included as a contribution to general revenue. It would appear that somewhere there is a firm directive from the British Treasury that the revenues from Crown Lands sale were to be used to 'offset' British costs of maintaining the Colony. The 'Blue Book' is evidence that as general revenues, these funds were already being used to pay for the costs of feeding, clothing, housing convicts, and we know they were specifically used to pay for 'sponsored immigrants', aboriginal 'protection', and now roads. The costs of the military establishment were charged against general revenues so in the quite large 'pot', nearly all Colonial expenditures were subsidised or offset by revenues from the Sale of Crown Land. Britain put its hand in the till only; it seems, to pay for the shipping and supplies costs of getting their prisoners to the Colony. After 1828, we know that convict production–both agricultural and mineral–went a long way to paying their expenses, so perhaps the British Treasury did in fact get off very lightly indeed, especially for the benefits it derived.

The vexing question of Crown Lands revenues still remains. It is apparent from the 'Blue Book' notations that this revenue was 'reserved' for specific allocation by the Crown and remained in the Colony as an offset against British Government fiscal obligations (e.g. Civil List salaries) until self-government in 1855. A relevant quotation from the 1887 Financial Statements of the Colonial Treasurer of New South Wales assists in clarifying the use of the revenues:

"Prior to the passing of the Constitution Act, the Territorial Revenues of the Colony belonged to the Crown, but upon that Act coming into operation in 1855, they were placed at the disposal of the local Parliament, and together with the taxes, imposts, rates and duties were formed into one fund, under the title of the Consolidated Revenue Fund. In lieu of the Crown Revenues thus given up to the Colony, an annual Civil List of 64,300 pound was made payable to Her Majesty out of the Consolidated Revenues of the Colony." What this means is that the British Treasury allowed the offset of all direct British payments made on account of the Colony against revenues raised by the sale, rent or lease of Crown lands.

G. Observations on Crown Land Transactions

There was a major improvement in record keeping and reporting after self-government in 1855. The "Financial Statements of the Colonial Treasurers of New South Wales from Responsible Government in 1855 to 1881" provide a detailed accounting mechanism for recording classifications, and compilation of budgets and reporting to the Authorities. They contain 'explanatory memoranda of the financial system of New South Wales, and of the rise, progress and present condition of the public revenue'.

The interest in this period (from 1822 to 1881) is that these records, firstly of the 'Blue Book' period and then of the printed Financial Statements to 1881, provide the first detailed identification of the items included in the revenue and expenditures for the Colony and the appropriation and approval process. This historical data is relevant to understanding the social conditions in the Colony, the application of duties, tariffs, tolls and fees which embraced the essential revenue of a Colony that was designed to be self-sufficient and which was being given minimal economic support by the British Government, even though the opportunity cost of housing 'prisoners' in the Colony was a fraction of the cost of housing them in England.

Governance of Public Finance

The appendix to the 'Financial Statements of 1887' (refer Appendix this work) records that:

"The Financial System of the Colony of New South Wales is regulated chiefly by the Constitution Act of 1855 and the Audit Act of 1870, and in matters relating to Trust Funds and Loans by special Appropriation Acts of the local legislature.

The Imperial Act granting a constitution to the Colony of New South Wales was assented to on 16th July 1855, and became effective on the 24th November 1855. This Act provides for a Legislative Council (Upper House) and a Legislative Assembly. The Upper House members were to be nominated by the Governor, while the Lower House members were to be elected by inhabitants of the Colony.

We know that the first official empowerment of the Legislative Council to impose 'taxes' by way of customs duties was in 1823, but the payment (commenced in 1788) by the British Government of Civil salaried officials remained until 1853. So before the 1853 self-government, the British authorities maintained a civil list of officials who were paid for by the Crown.

The British Treasury directed revenues from crown land sales and rents from squatters' and pastoralists' leases (imposed from 1853) are used to meet local expenses and running costs, as well as Civil List Salaries.

The reserve sale price of crown land had been originally set at 50 pence per acre in 1833, but by 1839 it rose to 12 shillings an acre and shortly thereafter (1842) it rose to one pound per acre, and it is likely, based on the revenues from Crown Lands and the annual surplus recorded in the Colonial 'Blue Books', that the British Treasury made a surplus on its Colonial possession of Australia.

To draw this conclusion, a number of premises were made:

a. The British Government lists its Civil payments to the key officials of the Colony e.g. Governor, Attorney-, Surveyor-General, Chief Justice etc, but makes no mention of revenue collected from the Colony.

b. The three related Acts (59 Geo III c.114; 2 Geo IV. c.8 and 3 Geo IV. c.96) give the Colonial Governor the power to impose local taxes in the shape of Customs Duties on spirits, tobacco etc from about 1823,

c. The Legislative Council of 1851 adopted a Select Committee Report protesting that the more recent 'constitutional' Acts (13 & 14 Vic c.59) did not place the control of all revenue and taxation from the Colony in the hands of the legislature. The key omitted and thus missing elements–in the eyes of the Council–were the control of waste lands (i.e. Crown lands–specifically excluded by Act 9 Geo IV c.83) and revenue from mining operations.

d. The discovery of gold and the burgeoning wealth of the Colony prompted the Legislative Council in 1852 to seek the British Government's acceptance of an offset arrangement whereby the Colony of New South Wales would accept responsibility for all civil (i.e. official) salaries, provided the British Government surrendered all Colonial revenues to the discretion (under a proposed new constitution) of the Legislature.

e. The British authorities accepted Colonial funds, raised from the earliest sale and lease of Crown Land to be used for the funding of 'free immigration' to the Colony.

f. The concurrent Napoleonic wars being undertaken by the British, as well as the ongoing American War of Independence placed a substantial burden on the public purse, and the British Treasury was seeking every opportunity to limit, defray or offset expenses relating to the Colony in the Great South Land.

The conclusion should be (by implication), that the British Government had, (all during the period from 1788 to 1852) been in control of crown land (wasteland) revenues, as well as the revenue from mining. It was thus some portion of the crown land revenue that was used to pay the transportation charges for the first 'free' immigrants from Britain, until, some three years afterwards, numerous Colonial merchants supported and underwrote the transportation costs of 'free' settlers and guaranteed them jobs on arrival.

(b.) The Crown Land charges rose from 5 shillings in 1833 to 12 shillings in 1839 and then 1 pound in 1842. This revenue was used to defray Civil expenditures in the Colony, by being retained in the Colony and the Governor directed its use, on behalf of the Crown, for the payment of salaries to officials on the Civil list, to Military personnel, for government expenses in day to day running of the Colony, and it would take a mere accounting or book-keeping entry to offset such revenue and expenses.

We know from the public record (Wealth & Progress in NSW–1887) that revenue from Taxation in 1886 amounted to over two million pounds. This was largely customs duty on wines, spirits, coffee, tea and sundry other imported items such as rice and dried fruits. Stamps and license fee raised a further almost five hundred thousand pounds making the total Taxation revenue a sum of 2,611,835 pounds for 1886.

TABLE REVENUES FROM TAXATION 1886

Colony	Rail	Water etc	Immign	Other	Total '000
NSW	31380	4122	569	10573	46646
Vic	29282	5638	0	2706	37627
Qld	15374	221	2621	7623	25840
SA	11374	3321	0	5739	20435
WA	824	.05310	0	541	1371
Tas	.0173	0	.0235	4609	5019

TABLE B REVENUE FROM SALE AND OCCUPATION OF CROWN LAND 1871-1886

1871	197978	1879	1632024
1872	840453	1882	2914394
1873	1137914	1884	1753345
1875	2020629	1885	1876452
1876	2773003	1886	1643955

The research undertaken in writing this paper has led the writer to certain conclusions, all of which reflect on the early economic progress of the Colony.

10. The British authorities were ignorant of the radically different nature of the climate, soils and natural environment of the new colony;
11. There was no sound planning to develop agriculture, and provide the basics of self-supported living for the early population;
12. Basic farming equipment and building tools were not supplied in sufficient quantities, nor training or guidance provided by experienced persons;
13. The members of the New South Wales Corps were more interested in pursuing their own interests than in supervising the convicts and promoting self sufficiency;
14. There was no system of proper supervision and training of convicts, leading to low levels of productivity; Governor Phillip had, on numerous occasions requested professional supervisors for the convicts but was repeatedly ignored.
15. The discovery of Gold was kept secret whilst convict transfers were still being undertaken, lest the 'dream' of great wealth became stronger than the requirement to work out a penal service.
16. Despite the lack of basic necessities and poor motivation of most of the population, the enterprise of a small number of individuals, both convict and 'free immigrant' provided a catalyst for the progress and prosperity of all.
17. Needless to say, in hindsight, progress to self sufficiency could have been hastened and much suffering avoided, if appropriate planning and economic encouragement had been provided.

18. The discovery of large tracts of good grazing land and its associated export development of wool, and the discovery of large gold deposits rapidly boosted the fortunes of the Colony, but the driving force and critical factor was the motivation, energy and determination of the early entrepreneurs, acting initially and mainly in their own interest, but inevitably taking the bulk of the Colony with them in the progress towards prosperity.

After 1828, we know that convict production–both agricultural and mineral–went a long way to paying their expenses, so perhaps the British Treasury did in fact get off very lightly indeed, especially for the benefits it derived.

Another question arises after analysing the pre-Federation period. How did the Colony build up a debt to the Mother Country of 159 million pound–This figure was quoted in 1893 at the Corowa Federation Conference by A.J. Peacock MLA (Mildura). Peacock was later to become the Minister for Lands in the first Government of 1900, and was knighted for his contribution to the Federation Movement. The answer is that Peacock quoted this figure in error and in truth the sum of 159 million pound is the total indebtedness by the Colonies to bondholders in the City of London. This was a Colonial obligation at attractive interest rates and due over an extended period of time.

Interpreting the Public Accounts

The purpose of this work has been accomplished–the purpose being that of identifying and analysing public financial statements from 1800-1899. A niche was identified and one worthy of filling. That there could be an interest in relating and understanding the economic fundamentals of the Colony onto Federation is not surprising but a study of the early Government financial reporting can unleash an understanding of so much information relating to the social economic and political progress of the early settlers. What was the progress of the early social infrastructure? The hospital, the roads, the water supply, the sewerage disposal; the growth of industries–retail, pastoral, mineral, timber, whaling and sealing; citrus? What was the progress of education? The health and the nutritional state of the nation? Were the settlers housed properly? Did the settlers enjoy the benefits of travel, telegraph, refrigeration and other results of the ongoing industrial revolution? What did their entertainment consist of; what were the working conditions?

The government accounting and reporting system answered all these questions, and more. So, if the aim of the Government accounts was to analyse the condition of the Colony and inform its people, then the system worked well. We learnt where the revenue of the Colony was derived from, and the advent and then taxation in the Colony. We learnt where all that revenue was expended, and the resulting measurable standard of living achieved by the settlers. Government accounting was the official measure of the performance of the Colonial administrators for the British Colonial Office in London.

Interpreting the Direct and Measurable Gain to the British Authorities from the Colony of New South Wales.

The original estimate of direct gains by the British authorities from the original and continuing investment in the Colony of New South Wales was based on 5 (five) identifiable and quantifiable events

2. The opportunity cost of housing, feeding and guarding the convicts in the Colony compared with the cost of doing the same thing in Britain.

The original estimates, in this category, were based on an estimated differential of ten pound per head–an arbitrary assessment of the differential cost.

However recent and more reliable information has come to hand which gives further validity to a number of 20 pound per head per annum, compared with the original 10 pound per head per annum.

A letter to Under Secretary Nepean dated 23rd August 1783, from James Maria Matra of Shropshire and London assists us in this regard.

It was Matra who first analysed the opportunity of using the new Colony as a Penal Colony; only his estimates were incorrect and ill founded. He had advised the Government that it would cost less than 3,000 pound to establish the Colony initially, plus transportation cost at 15 pound per head and annual maintenance of 20 pound per head.

In fact the transportation was contracted for the second fleet at 13 pound 5 shillings per head and Colonial revenues from 1802 offset annual maintenance.

However, Matra made a significant statement in his letter to Nepean, when he pointed out that the prisoners housed, fed and guarded on the rotting hulks on the Thames River were being contracted for in the annual amount of 26.15.10 per head per annum. He also writes that 'the charge to the publick fore these convicts has been increasing for the last 7 or 8 years' (Historical Records of NSW–Vol 1 Part 2 Page 7)

Adopting this cost as a base for comparison purposes, it means that the benefit to Britain of the Colony increased from 140,000,000 pound to 180,000,000 pound. This benefit assesses the Ground 1 benefit at 84,000,000 pound.

7. Benefit to Britain on Ground Two (2) is put at 70, 000,000 pound which places the value of a convicts labour at 35 pound per annum. Matra had assessed the value of labour of the Hulk prisoners at 35. 85 pound.

8. The valuation of convict labour in the new Colony should reflect the convicts not only used on building sites, but also on road, bridge and wharf construction. This would add (based on 35 pound per annum) a further 21,000,000-pound.

9. The Molesworth Committee (A House of Commons Committee investigating transportation) concluded that the surplus food production by the convicts would feed the Military people and this, over a period of 10 years, would save 7,000,000 pound for the British Treasury.

10. The benefits of fringe benefit grants of land to the Military etc can be estimated (based on One pound per acre) at over 5,000,000 before 1810.

11. We learn from Governor King's Report to Earl Camden (which due to a change of office holder, should have been addressed to Viscount Castlereagh as Colonial Secretary) dated 15th March 1806 that the Convicts engaged in widely diverse work. The Report itself (Enclosure #2) is entitled "Public Labour of Convicts maintained by the Crown at Sydney, Parramatta, Hawkesbury, Toongabbie and Castle Hill, for the year 1805

Cultivation–Gathering, husking and shelling maize from 200 acres sowed last year–Breaking up ground and planting 1230 acres of wheat, 100 acre of Barley, 250 acres of Maize, 14 acres of Flax, and 3 acres of potatoes–Hoeing the above maize and threshing wheat.

Stock–Taking care of Government stock as herdsmen, watchmen etc

Buildings–

- At Sydney: Building and constructing of stone, a citadel, a stone house, a brick dwelling for the Judge Advocate, a commodious brick house for the main guard, a brick printing office
- At Parramatta: Alterations at the Brewery, a brick house as clergyman's residence
- At Hawkesbury: completing a public school
- A Gaol House with offices, at the expense of the Colony
- Boat and Ship Builders: refitting vessels and building row boats
- Wheel and Millwrights: making and repairing carts

Manufacturing: sawing, preparing and manufacturing hemp, flax and wool, bricks and tiles

Road Gangs: repairing roads, and building new roads

Other Gangs: loading and unloading boats"

(Historical Records of NSW–Vol 6 P43)

Thus the total benefits from these six (6) items of direct gain to the British comes to well over 174 million pound, and this is compared to Professor N. G. Butlin's proposal that the British 'invested' 5.6 million.

Historical Records of NSW Vol 1 Part 2

THE OPINIONS OF CAPTAIN ARTHUR PHILLIP AS GOVERNOR OF THE COLONY OF NSW

HRNSW VOLS 1-7

e.   (P7)–Cost of Convicts (-J.M. Matra Letter)

  - The estimate to create a settlement there (in Africa) amounted to 9865 pound, and the annual charge for each convict would be 15.14.0. The Government pays annually to the Contractor for each convict employed on the hulks 26.15.10
  - the 1,000 felons is currently costing over 20,000 per annum

f.   (P10)–The plan by Sir George Young as presented to Lord Sydney included a list of benefits for Britain. These included:

  - The geographical position
  - Trade with South America
  - The commercial position
  - Variety of climate and productions
  - Facilities for trade
  - Tropical products
  - Flax
  - Commercial centre
  - Metals of every kind
  - Settlers from China
  - The American Loyalists
  - Felons
  - Expense
  - Number of ships required
  - Guard-ship
  - Exploring ship

- Cheap transportation
- Back-loading

g. (P32) Estimates of Expense for equipment & supplies
h. (P67) Phillip's Commission

- "Our will and our pleasure is that all public monies which shall be raised be issued out by warrant from you and disposed of by you for the support of the Government or for such other purpose as shall be particularly directed and not otherwise"
- "We do likewise give and grant unto you full power and authority to agree for such lands, tenements as shall be in our power to dispose of and them to grant to any person upon such terms and under such moderate quit rents services to be thereupon reserved . . . ."

h. (*P87*) Economy

- "You shall use every proper degree of economy and be careful that the commissary so transmit an account of the issues to our Treasury, from time to time . . . ."

i. (P91) Emancipation and land grants

- "You have full power and authority to emancipate and discharge from servitude any of the convicts under your superintendence who shall be deserving of such favour"
- "You may issue your warrant to make full and careful surveys of land and may pass grants to any of the convicts emancipated e.g. to every male 30 acres, and if married, a further 20 acres more."

j. (P146) Bricklayers Wanted

- In at least two despatches–those of 9th July 1788 to Lord Sydney and that of 28th September 1788 to U/Secretary Nepean, Governor Phillip drew the British attention to the severe shortage of carpenters and bricklayers in the Colony.

BIBLIOGRAPHY

Shann, E. O. 'Economic History of Australia'

Yarwood, A. T.–Samuel Marsden (1977)

Collins, David 'An Account of the English colony in NSW' (1798)

Steven, Margaret 'Merchant Campbell 1769-1846)

Bigge, John Thomas 'Report of Commissioner of Inquiry, on the State of Agriculture and Trade in New South Wales' (1823)

Palmer, L.H. 'Our John's Adventures' (1988)

Carter, W. E. R. 'John Palmer: Father of the Colony' (1986)

Beckett, G. W. 'The Development of Public Finance in the Colony'

Crawley, Frank 'Colonial Australia' Vol 1

The Sydney Gazette 1803-1809-1816-1821

The Australian Chronicle

H.R.A. series 1 vol 1-10 (10-p651)

HRNSW Vols 1-IV

Marjorie Barnard–"A History of Australia"

Foster, Josephine "John Palmer' Journal Royal Aust History, Soc Vol 11 (1925)

Mackaness, G. 'The Life of William Bligh'

Coghlan, T. A. 'Labour & Industry in Australia Vol 1-IV (1918)'

Butlin, N. G. 'Forming a Colonial Economy'

Report of the Committee of Inquiry into Transportation–Evidence by John Palmer 1812

The Late John Palmer. An article in "New South Wales Magazine–vol 1834"

Lea-Scarlett, Errol 'Queanbeyan–The District & Its People.

Evatt, H. V. 'The Rum Rebellion' (1938)
Illustrated History of Australia
Flannery, T (Ed)–'The Birth of Sydney'
The Oxford History of Australia
Hughes, R–'The Fatal Shore'
Macquarie Publishing 'A Colonial Time-Line'